MAKING SENSE OF SEXUAL CONSENT

Making Sense of Sexual Consent

Edited by

MARK COWLING
University of Teesside

PAUL REYNOLDS
Edge Hill University College

ASHGATE

Published by
Ashgate Publishing Limited
Gower House
Croft Road
Aldershot
Hants GU11 3HR
England

Ashgate Publishing Company
Suite 420
101 Cherry Street
Burlington, VT 05401-4405
USA

Ashgate website: http://www.ashgate.com

British Library Cataloguing in Publication Data
Making sense of sexual consent
   1. Sexual consent 2. Sex and law
   I. Cowling, Mark II. Reynolds, Paul, 1962-
   306.7

Library of Congress Cataloging-in-Publication Data
Making sense of sexual consent / edited by Mark Cowling and Paul Reynolds.
      p. cm.
  Chiefly revisions of papers presented at a conference on "Making Sense of Sexual Consent" held at Edge Hill College in June 2000.
  Includes bibliographical references and index.
  ISBN 0-7546-3687-9
  1. Sexual ethics--Congresses. 2. Sexual consent--Congresses. 3. Rape--Congresses.
 I. Cowling, Mark. II. Reynolds, Paul, 1962-

  HQ32.M35 2004
  176--dc22

2004007440

ISBN 0 7546 3687 9

Printed and bound in Great Britain by MPG Digital Solutions, Bodmin, Cornwall

Contents

List of Tables and Figure

Notes on the Contributors

Andrea Beckmann is a Lecturer in Criminology at the University of Lincoln. Her PhD was *The social construction of 'Sadomasochism'; subjugated knowledges and the broader social meanings of this bodily practice*. Publications include: 'Deconstructing myths: the social construction of "Sadomasochism" versus "subjugated knowledges" of practitioners of consensual "SM"', *Journal of Criminal Justice and Popular Culture*, 8 (2) (2001) pp. 66-95 and 'Researching consensual "sadomasochism", perspectives on power, rights and responsibilities-the case of "disability"', *Social Policy Review* (13) 2001, pp. 89-106. Further publications in the areas of 'sexual deviance', 'bodily practices' and/or 'body cultures' as well as social theory are forthcoming.

Gideon Calder is a Senior Lecturer in the School of Social Studies at the University of Wales, Newport, where he teaches across a range of areas in philosophy, social theory and applied ethics. Recent publications include *Rorty* (Weidenfeld and Nicholson, 2003), and the co-edited *Liberalism and Social Justice: International Perspectives* (Ashgate, 2000), along with pieces in *Radical Philosophy*, *Imprints*, *Human Affairs*, *Political Studies* and elsewhere. He is currently reviews editor for the journal *Res Publica*, and helps to run the Society for Applied European Thought.

Dr Moira Carmody is a Senior Lecturer in Sociology and Criminology at the University of Western Sydney, Australia. She has been researching, writing and developing policy around sexual violence prevention for the last twenty years. Her most recent publication is 'Sexual ethics and violence prevention' in *Social and Legal Studies: An International Journal* Vol. 12, No. 2, pp. 199-216. She is currently interviewing women and men of diverse sexualities about how they negotiate ethical sex.

Karen Corteen is a Lecturer in Critical Criminology in the Centre for Studies in Crime and Social Justice at Edge Hill in Ormskirk. She has written book chapters and articles on children's rights, sexuality and Sex and Relationship Education and violence, sexuality and space. Her recently completed PhD was concerned with the role of Sex and Relationship Education in the sexual and gender ordering of society. Specific focus was given to role of Section 28 of the Local Government Act 1988. Currently she is working on a co-edited book entitled *Critical Reflections in Criminology*.

Mark Cowling is Reader in Criminology at the University of Teesside. His previous publications include: *Approaches to Marx* (ed. with Lawrence Wilde), Open University Press, Milton Keynes, 1989, *The Communist Manifesto: New*

Interpretations (edited), Edinburgh University Press, Edinburgh, 1998, *Date Rape and Consent*, Ashgate, Aldershot, 1998, *Marxism, the Millennium and Beyond* (edited, with Paul Reynolds), Macmillan, 2000, and *Marx's Eighteenth Brumaire: (Post) Modern Interpretations* (edited, with James Martin), Pluto Press, 2002.

John Gibbins is a Principal Lecturer in Research Management in the School of Social Sciences and Law at the University of Teesside, and a member of Wolfson College Cambridge. He recently published *The Politics of Postmodernity*, a book on value change and political futures with Bo Reimer. He has written extensively in the fields of political and social theory, but is currently working in the fields of criminology, social epistemology and the history of university curriculum, focused at Cambridge University.

Terry P. Humphreys is an Assistant Professor in Psychology at Wilfrid Laurier University, Waterloo, Ontario, Canada. His current research focuses on young adults' attitudes and behaviours with respect to sexual communication, negotiation, and consent. Terry is a long-standing member of the Annual Conference and Training Institute on Sexuality at the University of Guelph, in Guelph, Ontario, Canada. This conference has been recognised as Canada's leading training and education forum for sexual health professionals.

Michelle McCarthy is a Senior Lecturer in Learning Disability at the Tizard Centre, University of Kent, UK. Originally a social worker, she has worked with people with learning disabilities in a variety of settings. For four years she led a team which provided a specialist sexuality service to people with learning disabilities and staff. She has a particular interest in working with women with learning disabilities on issues of sexual abuse and sexual health. Publications include *Sexuality and Women with Learning Disabilities* (1999, Jessica Kingsley); *Sex and the 3R's: Rights, Responsibilities and Risks* (with D. Thompson, 1998, Pavilion).

Margaret S. Malloch is a Research Fellow in the Department of Applied Social Sciences at the University of Stirling. Her research has focused on state responses to drug users and drug-related crime, and the evaluation of criminal-justice based initiatives such as the Glasgow and Fife Pilot Drug Courts. Her book *Women, Drugs and Custody* was published by Waterside Press in 2000.

Allison Moore is Research and Information Co-ordinator at the Lesbian and Gay Foundation in Manchester. She is currently completing her PhD on the relationship between public discourses of sexual citizenship and the 'lifeworld' experiences of people with diverse sexual identities

David Renton is a Research Fellow at the University of Sunderland. He has written for many different journals and magazines, including *Cahiers Léon Trotsky*, *Changing English*, *Contemporary Politics*, *Fragments*, *International*

Socialism Journal, Jewish Culture and History, Jewish Socialist, Labour History Review, Lobster, Race and Class, Searchlight, Socialist Review, Socialist Worker, Soundings and *What Next?* His recent books include *This Rough Game: Fascism and Anti-fascism in History* (Sutton, 2001), (with James Eaden) *A History of Communism in Britain* (Palgrave, 2001) and *Marx on Globalisation* (Lawrence and Wishart, 2001).

Paul Reynolds is Senior Lecturer in Sociology in the Centre for Studies in the Social Sciences at Edge Hill College. His research interests include sexual politics, cultures and ethics, contemporary social theory and Marxist and radical theory and politics. Recent publications include: (ed. with Mark Cowling): *Contemporary Issues in Law* Volume 6 No. 1, 2002 – Special Edition on Rape and Sexual Consent, including the introduction and 'Rape, Law and Consent: The Scope and Limits to Sexual Regulation by Law'; 'Accounting for Sexuality: the Scope and Limitations of Census Data on Sexual Identity and Difference', *Radical Statistics* Issue 78 pp. 63-76, 2001; and Mark Cowling and Paul Reynolds (eds) *Marxism, The Millennium and Beyond* London: Palgrave, 2000, including the introduction and 'Post-Marxism : Radical Political Theory and Practice Beyond Marxism?'. He is currently preparing a co-authored book with Tony Fagan on *The Politics of Disability: Identity, Policy, Ideology* for Sage and editing a special edition of the journal *Radical Statistics* on Sexuality and Radical Research.

Philip N. S. Rumney is Reader in Law at Sheffield Hallam University. He has written numerous articles on such issues as rape sentencing, rape law reform, juror education and the rape and sexual assault of males. He is currently researching an article on false rape allegations, along with a book on the impact and effectiveness of rape law reform.

Barbara Sullivan is a Senior Lecturer in the School of Political Science and International Studies, University of Queensland, Australia. She has published on prostitution and pornography in Australia (*The Politics of Sex*, Cambridge University Press 1997) and is presently undertaking comparative, international work on prostitution and trafficking (*International Feminist Journal of Politics* March 2003). Her theoretical work has addressed feminist approaches to prostitution, post-structuralism and liberal-democratic theory.

Martin Morgan-Taylor is a Senior Lecturer in Law at De Montfort University, Leicester. He has written on aspects of serious sexual offences, particularly male rape and the use of syndrome evidence in rape trails. He also writes on consumer protection law.

David Thompson is currently supporting the implementation of England's new learning disability policy (*Valuing People*) with a particular focus on family support and lecturing at Thames Valley University, London, UK. His main areas of interest and research have been sexual issues for men with learning disabilities and how growing older effects the lives of people with learning disabilities.

Publications include *Sex and the 3Rs: Rights, Responsibilities and Risks* (with M. McCarthy, 1998, Pavilion) and Response-Ability: Working with men with learning disabilities who have difficult or abusive sexual behaviour (with H. Brown, 1998, Pavilion).

Matthew Waites is Lecturer in Sociology in the School of Social Science and Law at Sheffield Hallam University, Sheffield, U.K. He has published a variety of book chapters and journal articles on debates over age of consent laws and lesbian, gay and bisexual politics. His current research focuses on critiquing proposals for reform of age of consent laws emerging from the recent Home Office review of Sex Offences in the U.K. He is co-editor, with Jeffrey Weeks and Janet Holland, of *Sexualities and Society: A Reader* (Cambridge: Polity Press, 2003).

Preface

This book has its roots in discussions and disagreements between the editors in the late 1990s, triggered by Cowling's publication of his *Date Rape and Consent* in 1998. Some of the initial ideas and contestations were played out at the second conference of the International Association for the Study of Sexuality at Manchester Metropolitan University in 1999 on a panel with David Archard, author of *Sexual Consent*. David's work deserves special mention for its sophistication and clarity of thought, and David for his generosity of spirit and erudite comment – it was regrettable that other commitments caused his departure from deliberations after 1999.

The editors then decided to co-convene a conference – 'Making Sense of Sexual Consent' at Edge Hill College in June 2000. This was quite a bold decision of the college. A proposal to hold the conference at the University of Teesside was not supported on the grounds that a public scandal might ensue. Particular thanks are due to Professor Alistair McCulloch, Head of Research at Edge Hill College, for his encouragement and support for the project. The conference involved two days of intellectually rigorous and extremely pleasurable discussion from which solid working relationships were born. There proved to be considerable overlap of concerns between researchers looking at different areas of the issue of consent, and people who in other contexts might well have been shouting at each other engaged in sensible discussion. Although our time certainly did not lead to consensus it helped many of us to clarify our ideas. Another valuable feature of the discussion, which is reflected in the present collection, is the mix of disciplines present. Participants' backgrounds included law, philosophy, politics, criminology, sociology and psychology. Those working in support of rape victims – whether in activist or voluntary groups or within the legal system – felt free to discuss issues with academics and more theoretically minded participants, and debate extended from heterosexual consent to cover other sexualities and the consent issues they raised. Thanks to all the participants at the conference for what, for many of the authors in this volume, was helpful comment and discussion of their papers.

Most of the chapters in this collection have been revised and updated from papers delivered at the conference. Some other papers were organised into a special edition of the journal *Contemporary Issues in Law*, Volume 6 No.1, focused on 'Rape, Law and Sexual Consent', guest edited by the editors of this volume. Whilst the tragedy of rape and sexual violence finds echoes in many of the chapters of this book, the division of papers between those focused on rape and those more focused on consent seemed to make much sense. The journal was published in 2002, whilst the book had a slightly longer gestation. Partly, this arose from one publisher's rather cavalier attitude to the project, a position that changed when Ashgate agreed to take on the project. Thanks to Katherine Hodkinson, Anne

Keirby and others at Ashgate who moved the project forward and forgave the editors their delays in handing over the manuscript.

Mark and Paul would like to thank all the contributors to both this collection and the special edition of *Contemporary Issues in Law* for their patience and good humour in moving the project from discussion to publication. They would also like to thank Allison Moore for her constant support with this project, far above and beyond her own academic contribution, which stretched from assisting in organising the 2000 conference to painstakingly reading through the final draft of the text when she had many other demands upon her time. Mark would particularly like to thank his wife Amani and children for looking after him during the project and for picking him up when he is low – in the most literal sense. Paul would like to thank six people whose willingness to tolerate endless discussion about sexual consent, often at the expense of their personal time, says as much for their friendship as it does the fascination of the topic – Alistair McCulloch, Gideon Calder, Mark McGovern, Allison Moore, Alison Walker and Stephanie Bradley.

Introduction

Mark Cowling and Paul Reynolds

Just a Simple Matter of Yes or No?

Before the 1990s, students and researchers with an interest in reading about sexual consent would have struggled to find an academic literature. Except within feminist critiques of hetero-patriarchal society, and principally the work of radical feminists like Andrea Dworkin (1974, 1981, 1988) and Catherine MacKinnon (1989, 1996), the idea of sexual consent did not attract critical interest. The focus of discussion, understandably, was on the prevalence and incidence of non-consenting sex and the crisis of rape, forced sex and sexual abuse against women – both in the public epidemic of sexual violence and abuse and the more insidious and normalised abuse within private relationships. This focus on non-consent had the effect of producing diverse and widely varying definitions of consent/non-consent, used by different researchers with different disciplinary focus, leading to widely varying arguments and statistical interpretations of rape and sexual violence and abuse, with much attendant public controversy (for discussion see Cowling, 1998, 2003; Muehlenhard, 1992; Johnson and Sigler, 1997).

Sexual consent was articulated through radical feminist or liberal views of rape and non-consent. To radical feminists, sexual consent was reduced to a marginal and superficial representation of a 'sexual contract' that obscured the exercise of male power and violence over women, thereby differentiating consent from non-consent only by degrees of physical or emotional coercion. Outside of that perspective, the common understanding and legal codification of sexual consent adopted, by default, a liberal assumption of the sexual contract – free individuals say yes or no. Using the example of UK law, women were (and still are, to a great extent) supposed to demonstrate resistance to attempts at forced sex, and their conduct was the object of close scrutiny, whilst men's – hetero-patriarchal constructed – 'honest belief' in consent constituted a defence against rape – the *Morgan Defence* (see Jones, 2002 and Hinchliffe, 2002 for contrasting discussion). The law thus completely failed (and arguably still fails) to address gendered inequality, and seemed to offer compelling testimony to the radical feminist critique. It stereotyped women as sexual objects and victims yet also as the responsible party where questions of sexual consent were concerned, and effectively repeated much of the character of the sexual abuse of women raped or forced to have sex – the violation and denigration – in the legal process (see, for example, Adler, 1987; Brown, Jamieson and Burman, 1993; Cook, 2002; Reynolds, 2002a; Temkin, 1987). However much recent and current changes in legislation in the UK will make constructive changes to the legal system and process – for example, the Sexual Offences Bill processing through Parliament in 2003 – the radical feminist focus on the structural foundations of the subversion of women's consent and the liberal focus on women as free and autonomous individuals has formed (and continues to form) the boundaries for debate on understanding sexual consent in the UK, as in other societies and legal systems (see Home Office, 2003).

This book reflects the development of more sophisticated approaches to sexual consent within these boundaries in the last decade. This is not to dismiss radical feminism, which has been persuasive in putting sexual consent and non-consent within the context of hetero-patriarchal power relations in society, and catalysed political struggle to change the inadequate legal and political discourses that applied to questions of consent. Nevertheless, debate has developed that subjects sexual consent to greater and more direct scrutiny, for a number of reasons. First, developments within feminism(s) have moderated radical determinations within greater subject contingencies (this is covered in detail in the chapter by Moore and Reynolds in this volume). Post-feminists have rejected what they regard as the radical feminist 'victimology' of women's sexuality and denial of heterosexual women's sexual pleasure (notably Roiphe, 1993). At the same time, feminists more resistant to association with particular schools of feminist thought, such as Sylvia Walby and Lois Pineau, began to develop more contingent frameworks for feminist critiques of gendered inequalities (Walby, 1990; Pineau, 1995).

Similarly, women's groups such as rape crisis campaigning groups and victim support groups began to generate support for rape to be taken more seriously by legal and political authorities (and were extremely influential in the shaping of the current Sexual Offences Bill in the UK). They argued for, with varying degrees of success, tougher legislation against sex crimes against women with tougher sanctions and penalties, reduced sentences or sympathetic verdicts for abused women, and a review of legal system's treatment of abused women – these struggles continue (for a good summary of many of the issues see Lees, 1997, and for two discussions by contributors to the Home Office Review that led to the current UK Sexual Offences Bill, see Cook, 2002 and Jones, 2002). In doing so, they pushed the 'problem' of sexual non-consent – and so sexual consent – into the legal and public domains.

Further, for reasons still under debate, the crime of rape began to be subdivided to recognise different forms of rape with different attendant problems. The classically stereotyped 'stranger rape' was contrasted with 'acquaintance rape', responding to evidence that located the majority of rapes within friendship, work colleague, broad family or general acquaintance relationships, thus changing perceptions about the 'otherness' of rape. Rapists were not anonymous, but known. 'Spousal' or 'Domestic' rape highlighted rape within marriage and interpersonal relationships of some intimacy or duration, and again changed perceptions of rape as an alien act to rape as something that happened within intimate or close relationships. This, for example, brought about changes in UK law in 1991 that recognised rape in marriage. The 1990s got its own form of rape – 'date rape' – that highlighted rape as a feature of the process of negotiating (or failing to negotiate) the sexual contract of consent within intimate relations.

These subdivided categories have prompted a rethink of how rape and forced sex are distinguished from consenting sex, which has further awakened public interest in what it means to sexually consent. Such sub-divisions could be seen to correspond with a contemporary (post-feminist) sense that women can assert greater control of their sexuality and desires and so both reject forced sex within their interpersonal relations and take a greater degree of initiative. This has catalysed public debate on sex, sexuality and sexual 'problems' in the media and public discourse, which has applied a less uniform 'victimology' to women's sexual experience. At the same time as it has projected a stronger representation of women's sexuality, it has also arguably underplayed prevailing structural inequalities between men and women.

The idea of date rape allows a space for some men to redefine their actions, and provide mitigation that rearticulates abuse as miscommunication, and emphasises the challenges of more complex notions of consent to men's traditional stereotypical active and acquisitive sexuality. Nevertheless, men are expected to take more responsibility and be more accountable for their sexual conduct. These developments were manifest in arguments between charitable and critical views of 'date rape' as a consequence of miscommunication in intimate relations or continuing examples of male power, insensitivity and lack of responsibility. Of the editors, Cowling has written a book on date rape which stresses that the boundaries between rape and bad sex are somewhat arbitrary (1998), whereas Reynolds on balance is more hostile to the term 'date rape', seeing it as a form of apologia for rape.

Whatever the position taken, the increasing recognition that most rape occurs within relationships that are to some degree intimate has encouraged public attention on how people made decisions about sex as well as when they are denied the right – a focus on sexual consent.

These specific determinants have been contextualised by other social factors that have changed attitudes to sex more generally, and stimulated interest in how we make decisions about sex and sexuality. The portrayal and discussion of sex has become increasingly explicit. Since the 1960s, there has been a growing visibility for both sexual imagery and sexual discussion, from advertising through pornography and sex in the media to more openly sexual affection in public places. An increasing proportion of television is devoted to displaying intimate interpersonal and sexual matters for public discussion and reflection. This inevitably triggered interpersonal and social discussions, already excited by a more openly sexual culture.

Sexual debate, and particularly debate around the role of public authorities in the regulation and monitoring of sex, has been further provoked by the (partial) legitimation of diversity in sexuality, loosening the strictures of 'compulsory heterosexuality' (Rich 1981). The development of nascent lesbian and gay rights, the visibility of legal and legislative cases such as the 'Spanner Case' and the 'Bolton Seven', where consenting sado-masochistic sex was criminalised, and the development of televisual media with a focus on diverse sexuality have all prompted increased public knowledge of and interest in questions of sexual conduct (selectively, see Bell and Binnie, 2000, Moran, Monk and Beresford (eds.), 1998; Richardson, 2000).

This recent interest in sexual consent has been evident in different disciplinary contributions to recent debates. Philosophical interest has centred upon exploring the problems of the presence or absence of consent as an act, utterance or communicative process (Pineau, 1995; Burgess-Jackson, 1996; Cowling, 1998; Archard, 1998). Mainly in the last five years, psychologists have sought to explain both the mechanisms and processes by which the consent decision is made and the psychological processes that inform it (McCormick, 1979; Perper and Weis, 1987; Byers and Lewis, 1988; Rosenthal and Peart, 1996; Hall, 1998; Hickman and Muehlenhard, 1999; Humphreys in this volume). More contentiously, evolutionary psychologists have offered explanations of why the consent decision appears to be structured unequally, with a proactive and arguably acquisitive male and passive and arguably temperate female, through scientific models of brain, biology and behaviour (Hamilton 2002; Thornhill and Palmer, 2000). Sociologists (and much of feminist writings have straddled philosophy, legal theory and sociology) have stressed the social, cultural and structural contexts of gender in analysing the way in which individuals' consent decisions are made (Jeffreys, 1990; Walby, 1990). These different positions constitute considerably different approaches to the idea of consent that sometimes contradict each other in what they see as free sexual consent, but do provoke debate and research to understand sexual consent better.

What these different approaches have come to agree on – insofar as they have any agreement at all – is that when taken as a subject in itself and not only problematised in respect of its absence in forced sex and rape, thinking about sexual consent involves more complex questions than might at first be imagined. Does consent have to be conveyed verbally, and how safe are understandings of consent decisions by both partners in a prevailing culture where sexual communication is non-verbal, such as through body language and 'hint'? If consent is usually given either through gestures or in metaphorical and symbolic language, can we be confident that everyone involved in a particular sexual episode has the same understanding of the gestures and metaphors? Assuming that consent to have sex has been clearly conveyed, what does it actually include? What assumptions are being made about contraception? Where are the lines drawn between consent to sex as a general proposition, and consent to sex as a set of consent decisions concerning different sexual practices – for example, breast kissing, toe sucking, penetrative sex, anal sex, spanking or caning? This is particularly problematic around the area of what is regarded as either 'petting' or 'foreplay' and the move to penetrative sex, or the move from what is conventionally regarded as 'vanilla' sex (same sex or 'straight') to more 'exotic' pleasures, involving additional partners, bondage, partial asphyxiation, water sports, flagellation and so forth. What additional consent is needed? How should it be negotiated? Should the state step in and stop people if they want to, for example, nail each other's scrotums or foreskins to the coffee table, even if those engaging in this sexual conduct are consenting and enjoying themselves (as in the 'Spanner Case')?

There are also contextual issues to consider. While rape is certainly possible within established relationships, does consent in these relationships work differently from new relationships and first-time negotiations? For example, is there an assumed 'permanent' consent to kissing and mild sexual fondling unless it has specifically been revoked in long term partnerships? How are a range of issues around consent decisions judged within inter-personal relationships that might see sex incorporated within other aspects of their relationship, rendered in exchange for maintaining the 'status quo' or in the context of some history of the threat of or incidence of violence, sex as 'gift' or surrogacy for problems at work, withdrawal or absence of affection, or so forth? How situations are read will also depend upon the personal histories of the participants, their experience and their understanding of the meaning of sexual consent in their lives. Whilst these idiosyncratic features of inter-personal relations should not constitute apologia for rape and forced sex, context matters in deciphering and understanding sexual consent, particularly in a society where sexual consent is normally private and intimate.

Even considering these concerns, there is an assumption that participants in consent decisions are rational adults. This discounts the issue of consent where rational choice is constrained, if participants are drunk or drugged, for example. They might be intoxicated because of their own voluntary intake, because someone else has been plying them with drink or drugs but they fully know the effect of them and desire the absence of control they might bring, or because someone else has slipped something in their drink and they have neither knowledge or control. One or both of them might be under the legal age of consent, or might be under a special age of consent applying to prostitution or to relations between teachers and school children. People under a particular legal age of consent may be anything through from helpless and deeply vulnerable to more rational and capable of looking after themselves than many people who are over the age of consent. Again, maybe one or both of the participants has learning difficulties. Who should decide whether they are capable of consenting to some particular sexual act? On what grounds should such a decision be made?

There is some degree of overlap between many of these issues, and they have contributed to recent reviews of legal understandings of consent and non-consent in the UK. The Labour government that was elected in 1997 shared the view that the laws that govern sexual conduct were out of date and full of anomalies and set up a Home Office committee to propose how the laws should be changed. The committee consulted widely with interested groups and commissioned much research of its own, finally producing the report *Setting the Boundaries* in 2000. The committee recognised the centrality of consent by starting the serious work of its report with a discussion of rape. It proposed to retain the basic idea that rape is sex without consent, but to spell out that consent means free agreement, and to write into statute existing common law decisions that no one can give consent on behalf of somebody else; that someone who is asleep, unconscious or extremely drunk cannot give consent and that consent given to someone pretending to be a husband or boyfriend or to be carrying out a 'medical procedure' is not valid. It then proceeded to go through other areas that are related to this central idea of rape as sex without consent, looking, for example, at how this idea applies to indecent assault, at the age of consent and related issues and at the question of mental capacity. This report represents a shift in legal standards for distinguishing sexual consent and non-consent, and is the basis for the current Sexual Offences Bill before Parliament as this introduction is written. It is hoped that as well as making a tangible difference to how rape and sexual violence are treated through the police and judicial process, such legislation proves to be one step forward on the road to a more public concern about sexual ethics that refines and develops public interest in and understanding of the problems of sexual consent. The UK example is indicative of a general if uneven movement towards a more constructive view of the 'problems' of sexual consent in democratic societies.

The Chapters

The editors have argued at some length about how our volume should be divided into parts. Our disagreement is based on a high degree of overlap between the themes of the chapters. Whatever the reader's immediate concern, *all* the chapters will offer some ideas and insights. In the end we have settled for a fairly arbitrary division between a more general and theoretical first part and a more specific and practical second part. Where discussions of sexual consent are concerned the Kantian dictum that concepts without percepts are empty; percepts without concepts are blind remains valid.

Part 1: (More) General and Theoretical Themes

The issue which Cowling tackles in the first chapter is that of what form of approach to consent should underpin anti-rape education. Should it take the form of student codes at colleges, specific educational activities, or public discussion aimed at avoiding rape amongst young people? After pointing out that the very widespread extent of unrecorded and unprosecuted rape makes it highly unlikely that the problem of rape will be solved exclusively by a more vigorous prosecution regime he moves on to look at the Antioch College Ohio Student Code. This demands that students at the college should secure explicit verbal consent to each new level of sexual escalation. Cowling considers what this might mean, and argues that it is not very clear. The best way to make it clear, he observes, is to carefully specify each act which requires verbal permission, but he regards this as being unduly elaborate and cumbersome. He then discusses the possibility of using a Guttman scale. The idea of this is that someone who consents to, for example, penile/vaginal sex would also consent to kissing and having her breasts felt, but not vice-versa. Although this might simplify matters for many people it is ultimately unsatisfactory because there is no clear agreement on Guttman scale rankings, only an average. Moreover, the Guttman scale would institutionalise the heterosexual and patriarchal pattern of escalation from kissing to petting to sex which some campaigners are keen to question. He then moves on to propose an approach based on recent research about how sexual consent is actually given, and argues that proposals developed from this would be the most realistic.

Allison Moore and Paul Reynolds focus on feminist approaches to sexual consent. In a critical view of a range of recent theory, they seek to retrieve what is valuable within feminist critiques whilst avoiding their attendant pitfalls. They discuss radical feminist approaches that see rape and sexual violence as an extension and condition of hetero-patriarchal society and take issue with the way non-consenting sex becomes indistinct from sexual consent, and women's sexual consent and sexual pleasure is neglected or denigrated. They are not impressed, however, with post-feminist rejections of radical feminism, arguing that their portrayal of individual women's power, choice and responsibility for her sexual fortunes ignores the structural bases of gender inequality and reproduces liberal problems of representing sexual coercion and harassment as problems that individual women should manage or ignore. Between over-determinant structure and over-emphasis on agency, Moore and Reynolds find feminists like Lois Pineau and Sylvia Walby, who recognise gender inequality in sexual relations but equally recognise women have some degree of contingency and autonomy, allowing for discussion of the terms within which women can engage in meaningful consent decisions. Moore and Reynolds conclude that feminist approaches to sexual consent have considerable value to debates on sexual consent, and regardless of their limitations, they form a central part of the debates from which a more sophisticated and enlightened view of sexual consent will emerge.

Moira Carmody pursues a parallel theme to the first two chapters, starting from a very different background. She has been involved for many years in Australian activism against sexual violence to women. She comments that several rounds of legislative and social policy reform have failed to deliver much by way of deterrence to sexual violence. This has led her to reject of a number of dominant feminist discourses that have shaped anti-violence strategies to date. She argues that some essentialist feminist traditions have marginalised women's desire and pleasure by placing an emphasis on avoiding sexual exploitation. Central to these political strategies has been consent or the lack of the woman's consent to sexual activity. The responsibility for managing consent, she maintains, has been placed firmly with women to manage men's desires. Her critique of the continuing dominance of radical feminist belief systems has led her to an exploration of sexual ethics: all sexual encounters, regardless of the gender of the people involved, invite the possibility of ethical or unethical sexual behaviour. She then presents some preliminary ideas about how to conceptualise sexual ethics, arguing that sexual consent is a significant part of a broader concern about sexual ethics. She considers how Foucault's ideas about constituting an ethical self can broaden debates about sexual behaviour that is pleasurable, non-exploitative and has the potential for developing an ethics of consent.

Gideon Calder attacks Sharon Marcus's post-structuralist treatment of rape as a 'linguistic fact'. She says:

> Rapists do not prevail simply because as men they are really, biologically, and unavoidably stronger than women. A rapist follows a social script and enacts conventional, gendered structures of feeling and action which seek to draw the rape target into a dialogue which is skewed against her (Marcus, 1992, p. 390).

Calder argues that this transforms language 'into something suspiciously like God..: the ultimate source of absolutely everything which might otherwise seem to be the result of other contributing factors, including 'material' ones in a fairly basic sense' such as physical strength. Rape appears as something produced by language, and which can be resisted only by language. In contrast Calder asserts that material reality exists and has real effects, but also changes and can be changed by human intervention. An approach that recognises the effect of material reality offers the possibility of dealing with issues which are impossible within post-structuralism. These include the fact that the word 'no' is neither a sufficient nor a necessary component of refusals, the possibility that a date rape drug might nullify the apparent meaning of consenting words or actions, or the necessity for women to be regarded as, to some extent, authors of their language if their refusals are to be treated as meaningful.

Matthew Waites tackles the difficult and controversial area of the age of consent for gay sex. He examines the different models used to argue for particular ages of consent. A medical model was influential at the time of the legalisation of homosexuality in England. It was said that male sexual preferences were unstable until the age of 21. Since then the medical profession has become less confident about this issue, and questions of rights have come more to the fore. Waites also doubts whether an approach based on the idea that people develop into rational and autonomous beings able to make sensible sexual choices at a particular age can be sustained. Waites argues for a different, sociological, approach in which we concentrate upon the practical effects of a particular age of consent. Thus we look at, for example, whether teenagers feel happy about getting advice on health and contraception if they are having under-age sex. If this consideration suggests that the age of consent should be lowered, the great gap in power between a 14 year-old and an adult is a good reason for maintaining an age of consent even if the 14 year-old has a good intellectual and emotional grasp of what is involved in having sex. Although the age of consent for male homosexuals has now been settled at 16 in mainland Britain, the issues Waites raises are very much alive. Consenting sex between teachers and pupils aged 16 and 17 in the same school has been made illegal, whereas sex between a teacher and pupil of 16 in a different school is legal. Currently it is proposed in the Sexual Offences Bill that the age of consent for sex should remain at 16, while the age of consent for being photographed in indecent poses becomes 18. Sex with a prostitute aged at 16 or 17 will be treated as paedophilia and attract a seven-year sentence, whilst sex with an 18 year-old prostitute is legally acceptable. Waites' sociological approach should be helpful for these and other age of consent issues.

The more theoretical chapters end with Paul Reynolds' discussion of the quality of sexual consent. Reynolds argues that whilst it is quite understandable that the recent development of interest in sexual consent has concentrated on distinguishing between consent and non-consent, it is also necessary to look at the quality of sexual consent when given. He argues that there are significant problems and difficulties of culture, communication and knowledge in understanding sex and sexuality that persist in contemporary societies. These problems are manifest in a low quality of sexual consent decisions, which might constitute the giving of sexual consent but remain unsatisfactory as decisions that might be regarded as free, healthy or positive self-expression. What is at stake, Reynolds argues, is the development of a public sexual ethics that enables and emancipates subjects from fear or a fetishised and distorted fascination with sex. Reynolds argument is that this goes beyond legal change to more substantial changes in sex education, the way sexual knowledge is communicated and the sexual cultures that emerge in contemporary society. As such, Reynolds is concerned to develop and deepen the focus on sexual consent within a broader context of sexual ethics as a central aspect of social, cultural and political change.

Part 2: (More) Specific and Practical Themes

In the first of our more specific chapters Margaret Malloch is concerned with the treatment in court of women who engage in 'risky' behaviour because of their use of drugs or alcohol. But her argument is that drug and alcohol use are deemed to invalidate consent by a patriarchal judicial system. She argues that 'risk' in rape cases lies with women, thereby shifting the focus away from the perpetrator. Although the law does theoretically provide protection to women who are drugged or given spiked drinks, the protection is seriously inadequate. Much more frequently women who have voluntarily taken some drink or drugs have been portrayed in the court setting (as both victims of crime and as lawbreakers) as irrational and untrustworthy. Their narratives are delegitimised and their rights to justice are frequently undermined through these negative representations. Further, the legal system also finds it difficult to accept that women who freely express their sexuality retain the right not to consent. Perhaps this reached its extreme with the suicide of Lindsay Armstrong in the summer of 2002 following her cross examination in the course of a rape trial. This chapter illustrates the operation of this process through an analysis of the social construction of women as 'risky' women, and in doing so critically explores the status of women's consent.

Barbara Sullivan shifts the ground to focus on consent issues for sex workers. She comments that most of the current literature on prostitution and consent tends to – wholly or largely – reject the possibility of consent to prostitution sex (for sex workers). She acknowledges that this is not an entirely unreasonable position. Economic and other coercions clearly play an important part in sex work – as they do in most other forms of work. From a traditional liberal perspective, coercion or the lack of autonomy makes valid consent impossible. However, more attention needs to be paid to the power relations which both coerce sex workers *and* construct their consensual capacities. An examination of recent case law addressed to the rape of prostitutes demonstrates that consensual capacity can and has been constructed in this arena over the last twenty years. Where once a prostitute could not pursue a complaint of rape her non-consent can (under some circumstances) now be registered in law. This suggests that a positive consensual capacity might also be constructed. Sullivan's chapter argues that certain conditions will maximise the freedom and thus, consensual capacity of sex workers. These include safe and legal working conditions, access to other employment options (or other forms of income support), access to the criminal justice system and a politico-legal system that encourages the development of new rights as workers for prostitutes.

A similar mix of theory and more practical concerns can be found in our next chapter. Philip Rumney and Martin Morgan-Taylor examine the relationship between rape supportive attitudes and the prevalence of male rape, male sexual victimisation within the prison system and the construction of male sexual consent in the courtroom. In many respects their chapter illustrates a situation close to that which applied to female rape thirty years ago. A male version of the myths of rape is quite pervasive. Although the police are sometimes sympathetic the situation of male victims is much more of a lottery than that of females. Services for victims are scanty. There is some tension between activists and researchers on female rape and those studying male rape, with radical feminists concerned to preserve the idea of rape as a gendered act in which men oppress women and worried that the acknowledgement of male rape will erode concern and services for female victims. Rumney and Morgan-Taylor argue that relations between male prisoners are frequently so coercive that consent to sex in prison is highly problematic. Examples are given of judges mistaking physiological responses for consent. The chapter concludes by exploring the similarities and differences between male and female rape and making suggestions for future research.

Discussions of consent have generally concentrated on adult heterosexual consent. In contrast to this, Karen Corteen is specifically interested in consent and socially marginalised sexualities. She goes back to early twentieth century discussions of sexual conduct such as that by Marie Stopes in order to point out that it focuses on a rigid and constrained heterosexual sexuality, and argues that much discussion since has followed the same lines despite a somewhat increased recognition of complexity more recently. She argues that public space is dominated by heterosexual sexuality so that discussions of consent do not consider gay or lesbian sex. Although notionally acceptable in private, gay and lesbian sex is prone to suffer state intervention in ways to which heterosexual sex is not subject. And increasing media attention to gay and lesbian at sex in recent years, although welcome in reducing isolation, has tended to be voyeuristic and commodified. A creative response to marginalisation has been the development by minorities of dress codes which indicate their sexuality and their preferences. But because of marginalisation there is an increased possibility of misunderstanding or simply of individuals disregarding signals of consent and non-consent; yet being more explicit about one's sexuality is a dangerous strategy for minorities, risking physical violence from those who espouse a rigid heterosexuality.

Sado-masochism is highly marginalised sexuality. Sado-masochists have been prosecuted for engaging in consenting sex in Britain in the 1990s, notably in the Spanner case and the case of the Bolton Seven. In contradiction to the marginalisation and legal prosecution of sado-masochists, Andrea Beckmann's chapter finds that communicative sexuality is carefully and explicitly practised amongst the consenting sado-masochists of the New Scene where Beckmann carried out her participant observations. Probably because sado-masochism is dangerous if not undertaken carefully, Beckmann found that those involved were very careful in setting up a 'scene' to make sure that there was a good understanding of what was going to happen and of safe words and gestures. Beyond these relatively formal understandings there was also a sense that the 'top' (sadist) has to be sensitive to the needs and feelings of the bottom (masochist) in order to avoid injury. These ideas are well understood in the community which comprises the New Scene, and those who do not comply with them are excluded. Beckmann concludes by arguing that the form of consent required by consenting S/M goes beyond the formal model characteristic of liberalism and can only be understood in a framework based on Foucault's ideas.

A common observation made by the authors of the first three chapters in the book is that discussion of sexual consent has been dominated on the one hand by media representations and on the other by psychologists and activists concerned to minimise sexual assault. Thus despite the frequent theme in films, soap operas and television dramas of a couple making love for the first time, and despite very numerous surveys of the extent of rape and sexual assault, there has been surprisingly little investigation of how real people negotiate sexual consent in their daily lives. Terry Humphreys' chapter is one of a very few empirical investigations of the negotiation of sexual consent. It also has the merit of asking student opinions of the renowned Antioch Ohio code. Humphreys concludes that people frequently do not think about consent, as such, when negotiating sex. Instead they tend to engage in escalating physical activities, which are taken further if they meet with an encouraging response, itself frequently physical, or stopped if they meet with (typically) verbal resistance. Although Humphreys' student subjects were sympathetic to the objectives of the Ohio code, they regarded it a potential bureaucratic nightmare and an unwarranted intrusion into their bedrooms. Constantly obtaining verbal permission was seen as a passion killer.

The assumption in all the chapters to this point other than Waites' is that consent is between more or less rational adults. What about people with learning disabilities? Michelle McCarthy and David Thompson start by observing that within the learning disability field, there has for some time been an ongoing debate about how to balance people's rights to sexual autonomy with appropriate protection from abuse and exploitation. They start by looking at what boundaries previous legislation in England and Wales put on the sexual lives of people with learning disabilities. They argue that these laws failed to protect people with learning disabilities from abusive sexual contact whilst simultaneously contributing to a prohibitive sexual climate. They generally welcome the proposals for change contained in the White Paper *Protecting the Public*, particularly the designation of categories of people who should be prohibited from having sex with people with learning difficulties. In the same vein they are critical of the view in *Setting the Boundaries* that the law should not prohibit incest between adults, as people with learning difficulties are often abused by family members. In the course of a thorough review of existing and proposed laws they make several recommendations, notably that the test of competence to understand sexual consent should basically be a functional one which looks at the consequences of particular acts, but that this should include a basic understanding of laws and customs relating to sex (e.g. it is usually done in private); and that there is a particularly strong case for putting the onus on someone having sex with a person with learning difficulties to demonstrate that he (or she) has taken reasonable steps to obtain consent.

The last two chapters look at specific themes which have arisen in researching sexual consent. In his chapter David Renton argues that violence should not be used as the sole indicator of non-consensual sex. His particular target is Susan Sontag's essay 'Fascinating Fascism', which links the art of Leni Riefenstahl to the practice of S/M. He rejects Susan Sontag's claim that sexual violence is fascistic for two reasons. First, her argument is not a convincing account of the sexual dynamics of fascism. In this context the converse of Renton's argument is valid too: a regime does not have to fetishise black leather and sexual violence in order to be fascist. Second, Sontag also misunderstands violent sex. Renton claims that it is wrong to see all violence as possessing one unitary set of properties. Violence is a broad term, whose common meaning is hard to pin down. Non-oppressive forms of violence can be envisaged. The most important question to ask of all sexual activity is 'did consent take place?' If this is the key issue, then the presence of violence is only a secondary question.

Finally John Gibbins is interested in what guidelines should an academic researcher follow when investigating sexuality, particularly extreme sexualities such as paedophilia or sado-masochism, when having the wrong images stored on your computer can get you imprisoned? Can the researcher control exactly what ends up stored on his or her hard drive, when the content of websites is not always clear from their home page, and, indeed, when pornographic spam arrives entirely unsolicited? Gibbins argues that University codes of ethics and protocols on internet use can be of some help, and can be an aspect of a developing culture of ethical self-regulation. Nonetheless one still cannot be certain what will be the content of, say, the *Safe, Sane and Consensual Spanking* website – will it be a discussion suitable for this book or something on the borders of illegality? (The editors have not checked!) He also recognises that real harm can be done to people by some sexual practices, but argues that academics should get the benefit of the doubt, and not be assumed to be, for example, paedophiles on the basis of stored images unless there is an overwhelming and clear cut case against them. For seminars and courses within the university a principle of informed consent to proposed content is a valuable resource.

Sexual Consent: What is at Stake?

This collection seeks to make an important contribution to an area that, despite its importance to our everyday lives and to our sense of both self-esteem and social justice, has been for too long overlooked. It is in part a product of the current politics of bringing responses to rape and sexual crimes 'up to date', and establishing a more egalitarian attitude to sexual rights and responsibilities. It also represents a growing interest in sexual ethics. This interest in partly deeply personal – consent decisions are integral to our enjoyment of healthy, imaginative and pleasurable sexual experiences. Equally, as sex becomes more and more the subject of discourse in the public domain, and discourse that stretches beyond pornography, fetishised sexual representations and stereotypes or sensationalist 'storytelling' for the media, the problems of ethical sex become more and more evident. What we are confronted with is an ethical terrain strewn with problems and difficulties and beset by traditional views and custom and practice that shrouds the openness necessary for ethical discourse and stands against sexual openness as a feature of contemporary society.

What is at stake in demystifying and understanding sexual consent is enhancing personal happiness and personal ethical conduct, and the uncovering of a significant dimension of our lives and social representations and articulations of sex to ethical discourse. At one level, the editors hope that they have brought together some critical and valuable texts that will contribute to intellectual, academic and legal and political debate. At another, we hope that readers will do something as difficult as taking on the intellectual questions posed and addressing the different arguments around consent decisions – that is to look at their sexual ethics, their peers, and those of their children and those they have responsibilities to and for, and use this text to start discussions on just one aspect of this ethical discourse. In a sense, if one person can say they have felt empowered as a result reading this book and thinking and talking about their consent decisions, this book will have served a purpose.

Bibliography

Adler, Z. (1987), *Rape on Trial*, London: Routledge.

Archard, D. (1998) *Sexual Consent*, Oxford: Westview Press

Bell, D. and Binnie, J. (2000) *The Sexual Citizen*, Cambridge: Polity

Brown, B., Burman, M. and Jamieson, L. (1993), *Sex Crimes on Trial: The Use of Sexual Evidence in Scottish Courts*, Edinburgh: Edinburgh University Press.

Burgess-Jackson, K. (1996), *Rape: A Philosophical Investigation*, Dartmouth: Brookfield, Vermont.

Byers, E. S. and Lewis, K. (1988), 'Dating Couples' Disagreements over the Desired Level of Sexual Intimacy', *The Journal of Sex Research*, Vol. 24, pp. 15-29.

Cook, K. (2002) 'Rape Law.Consent@FreeAgreement.co.uk: An Assessment of the Legal Definition of Consent, in the light of the Current Review of Sexual Offences Law', *Contemporary Issues in Law*, Vol. 6, No. 1, pp. 7-22.

Cowling, M. (1998), *Date Rape and Consent*, Aldershot: Ashgate Publishing Ltd.

Cowling, M. (2003), 'Surveying Sexual Assault: the Benefits, Problems and Pitfalls', *Radical Statistics*, Vol. 83, forthcoming.

Dworkin, A. (1974), *Woman Hating*, New York: E. P. Dutton.

Dworkin, A. (1981), *Pornography: Men Possessing Women*, London: The Women's Only Press.

Dworkin, A. (1988), *Intercourse*, London: Arrow.

Hall, D. S. (1998), 'Consent for Sexual Behaviour in a College Student Population', *Electronic J. of Human Sexuality*, Vol. 1, [WWW document] URL http://www.ejhs.org/volume1/consent1.htm

Hamilton, R. (2002) 'How to Get Real about Rape: Evolutionary Psychology, Coercion and Consent' *Contemporary Issues in Law*, Vol. 6, No. 1, pp. 79-91.

Hickman, S. E., and Muehlenhard, C. L. (1999), '"By the semi-mystical appearance of a condom": How young women and men communicate sexual consent in heterosexual situations', *The Journal of Sex Research*, Vol. 36, pp. 258-272.

Hinchliffe, S. (2002) 'Morgan Reviewed: In Defence of Freedom of Will', *Contemporary Issues in Law*, Vol. 6, No. 1, pp. 37-46.

Home Office (2003), Information on the progress of the current Sexual Offences Bill – http://www.homeoffice.gov.uk/justice/sentencing/sexualoffencesbill/bill_prog.html

Jeffreys, S. (1990) *Anti-Climax: A Feminist Perspective on the Sexual Revolution*, London: The Woman's Press.

Johnson, I. M. and Sigler, R. T. (1997), *Forced Sexual Intercourse in Intimate Relationships*, Brookfield, Vermont: Ashgate.

Jones, H. (2002) 'Rape, Consent and Communication: Resetting the Boundaries?', *Contemporary Issues in Law*, Vol. 6, No. 1, pp. 23-26.

Lees, S. (1997), *Carnal Knowledge: Rape on Trial*, Harmondsworth: Penguin.

McCormick, N. B. (1979), 'Come-ons and Put-offs: Unmarried Students' Strategies for Having and Avoiding Sexual Intercourse', *Psychology of Women Quarterly*, Vol. 4, No. 2, pp. 194-211.

MacKinnon, C. (1989), *Towards a Feminist Theory of the State*, Harvard: Harvard University Press.

MacKinnon, C. (1996), 'Feminism, Method and the State: An Agenda for Theory' in Jackson, S. and Scott, S. (eds.), *Feminism and Sexuality*, Edinburgh: Edinburgh University Press.

Moran, L. Monk, D. and Beresford, S. (eds.) (1998), *Legal Queeries: Lesbian, Gay and Transgender Legal Studies*, London: Cassell.

Muehlenhard, C. L. et al. (1992), 'Definitions of Rape: Scientific and Political Implications', *Journal of Social Issues*, Vol. 48, No. 1, pp. 23-44.

Perper, T., and Weis, D. (1987), 'Proceptive and Rejective Strategies of US and Canadian College Women', *Journal of Sex Research*, Vol. 23, pp. 455-80.

Pineau, L. (1995), 'Date Rape: A Feminist Analysis' in Francis, L (ed.), *Date Rape: Feminism, Philosophy and the Law*, Pennsylvania: Pennsylvania State University Press.

Reynolds, P. (2002a), 'Introduction', *Contemporary Issues in Law*, Vol. 6, No.1, pp. 1-6.

Reynolds, P. (2002b), 'Rape, Law and Consent: The Scope and Limits to Sexual Regulation by Law', *Contemporary Issues in Law*, Vol. 6, No.1, pp. 92-102.

Richardson, D. (2000), *Rethinking Sexuality*, London: Sage.

Roiphe, K. (1993), *The Morning After: Sex, Fear and Feminism*, London: Hamish Hamilton.

Rosenthal, D. and Peart, R. (1996), 'The Rules of the Game: Teenagers Communicating about Sex', *Journal of Adolescence*, Vol. 19, pp. 321-32.

Temkin, J. (1987), *Rape and the Legal Process*, London: Sweet and Maxwell.

Thornhill, R. and Palmer C. T. (2000), *A Natural History Of Rape: Biological Bases Of Sexual Coercion*, Cambridge Ma: MIT Press.

Walby, S. (1990), *Theorising Patriarchy*, Oxford: Blackwell.

PART 1
(MORE) GENERAL AND
THEORETICAL THEMES

Chapter 1

Rape, Communicative Sexuality and Sex Education

Mark Cowling

Introduction

In this chapter I discuss what approach to consent should underpin anti-rape education, whether this takes the form of student codes at colleges, specific educational activities, or public discussion aimed at avoiding rape amongst young people. After pointing out that the very widespread extent of unrecorded and unprosecuted rape makes it highly unlikely that the problem of rape will be solved exclusively by a more vigorous prosecution regime I discuss the Antioch College Ohio Student Code. This demands that students at the college should secure explicit verbal consent to each new level of sexual escalation. It is not, I maintain, at all clear what this would mean in practice. The best way to make it clear would be to carefully specify each act which requires verbal permission. This would be unduly elaborate and cumbersome. Might it be possible to simplify things by using a version of the commonsense idea that – for example – a woman who consents to sex also implicitly consents to kissing on the mouth and having her breasts felt but does not implicitly consent to group sex? Unfortunately this idea is too vague to work on its own. I propose instead an approach based on recent research about how sexual consent is actually given, and argues that proposals developed from this would be the most realistic.

Why Sex Education?

There is widespread agreement that most instances of rape and sexual assault do not result in convictions in court. In England and Wales in 2001-2, for example, the police recorded 9,008 women as having been raped, resulting in 559 convictions or cautions (Home Office recorded crime statistics). Myhill and Allen, using data from the British Crime Survey, estimate that in 2000 61,000 women aged between 16 and 60 were raped, i.e. 12.6% of victims reported the incident to the police (Myhill and Allen, 2001, pp. 48-9). In my book *Date Rape and Consent* (Cowling, 1998) I looked at various estimates extrapolated from surveys which would show that there were anything up to 270,000 incidents of rape and attempted rape each year in England and Wales. Whilst it is very difficult to find an exact estimate on which most people would concur, it is clear to all that there is far more rape and sexual assault than appears in either recorded figures or convictions. Further, if rape was prosecuted at anything like the rate at which it occurs the prison population of England and Wales, currently at a record of around 73,000, would need to at least double.

Efforts should certainly be made to raise the rate of conviction for rape. The Sexual Offences Act currently before Parliament is partly intended to do this, as was the Youth Justice and Criminal Evidence Act, 1999. However, there is no massive programme of prison building; my impression is that only a modestly increased rate of conviction is anticipated. Rape legislation, therefore, is partly a matter of publicly stating what is acceptable behaviour as a form of education. The hope is that by stating what is allowed and what is not in the law there will be a shift in what men see as tolerable. This can certainly happen on the basis of very few convictions, as can be seen with the legislation on race relations, and as may have happened to some extent with the criminalisation of marital rape in 1994.

Education is certainly one of the goals of the Sexual Offences Act . Its very first clause extends the definition of rape to include forced fellatio on the basis that this causes just as much distress to victims as vaginal or anal rape. This in turn led to a debate in the House of Lords, with critics asserting that although they accepted the point about seriousness there is a public perception that a 'shiner' is distinct from, and possibly a bit less serious than, vaginal rape (see House of Lords debates, 31st March 2003). Arguably much more important, the proposed Act fleshes out the current definition of rape as sex without consent by defining consent as 'free agreement', and includes in the statute a non-exhaustive list of examples of situations in which free agreement does not exist. I have argued that this goes as far as the law should to writing the ideals of communicative sexuality into statute (see Cowling, 2002a).

The Antioch Code

Although the law can act as a form of sex education, it has a relatively limited role. There has been more discussion in the British press about the clause in the Sexual Offences Bill which would have made it illegal to have sex in your garden than there has been about the issue of free agreement. I teach a final year university course on rape and sexual assault, and I am afraid to say that only two or three of the 50-odd students on the course had heard of the Sexual Offences Bill.

Surveys suggest that the peak age for rape and other forms of sexual assault, both for victims and for perpetrators, is the late teens and early twenties. It is also clear that the rapes which are least reported are those by dates and acquaintances. All of this suggests that there should be a role for forms of sex education focused on rape and directed at this age group. The most famous attempt at this is the Antioch College Ohio code, written by students at Antioch College, Ohio, but with widespread campus discussion, in 1990. The code is based on the idea of communicative sexuality, i.e. that sex should ideally be based on mutuality and friendship. Elsewhere I have offered some criticisms of this ideal (Cowling, 1998,

2002a), briefly that it does not work directly for established relationships, and that it points to an artificial criterion for rape which would be rapidly discredited if passed into law. Here I want to look more extensively at sex education. By this I do not mean the pedagogical details but the basic underlying principles of sex education directed at minimising rape. Let us start by examining the Antioch code.

Antioch College Sexual Offence Policy (part)

1.   For the purposes of this policy, 'consent' shall be defined as follows:
the act of willingly and verbally agreeing to engage in specific sexual contact or conduct
2.   If sexual contact and/or conduct is not mutually and simultaneously initiated, then the person who initiates sexual contact/conduct is responsible for getting the verbal consent of the other individual(s) involved.
3.   Obtaining consent is an ongoing process in any sexual interaction. Verbal consent should be obtained with each new level of physical and/or sexual contact/conduct in any given interaction, regardless of who initiates it. Asking 'do you want to have sex with me?' is not enough. The request for consent must be specific to each act.
4.   The person with whom sexual contact/conduct is initiated is responsible to express verbally and/or physically his/her willingness or lack of willingness when reasonably possible.
5.   If someone has initially consented but then stops consenting during a sexual interaction, she/he should communicate withdrawal verbally and/or through physical resistance. The other individual(s) must stop immediately.
6.   To knowingly take advantage of someone who is under the influence of alcohol, drugs and/or prescribed medication is not acceptable behaviour in the Antioch community.
7.   If someone verbally agrees to engage in specific contact or conduct, but it is not of her/his own free will due to any of the circumstances stated in a. through d. below, then the person initiating shall be considered in violation of this policy if:
a.   the person submitting is under the influence of alcohol or other substances supplied to her/him by the person initiating;
b.   the person submitting is incapacitated by alcohol, drugs and/or prescribed medication;
c.   the person submitting is asleep or unconscious;
d.   the person initiating has forced, threatened, coerced or intimidated the other individual(s) into engaging in sexual contact and/or sexual conduct.

The policy then spells out a series of offences which are implicit in the above: rape, i.e. 'Non-consensual penetration, however slight, of the vagina or anus; non-consensual fellatio or cunnilingus', sexual assault, i.e. basically attempts at rape; sexual imposition, i.e. non-sexual touching of 'thighs, genitals, buttocks, the pubic region, or the breast/chest area, followed by other offences less interesting from our point of view such as sexual harassment or failure to disclose HIV positive status. The rest of the policy describes how it will be enforced.

Critique of the Antioch Code

The Antioch code led to extensive American, and indeed, world-wide controversy and ridicule. Like everyone else involved, Alan Guskin, the president of Antioch College at the time the policy was developed, was surprised at the intense media interest in the policy. He puts this down partly to a public interest in sex, but more specifically to the requirement that students should talk about it (Guskin, 1996, p. 157). Whilst I am sure he is right about these two factors, the degree of ridicule which the policy aroused leads me to think that there is a further factor: the code was widely felt to impose artificial requirements on an intimate area of life in a mechanical fashion. There is a popular image of Antioch students setting off for dates with a pile of consent forms, a lawyer and a breathalyser. Although this caricature goes well beyond the code, I think its mechanistic quality is why, despite the fact that I defend the code as an attempt at a serious solution to a serious problem, my students always seem to laugh when I first mention the code (which they have usually at least vaguely heard of). In the course of his article explaining and defending the policy Guskin quotes a letter written to *The New Yorker* in its support. The author, Julia Reidhead, describes the code as an 'erotic windfall': 'What man or woman on Antioch's campus, or elsewhere, wouldn't welcome the direct question "May I kiss the hollow of your neck?" The possibilities are wonderful...' (Guskin, 1996, p. 158).

In its way this letter sums up many people's general reservations about the code: it is requiring everyone to rewrite their erotic conduct, most of which seemed to be working adequately before. The Antioch policy seems to me to be flawed on this point. It talks of obtaining specific verbal consent to 'each new level of physical and/or sexual contact/conduct', but does not specify what exactly is involved in this. Would most people surely understand what is meant by a level? The more I have thought about this the less clear I have become. Kissing somebody on the mouth presumably requires permission. Would kissing someone upon the mouth with tongue contact require further permission? How many times would a man who wants to kiss his date's breasts have to ask permission? Which of the following are otiose and silly? (I am assuming that right and left breasts are on the same level.)

Table 1.1 Possible Steps to Breast Kissing Following Antioch Policy
1.   May I touch your breast through your clothes?
2.   May I remove your overcoat?
3.   May I unbutton the top two buttons of your blouse?
4.   May I put my hand inside your bra?
5.   May I take off your blouse?
6.   May I take off your bra?
7.   May I kiss your breasts?

Except as a one-off special event, sex following the Antioch code is getting to look tedious, particularly in a long-standing relationship where the couple have come to know each other's preferences well. How many levels are there in total? The following is a Guttman scale produced by Cowart and others:

Table 1.2 Example of a Guttman Scale	
31	Bondage
30	Use of mild pain
29	Finger penetration of partner's anus
28	Sexual intercourse, sitting
27	Sexual intercourse, standing
26	Hand contact with partner's anal area
25	Sexual intercourse, from rear
24	Male tongue manipulation of female genitals to orgasm
23	Shower/bathing with partner
22	Sexual intercourse, female superior
20	Sexual intercourse, face-face, side
19	Mutual oral stimulation of genitals to orgasm
18	Male tongue manipulation of clitoris
17	Male tongue penetration of vagina
16	Sexual intercourse, partly clothed
15	Male mouth contact with vulva
14	Clitoral manipulation to orgasm by male
12	Sexual intercourse, male superior
11	Male manipulation of vulva
10	Female mouth contact with penis
9	Male lying prone on female, no penetration
8	Manipulation of penis by female
7	Clitoral manipulation by male
6	Partner's observation of your nude body
5	Your observation of nude partner
4	Male finger penetration of vagina
2	Male mouth contact with female breast
1	Feeling female's nude breast

(Table adapted from Cowart and Pollack, 1979 and Cowart-Steckler, 1984, found in Hall, 1998. This table is for males; the one for females is very similar, with minor differences in order. Omitted activities are presumably solitary, notably masturbation and the contemplation of pornography.)

Although this is a good start on a possible list of levels, readers will have no difficulty in making additions. The list should surely mention kissing, and probably

French kissing, before anything more directly sexual is dealt with. At the other end, what about anal intercourse and rimming? Some levels might need sub-division – do the couple become nude at one bound? What about using or not using condoms and/or contraception for various activities? There is nothing here about having more than one partner. What about the use of ice, oils, whipped cream, chocolate spread, orgy butter? What about sex toys, vibrators, Thai beads, dildos, nipple clamps and the like? What about the use of assorted drugs on a voluntary basis? What are the partners to do with the metal ornaments which are the result of body piercing? The sado-masochistic possibilities considered are very limited. What about filming the event on video? Perhaps, also, combinations of possibilities should form additional levels: an additional partner, chocolate spread and an anal vibrator could be seen as different in combination than these items taken singly. It looks as though an appendix to the code offering examples of levels would run into at least the low hundreds. Things would get worse if the code also specified levels for gay and lesbian sex, which it certainly should. As the basis of sex education for, say, fourteen year olds this is beginning to look much too complex and alarming.

One possibility might be a simplification based on the idea of a Guttman scale, which is that someone who has carried out the acts in the higher levels (with higher numbers in the list above) has also carried out the acts in the lower levels. This could be the basis of a convention about consent: if you consent to an act with a higher number you consent by implication to the acts with lower numbers. Thus a woman happy in a particular situation about sexual intercourse from the rear would also be happy to have her nude breast felt, but not vice-versa.

There are several reasons for resisting this seductive approach. It tends to reinforce the patriarchal teleology in which heterosexual encounters lead inevitably onwards and upwards towards genital sex. In contrast, one of the ideals of communicative sexuality is that the partners should explore all sorts of activities which may give them pleasure. In addition, people do not agree fully about the levels on a Guttman scale, which are the product of averaging. Thus part of what was at stake in the House of Lords debate already mentioned was whether or not fellatio is on the same level as genital and anal sex. Similarly, Hall asked his subjects in which order they had moved through 12 levels of engagement ranging from kissing and hugging through to anal sex in their most recent sexual encounter. It seems a reasonable assumption that people would normally progress from the lowest levels such as kissing and hugging through to intercourse, but out of 300 subjects the best exact correlation of sequences he could come up with was four women who had moved through eight levels in the same order as each other. Agreement about higher or lower levels might be rather better than this, but any list would obviously involve an average which violates some people's preferences. There is nothing to stop individuals having their own, idiosyncratic, order of levels. For example, a man who was happy to do virtually anything else might object to having his chest stroked. There might also be straightforward reasons for someone who was quite happy to engage in extensive play with whipped cream followed by rear entry sex to object to having her right breast felt because it was sore. The idea that a woman who was happy to go along with anal sex with multiple partners whilst wearing bondage gear was right at the top of the Guttman scale and would therefore be happy to do anything else whatsoever is alarmingly similar to the assumption in rape trials that a woman who has been promiscuous would consent to anything, and should be not be accepted.

If we follow the Antioch code, we thus seem to be left with an enormous number of acts which require explicit verbal permission. Would people be expected to memorise lists? It is time to look at an alternative approach based on what we know of how people actually negotiate sexual consent.

Building from Real Life

In *Date Rape and Consent* I commented that it is strange that there are a large number of studies by American psychologists of rape and sexual coercion in dating situations, but very few of the process of consent, most of these being based on what women might do in situations where they were interested in having sex rather than on the process of consent itself (Cowling, 1998, p. 93. The studies in question were Perper and Weis, 1987, Byers and Lewis, 1988, Moore and Butler, 1989, McCormick and Jones, 1989, McCormick, 1979, Rosenthal and Peart, 1996). I was not alone in thinking this, and fortunately there have now been a few more studies of the process of consent, notably Humphreys (in this volume), Hall (1998) and Hickman and Muehlenhard (1999).

These studies are reasonably consistent with each other and with the previous literature. The general conclusions are admirably summarised in Humphreys' chapter in this book:

- People of both sexes frequently do not think about consent as such, but about whether a sexual encounter is going well. They might start thinking about consent and talking about it if there is disagreement.
- Consent in the situation of a one night stand might well take the form of an invitation to 'come back to my place' followed by an assumption that there is consent to the ongoing heavy petting etc, perhaps followed by a quick verbal confirmation of consent ('You do definitely want to do this?') before sex actually takes place.
- Continually talking about consent is seen by men and women as tedious and as detracting from the romance of the situation.
- Provided there is general consent to sex taking place a degree of uncertainty about what one's partner is going to do is seen by at least some people as part of the excitement of a sexual encounter.
- To the extent that consent is sought as an encounter progresses it is mainly non-verbal. One partner, typically the man, takes an initiative and the other responds by hugging and caressing, smiling, not moving away, getting closer, kissing, intimately touching (Hall, 1998). Men tend to prefer to assume that there is consent unless there plainly is not; women may prefer to put more stress on ongoing physical consent. Men are slightly more optimistic that female signals imply consent than are women when interpreting male signals

(Hickman and Muehlenhard, 1999). These gender differences are not overwhelming, and may, perhaps, represent two different ways of looking at the same process.

- Strategies to encourage sex tend to be indirect and physical (for example, producing a condom, undressing one's partner); strategies to avoid it tend to be direct and verbal ('tell him he's gone far enough').
- When asked about the Antioch policy students tend to respond that although they sympathise with the underlying intentions it is unduly mechanical and potentially a bureaucratic nightmare if implemented seriously.

The limited studies to date would suggest that the existing process of obtaining consent is generally felt to work reasonably well, but that it is largely non-verbal and operates for at least some of the time by assuming consent unless there is a clear indication to the contrary. One immediate observation is that the somewhat artificial ideas of an ideal process of consent which have been derived from advocates of communicative sexuality may actually have contributed to the exaggeration of the extent of date rape (for discussion see Cowling 2003). Perhaps existing practices do facilitate miscommunication, and perhaps if everyone followed the ideals of communicative sexuality there would be less miscommunication. However, perhaps women are willing to risk a certain amount of miscommunication as part of an overall process of dating which works reasonably well.

What would an alternative to the Antioch code, which I shall tendentiously call the 'real life approach' actually look like? Based on the literature described above I think that it should start by describing some episodes of consenting sex, paying careful attention to the process by which consent was negotiated in each case. One example should definitely be a one night stand, and another should be of a couple growing increasingly intimate over a few weeks and finally deciding to sleep together. The forms of verbal and non-verbal communication employed should be examined. Hopefully these would then be the basis for a discussion of personal preferences in sexual negotiation, of forms of miscommunication which might arise in each situation, and of various sorts of things which might go wrong. One example would simply concern failure to use contraception or failure to take precautions against HIV infection. Another would be to look at a situation where both partners got too drunk to be able to understand the other one's communications properly. Another might perhaps concern a woman who out of a misconceived sense of politeness went along with a whole series of male initiatives until she was naked in his bedroom but then decided she did not want to have sex: one worry raised by Hickman and Muehlenhard (1999) is that doing nothing can be either a form of consent or a result of paralysis and fear. The moral of all of these would be quite compatible with the communicative sexuality approach: better, sober, communication would make each of these problems less likely.

The reliance on language in the communicative sexuality approach would, however, be lessened in the real life alternative. Consider the following date rape vignette:

Mary and John had been dating for two weeks. Both Mary and John had slept with people in the past but they hadn't had sexual intercourse with each other. On their fourth date, after John took Mary out for a lobster dinner and then to a wild party to meet some of his friends, the couple went to John's apartment. Mary was wearing a sexy, provocative dress. She had spent a lot of time getting ready, because she wanted to look her best for a special evening. After they got to his apartment, they shared a bottle of wine, listened to music, talked, laughed and kissed. Mary told John what a wonderful time she was having with him. John suggested that they move to his bedroom where they could get more comfortable. She nodded in agreement. In the bedroom, they started dancing erotically and kissing passionately. John caressed Mary's breasts, and Mary moaned. When he started to unbutton her blouse, Mary asked him to stop. He kissed her gently and continued to undress her. She begged him to stop. She told him 'No!' emphatically and said that she was not ready for sex with him. He continued anyway, telling her that he knew she wanted it. He told her to relax and that she was really going to like it. John assured Mary that he loved her and that he had been thinking about this moment ever since they first met. He pulled up her skirt and pulled down her panties. While holding both of her arms with one of his hands, he unzipped his fly, took out his erect penis, and penetrated her (Parrott, 1991, p. 9).

Parrott's point is that this is rape just as much as stranger rape. Advocates of communicative sexuality would stress that Mary verbally and emphatically did not consent. From the real life approach I would agree that this is rape because Mary does not consent and John forces her. This case seems very similar to ones in surveys about date rape in which the man 'just carries on'. However, in terms of the pattern of non-verbal initiative encouraged by 'hugging and caressing, smiling, not moving away, getting closer, kissing, intimately touching' described above Mary has a series of eleven choices where she encourages John before deciding she does not want to go any further. It would be better if she cried off at an earlier stage, or alternatively supplied John with a more decisive explanation: 'Oh, no, the lobster, I think I'm going to throw up', 'I'm sorry, I've just suddenly got a blinding headache', 'Oh no! I've been having such a lovely evening I've just remembered I was supposed to look after my sister's children from midnight to allow her to go to work', etc. etc.

Again, consider the following possibility. Instead of asking John to stop, etc., Mary says: 'Go on if you must'. This is certainly consent, and John would not be guilty of rape unless the statement had been produced by force or by threats. However, on the basis of the statement a considerate man would certainly have grave doubts about proceeding with sex. He would surely be asking the woman 'What's wrong?' 'Don't you really want sex?'. Or consider a situation where the women gives every indication of going along with the man's desires, but where in practice she simply does not seem happy. Perhaps she seems distracted, perhaps she cannot ever quite get comfortable, perhaps she keeps finding objections to things the man does which she would normally find stimulating or neutral. Again, a considerate man at would surely stop and try to sort out what was wrong. In other words what I am looking for is the feeling that in addition to any specific words or actions of the woman there is a general atmosphere such that the man can be confident that she is happy with what is happening.

A further point about the vignette arises from Archard's critique of an article by Husak and Thomas which advocates something close to the real life approach, stressing that much of the communication surrounding sex relies on conventions (Husak and Thomas, 1991; Archard, 1997). In brief, Archard argues that conventions may not be fully universally established, that relying on them may lead to considerable suffering for particular women whilst checking them verbally is not difficult, that much of the behaviour which Husak and Thomas identify as consenting to sex doubles as friendly or flirtatious behaviour, which may well lead on to sex but which by no means amounts to consent to sex. He is happy with the idea that a verbal question may be given a physical response. Thus, crudely, the man might say 'do you want sex'? and the woman might remove more of her clothes and make a beckoning gesture. He is thus advocating communicative sexuality, but not a full-blown verbal consent standard.

Archard is certainly right if he means that ambiguous but encouraging invitations such as 'come up for coffee' should not be relied on as invitations to sex in the face of clear verbal or physical indications to the contrary. But Archard does not seem to take on board that there are elements of convention in all communications. For example, in much of India nodding your head is a way of saying 'no'. Thus all our communications, including verbal communications, depend on conventions. Let us go back for a minute to Archard's couple. The man says 'Do you want sex?', and the woman effectively answers 'Yes' using gestures. But what has she actually consented to? Has she consented to having her hair stroked? Has she consented to having her toes sucked? Has she consented to having her breasts kissed? Has she consented to anal sex? Most of us would have preliminary answers to these questions, but there would be likely to be some level of debate about some of them. If they are making love for the first time I would suggest that they rely on three ways of communicating. First, some sort of set of conventions about what an affirmative answer to 'Do you want sex?' entails. This enables us to say that the man is reasonable in thinking of that the woman does not need to be asked, in addition: 'May I stroke your hair?', but would not be reasonable in assuming that he has consent to anal sex. However, we can see from the literature that these conventions are not very precisely established, and certainly could not be relied on as if a Guttman scale provided an exact guide to consent. Second, a considerate and tolerant approach on both sides, so that he notices if she does not like having her hair stroked, but she does not equate hair stroking without permission with rape. Third, verbal or physical encouragement or discouragement of particular supplementary activities takes place.

A discussion of conventions should move on to look at the metaphorical and symbolic aspects of sexual communication, for example a discussion of invitations to go to bed and how such an invitation could be issued with the intention is a very firmly that it will lead to sleep. Susan Ehrlich's book, *Representing Rape: Language and Sexual Consent* (2001), based around the trial of a student who persistently refused to remain within the boundaries of such limited invitations would be an appropriate focus of discussion. The women he victimised, in my view, felt impelled to go along with the man's wishes because of politeness or not wishing to cause a rumpus. I think that the convention of not disturbing others unduly might be more widely relevant in cases of date rape (see Cowling, 2002).

Linked to this is the point that sexual signals and sexual acts are liable to take on different meanings in different contexts. To take two extreme examples within an ongoing relationship, contrast a situation in which the woman's much-loved uncle has just died and where what she wants is really comfort rather than sex with the one where she has just returned from a break in Amsterdam complete with an assortment of interesting videos and devices. Or contrast a situation in which the man is exhausted and stressed out as a consequence of his work, and may therefore perhaps not perform at his best, with one where he has returned from a healthy but celibate field trip.

This is, of course, also true of differing personal histories. A woman who has previously suffered attempted strangulation or domestic violence is likely to react adversely to caresses around her neck and boisterous but well-intentioned physical 'threats' (see Estrich's discussion of the Rusk case, 1987, pp. 63-66).

Discussions of rape should also, of course, cover acts which are closer to stranger rape: the deliberate use of spiked or drugged drinks or rape under the cover of a date (see Lees, 1996). All through it is important to stress strongly the devastating consequences of rape, in order to make men more aware of the potentially serious results of their actions.

Conclusion

A basic principle of good education is that it takes account of the students' existing knowledge and experiences. My quarrel with the approach to sex education aimed at avoiding date rape which is based on the ideal of communicative sexuality and which I describe above is that it fails to do this. Instead it attempts to impose patterns of sexual conduct which are remote from students' real experiences, and is thus perceived as artificial. Instead I suggest the beginnings of a 'real life' approach, based on what we know of how sexual consent is negotiated and recognised. It plainly requires further development as more research is undertaken, and it needs, of course, to be turned from an academic discussion into material suitable for workshops or discussion groups.

Bibliography

Antioch College (2002), Antioch College Ohio Policies on Sexual Offences and Sexual Harassment: http://www.antioch-college.edu/community/html/cg.html

Archard, D. (1997), "'A Nod's as Good as a Wink": Consent, Convention and Reasonable Belief', *Legal Theory*, Vol. 3, pp. 273-290.

Byers, E. S. and Lewis, K. (1988), 'Dating Couples' Disagreements over the Desired Level of Sexual Intimacy', *The Journal of Sex Research*, Vol. 24, pp. 15-29.

Cowart, D. A., and Pollack, R. H. (1979). A Guttman scale of sexual experience. *Journal of Sex Education and Therapy*, Vol. 1, pp. 3-6.

Cowart-Steckler, D. A. (1984). A Guttman scale of sexual experience: An update. *Journal of Sex Education and Therapy*, Vol. 10, pp. 49-52.

Cowling, M. (1998), *Date Rape and Consent*, Aldershot: Ashgate.

Cowling, M. (2002), Review of Ehrlich (2001), *International Journal of the Sociology of Law*, Vol. 30, No. 4, pp. 312-4.

Cowling, M. (2002a), 'Should Communicative Sexuality be Written into the English Law on Rape?', *Contemporary Issues in Law*, Vol. 6, No. 1, pp. 47-63.

Cowling, M. (2003), 'Surveying Sexual Assault: the Benefits, Problems and Pitfalls', *Radical Statistics*, Vol. 83, forthcoming.

Ehrlich, S (2001), *Representing Rape: Language and Sexual Consent*, London: Routledge.

Estrich, S.(1987), *Real Rape*, Cambridge, MA: Harvard University Press.

Guskin, Alan E. (1996), 'The Antioch Response: Sex, You Don't Just Talk About It', in Francis, Leslie (ed.), *Date Rape: Feminism, Philosophy and the Law*, Pennsylvania State University Press: Pennsylvania, pp. 154-165.

Hall, D. S. (1998), 'Consent for Sexual Behaviour in a College Student Population', *Electronic J. of Human Sexuality*, Vol. 1, [WWW document] URL http://www.ejhs.org/volume1/consent1.htm

Hickman, S. E., and Muehlenhard, C. L. (1999), '"By the semi-mystical appearance of a condom": How young women and men communicate sexual consent in heterosexual situations', *The Journal of Sex Research*, Vol. 36, pp. 258-272.

Husak, D. N. and Thomas, G. C. III, 'Date Rape, Social Convention and Reasonable Mistakes', *Law and Philosophy*, Vol. 11, 1992, pp. 95-126

Lees, S. (1996), *Carnal Knowledge, Rape on Trial*, London: Hamish Hamilton.

McCormick, N. B. (1979), 'Come-ons and Put-offs: Unmarried Students' Strategies for Having and Avoiding Sexual Intercourse', *Psychology of Women Quarterly*, Vol. 4, No. 2, pp. 194-211.

McCormick, N. B., and Jones, A. J. (1989), 'Gender Differences in Nonverbal Flirtation', *Journal of Sex Education and Therapy*, Vol. 15, No. 4, pp. 271-282.

Moore, M. M., and Butler, D. L. (1989), 'Predictive Aspects of Nonverbal Courtship Behaviour in Women', *Semiotica*, Vol. 76, Nos 3/4, pp. 205-215.

Myhill, A. and Allen, J. (2001), *Rape and Sexual Assault of Women: the Extent and Nature of the Problem – Findings from the British Crime Survey*, Home Office Research Study 237, London; also at: http://www.homeoffice.gov.uk/rds/pdfs2/hors237.pdf

Parrott, A., and Bechhofer, L. (1991) *Acquaintance Rape: The Hidden Crime*, New York: John Wiley.

Perper, T., and Weis, D. (1987), 'Proceptive and Rejective Strategies of US and Canadian College Women', *Journal of Sex Research*, Vol. 23, pp. 455-80.

Rosenthal, D. and Peart, R. (1996), 'The Rules of the Game: Teenagers Communicating about Sex', *Journal of Adolescence*, Vol. 19, pp. 321-32.

Chapter 2

Feminist Approaches to Sexual Consent: A Critical Assessment

Allison Moore and Paul Reynolds

Introduction

> When force is a normalised part of sex, when no is taken to mean yes, when fear and despair produce acquiescence and acquiescence is taken to mean consent, consent is not a meaningful concept. (MacKinnon, cited in McIntosh, 1992, p. 156)

> ....a process whereby gender inequality is maintained, supposedly sufficient to negate the apparently willing consent of all women, cannot at the same time be such to allow for resistance to and dissent from that process by some of its supposed victims. (Archard, 1998, p. 89)

The 'problem' of sexual consent – and more specifically the prevalence and incidence of forced sex and rape – is acutely political for women. Studies of the legal and judicial process of prosecuting sex without consent demonstrate persistent and profound inequalities in the treatment of women who are raped or forced to have sex in comparison with the men who rape/force them (Lees, 1997, Cook, 2002). At the same time, the historical study of sexual conduct and social inequality in society has demonstrated the extent to which women's consent has been constructed referentially to male sexuality. That is to say, women have historically understood and measured their capacity to consent to sex by male referents of who has power, who actively initiates and who passively responds, and what is constituted as the 'normal' parameters of sexual pleasure. All of these are contextualised within the masculine and feminine gendered constructs of hetero-patriarchy (Jeffreys, 1990).

In such a context, it is not surprising that feminist conceptions of sexual consent have arisen from an understanding of sexual relations that variously denies the possibility of meaningful consent under the conditions of hetero-patriarchy, or argues that the extent of sexual consent by women reflects the extent to which women are allowed or struggle for a degree of agency under hetero-patriarchal regimes. The concept of sexual consent is stripped of wilful and willing participation, agency and autonomy, and reduced to a measurement of partial engagement in an unequal sexual contract that brings limited benefits to women, or denied as the ideological misrepresentation of hetero-patriarchal sexual ownership, control and abuse (Pateman, 1988).

The problem with this position is that it denies the idea of women's sexual consent an *a priori* meaning beyond or apart from the conditions of hetero-patriarchy. Women are always and everywhere the objects of sex, the passive recipients of male aggression – denied enjoyment, forbidden pleasure and deterred from liberating and owning sexual pleasure outside of total rejections of heterosexuality, such as lesbianism or 'political lesbianism' (Dworkin, 1981, Dworkin, 1997, Kitzinger, 1987, MacKinnon, 1989, Radicalesbians, 1970, Wilton, 1995). There may be some diversities in and divergence from this position, according to class position, particular societal or cultural norms and values or subjective and interpersonal factors, for example, but these lie within gendered structural and determinant inequalities that mitigate against anything but marginal and temporary change. In contrast, post-feminist critiques of the 'victimology' of structural or ideological determinations of women's experience and ability to act autonomously have raised questions of how women can claim power and ownership of what they do, including pleasure in engaging in heterosexual sex (Roiphe, 1993, Wolf, 1993). A concept of sexual consent that cannot appreciate the meaning of women's agency and autonomy, even under conditions of social and sexual inequality, will be of little use in theorising women's ownership of their sexuality short of radical social and structural change. If feminism is to offer women an agenda for greater ownership, control and enjoyment of their sexuality, it has to offer an agenda that accepts the pleasure in and desire of women for heterosexual sex. It also has to offer a transformative politics whereby not only are structural inequalities inherent in patriarchy and heterosexist society challenged, but intermediate gains in sexual pleasure, conduct, ethics are achieved. To deny the language and concepts of the 'battleground' in sexual and gendered politics is to deny or fail to recognise women's existing everyday struggles and the range of potent weapons available to women in struggles in contemporary society.

This contribution to feminist debates begins from a position that values radical feminist approaches to sexual consent, but accepts their limitations, arising principally from their emphasis on structural determinisms at the expense of women's agency. At the same time, it seeks to avoid the post-feminist restatement of liberal freedoms that reifies women's agency and does not adequately consider structured social inequalities. It seeks to provide a broad overview of feminist positions on sexual consent, in order to avoid the stereotyping of feminism either as singular in its approach to debates around sexual consent or as offering nothing to debates around consent. It then seeks to retrieve some grounds for a feminist theoretical position that problematises the structural shaping of women's sexuality but leaves conceptual space for agency in women's consent in hetero-patriarchal socio-cultural contexts.

Competing Perspectives: Radical Feminism versus Post-Feminism

The most common representation of a feminist position on sexual consent is that of the radical feminist critique, typified in the work of Catherine MacKinnon (1989). MacKinnon theorises sexual consent in hetero-patriarchal society as resting on two fallacies. It rests upon notions that women control and are empowered by their sexuality, and have the freedom to choose the type of sex they engage in, and with whom they have sex. MacKinnon rejects this as a view predicated on assumptions of human equality that does not reflect the systematic and structured inequality and brutalisation of women under patriarchy. The concept of consent in hetero-patriarchal societies is premised on the idea of an autonomous negotiation of a sexual 'contract' within which women derive at least some satisfaction. For MacKinnon, in a 'male supremacist' society women lack the power to negotiate with men about what would bring them sexual pleasure. Indeed, women are property, domestic servants, reserve labour and objects of sexual lust, none of which are positions from which they can renegotiate their social relations with men. Under a system of hetero-patriarchy, women are unable to exercise choice and therefore are not able to give valid consent to sexual intercourse.

MacKinnon sees forced sex as a 'normal' part of sexuality and rape as 'indigenous, not exceptional, to women's social condition' (MacKinnon, 1989, p. 172). Traditionally, what has separated rape from 'normal' sex is the notion that rape is violent. However, in a society where sexuality and violence have become conflated, it is increasingly difficult to distinguish between forced and unforced sex (MacKinnon, 1989, p. 174). Therefore, it becomes meaningless to talk about consent in the context of a mutuality of violence and sexuality. Rape is simply an extension of male sexual power from less violent but equally brutalising sexual relations.

In legal terms, it is the absence of consent that differentiates rape from 'normal' sex and it is a woman's relationship to a man that determines whether consent has been given (MacKinnon, 1989, p. 175). She suggests that women are categorised according to a dichotomous 'Madonna/Whore' model of female sexuality. Virtuous and virginal girls do not consent, while wives, prostitutes and unvirtuous women do nothing but consent. Even in a situation where an explicit verbal consent has been given, it takes place within a context of unequal power relations between men and women and, therefore, the quality of that consent is flawed (MacKinnon, 1989).

MacKinnon's argument is premised on the notion that sexuality is determined by and for men – through an all-pervasive hetero-patriarchy. Sexuality is defined and characterised through a male referent, predicated on male desire, pleasure, fantasy and power. She maintains that it is not enough to examine historical evidence of the changing definition of sexuality, or to consider the role and meaning of language, reflecting recent development in feminist and post-feminist discourse analysis. A feminist theory of sexuality must take into account empirical evidence. It must examine the way in which sexuality, and the social relations that underpin it, impact on women's everyday lives (MacKinnon, 1989, p. 129).

MacKinnon (1996) compares a feminist theory of sexuality with a Marxist theory of work. Just as labour is bought and sold for the benefit of a few, so too is sexuality 'expropriated' for the benefit of some. Those who have their sexuality taken away from them are defined as a class – women (MacKinnon, 1996, p. 182). Sexuality moves from being centred on pleasure, desire and fantasy to analyses of the distribution of power between genders and the relationships that arise from it. (MacKinnon, 1989).

In a hetero-patriarchal society, power and inequality are eroticised, 'sexuality equals heterosexuality, equals the sexuality of (male) dominance and (female) submission' (MacKinnon, 1989, p. 131). In a society where women's lives are conditioned by systems of institutionalised domination and subordination (Jeffreys, 1990), it is hardly surprising that women learn to eroticise relations of power and inequality, because 'it beats being forced' (MacKinnon, 1989, p. 177). Female sexuality is socialised into passivity and comes to be defined as masochistic (Jeffreys, 1990).

The eroticisation of dominance and submission leads MacKinnon to argue that heterosexuality is a system whereby the powerless are feminised and the powerful are masculinised, irrespective of their biological sex (MacKinnon, 1989). She is not alone in adopting this position. Sheila Jeffreys (1990) suggests that any sexual relationship that eroticises power is a manifestation of heterosexual desire. The only way to dismantle heterosexual desire is to reject it and replace it with a homosexual desire. Indeed, according to this position, a lesbian-feminist relationship is seen as an important strategic tool to end women's oppression because compulsory heterosexuality is the root of all oppression and the measure against which all other relationships are judged (Rich, 1981, Brunet and Turcotte, 1988).

Heterosexuality is thus reduced to being a form of violation or possession (Segal, 1992, p. 80). For example, MacKinnon (1989) suggests that female heterosexual sexuality comes to be understood as the desire or love of violation, whilst for Dworkin (1981) penile-vaginal penetration represents an act of possession or ownership. This line of reasoning asserts a strict and structural dichotomy – male/masculine sexuality is constructed as powerful, active and aggressive while female/feminine sexuality is constructed as powerless, passive and submissive. Seen in these terms, heterosexuality is oppressive and consent does indeed become a meaningless concept.

The arguments advanced by MacKinnon, Dworkin and Jeffreys are persuasive if heterosexual sex is reduced to power and abuse forced upon women or embraced through the ideological conditioning of hetero-patriarchy. As soon as heterosexual sex is seen as more complex, or involving pleasure for women, the radical position become far more fragile.

The claim that consent is meaningless under hetero-patriarchy is epistemologically flawed. It is based on a false universalism whereby all men oppress all women. Indeed, such is MacKinnon's universalism that she argues that gender inequality and male dominance exist cross-culturally, although she does acknowledge local variations (MacKinnon, 1989, p. 130). Critics like McIntosh, (1992) highlight a fundamental contradiction with this radical feminist position.

Whilst claiming, on the one hand, to be woman-centred and committed to fighting women's oppression by listening to women's voices (Rowland and Klein, 1990), on the other hand, they dismiss the accounts of women who report positive experiences of heterosexuality. By claiming, as both MacKinnon and Dworkin do, that all heterosexual sex is a violation or possession and consent is therefore meaningless, they effectively reduce all heterosexual sex to an act of rape. Not only does this undermine those women who view their heterosexual encounters as consensual, it also negates the specificity of the experiences of women who have had unconsenting/forced sex done to them. To suggest that rape and 'normal' sex are almost indistinguishable is an absurdity that denies both women's subjective experience of consenting sex and their suffering from rape or sexual violence. Women who report rape do so because they know they have not had consensual sex and they are aware that what was done to them was definitely not 'normal' sex (Archard, 1998, p. 93). Their argument devalues women who choose heterosexual relationships and invalidates the category of rape. This is not to say that a focus on the structural constraints and systemic characteristics of hetero-patriarchy is not useful, but when it becomes determining, and conflates forms of sexual experience, there is the danger that such feminist critiques – paradoxically – objectify women by not recognising the subjectivity of women.

There are some radical feminists, such as Susan Brownmiller, who identify a clear distinction between consensual and non-consensual heterosexual sex. Although she sees rape as 'nothing more than a conscious process of intimidation by which *all* men keep *all* women in a state of fear' (Brownmiller, 1975, p. 15), she defines it as a man continuing to have sexual intercourse with a woman against her wishes. Despite the apparent ambiguity of her position, there is at least an acknowledgement that women can, and indeed do, consent to heterosexual intercourse and that there is a qualitative difference between consensual sex and rape that is defined through women's agency.

In order to sustain the argument that there is little difference between normal sex and rape, MacKinnon must either privilege the experiences and the consciousness of some – feminist – women over others or assert that women who report consensuality in their heterosexual relationships are suffering from false consciousness (Archard, 1998, p. 93). The result of either approach is the perpetuation of the myth that women are incapable of exercising control over their sexuality, or that hetero-patriarchy so characterises heterosexual sex as oppressive that it is meaningless to retrieve it. This is somewhat paradoxical given MacKinnon's understanding of sexuality as 'that which is most one's own, yet most taken away' (MacKinnon, 1996, p. 182). A feminist analysis that denies the possibility of consent takes away the sexuality of those women who give positive accounts of heterosexuality and the notion of women's agency in different forms of social relations.

The radical feminist position is based on an understanding of heterosexuality as the eroticisation of power, where male sexuality is constructed as active and powerful and female sexuality as passive and powerless. However, these constructions of sexuality belie the 'corporeal reality' (Segal, 1994, p. 219). According to Lynne Segal,

> The hominid penis is anything but permanently erect, anything but endlessly ready for unencumbered sex, anything but triggered by the nearest passing female – even when she happens to be his wife, mistress or lover, and eager for sex. (Segal, 1994, p. 219)

The idea that the penis is the site of male sexual power (Dworkin, 1981) is a myth that masks the reality of male sexual dysfunction (Segal, 1994). The totemic power of the penis is reinforced and reproduced by a feminist discourse that adopts a phallocentric and essentialist understanding of sexuality (Segal, 1994). Whilst feminist discourse reinforces patriarchal power, elsewhere studies in masculinity represent its unravelling under its own contradictions (Connell, 1987, Connell 2000, Mac An Ghail, 1996).

This is not to deny radical feminist critiques of sexual consent some insight, particularly in relation to the contested constructions of rape and sexual violence, where they have highlighted the inadequacies of a legal system that defines rape in terms of male sexuality (MacKinnon, 1989). However, by concentrating on the structures and institutions of heterosexuality, radical feminist theorists have failed to address the diversity in how men and women are able to communicate with each other in heterosexual relationships (Hollway, 1995, p. 87). The focus has been on the structures and systems that support compulsory heterosexuality, rather than on the sexual agency of men and women engaged in heterosexual relationships. The radical feminist solution to compulsory heterosexuality and women's subordination is the development of a homosexual desire within a lesbian-feminist framework. This is based on an ill-founded assumption that lesbian relationships are more egalitarian and lack the power inequality that exists in heterosexual relationships. Power, whether it is oppressive or empowering, is present in all human interactions (Plummer, 1995), but a radical feminist analysis cannot account for, or refuses to be critical of the power dynamics of a lesbian relationship. Unable to theorise positive heterosexual relations or indeed, negative lesbian relations, radical feminism is unable to provide an adequate theory of sexual interplay and for strategies for social change. Change is achieved through all social relations, '"private" ones included' (Holloway, 1995, p. 130).

It is the inadequacies of radical feminism, particularly the reductionism and universality of this approach, that has led to the accusation that feminism makes women into victims, and it is in the work of the new generation of post-feminists that this criticism is at its most vehement. In her first book, *The Morning After: Sex, Fear and Feminism* (1993), Kate Roiphe launched a scathing attack on the way in which feminist discourse represented female sexuality. She displays an open cynicism at the role of feminists involved in, what she calls, the rape-crisis movement. She uses this term to refer to the assertion that there is an endemic rape culture, which portrays forced or coerced sex as normal (Roiphe, 1993, p. 56). She suggests that the idea of a rape crisis is used as a strategic tool to 'get from here to there' (Roiphe, 1993, p. 57) and that 'Rape is a natural trump card for feminism. Arguments about rape can be used to sequester feminism in the teary province of trauma and crisis' (Roiphe, 1993, p. 56). Although she focuses her discussion primarily on 'acquaintance rape' and sexual harassment, which might be considered to involve greater questions of interpretation and contestation than 'stranger' rape and physical violence, Roiphe's analysis does have significance for the wider debate on sexual consent.

Roiphe's principal position is that women are sexual agents who are capable of exercising free choice. She suggests that it is problematic to call an unwanted encounter rape if it occurs because a man has given a woman drugs or alcohol. She maintains that whilst a woman may be offered such substances, she chooses whether or not to take them (if she is aware of consuming toxic substances and of their physiological consequences) (Roiphe, 1993, p. 53). Similarly, in a situation of verbal coercion, where a woman is pressured into having sexual intercourse with a man, Roiphe maintains that she still exercises free choice in response to this pressure and must therefore be responsible for her actions (Roiphe, 1993, p. 68).

According to Roiphe, whether sexual intercourse is defined as consensual or non-consensual is dependent on our understanding of sexuality. A theory that views all penetrative sex as violation and possession is based on, and reinforces, the assumption that female sexuality is passive, virtuous and in need of protection (Roiphe, 1993, p. 70). At the same time, if one accepts the argument that any theory of sexual consent is informed by a particular understanding of sexuality, does it follow that the same relationship exists in Roiphe's work?

Roiphe's analysis is based on a liberal individualism, whereby all sexual relations are contingent upon the parties involved exercising free choice and taking responsibility for their actions. Within this context it is hard to imagine, except in the most extreme of circumstances, a sexual encounter that would be deemed non-consensual. Whilst accepting that sexual intercourse involving actual or threatened physical force does constitute non-consent, Roiphe maintains the use of verbal coercion or manipulation does not. These are techniques of seduction or persuasion, not exercises of power. She believes that women are able to exercise choice and consequently most women are able to withstand both verbal and emotional pressure. Those women who succumb under such circumstances are the exception, rather than the rule (Roiphe, 1993, p. 68). For Roiphe, the suggestion that verbal coercion constitutes non-consensual sex portrays·women as mentally and emotionally weak, and effectively infantalises them (Roiphe, 1993, p. 67). Furthermore, she maintains that if verbal coercion is taken to constitute rape, the definition of rape is expanded to include any sexual encounter that women regret or found negative. For Roiphe, women's sexual consent involves a meaningful choice that women make and should take responsibility for, for good or ill, unless it is clear that they have been deprived of that choice.

There are a number of problems with this post-feminist position. First, there is no real empirical evidence to support this argument. Studies indicate that women are aware of a fundamental difference between coerced sexual intercourse and an unsatisfactory sexual encounter. Even when conscious of having non-consensual sex done to them, women are inclined not to categorise it as rape (Lees, 1997, p. 70). Roiphe's polemic against radical feminists and the 'endemic rape culture' seems somewhat exaggerated if not misinformed.

For Roiphe, the act of consent is an act of free choice. This privileging of individual free choice does give rise to concerns about the gendered nature of

sexual choice and the focus on the subjective perception of women choosing rather
than broader notions of pervasive gendered discourses of power in society. If
radical feminists understand language, culture and the 'lifeworld' as inherently
determined by hetero-patriarchy, Roiphe sees no determination within language,
culture and 'lifeworld', which clearly idealises autonomous womanhood and
underplays structural and social forces. Written at the age of twenty-four and based
on her experiences of life on a university campus, Roiphe's account is an
extremely personal one. It is based on her own experiences, her own insights and
opinions. She makes no apologies for her perspective and does not claim to offer
an overarching truth about female sexuality. This personal approach limits her
work. As already suggested, a feminist analysis that does not listen to the diversity
of women's experiences or privileges some experiences over others is
fundamentally flawed. Replacing the perspective of a radical (structure) with a
liberal (agency) perspective does not progress beyond that universalism, since
women's subjective experience is given an equal sense of having the power to
choose as a universal truth. However, it is not the intention to dismiss or invalidate
Roiphe's work, simply because it is based on personal experiences. Indeed, the
process of women relating the stories of their experiences is both an empowering
and necessary part of the emancipatory project (Plummer, 1995). Roiphe's account
is valid and relevant to some women, who are able to identify with her story and
start to develop new communities (Plummer, 1995).

   The limitation of Roiphe's analysis lies in the fact that she focuses on personal
experiences and women's sexual agency to the exclusion of structural barriers that
may problematise the meaning of consent. Indeed, it could be argued that despite
appearing to be diametrically opposed, both Roiphe and MacKinnon fail to
acknowledge the significance of social structure. Roiphe ignores structural
influences because she sees women as individuals responsible for their own
actions, while MacKinnon marginalises the social because she gives precedence to
private patriarchal relations, whereby all men oppress all women. Roiphe's social
structure is simply the context for individual choice, with no dominant or
prejudicial discourses of power and oppression. MacKinnon's structuralism is a
rigid representation of a universalist gendered relation that does not focus upon
social structure as systemic and dynamic sites of institutions, actors and
orthodoxies suffused with multiple forms of oppression and discourses of
liberation. Both are static and driven by one-dimensional representations of
women.

Between Structural Determination and Individual Agency and Autonomy

One attempt to address the inadequacies of both radical and post-feminists has
come from Sylvia Walby. Adopting a multiple systems approach which takes into
account class, race and gender (Hester, 1992), Walby suggests that there are six
structures of patriarchy: the mode of production, paid employment, the State, male
violence, sexuality and culture (Walby, 1990, p. 20). The structures are related, as
they reinforce and block one another, but each structure retains a degree of

autonomy. To focus on one structure as the site of women's oppression is too simplistic – it is the interconnected experience of multiple structures that characterises oppression and inequality. Walby argues that the six structures can be further categorised as either public or private patriarchy, and that the twentieth century has seen a shift from private to public patriarchy, where women's subordination is maintained at a social and institutional level (Walby, 1990, p. 20).

Walby does accept radical feminists' concern with structural determinations but maintains that they underestimate the impact of recent social sexual change on the lives of women. Heterosexuality is a patriarchal institution, but it has altered dramatically during the last century, and particularly the 1960s. There has been a move away from a desexualisation of women to a situation in which women are encouraged to seek pleasure from their sexual encounters (Walby, 1990, p. 124) Despite living in a hetero-patriarchal society, women cannot simply be reduced to 'passive victims' (Walby, 1990, p. 125). Women do actively seek out heterosexual encounters and whilst this might be seen at worst as a strategy of assimilation into a patriarchal system, it cannot simply be ignored or read as pre-determined in its character and outcomes. For Walby, women are engaging in sexual relations on what might be regarded as an 'uneven playing field', but they are still 'playing', and can achieve some general 'victories' towards equality, particularly in inter-personal relationships, and have subjective satisfactions from their 'playing'. Such a position argues for a more intermediate approach to deconstructing sexual consent and assessing its meaning as a concept for women.

In her research into the sexual experiences of young women, Ine Vanwesenbeeck (1997) found that whilst her respondents were able to say 'yes' or 'no' to sexual intimacy, they were unable to negotiate further. Sex was seen as a way to secure a relationship rather than a means of achieving sexual pleasure, and the women were more concerned that their male partners were sexually satisfied (Vanwesenbeeck, 1997, p. 175). This poses the question of whether these 'accommodatory strategies of sexuality' (Walby, 1990, p. 125) invalidate any consent given or focuses on the quality of consent rather than its presence or absence. For Vanwesenbeeck (1997), the only way to improve the quality of consent is to portray female sexuality in a positive way, so women are better placed to negotiate the type of sex they want. This sort of evidence suggests that women can be observed to be beginning to take ownership of consent decisions, if only partially.

This idea that the ability to negotiate is central to the issue of consent underpins recent attempts to develop a model of communicative sexuality that adheres to feminist principles. In her influential essay, Lois Pineau (1995) advocates a move away from a contractual conception of sexuality to a communicative model. She argues that implicit within the contractual approach is an assumption of female powerlessness. The active, aggressive male offers a sexual contract to the passive, submissive female, which she does or does not consent to (Pineau, 1995, p. 17). In other words, it is a model premised on the playing out of an inherent inequality. One party, usually the woman, submits to the desires of the other party, usually the man.

A contract is concerned primarily with achieving a desired outcome, with little emphasis on the process of negotiation required to meet that objective (Pineau,

1995, p. 19). A communicative model of sexuality, however, stresses the need for 'mutuality of desire' (Pineau, 1995, p. 20) and the obligation to take into account the interests of the parties involved. Pineau analogises between communicative sexuality and a good conversation. Individuals will be 'intuitive, sympathetic and charitable' (Pineau, 1995, p. 19) to their partner's needs. Such a view locates the contractual 'act' of sexual consent, represented elsewhere as an action, within a process of communication, where consent is one part of a set of relational discourses.

If we accept that people engage in sexual activity for the purpose of gaining sexual pleasure, it is necessary for individuals to communicate how sexual satisfaction can be achieved. Pineau suggests that even sex that is not pleasurable can be consensual, as long as both parties have discussed why they are engaging in a sexual activity that does not result in mutual satisfaction (Pineau, 1995, p. 22). Sex becomes something that can be consensual within the contexts of processes of obligation, feelings of responsibility or *quid pro quo*, which might involve inherent inequalities in preference or desire for sex. The only way to ensure that the quality of consent given in any sexual encounter has some value is to practice communicative sexuality.

Whilst writing specifically about 'acquaintance' rape, Pineau's analysis does provide us with a framework in which consent is infused with meaning through negotiation and mutual decision-making, with a more developed sense of the diversity of interplay of consent and context. However, her model of communicative sexuality does have limitations. Despite claiming to write from a feminist perspective, Pineau fails to adequately address the issue of communication within a gendered context – such as the gendering of language and culture – and her analysis is based on the assumption that men and women communicate in the same way (Adams, 1995, p. 32). Evidence from socio-linguistic research suggests otherwise. According to Deborah Tannen (1992) men and women view the world differently and therefore have different motivations for engaging in conversation. She suggests that men tend to view themselves as part of a social hierarchy and see conversation as a means to maintain or improve their position within it. Women, on the other hand, position themselves within a wider network and use conversation as a way of developing closer relationships (Tannen, 1992, p. 24). Given these differences, a communicative sexuality based on mutuality seems difficult to construct if men and women are talking for different purposes and with different reasons. It may be problematic to suggest that men and women exist in separate linguistic worlds because it reinforces the notion of 'otherness' that separates men and women into structurally determined power relations that deny a meaning for consent discourse (Roiphe, 1995, p. 76). Yet we do live in a society in which there exists defined gender roles. Whilst it is not impossible to transgress those roles, it is probable that they influence, to some degree, the way in which we communicate, and thus make communicative sexuality a more complex project (Adams, 1995).

A further criticism of Pineau's theory of communicative sexuality is that, like Catherine MacKinnon, she prescribes how female sexuality should be expressed. A model of sexuality premised on negotiation does not allow for a female sexuality that enjoys non-communicative but consensual sexual intercourse. Robin West (1991) argues that there is substantial evidence that women have erotic fantasies of domination and submission (West, cited in Adams, 1995, p. 34). Once again, these accounts are either dismissed as non-consensual or as examples of false consciousness, or the concept of communication envelopes all sexual interactions, which weakens the specificity of the communicative sexuality that Pineau argues for. Pineau's theory is unable to acknowledge that women are able to eroticise and consent to sex based on domination and submission. Her communicative sexuality is value-laden, and sees the negotiation of sexual desire and participation in a rationalist context of best interest, rather than a gendered context of discourses of power, inequality and the eroticisation of both.

Feminist Concepts of Sexual Consent – Tensions and Possibilities

Walby and Pineau's analyses of gender inequality and its impact on sexual consent leave feminists between the tensions of social, cultural and structural determinations and subjective agency and autonomy. The problem they face is in defending the idea that gender is significant and important in shaping, if not determining, women's experience of consenting to sex, without usurping or disparaging women's subjective experiences of sexual consent and sexual pleasure, which are to some degree diverse, contradictory and contingent. This is a problem of saying something about women's sexuality that is distinctive of women, whilst recognising that being 'women' is not a universalised characteristic of women's sense of self.

At the same time, post-feminist objections to feminist tendencies to claim universalities in the experience of women are somewhat offset by the way in which they themselves universalise their subject, so that all women are able to shuffle off gendered cultural and social determinants to exercise contingency. Post-feminists' resistance to women being reduced to a homogenised category by hetero-patriarchy or radical feminism constitutes a critical discipline of feminist thinking. It may be a crude analogy, but the challenge for feminist critiques of sexual consent is that they have to locate a space somewhere between women as slaves or amazons.

This space seems to be at least partly occupied by the continuous and synchronous relationship between women and their contexts. Whilst social contexts are gendered and hetero-patriarchal, they are also diverse in the balance of gendered discourse and equality discourse, and in part contingent in the patterns of interpersonal relations and particular public and culturally-mediated relations women have with individuals, groups and institutions in society.

It is further occupied by an understanding that these contexts and relations are processes within which negotiation and 'narrative-building' take place, so that the negotiation of sexual consent operates within a social and a temporal context. In other words, a further factor in this space is the period of time a relationship develops within and how subjective narratives establish patterns of inter-personal relationships which may reflect but equally mediate socio-cultural discourse. Such contexts of sexual consent are important, whether in a long term relationship or a one night stand, whether in an intoxicated state at a party or after long deliberation and discussion with a previously platonic friend, or whether in introducing different sexual acts into a relationship or initiating such a relationship for the first time. They are critical in assessing the meaning of sexual consent, both as a generally understood concept from which standards can be established, and as a specific subject of conventions and negotiations within particular inter-personal relationships. This focus on context allows for some understanding of sexual consent not simply as an utterance or act – a formal step, to be variously represented as contingent and chosen or manipulated and forced. Consent becomes a characteristic of process, a feature of a set of previous negotiations and articulations and a part of the relation within which sex is expressed. Consent does not, therefore, simply reside within a particular utterance but in a narrative in which the contextualising of the particular sexual relationship allows a greater understanding of the meaning of consent decisions and therefore their validity.

There are two immediate caveats to make about this contextualisation of consent. It does not allow the easy claim of rape as 'misunderstood' consent – indeed it requires partners to accept that they are part of a narrative in which the quality of the act of sexual consent is a necessary part of the intimacy they enjoy. In other words, the representation of sexual consent as communication and narrative within an inter-personal relationship implies that the constituent actors both understand and take responsibility for the narrative and that consent is a feature constituting and characterising their relations. Equally, it does not allow for a defence of rape in marriage or long-term relationships. The context of an interpersonal narrative may lead to an understanding of sexual consent as something not based on pleasure alone, but as part of a complex mediation of a range of wants and desires within the relationship. It does, however, require both parties to acknowledge and participate in that mediation. It does allow for the possibility of contexts in which both parties might be responsible for not constructing a meaningful narrative, and erroneous and false consent might be a product of bad communication. There will be occasions when narratives are constructed in such a way that all parties contribute to a situation where consent is problematic. Bad sex, whilst it is a problem that can be addressed within the context of sexual ethics, should not be presumed to be synonymous or integrally linked to non-consent.

This notion does provide for a 'messy' area that feminists would traditionally argue is the defence for male power, on that grounds that raising issues of agency creates problems, contradictions and inertia against the continuing structurally and culturally constituted boundaries of gender inequality. The challenge for contemporary feminist theorists is to colonise that 'messy' area and locate gender in constant juxtaposition, or more precisely in a dialectical relationship, with subjective and other factors that influence decisions of sexual consent.

What is distinctive about a feminist critique is that it will always emphasise the power of gender in the structural, social and cultural conditioning of context and in the way in which subjects make their narratives. Whilst that opens them up to arguments of reductionism, determination or essentialism in their analysis, it is what makes them feminist. Further, the evidence available on rape and sexual violence and on the normalisation of processes of objectification and commodification in women's sexuality and the coercive strategies some men use to pursue their sexual agendas is adequate justification for such a position. What Walby and Pineau offer are different ways of providing more sensitive conceptual mechanisms for considering gendered inequality but recognising what varying power different women have in their own sexual negotiations. These mechanisms should underline the importance of gender – give gender a significant 'place at the table' in discussions of sexual consent, whilst avoiding a position that separates a gender informed view of consent from other views of sexual consent. Gender is always a *tendency* – always of importance but of varying impact – in any discussion of the nature and meaning of sexual consent.

This is reflected in current debates over changing rape law in the UK, shifting away from the current conventions in determining consent or its absence, that requires women to prove that rape has taken place and allows men a defence of 'honest belief' in consensuality (Cook, 2002; Jones, 2002; Hinchliffe, 2002). Cook has suggested that the 'free agreement' model of deliberating sexual consent, used in Victoria in South Australia, offers a more satisfactory approach to rape law in that both parties' narratives receive the same scrutiny and require the same justification. If the woman asserts that she did not consent, the man does not simply require her to prove her case, but has to account for how a 'consensual' sexual encounter could have been so misunderstood. This idea requires consent acts that do not allow reckless or self-centred abandonment of thinking about the quality of sexual consent in sexual relations.

This might be a concrete example of a more sensitive conceptual mechanism for considering and resisting the inequality inherent in women's sexual consent under hetero-patriarchy. In addition, a feminist might argue the need for a juridical process to recognise the social and cultural contexts of gender inequality in the consent 'transaction', and hold the man to greater account for the position of power he occupies in a society gendered in power and context.

Reynolds (2002), observing the problems and contradictions the law has in accounting for these inequalities, argues that the shortfalls of law need to be taken up by political change and a broader political strategy that takes in the cultural, educational, ethical and ideological terms of hetero-patriarchal society.

> Undoubtedly there would still be problems of transition, and at a broader level political decisions are predicated in ideological values and commitments...It presupposes that political change will result in some individual injustices to men but views this as a transitional problem outweighed by the benefits of dissembling the present crisis of rape in contemporary societies (Reynolds, 2002, p. 101).

It is doubtful if many feminists are going to regard this position as adequate in its focus and its emphasis on the gendered nature of sexual consent, and more particularly in the consequences of the continued prevalence and incidence of sexual violence, which is still borne principally by women. It does, however, represent a political will to press a social and cultural transition towards a more equal society and does balance the varying political claims of different schools of feminist thought against the need to consider women as diverse subject agents for whom gender is of variable importance amongst other social identities in contemporary society. It might be characterised as hegemonic in its strategic approach to sexual consent. It offers force against rapists through stricter legal scrutiny and penalty, and engaging in a 'hearts and minds' manufacture of awareness of the structural inequality of consent contexts, which requires greater reflection from men and thereby begins to undermine the very foundations of patriarchy that demand it. What is important is that such debates continue to take seriously, however flawed or partial, feminist ideas and critiques of sexual ethics and sexual consent. The continued work of feminist writers, in laying bare the current prevalence and incidence of forced sex upon women and the inadequacy of current standards for understanding women's sexual consent, is critical to a more sophisticated, equal and empowering conception of sexual relations for men and women.

Bibliography

Adams, D. M. (1995), 'Date Rape and Erotic Discourse', in *Date Rape: Feminism, Philosophy and the Law*, Francis, L. (ed.), Pennsylvania: The Pennsylvania State University Press.

Archard, D. (1998), *Sexual Consent*, Oxford: Westview Press.

Brunet, A. and Turcotte, L. (1988), 'Separatism and Radicalism: An analysis of the differences and similarities', in Hoagland, S. L. and Penelope, J. (eds), *For Lesbians Only: A Separatist Anthology*, London: Onlywomen Press Ltd.

Connell, R. (1987), *Gender and Power: Society, the Person and Sexual Politics*, Cambridge: Polity.

Connell B. (2000), *The Men and the Boys*, Cambridge: Polity.

Cook K. (2002), 'Rape Law.Consent@Freeagreement.co.uk: An Assessment of the Legal Definition of Consent, in the Light of the Current Review of Sexual Offences Law', in *Contemporary Issues in Law*, Vol. 6, No. 1, Special Edition on Rape, Law and Sexual Consent, pp. 7-22.

Cowling, M. (1998), *Date Rape and Consent*, Aldershot: Ashgate Publishing Ltd.

Dworkin, A. (1981), *Pornography: Men Possessing Women*, London: The Women's Only Press.

Dworkin A. (1997), *Life and Death: Unapologetic Writings on the Continuing War Against Women*, London: Virago Press.

Hester, M. (1992), *Lewd Women and Wicked Witches: A Study of the Dynamics of Male Domination*. London: Routledge.

Hinchliffe, S. (2002) 'Morgan Reviewed: In Defence of Freedom of Will', in *Contemporary Issues in Law*, Vol. 6, No. 1, Special Edition on Rape, Law and Sexual Consent, pp. 37-46.

Hollway, W. (1995), 'Feminist Discourses and Women's Heterosexual Desire', in Wilkinson, S. and Kitzinger, C. (eds), *Feminism and Discourse: Psychological Perspectives*, London: Sage.

Hollway, W. (1995), 'A Second Bite at the Heterosexual Cherry', *Feminism and Psychology*, Vol. 5, No. 1, pp. 126-130.

Jeffreys, S. (1990), *Anticlimax: A Feminist Perspective on the Sexual Revolution*, London: The Women's Press.

Jones, H. (2002), 'Rape Consent and Communication: Resetting the Boundaries?' *Contemporary Issues in Law*, Vol. 6, No. 1, Special Edition on Rape, Law and Sexual Consent, pp. 23-36.

Kitzinger, C. (1987), *The Social Construction of Lesbianism*, London: Sage.

Lees, S. (1997), *Carnal Knowledge: Rape on Trial*, Harmondsworth: Penguin.

Mac An Ghail M. (ed.) (1996), *Understanding Masculinities*, Buckingham: Open University Press.

MacKinnon, C. (1989), *Towards a Feminist Theory of the State*, Harvard: Harvard University Press.

MacKinnon, C. (1996), 'Feminism, Method and the State: An Agenda for Theory', in Jackson, S. and Scott, S. (eds), *Feminism and Sexuality*, Edinburgh: Edinburgh University Press.

McIntosh, M. (1992), 'Liberalism and the contradictions of sexual politics', in Segal, L. and McIntosh, M. (eds), *Sex Exposed: Sexuality and the Pornography Debate*, London: Virago.

Pateman C. (1988), *The Sexual Contract*, Cambridge: Polity.

Pineau, L. (1995), 'Date Rape: A Feminist Analysis', in Francis, L (ed.), *Date Rape: Feminism, Philosophy and the Law*, Pennsylvania: Pennsylvania State University Press.

Plummer, K. (1995), *Telling Sexual Stories: Power, Change and Social Worlds*, London: Routledge.

Radicalesbians, (1970), `The Woman-Identified Woman', in Hoagland, S. and Penelope, J. (eds), *For Lesbians Only: A Separatist Anthology*, Onlywomen Press.

Reynolds, P. (2002), 'Rape, Law and Consent: The Scope and Limits to Sexual Regulation by Law', in *Contemporary Issues in Law*, Vol. 6, No. 1, Special Edition on Rape, Law and Sexual Consent, pp. 92-102.

Rich A., (1981), 'Compulsory Heterosexuality and Lesbian Existence', in Rich, A. (1987), *Blood Bread And Poetry – Selected Prose 1979-1985*, London: WW Norton.

Roiphe, K. (1993), *The Morning After: Sex, Fear and Feminism*, London: Hamish Hamilton.

Rowland, R. and Klein, R. D. (1990), 'Radical Feminism: Critique and Construct', in Gunew, S. (ed.), *Feminist Knowledge: Critique and Construct*, London: Routledge.

Segal, L. (1987), *Is the Future Female? Troubled Thoughts on Contemporary Feminism*, London: Virago Press.

Segal, L. (1992), 'Sweet sorrows, painful pleasures: Pornography and the perils of heterosexual desire', in Segal, L. and McIntosh, M. (eds), *Sex Exposed: Sexuality and the Pornography Debate*, London: Virago.

Segal, L. (1994), *Straight Sex: The Politics of Pleasure*, London: Virago.

Tannen, D. (1992), *You Just Don't Understand: Women and Men in Conversation*, London: Virago.

Vanwesenbeeck, I. (1997), 'The Context of Women's Power(lessness) in Heterosexual Interactions', in Segal, L. (ed.), *New Sexual Agendas*, London: Routledge.

Walby, S. (1990), *Theorising Patriarchy*, Oxford: Blackwell.

Wilton, T. (1995), *Lesbian Studies: Setting an Agenda*, London: Routledge.

Wolf, N. (1993), *Fire with Fire: New female Power and How It Will Change the 21st Century*, London: Chatto and Windus.

Chapter 3

Sexual Ethics and the Erotics of Consent

Moira Carmody

Introduction

The issue of sexual consent remains a controversial one with legal discourses of consent dominating debates about sex and sexual violence. However these discourses operate alongside other bodies of knowledge that also seek to regulate sexual practices. In particular there is evidence of psychological, socio/cultural, feminist and religious discourses present in much of the literature (Baumeister and Tice, 2001, Card, 1991, Cowling, 1998, Krahe et al., 2000, Mappes and Zembaty, 1997, Primoratz, 1999). Other authors in this collection will address some of these areas and their application to different social contexts, groups and settings. My approach will be somewhat different. What I wish to focus on is the role of sexual ethics. While consent is an element here, I will argue that this remains a limited concept without some consideration of how individuals as sexed and gendered bodies constitute themselves as ethical or unethical subjects within the social body and within interpersonal relationships and sexual encounters. My discussion draws on subjective perceptions and reflections based on the Australian experience and while I think the issues have universal resonance, recognition of cultural variations is important.

Some Background

This chapter is the continuation of work I have been doing in various ways for the last two decades (Carmody, 2003, 2001, 2000, 1999, 1997, 1992). My original work focused on the multiple ways in which sexual violence against women manifests in Australian society and what can be done to prevent it from continuing to be a daily reality in the lives of thousands of women. From early on, in my direct practice with survivors of sexual violence, policy work, research and education, I have been concerned to interrogate the cultural factors that have both encouraged and condoned violence against women and the discourses of the dominant culture's belief systems about the role of women in society. I, like many others, resisted the personal and institutional systems that privileged men's views of women as 'fair game' and actively denied the existence of violence to women on individual and systemic levels. Increasingly I believed, like many other feminists, that some hope of change was possible through actively re-writing the social policy agenda of government and key institutions such as health, law, welfare and education.

Since the early 1980s, numerous rounds of legislative reform, revised health, welfare and police procedures and several decades of community education have failed to deliver the much hoped for deterrence in crimes being committed or significant changes in the behaviour of those who continue to perpetrate violence against women (Carmody and Carrington, 2000). This reality has provoked me and others to call for an increased focus on primary prevention, to reflect on the successes and failures of the past and to begin to reconceptualise political goals and strategies and to develop different theoretical ways of understanding violence against women (Carmody and Carrington, 2000).

For me, this has led to a critique of the effectiveness of social policy in preventing intimate violence and a rejection of a number of dominant feminist discourses that have shaped anti-violence strategies to date. I will begin this chapter by firstly, demonstrating how some essentialist feminist traditions have marginalised women's desire and pleasure by placing an emphasis on avoiding sexual exploitation. Central to these political strategies has been consent or the lack of the woman's consent to sexual activity. While the regulation of sexual consent is codified by laws, I will also argue that the responsibility for managing consent has been placed firmly with women to manage men's desires. My critique of the continuing dominance of these belief systems has led me to an exploration of sexual ethics. It is my contention that all sexual encounters, regardless of the gender of the people involved, invite the possibility of ethical or unethical sexual behaviour. My second aim is to present some preliminary ideas about how to conceptualise sexual ethics. I will argue that sexual consent is a significant part of a broader concern about sexual ethics. Here I will consider how Foucault's ideas about constituting an ethical self can broaden debates about sexual behaviour that is pleasurable, non-exploitative and has the potential for developing an erotics of consent.

Feminist Responses to Sexuality and Violence

The dominance of radical feminist discourse has impacted greatly on constructions of women's desire especially in relation to heterosexuality. Sex and power are interwoven in this belief system that argues they are 'manifested in men's violence towards women through rape, pornography, child sexual abuse and sexual harassment, as well as in the more mundane arena of asymmetries in women's and men's relation to active sexuality' (Hollway, 1996, p. 93). Hollway argues further that radical feminism too often treats all men as sexual villains and the power that they manifest through their sexuality as monolithic in contrast to women's powerlessness and victim status. The universalisation of men as violent and women as passive recipients of violence is still a pervasive contemporary feminist theory (MacKinnon, 1987; Lees, 1997). There is nothing positive in such an over-arching negative conception of femininity or masculinity (Jefferson 1997, Carmody and Carrington 2000). It is not only misleading to represent all men as 'dangerous' (see

Connell, 1995, Messerschmidt, 1993), but such a totalising conception of masculinity constructs all men as criminal, or potentially so. It fails to take into account the multiple ways in which men can be men, cross-culturally, trans-historically and during different stages of their life cycle (i.e. during adolescence as opposed to adult-hood). It tends to assume that all men are either biologically, socially or culturally prescribed hetero-sexed creatures of patriarchy regardless of the multiple pathways and sexualities associated with masculinity (See Collier, 1998, pp. 6-33).

My colleague Kerry Carrington and I have argued elsewhere that accepting the notion of hegemonic masculinity is deeply problematic in the analysis of men, their gender and sexual crimes (Carmody and Carrington, 2000). The flipside of a totalising concept of masculinity is equally damaging. It is an equally totalising concept of femininity that robs women of any agency or ability to exert power, express desire, take control, resist, prevent or avoid their victimisation in intimate sexual encounters with men. Prevention is a virtual impossibility within this theoretical framework (see also Egger, 1997). Women are 'in waiting' to experience violence and men forever paused to engage in it. It also fails to acknowledge the diversity of women's subjectivities due to age, class, culture, sexuality or dis/ability and how these are inscribed in women's experience of sex. Therefore a central theoretical concern of this chapter will be to build on recent work in masculinity studies, post-structuralist feminism and queer theory which reject the false universalisation of all men as violent and all women as passive (Jefferson, 1997; Connell, 1995; Messerschmidt, 1993; Hollway, 1996; Butler, 1999; Segal, 1994; Rubin, 1993).

Discourses of Sexuality or Guilty Secrets

A key feature of radical left politics of the 1960s was the call for a sexual revolution (Millett, 1969). The much-touted sexual revolution, however, did not deliver liberation for women. Despite the call to sexual liberation as a way to dismantle the edifice of bourgeois order and the middle class suburban norms of the previous generation, women soon recognised that their desires and pleasures were not necessarily being met (Kwok, 1997). The 1960s was after all, 'most often arrogantly male: women were "chicks", to be plastered on every page, the younger and "softer", the better' (Segal, 1994, p. 22).

Much of the debate amongst feminists concerned with rejecting sexual violence developed from a particular construction of sexuality. Women whose sexual desire involved sexual encounters or relationships with men were accused of 'sleeping with the enemy' or participating in compulsory heterosexuality (Rich, 1980). Feminist readings of sexological discourses in the 1970s rejected and condemned sexual 'passivity' as demeaning and degrading to women and promoted the notion of feminine self-assertion through sexual 'activity'. Clitoral stimulation was seen as the key to female happiness and led to the view that anything to do with penetration was harmful for women. Penetration (read penis or penis substitute) and passivity were banished from correct feminist and female sexuality.

Instead, women were to band together as 'woman identified women' to provide protection from the excesses of patriarchy. Some interpreted this as a call for women to embrace same sex desire and to build a lesbian nation of lovers who it was assumed were more egalitarian and in which women would be safe from sexual exploitation (Daly, 1978). Others saw this as a way of opposing interactions with men at all levels especially the personal. The development of women's culture both inside and outside the bedroom was seen as an antidote to patriarchal oppression. Women's oppression therefore became tied to male sexuality that was seen as violent, exploitative and stamping out all feminine values in the society. Apart from the problems this poses for women who desire to express their sexuality with men, it also created other dilemmas.

Pornography became a key issue for feminist political action – 'Pornography was the theory, rape the practice'. Dworkin (1974) and MacKinnon (1987) argued that pornography led directly to violence against women. Male sexuality and in particular the penis thus became the central means of patriarchal domination and destruction. Increasingly the discourse narrowed to focus on the activities of male sexuality to the exclusion of wider analyses of male social power and its manifestations in the dominant institutions of the society.

Despite the continuing dominance of these phallocentric and essentialist discourses, alternative voices emerged to question the limits of this analysis. For feminists like Gayle Rubin (1993) sexual exploration, expression and liberation continued to be a crucial focus in feminist politics. The debate became polarised around what has been well documented as the sex wars (Kwok 1997). On one side were the supporters of Dworkin and MacKinnon who saw all women as victims of male sexuality. They were viewed by their opponents as anti-sex and detracting from the wider feminist struggles. The pro-sex supporters called for a reinvigorated feminist debate about women and sexuality that did not reduce women to victims of male sexuality.

The impact of these competing discourses was felt widely in many parts of Western urbanised feminist communities in the USA, UK and Australia. Heterosexual women often reported feeling alienated from feminist politics and resented the oppression they experienced in their desires to peruse pleasure in the arms of a man. Hollway (1996, p. 91) argued there had been little space in the political criticism of heterosexuality to develop feminist sexual desire outside of erotic domination by a man. She suggested the relative silence of heterosexual women has perpetuated the absence of such a discourse. It was 'further amplified by a historical lack of any discourse which offered women positions in which we can recognise ourselves as desiring sexual subjects, without moral opprobrium and sanctions'. One friend of mine who identified as a lesbian during this period described to me how she would escape from the city lesbian ghetto on the weekends and return home to have sex with a boyfriend. She did not tell anyone that her erotic desires involved women *and* men, as bisexuality was frowned on by 'good feminists' as a failure to give up heterosexual privilege and 'Queer Nation' had yet to emerge to challenge the 'fixed' boundaries of sexual desire and practice. Feminist sexual police had a strong influence in regulating what was considered not only acceptable sexual desire but the acts and pleasures of individual women.

Feminist lesbians were ostracised in some communities if their behaviour was seen as male identified, for example if our desires included erotic difference through butch-femme pleasure or penetration or s/m. For some of us the message we received was that we must constantly monitor ourselves and our lovers for desires and pleasures that replicated heterosexuality or were male identified. Sally Abrahams (1999, p. 116) speaks of her experience as a 1970s Sydney lesbian:

> It was particularly perilous in the 1970s for a lesbian like me. I tried hard. It was said that feminism was the theory and lesbianism the practice. But mine never quite lined up. I wore overalls and flying boots to all the demonstrations and marches: dragged my lover from the back of the police vans; sprayed the Tempe overpass; danced for Emma Goldman: I earned my stripes. But I had secrets. I lived in fear of any of my comrades discovering the (shamefully unburned) black lace bra under my slogan-emblazoned T-shirt. I covered up my male identified shaved legs, hid my razor – that sharp edged tool of the patriarchy – in my underwear drawer.

Indeed.

The strength of these repressive discourses was underpinned by a belief that women were responsible for avoiding direct sexual exploitation by men. In the case of heterosexual women, as Hollway (1996) suggests, this left no room for women to be desiring heterosexual subjects. 'Bisexual' women often hid part of their erotic desires from public scrutiny and only made visible relations with women that were universally assumed to be non-exploitative. For lesbian women there were two impacts. Feminist lesbians such as Abrahams (1999) and many others resisted the cultural dominant norms of the period but ran the risk of exposure and moral condemnation. I would suggest this also operated to inhibit the full expression of erotic desires and led to some tense moments in the bedroom until the preferences of a new lover could be ascertained. Lesbians who did not identify as feminists often felt alienated from feminist political agendas though they were often sought as lovers because they were not constrained by feminist political codes.

Within these discourses are sets of assumptions concerning consent. Rigid adherence to a universalised femininity, masculinity and consequent sexual practices precludes a flexible and negotiated consent specific to the sexual encounter. If all sexual encounters between women and men are assumed to be exploitative because they occur within patriarchal power relations, no freely given consent is possible for either party. This position assumes women have no agency over their own sexuality and that men are always exploitative. While it has been important historically to make visible the ways in which gender relations have benefited dominant forms of masculinity, assuming all relations are inherently exploitative is a deterministic view. It fails to acknowledge the multiple ways in which femininities and masculinities are constantly negotiated and performed in different social and cultural contexts.

The rupturing of essentialist and one dimensional views on sexuality in the wake of the 1980s sex wars has resulted in a reinvigorated debate about sexuality and the development of diverse sexualities, influenced strongly by postmodern critiques of grand narratives such as radical feminism and the growth of queer theory and studies of masculinities. A good deal of this fresh approach to theorising sexuality, power and gender derived from emergent philosophical debates, especially from the work of Michel Foucault. It is by considering these alternative discourses that the space is created to develop a different sense of sexual consent.

Development of the Ethical Subject

An exploration of ethical sexual behaviour invites a consideration of what philosophers have to say about ethics and sex. According to Primoratz (1999) philosophy has only recently become interested in sex. Foucault (in Rabinow, 1997, p. 253) suggests that even those supposedly sex loving Greeks were much more interested in food than sex. The metaphysical tradition of Plato and Pythagoras extolled the material and the soul not the body, viewing sex as purely physical. A life of reason was incompatible with passions such as anger, fear and sexual desire. To achieve reason passions must be subdued. This had a significant impact on Christian philosophers who confined sex to heterogenital interaction within monogamous marriage for the purpose of procreation. By the middle of the 19th century however philosophers such as Schopenhauer and Nietzsche began to re-assess traditional sexual morality influenced by critiques of bourgeois society. By the middle of the 20th century, philosophers like John-Paul Sartre, Maurice Merleau-Ponty, Simone de Beauvoir and Bertrand Russell were actively contributing to rethinking ideas about sexuality. It was not however until the 1960s when the philosophy of sexuality came into its own due to the new libertinism of the anti-establishment, the rise of feminism and gay liberation leading to changes in sexual mores. At the same time philosophy became more concerned with legal and political norms, morals and values.

In exploring ways of thinking through the role of ethics and sexuality I have found it useful to consider Foucault's ideas on the subject. My argument refers to three areas of his work; governmentality, the development of the ethical subject and power relations. Foucault argued that a new form of power emerged in the sixteenth century, which took as its object the government of the population and sought to strengthen, constitute and regulate government, not through force, repression or coercion but through the institution and dispersion of the norms of good government. This form of power displaced neither sovereign power (judicial or state power), nor more modern forms of disciplinary power (panopticonism). Rather it operated alongside, in a triangular relation with, these two forms of power. It did not emanate from the state – rather it was diffuse and multifarious. This new form of power he calls governmentality. The concept of governmentality is in part a critique of totalising discourses that conceive the state (whether capitalist or patriarchal) as the centre from which all power emanates. Rather than a singular reliance on repressive power through direct coercion or force to achieve social regulation, mechanisms within the social body enlisted individuals and groups (such as families) to act as instruments of government.

Foucault argued there were three elements to understanding sexual behaviour – acts, pleasure and desire. Greek society, he suggested, placed the emphasis on sexual acts and pleasure and desire are seen as subsidiary to them. He contrasted this with a Chinese approach where acts are put aside through the need to restrain acts to get the maximum duration and intensity of pleasure. The Christian formula puts an accent on desire and tries to eradicate it. Acts have to become neutral; you act only to produce children or to fulfil your conjugal duty. Pleasure therefore is both practically and theoretically excluded (Rabinow, 1997, pp. 268-269). Foucault took this analysis further and argued that the modern formula was desire, acts had become less important and nobody knew what pleasure was.

Foucault invites us to consider that acts are the real behaviour of people in relation to the moral code or prescriptions. The code tells us what is permitted or forbidden and determines the positive or negative value of the different possible behaviours. This is clearly where laws about consent come into play. The ability of laws to impact on regulating people's sexual behaviour is however contested. While many individuals support and follow consent prohibitions, the high incidence of exploitative sexual encounters in most communities suggests that the threat of coercive power over individuals is not enough. Intimate relations between individuals are more complex than this. Even if we accept how governmentality enlists individuals and groups such as families to act as instruments of government, the incidence of sexual violence points to a failure to achieve social regulation or create ethical sexual subjects. We also need to consider that families have been identified as a primary site of sexual exploitation of women and children through domestic violence, sexual assault and child abuse (Fawcett, Fetherstone, Hearn, Toft, 1996).

Individual subjects cannot stand outside the discourses that shape them. Here it is crucial that we understand how gender relations have historically shaped discourses about women and men's sexuality. Inherent in all relationships, as Foucault reminds us, are relations of power. His notion of power as mobile and productive and in a constant state of negotiation contrasts with grand narratives such as radical feminism in which it is always structurally defined by patriarchy. In this latter model ethical behaviour is to be achieved by gender equality or by regulation through laws and sexual conduct codes. The failure of these measures over the last thirty years to prevent exploitative sexual relationships suggests we need to find creative alternatives to the 'art of living'.

Foucault's central argument about ethics involves what he calls *rapport à soi* – the relationship you ought to have with yourself which determines how an individual is supposed to constitute 'himself' (sic) as a moral subject of 'his' (sic) own actions (Rabinow, 1997, p. 263). Foucault argues therefore that the care of the self is intimately linked with ethics and that ethics is the considered form that freedom takes when it is informed by reflection (Rabinow, 1997, p. 284). Further, 'The care of the self is ethical in itself: but it implies complex relationships with others insofar as this ethos of freedom is also a way of caring for others' (Rabinow, p. 287). The abuse of power manifested in exploitative sexual relations 'exceeds the legitimate exercise of one's own power and imposes one's fantasies, appetites and desires on others'. Therefore 'one has not taken care of the self and has become a slave of one's desires' at the expense of another (Rabinow, 1997, p. 288).

A reconceptualisation of sexual ethics therefore seems very pressing. Building on Foucault's conception of sexual behaviour as involving acts, desire and pleasure raises a number of interesting questions. If desire, acts and pleasure are considered singularly does this limit the possibility of ethical sexual behaviour? Let's first consider acts on their own. There is a long history of both medical and legal discourses that have focused on regulating or repressing certain sexual acts through laws or cultural sanctions, such as male homosexuality, oral sex, masturbation, public sex and sado-masochism. Despite these attempts to regulate sexual behaviour Foucault provides evidence through his genealogy of sexuality that there has always been a multiplicity of sexualities (Foucault, 1990). This is where his conception of power relations as productive and dispersed is crucial. On one level the powerful discourses of medicine and law aim to work in concert with sovereign power to repress and regulate unacceptable sexual behaviour. However alongside this is governmentality that enlists individuals and groups to act as instruments of government. The family becomes central in imparting norms of sexual behaviour and gender relations. However resistance to these norms creates alternative subjectivities and political movements to challenge the attempts at repression.

The tension between regulation and freedom of sexual expression is evident in several political strategies over the last thirty years. Both Gay Liberation and the Women's Movement have in part tried to make publicly visible aspects of sexual relations that were discriminatory and repressive. Gay Liberation and its later derivatives have argued that homosexual desire is part of the multiple ways in which sexual identity is experienced and the state has no place interfering in homosexual acts between consenting adults (Flynn, 2001). Despite the relative success of these movements, discrimination and violence towards lesbians and gay men is considered an epidemic by many researchers (Herek and Berrill, 1992; Mason and Tomsen, 1997). Feminist campaigns against violence towards women by men have focused on also making visible the multiple ways sexual exploitation is manifested and its devastating impact on women. As discussed previously much of the strategy has assumed a universalisation of women as victims and men as dangerous both as individuals and systemically. Rape in marriage is one area where freely given consent to sex was not possible as sexual access by the husband to his wife was built into the marriage contract. Legal condemnation of these acts did not occur in Australia until 1981, but despite this few prosecutions have been brought or succeeded in criminal sanctions. It would seem that developing notions of sexual ethics that focus purely on either liberating or repressing certain sexual acts are limited in achieving *rapport à soi*.

This suggests the development of the ethical self requires consideration of how we can understand desire. In radical feminist discourse, which retains a strong influence in anti-violence work, male sexuality is conceptualised as uncontrollable and women are required to manage it to avoid sexual exploitation. So men are consumed by sexual desire while women's desire disappears or is determined by male desire. The spectre of male violence therefore hangs over the bed in any hetero-sex encounter. Gay men are positioned as constantly desiring and this must be controlled and regulated to ensure public health and 'safety' of non-gay men. The picture is not much better in relation to lesbians. There are several possible subjectivities available; the political lesbian who is defined as asexual in male terms, angry, man-hater, ugly, or the 'special' friend or companion (read asexual). Alternatively, like gay men, women are saturated by sexual desire and any woman is fair game. Another competing discourse operates alongside this – the radical feminist idea of women loving women who are egalitarian and non-coercive. Emerging data on same sex domestic violence and rape has significantly challenged this myth (Elliott, 1996, Herek, 1990). Underpinning these desire discourses is the ever-present influence of romance narratives and how these are shaped by cultural norms of desire, desiring bodies and anticipation... Which leads me to pleasure.

It is the anticipation of sexual pleasure that builds from desire. But while desire and acts may be shaped by memory, fantasy or experience, pleasure requires presence in the moment. So how do desire and acts become pleasure? Is pleasure a singular or mutual experience? Leaving solo masturbation aside, if there is an absence of mutual pleasure does this mean the encounter was unethical? Foucualt is helpful here in reminding us that the care of the self – *raison à soi* – implies complex relationships with others and is also a way of caring for others. This suggests that self-care and reflection requires a consideration of the interrelationship between desires, acts and pleasure, not through a singular focus on one aspect of sexual behaviour alone. I want to suggest therefore that ethical sexual behaviour becomes possible when we pay attention to all three aspects.

Developing an Erotics of Consent

My discussion so far has rejected universalising discourses that view women as inherently and always potential victims of male desire, acts and violence. I have suggested that a conception of power relations that assumes structurally constituted masculine power is deterministic and creates an impossibility that sexual consent can be freely given. A brief overview of feminist discourses that have shaped anti-violence theory and practice highlighted how women's sexual desire and pleasure have been marginalised in an attempt to avoid and prevent sexual exploitation of women by men. These discourses have placed heterosexual male desire as central and have failed to acknowledge the multiple subjectivities available to both men and women. The responsibility for managing consent and therefore ethical sexual practice has been placed with women. There has been little change in these approaches when lesbians and gay men are acknowledged as sexual subjects.

Over the last thirty years we have witnessed more and more individuals and groups acknowledging that sexual violence is a reality in their lives. It has been important for the previously submerged voices of people with disability, diverse culture groups and a variety of age groups to be publicly heard and recognised as worthy of concern and the commitment of government resources to support them. Rather than simply adding increasing groups of people whose consent must be acknowledged and improving adherence to sexual consent laws and codes, we need to move beyond a limited conception of sexual ethics.

Foucault's ideas about the care of the self provides a productive space to explore more fully the complex relationship we have with ourselves in developing our own moral and ethical subjectivity. This approach has potential for heterosexual, same sex and queer sexualities. The failure to achieve non-violent communities through repressive power (via the state), the panoptical gaze or technologies of governmentality, suggest alternative ways of thinking are urgently required. I consider that much of the sexological, legal etc. discourses concerning sexual violence have focused on what is perceived as 'abnormal' and the desires, acts and pleasures of unethical subjects. It seems timely therefore to shift our thinking to consider that many women and men of diverse sexualities do behave as ethical subjects. Ethical subjects, following Foucault, not only reflect on how we constitute ourselves as moral subjects of our own actions, but essential to this subjectivity is caring for others. Therefore, desire, acts and pleasure are performed in an ethical manner in which freely given and constantly negotiated consent is inherent. This suggests that research into sex and sexual violence needs to shift its focus away from unethical subjects to explore ethical subjects. We need to understand how differently sexed and gendered relations are negotiated in casual, short-term and ongoing relationships. If we limit this purely to legal notions of consent we run the risk of failing to consider broader notions of sexual ethics. As such it would deny the complexity and dynamic nature of intimate relationships (Carmody, 2003). There is also a need to consider how different cultural groups give meaning to these issues, including the diverse understandings of the individual subject and the role of community. Maybe a critical reflection of all of these issues from a different theoretical standpoint will provide insights into how desire, acts and pleasure are understood from an ethical perspective and create a greater possibility of realising an erotics of consent.

Bibliography

Abrahams, S. (1999), 'Sticks and Stones' in Atkins, D. (ed.), *Lesbian Sex Scandals: Sexual Practices, Identities, and Politics*, USA: Haworth Press, pp. 113-122.

Armstrong, H., Carmody, M., Hodge, B., Hogg, R., and Lee, M. (1999), 'The risk of naming violence: an unpleasant encounter between legal culture and feminist criminology' in *Australian Feminist Law Journal*, Vol. 13, pp. 13-37.

Baumeister, R. F. and Tice D. M. (2001), *The Social Dimension of Sex*, Needham Heights: Allyn and Bacon.

Breckenridge, J. and Carmody, M. (eds) (1992), *Crimes of Violence: Australian Responses to Rape and Child Sexual Assault*, Sydney: Allen and Unwin.

Butler, J. (1999), *Gender Trouble: Feminism and the Subversion of Identity*, New York: Routledge.

Card, C. (ed.) (1991), *Feminist Ethics*, Kansas: University Press of Kansas.

Carmody, M. (2003), 'Sexual ethics and violence prevention', in *Social and Legal Studies: an International Journal*, Vol. 12, No. 2, pp. 199-216.

Carmody, M. (2001), 'Women and hate crime – a useful political strategy?' in *Women against Violence: An Australian Feminist Journal*, Issue 10, July, pp. 4-10.

Carmody, M. and Carrington K. (2000), 'Preventing sexual violence?' *Australian and New Zealand Journal of Criminology*, Vol. 33, No. 3, pp. 341 –361.

Carmody, M. (1997), 'Submerged voices – social work co-ordinators of sexual assault services speak of their experiences' in *AFFILIA Journal of Women and Social Work*, (USA), Vol. 12 No. 4, Winter, pp. 452-470.

Collier, R. (1998), *Masculinities, Crime and Criminology*, London: Sage.

Connell, R.W. (1995), *Masculinities*, Sydney: Allen and Unwin.

Cowling, M. (1998), *Date Rape and Consent*, Aldershot: Ashgate Publishing.

Daly, M. (1978), *Gyn/Ecology: The Metaethics of Radical Feminism*, Boston: Beacon Press.

Dworkin, A. (1974), *Woman Hating*, New York: E. P. Dutton.

Egger, S. (1997), 'Women and crime prevention', in O'Malley, P. and Sutton, A. (eds), *Crime Prevention: Issues in Policy and Research*, Sydney: Federation Press.

Elliot, P. (1996), 'Shattering Illusions: Same Sex Domestic Violence' in Renzetti C., and Mile C. H. (eds), *Violence in Gay and Lesbian Domestic Partnerships*, New York: Haworth Press.

Fawcett, B., Fetherstone, B., Hearn, J. and Toft, C. (eds) (1996), *Violence and Gender Relations: Theories and Interventions*, London: Sage.

Foucault, M. (1990), *The History of Sexuality: An Introduction, Volume 1*, USA: Vintage Books Edition.

Flynn, M. (2001), 'Lobbying into the new millennium: The Gay and Lesbian Rights Lobby 1988-2000', in Johnson, C. and Van Reyk, P. (eds), *Queer City: Gay and Lesbian Politics in Sydney*, Sydney: Pluto Press.

Herek, G. M. and Berrill, K. T. (eds) (1992), *Hate Crimes: Confronting Violence Against Lesbians and Gay Men*, USA: Sage Publications.

Herek, G. (1990), 'The Context of Anti-gay Violence: Notes on Cultural and Psychological Heterosexism', in *Journal of Interpersonal Violence*, Vol. 5, pp. 316-333.

Hollway, W. (1996), 'Recognition and heterosexual desire' in Richardson, D. (ed.), *Theorising Heterosexuality* Buckingham: Open University Press.

Jefferson, T. (1997), 'Masculinities and Crime', in Maguire, M. Morgan, R. Reiner, R. (eds), *The Oxford Handbook of Criminology: Second Edition*, Oxford: Clarendon Press.

Krahe, B., Scheinberger-Olwig, R. and Kolpin, S. (2000), 'Ambiguous communication of sexual intentions as a risk marker of sexual aggression', *Sex Roles*, Vol. 42, Nos 5/6, pp. 313-337.

Kwok, K. W. (1997), 'Sex and sexualities: contemporary feminist debates' in Pritchard Hughes, K. (ed.), *Contemporary Australian Feminism 2*, Melbourne: Addison Wesley Longman.

Lees, S. (1997), *Ruling Passions: Sexual Violence, Reputation and the Law*, Philadelphia: Open University Press.

MacKinnon C. (1987), *Feminism Unmodified: Discourses on Life and Law*, London: Harvard University Press.

MacKinnon, C. (1987), *Feminism Unmodified: Discourses on Life and the Law*, USA: Harvard Press.

Mappes, T. A. and Zembaty, J. S. (1997), *Social Ethics: Morality and Social Policy*, 5th edition, USA: McGraw-Hill.

Mason, G. and Tomsen, S. (eds) (1997), *Homophobic Violence*, Sydney: Australian Institute of Criminology, Hawkins Press.

Messerschmidt, J. W. (1993), *Masculinities and Crime: Critiques and Reconceptualisation*, Lanham: Rowman.

Millett, K. (1969), *Sexual Politics*, London: Abacus.

Primoratz, I. (1999), *Ethics and Sex* London: Routledge.

Rabinow, P. (ed.) (2000), *Michel Foucault: Ethics, The Essential Works 1*, London: Allen Lane/The Penguin Press.

Rich, A. (1980), 'Compulsory heterosexuality and lesbian existence', *Signs*, Vol. 5, No. 4, pp. 631-660.

Rubin, G. S. (1993), 'Thinking sex: Notes for a radical theory of the politics of sexuality' in Abelove, H. et al. (eds), *The Lesbian and Gay Studies Reader*, New York: Routledge.

Segal, L. (1994), *Straight Sex: The Politics of Pleasure*, London: Virago.

Chapter 4

The Language of Refusal: Sexual Consent and the Limits of Post-Structuralism

Gideon Calder

Senses of 'Consent'

A randomly consulted dictionary entry gives fives senses of 'consent' as a verb:

> to be of the same mind: to agree: to give assent: to yield: to comply

... followed by three of the noun:

> agreement: accordance with the actions or opinions of another: concurrence (Various, 1990, p. 303)

At one level, one need look no further for explanation of why, legally and otherwise, 'sexual consent' remains such a difficult, contested issue. These definitions fail starkly to agree amongst themselves. Being 'of the same mind' connotes something quite different from 'complying' – while one implies spontaneous, uncoerced harmony of thought, the other implies adapting to another's point of view. Similarly, 'yielding' need not entail 'giving assent' (or vice-versa). And it's by no means self-evident that 'agreement' is synonymous with 'accordance with the actions or opinions of another'. Any simple assumption that 'consent' implies free agreement might seem, then, to be scuppered at the outset by the very slippages and ambiguities of its dictionary definition.

This isn't, of course, just a narrowly semantic issue. If you can't define 'consent', or find a framework in which it can be separated from 'non-consent', the implications for rape law, for the practices of moral blame and retribution, for approaches to date rape, for the very articulation of what rape is in the first place, are many and onerous. Indeed, the various ambiguities conveyed even in its dictionary definition serve as easy ammunition for the claim that 'consent' is so ideologically loaded as a term – so saturated in contestable assumptions – that it should have no application in rape law whatsoever: that it works as a kind of distorting lens which projects questionable gender stereotypes and a pre-given order of priority between them.

Reasons for such a change can pretty much be read off the list of alternative definitions given above. If 'to be of the same mind', figurative as the phrase may be, means the same as to 'agree', then this implies that men and women must think the same in order for consent to happen. This in turn implies that the mind has no sex, that men and women 'really', or at least *should* potentially, think the same, that there is something like a meeting of minds that can take place on some neutral, ideal territory untouched by power relations, that bodies and other aspects of material reality are strictly subsidiary, and so on. One picture of 'consent' assumes that it has to be a pure, rational, self-present, self-transparent, act in which the words themselves serve as a kind of dispensable ladder, a means to the end of the unifying of different minds.

Opponents of this view tend to argue, with some plausibility, that you can trace it straight back to Descartes' 'substance dualism', according to which the mental realm, the realm of thought and reason, floats free of the realm of mechanistic matter, and with it mere instinct and desire. They might question whether 'rationality' has to be conceived in these highly abstract, idealistic terms – or whether, more technically, 'agency' must be constructed on the basis of the self-legislating 'subject presumed to know', as pure, sole author of its own thoughts and judgements. Alternatively, going further, they might suggest that the very idea of 'rational consent' has (after Freud and Nietzsche, for instance, in addition to the work of feminist theorists in showing the masculine biases of mainstream understandings of reason) long since gone out the philosophical window. Most especially, it looks drastically naive in light of poststructuralist emphases (in many places now *de rigeur*) on the ways in which the language we utter works in ways which are strictly beyond our control, neither matching our own intentions nor mapping the material world, but in important ways *producing* both of these.

Again, poststructuralist feminists looking to deconstruct any rational-communicative account of sexual consent might start by pointing to the next three senses of the verb 'to consent', which associate 'assenting' with 'yielding' and 'complying'. The sense is given that 'consenting' is necessarily reactive: that it is always a response to a demand, and one which requires a sort of capitulation or surrender to an external imposition. To have 'accordance with the actions or opinions of another', you must first be presented with those actions: and thus you must always, as consenter, be subordinate or secondary in the encounter – a *consentee*, perhaps, rather than an equal participant. If 'yielding' implies 'giving assent', this presumes that the volition of the yielder can simply be inferred from their submission. This in turn would suggest that we can simply assume firm consent wherever there is *not* active refusal to yield. In a different context, David Hume once described such assumptions as 'delirious' and 'absurd' (1994, p. 168). As he didn't say, but might have added: they are also inherently dangerous.

For all of these and other reasons, the very language of 'consent' is inapplicable when talking about crimes of sexual violence because it is loaded from the start. In its hedgings and qualifications, the very dictionary definition of 'consent' seems to deny that consent, as unforced agreement, is actually possible. Unless it pins itself to some sort of abstract, socially disengaged, pure, immediate 'meeting of minds', 'consent', viewed thus, seems in practice to require its opposite. It presents a scenario involving active and passive subjects ('consenter', perhaps, and 'consentee'): the one assenting to or refusing, but in any case responding to, the proposition of the other. If these roles are to be filled by man and woman, this presupposes that men initiate sexual interaction, and that women's role is to accept or reject the advance. Legally, as many have argued, the emphasis on consent means that what matters in establishing a rape charge is whether the perpetrator had reason to think that the woman was consenting (i.e., that their 'yielding' implied 'assent'), not whether she actually consented (see Haslanger, 1996, for a discussion of this approach). How can there be anything like purity of agreement when 'consent' is conceived in such terms? It seems, on this level, a self-destabilising notion, and one which will be too contaminated by power relations to do justice to the issues at stake.

Further Issues

So much for the instabilities of 'consent' as a term – muddinesses which must be confronted by those who would defend it as a central component of the legal definition of rape. This chapter will make no attempt to deny these problems of definition. Rather, it discusses a further, recently fairly commonplace way of calling into question certain 'traditional' assumptions about what rape is and how we should best approach it. This is the argument that the legal language of rape definition is endlessly problematic partly because rape itself is best viewed as a sort of language – a 'linguistic fact' which is generated by a particular set of grammatical rules, and thus has a sort of inscribed logic.

My attention to this approach is given with two background considerations in mind. One is the UK government's recent introduction of tight controls on the sleeping pill Rohypnol, the so-called 'date rape' drug, after its linking to rape cases in Britain and the United States. Its effects have been widely documented. Odourless, colourless and tasteless when added to alcohol, it is ten times stronger than other sedatives, and can confuse the memory of takers for days once administered – by which time the drug will have disappeared from the blood and, if one has taken place, there will be no forensic evidence of a rape (details: <http://news2.thls.bbc.co.uk/low/english/uk/newsid>). The use of this drug as a prelude to sexual assault derives precisely from the fact that it leads to memory loss, decreases resistance, and may in fact lead the taker to pass out. In most cases, takers experience difficulty in speaking (data from: <www.4woman.org/faq/rohypnol.htm>).

Secondly, I want to raise implications of studies in conversation analysis that for some critics have challenged the effectiveness of the familiar anti-rape slogan 'yes means yes and no means no'. The argument here owes nothing to the counter-feminist retort that women 'really' want sex despite their verbalised protestations – it is not suggesting that women's speech-acts should not be taken at face value. Rather, it presents the quite separate case that (a) women (and indeed people in general, in all sorts of situations) have a far from straightforward attitude towards their own capacity to say 'no', and (b) in everyday conversation, we very rarely utter a simple, forthright 'no' even when we most categorically mean it. On the contrary: everyday refusals are complex, finely organised, and nuanced. As one description has it, 'acceptances do, indeed, often involve "just saying yes", but refusals very rarely involve "just saying no" – indeed, it is conversationally most unusual to "just say no"' (Kitzinger and Frith, 1999, pp. 300, 302). That, all the same, we usually know a refusal when confronted by one, is down to a sort of background understanding between speakers to the effect that certain conversational patterns, while not *explicitly* refusing, amount *practically* to much the same thing. We do not speak literally, even when making ourselves clear.

Hence any defence on the part of anyone charged with rape that their alleged victim did not say 'no' is challenged by the fact that speakers of a shared language register refusal in a great many, subtler ways than that. 'It should not,' as Kitzinger and Frith conclude, 'be necessary for a woman to say "no" in order to be understood as refusing sex' (1999, p. 306). Outside the courtroom, we do not conduct conversational exchanges at that level of explicitness: 'the word "no" is not a necessary semantic component of refusals. It is not normally necessary to say "no" in order to be heard as refusing an offer or invitation – pausing, hedging, producing a palliative, and even delayed or weak "acceptances" are typically understood as refusals in everyday talk' (1999, p. 309).

Without wanting to take such 'micro' examples as conclusive in terms of analysis of the nature of consent, I do want to suggest that they highlight key problems with the post-structuralist account favoured by many recent feminist critics. My basic argument is that, if this is supposed to be a way round the problems of defining consent, it doesn't work. In fact, it suggests that 'consent' talk, though ridden with pitfalls, must be (critically) retained. My hunch in so arguing is that making allowance for an ontological gap between word and deed, word and material reality, is crucial to any adequate theoretical approach to sexual consent. Put more technically, the speech-act is never fully adequate to bodily interaction, is always discrepant, precisely because consent is always about more than language, either at the level of the individual utterance, or in a wider, discursive sense. Describing rape as a 'linguistic fact' offers little in the way of explanatory power, and in fact creates something of a diversion for productive feminist analysis.

'A Gendered Grammar of Violence'?

Just that description of rape occurs in an illuminating, frequently insightful piece by Sharon Marcus on the possibility of a feminist counter-politics to rape. She defines rape as 'a scripted interaction which takes place in language', as a 'linguistic fact', as something 'structured like a language, a language which shapes both the verbal *and* physical interactions of a woman and her would-be assailant' (Marcus, 1992, pp. 389, 390; Marcus's essay deals exclusively with heterosexual rape, and for the purposes of argument I'll follow her lead on this). She presents this view as a counterposition to the 'common-sense', empiricist view 'that rape is real; that to be real means to be fixed, determinate, and transparent to understanding; and that feminist politics must understand rape as one of the real, clear facts of women's lives' (Marcus, p. 385). Against this, she puts forward:

one of feminism's most powerful contentions about rape – that rape is a question of language, interpretation, and subjectivity. Feminist thinkers have asked: Whose words count in a rape trial? Whose 'no' can never mean 'no'? How do rape trials condone men's misinterpretation of women's words? How do rape trials consolidate men's subjective accounts into objective 'norms of truth' and deprive women's subjective accounts of cognitive value? (Marcus, p. 387)

Few would dispute that these are valid, indeed essential questions for any oppositional politics to the culture of rape. But Marcus wants to go further than just suggesting that we pay special analytical attention to the linguistic aspects of sexual violence and its treatment in the law. On the one hand, she argues, unproblematically, that 'A politics which would fight rape cannot exist without developing a language about rape'. But then she adds a deeper, *non sequitur*-ish claim: that such a politics cannot exist 'without understanding rape to be a language' (p. 387). It is this aspect of her case that seems in urgent need of contestation.

What is Marcus's problem with the 'empiricist' view of rape as something which is 'real' and factual? It is roughly this: that it presents rape as 'an inevitable material fact of life', and, in viewing it as something material, assumes that 'a rapist's ability to physically overcome his target is the foundation of rape'. This in turn makes rape into 'a reality that lies beyond our grasp', 'encircling us', 'terrifyingly unnameable'. It also (and I'm not sure this is at all consistent) assumes rape to be 'a fact to be accepted or opposed, tried or avenged' (p. 388).[1] To combat the conservative and defeatist tendencies embodied in the assumption that rape is thus some sort of physical fact of our lives, some sort of unchangeable reality, we'd do better:

to treat it as a *linguistic* fact: to ask how the violence of rape is enabled by narratives, complexes and institutions which derive their strength not from outright, immutable, unbeatable force but rather from their power to structure our lives as imposing cultural scripts. To understand rape in this way is to understand it as subject to change. (Marcus, p. 389)

In what senses is rape a 'linguistic fact'? Marcus gives three: its representation in cultural and ideological images in which mythical assumptions about women's attitudes to rape are sustained; the (surely rather *empiricist-minded*!) observation that speech is often present in rape (which is rarely wordless); and most importantly, that rape itself is structured like a language.[2] Language here is conceived as 'a system of meanings which enables people to experience themselves as speaking, acting, and embodied subjects', which 'solicits women to position themselves as violable, and fearful and invites men to position themselves as legitimately violent and entitled to women's sexual services' (p. 390). Rape, then, is one of culture's many ways of 'feminising' women. It follows a sort of pre-existing script which defines some of us (men) as legitimate *subjects* of violence, and others (women) as its rightful *objects*. Hence women are cast into the role of victims in a script not of their own authorship.

The utility of this approach, argues Marcus, is that it lies in its potential to undermine any idea that rape is some kind of inevitable feature of the landscape, something 'natural' (because 'real' in some fixed sense) to which we must conceive an adequate theoretical or legal response. If rape follows a 'script', then that script must be changeable. We can interrupt its flow, re-direct its logic. This means, again, that rape is not primarily a physical process, featuring factual givens:

> To take violence or female vulnerability as the first and last instances in any explanation of rape is to make the identities of rapist and raped pre-exist the rape itself. If we eschew this view and consider rape as a scripted interaction in which one person auditions for the role of rapist and strives to manoeuvre another person into the role of victim, we can see rape as a *process* of sexist engendering which we can attempt to disrupt. (Marcus, 1992, p. 391)

'The rape script pre-exists instances of rape but neither the script not the rape act results from or creates immutable identities of rapist and raped' (p. 391). It 'structures physical actions and responses as well as words'. Though the feelings involved – say, powerfulness on the part of the would-be rapist, powerlessness on the part of the threatened party – *seem* like 'real' physical sensations, 'they appear so because the language of rape speaks through us, freezing our own sense of force and affecting the would-be rapist's perception of our lack of strength. Rapists do not prevail simply because as men they are really, biologically, and unavoidably stronger than women. A rapist follows a social script and enacts conventional, gendered structures of feeling and action which seek to draw the rape target into a dialogue which is skewed against her' (p. 390).

What is this rape script then? It is something that dictates the course of actions without being immutable. It is something that structures sexual violence while still allowing for either party to interrupt things. It is whatever enables us to carry out certain roles without rigidly delimiting those roles. Both would-be rapist and his target can always 'shift the terms of discussion': rather than seeing women as able only to consent or not consent, acquiesce in the demands of the would-be assailant or dissuade him from them, this account sees the script as something open and malleable. Rape is best viewed not as 'the forced entry of a real inner space', but as 'a form of invagination in which rape scripts the female body as a wounded inner space' (p. 400). We can always imagine things differently: men are not the unfragile violators which the rape script presents them as. We need not wait for men to decide to stop raping. We can intervene now, physically and verbally, to resist the logic of the script, interrupt it, challenge 'rape culture', demonstrate its contingency, and replace it with something else.

What Kind of Script? What Kind of Performance?

For obvious reasons, this approach has little time for any claim that the notion of 'consent' is salvageable from the rubble of its deconstruction. It explicitly rejects 'the communicative stance of *responsiveness*' which 'encourages women not to take the offensive in a dialogue with a would-be rapist but to stay within the limits he sets' (p. 393). Put in *those* terms, consensuality does indeed seem to be analytically irrelevant. Even so, several points seem worth raising here.

This whole approach assumes that we know what rape *is*, that it can be recognised when we see it, that there is a pre-existing pattern which rape as a cultural effect will follow, and so forth – while simultaneously denying that there is *any such thing* as 'rape' in any real, stable, definable sense, and that talking in such terms is regressive and acquiesces in rape culture. Marcus, for all her suspicions of the notion of 'consent', seems sure enough in the belief that we can establish the *non*-consensuality of a sexual act with firm epistemological certainty. That rape exists, on her terms, and that it is a bad thing, sits less than easily with the insistence that we do not take it as in any sense 'given'.

This contradiction parallels an ambiguity in the notion of a 'rape script', which on Marcus's account seems to script our behaviour without actually scripting our behaviour. This raises questions about the status of *agency* which tend often to hamper post-structuralist theory. The sort of sophisticated social constructionism endorsed by Marcus, and most notably by Judith Butler, claims that the social construction of reality is always more elaborate, more complexly scripted, more deeply linguistic, than appearances suggest. Butler puts great emphasis on the 'performative' – that form of speech-act which brings into being what it names.[3] This, she remarks, is the sense in which:

> discourse becomes productive in a fairly specific way. [...] If you want the ontology of this, I guess performativity is the vehicle through which ontological effects are established. Performativity is the discursive mode by which ontological effects are installed. (Butler, 1996, p. 112)

This is crucial when it comes to consent or non-consent in sexual actions, to the extent that it problematises that very opposition. 'My presumption,' as she puts it, 'is that speech is always in some ways out of our control' (Butler, 1987, p. 15) – we are never simply authors of our own speech-acts, be they of refusal or consent.

Performativity works on other levels, too. In her work over the past few years Butler has given constant attention to the question of how it is that our bodies are linguistically constructed. This makes the body into something with an ontological status which is very deliberately indeterminate – but not, as Butler insists, something that thereby is any less substantive. She refers to 'the chant of antipostmodernism', which runs: 'if everything is discourse, then is there no reality to bodies? How do we understand the material violence that women suffer?' (Butler, 1992, p. 17). In response, she insists that 'the discursive ordering and

production of bodies in accord with the category of sex is itself a material violence'
(Butler, 1992, p. 17), and continues:

> Consider the legal restrictions that regulate what does and does not count as rape: here
> the politics of violence operate through regulating what will and will not be able to
> appear as an effect of violence. There is, then, already in this foreclosure a violence at
> work, a marking off in advance of what will or will not qualify under the signs of 'rape'
> or 'government violence', or in the case of states in which twelve separate pieces of
> empirical evidence are required to establish 'rape', what then can be called a
> governmentally facilitated rape. (Butler, 1992, p. 18)

In other words, it is the practices of legal classification which are entirely
responsible for what counts as 'rape', and thus, by extension, for the 'rape' itself.
Now there are questions here concerning Butler's consideration of sex and gender,
and of the nature of the body, which would merit extended treatment in
themselves. Put briefly, Butler insists that while she does not want to deny 'certain
kinds of biological differences', she always asks 'under what discursive and
institutional conditions do certain biological differences become the salient
characteristics of sex' (Butler, 1996, p. 113). Butler contends that matter is an
effect of power: the body is thus both material *and* a social construction. As well as
being material, it is an effect of regulatory norms.[4] The same will go for sexual
violence: it is not that it does not 'really exist', but rather that its important aspects
gain that importance only as a result of certain discursive and institutional
conditions. We simply can't imagine the 'impossible scene' of 'a body that has not
yet been given social definition' (Butler 1997, p. 5). The same goes for rape. It is
not reality prior to our approaching it.

But this seems deeply skewed. To claim that language is a crucial dimension of
analysis of rape, that speech features in and contributes to acts of sexual violence,
that our culture abounds with dubious representations of rape as something which
women like more than they let on, as somehow natural or not as bad as all that,
abound in our culture – all of this is relatively uncontroversial. But there is a huge
conceptual leap from this to the idea that rape is only, or simply, a 'linguistic fact'.
Put differently, the conclusion 'rape is a linguistic fact' is utterly underdetermined
by the many ways in which language features in our analysis of it. Indeed, no
explanatory power is added by this claim. The idea that to claim that 'rape is real'
is to make some naive empiricist claim that rape exists in the same way that a rock
or a pedestrian crossing does is (to state the obvious) to assume that when it comes
to defending the notion of 'reality', naive empiricism is the only game in town.
Material reality need not be static, unchangeable, or hypostatised. It just needs to
be real, in a sense which is not *simply* reducible to discourse.

Or simply, by the same token, simply a product of it. Take this description of
the 'language of rape':

> This language structures physical actions and responses as well as word, and forms, for
> example, the would-be rapist's feelings of powerfulness and our commonplace sense of

paralysis when threatened with rape. As intractably real as these physical sensations may appear to us, however, they appear so because the language of rape speaks through us, freezing our own sense of force and affecting the would-be rapist's perception of our lack of strength. Rapists do not prevail simply because as men they are really, biologically, and unavoidably stronger than women. A rapist follows a social script and enacts conventional, gendered structures of feeling and action which seek to draw the rape target into a dialogue which is skewed against her. (Marcus, 1992, p. 390)

The problem here is that positing 'language' as something which 'enables' (in a pretty unspecific way) violence, to the exclusion of more physical factors, is to fall into two looming traps which lie in wait for most post-structuralist analysis. One is that of inflating 'language' into something suspiciously like God, or a sort of life-giving spirit: the ultimate source of absolutely everything which might otherwise seem to be the result of other contributing factors, including 'material' ones in a fairly basic sense – physical strength, the possession and administering of the 'date-rape drug' Rohypnol, etc. To this extent, it becomes pretty much useless as an explanatory device, rather like God is to atheists. On Marcus's account of the rape script, it is something like a 'first cause', 'enabling' all subsequent events to happen. But like the Bible is for liberal theologians who want to soften St Paul's pronouncements on homosexuality, or for clerics in general seeking to explain the extent of famine, war, genocide, misery and evil in the world of a benign Creator, the 'rape script' for Marcus becomes something which appears quite differently depending on the rhetorical use she wants to make of it. It provides for everything while at the same time being expendable.

The other problem is that, in its great fear of any appeal to 'nature' as somehow inevitably involving a confirmation of the legitimacy of the status quo, post-structuralism's heavy-duty cultural determinism denies the physical dimension of rape. The world, the material, the physical, the real – however you want to describe it – becomes an utterly blank slate, an open space onto which discourse projects whatever it likes. To go back, for instance, to the description of rape as a 'linguistic fact'. Bear in mind that this description must, if it is to have any real resonance, seek to collapse any clear distinction between the way in which we talk about rape, or rape is culturally constructed, and the act itself. In fact, there can be no 'act itself' if this implies that we can somehow talk of sexual violence as something 'objective', a discrete event. If 'rape is a linguistic fact' doesn't mean more or less this, then it seems a pointless statement to make: otherwise, it's just making the fairly mundane point that the 'factuality' of rape, like everything else, may be construed differently according to the perspective from which it's viewed, the vocabulary that we use, ideological manipulations, its definition, and so forth. That if we define 'rape' in different ways, then different things will count as rape. No, the claim goes further: that it is as a piece of language that we will most profitably analyse any act of rape, and that, since language is not best viewed as a tool which human beings manipulate, but rather as the source of our existence as selves, rape is not just something about which our perceptions are linguistically organised, but is something *produced* by language. If you think differently, you are chained to the (on these terms) hopelessly delusional assumption that there is a material reality separate from our descriptions of it, or other determining factors (socio-historical, economic, biological) other than the cultural or linguistic which affect the ways in which we talk about rape. You are condemned, in other words, to the assumption that legal discourse might be more or less *accurate* in its treatment of the nature and conditions of, and indeed the harm caused by, rape.

For the implications of this line of analysis, we might apply it to something else – say, starvation due to famine in sub-Saharan Africa. According to Marcus, the only way in which we can talk about such things as being 'real' (and as involving, at a crucial level, the effects of nutritional deprivation on the bodies, the biology of those affected) is by adopting some sort of boneheadedly crude empiricist account of factuality according to which to be 'true' our statements must map a static, unchanging, immutable reality. But to understand something as 'real', as a material aspect of our lives, is *in no way* necessarily to understand it as 'immutable', or 'unchangeable', or somehow possessing a permanent identity entirely separate from all human activity. Theorists of the material circumstances of capitalism by no means treat any aspect of it as having an eternal, unchanging essence, or any necessity or inevitability about it. 'Sweatshop labour' exists – and exists, as I would have it, in ways which are not reducible to its discursive construction. But it neither has an immutable nature, nor, one would hope, is there anything ineluctable about its long-term survival.

One can conceive material reality as precisely being in a state of flux: as something which is not *constructed* by culture, but is nonetheless transformed by human agency. If you want to say that you can't *know* about the real nature of material reality, then that's a different, epistemological question. But to say that there is *no* reality outside of language, that language scripts reality *tout court*, is just one of those weird intellectual extravagances that a great many people have slipped into without really meaning anything of the sort. It is to suggest that material conditions not of our own choosing (or more accurately, conditions which aren't always already socially constructed) neither impose constraints upon us, shape our potential nor offer any resistance to our redescriptions of them.[5] To say that global warming, or having a broken leg, can be accounted for exclusively in terms of their social construction is, well, a tall order. More than that: it runs the risk that the power and effects of social construction slip entirely out of analytical view – precisely because, being everything, there is nothing to distinguish them from, or contrast them against. To say that the only way women can be encouraged to defend themselves in rape situations, to challenge the role into which they are conventionally cast, to retaliate, is by viewing rape as a language is a bit like saying the only way to end famine is to view the World Trade Organisation and the charity War on Want as languages. In terms of explanatory power, it leaves things remarkably untouched.

So much for the problems of the post-structuralist account of the relationship of materiality and language, body and discourse, deed and word. So what? Need this have any implications for the possibility or desirability of defining 'consent'?

Reclaiming Materiality, Reconceiving Consent

What leads Marcus and Butler into their untenable positions is, I think, the common poststructuralist assumption that, as Toril Moi has put it, 'if something is not discursively constructed, then it must be natural'. To speak of the 'natural' becomes the devil's language, on this account, because 'nature is taken to be immutable, unchanging, fixed, stable, and somehow "essentialist"' (Moi, 1999, p. 51). The mistake here, as we've seen, is twofold: that whatever is 'real', or not simply discursively constructed, must somehow by fixed and stable; and that whatever is 'constructed' must somehow be easily changed. Hence we must insist that rape is a social construction, because otherwise it would be reified as an eternal feature of the landscape, some sort of human necessity.[6] The fact that we might stubbornly continue to believe that rape is a 'fact' can only be explicable in terms of the mysterious workings of 'power'.

This can be traced back to the assumption that there is no meaningful distinction between matter and discourse, that 'materiality is ... bound up with signification from the start' (Butler, 1993, p. 30). This in turn leads to the twin rejection of both materiality and consent. I think it is essential to reclaim the possibility of talking about both, and that the reclaiming of both goes hand in hand. Post-structuralism's twofold mistake is to employ a warped conception of 'nature', and then to insist on the basis of its rejection that everything must be discursively constructed. Discourse for Butler is never purely ideal, nor ever simply a reflection of prior reality (Hull, p. 23). Hence we can never say that, going back to our dictionary definitions, 'minds' can 'meet' in some neutral rational space free of social or material circumstance. But equally, we can never assume that there is a material realm outside discourse or language about which we might agree.[6] Rape can only be defined from a point of view; points of view are discursively constructed; hence, there is no reality of 'rape' independent of language.

But to reject the very possibility of adequate linguistic communication, and so 'consent', for this reason is to assume a very oddly defined notion of 'consent' and to take it as the only available option. To be more precise: it is to assume that consent, to be a workable legal notion with any form of purchase or explanatory power, must obtain in a realm where ideas relate only to ideas, severed from the intrusions of concrete, lived reality. This assumption stems from a familiar enough habit of thinking, at its root Cartesian. It assumes that due attention to the nature of ideas on the one hand, and to material reality on the other, requires their packaging up into cleanly separate ontological compartments. A philosophical spin-off is that the rejection of a fully autonomous, mentalistic, Descartes-style version of subjectivity very often goes hand in hand with the rejection of the corresponding 'objectivity' traditionally assumed to be its counterpart. Thus, if there are problems with conceiving subjectivity as something pure, stable, self-present, and uncontaminated by determining factors, then equally there are problems with conceiving of any sort of objectivity which is separable from the way in which we happen to talk about it. It's a double displacement: there is no 'reality' beyond what we construct from particular perspectives, and furthermore we don't construct that reality on our own terms. But this equation doesn't hold. As Adorno once pointed out (see Hull, p. 28), it's the idealist premise that thought equals its objects that has led people into the (certainly rather odd, almost theological) belief that matter is reified and stable. But still, 'there *is* a material realm outside discourse or language'. Thought and language might never be able fully to capture their object. But this does not mean that the object is unnecessary, or incidental, or a mere effect of discourse. In fact, reality constrains subjectivity in a way in which subjectivity simply does not constrain objectivity: material reality, in the end, simply doesn't care how we describe it.

This distinction is crucial when considering the administering of the so-called 'date-rape drug'. The preconditions, or the background, for this might in many senses be script-like: the roles involved, the construction of 'acceptable' modes of behaviour towards the opposite sex, the influence of discourses about the ideally compliant female, and so on. But here, if the script is interrupted, or the standard pattern of behaviour is changed, it is precisely because a non-discursively constructed event (i.e., the action of chemical content of Rohypnol in the bloodstream of the recipient) intervenes and interrupts the prior logic of things. Changes, for example, a script in which the female is cast as 'really' wanting sex despite her 'apparent' refusals, to one in which (as an admission of her likely resistance) she must be drugged in order to be compliant. Again: this interruption is not an effect of discourse unless *everything* is at some step removed an effect of discourse, in which case language has become God: the first cause of everything. And if discourse is the undifferentiated first cause of everything, then (as I argued earlier) its sense is stretched beyond the stage where it has any explanatory power. It seems particularly deficient when it comes to delineating a distinction between consent as something which can simply be read by the would-be rapist into the appearance of non-resistance, and consent as representing active *willingness*.

Secondly, turning to the other factor we raised at the start – namely, the routine dimensions of conversational interaction which do not involve the word 'no' but nonetheless clearly signal refusal. As I said, to highlight these factors is not to suggest that 'no' really means 'yes', but rather that there is more to meaning 'no' than the direct utterance of the word itself. Now both Marcus and Butler would of course want to distance themselves from any reductive, or purely formalistic, account of language as simply the utterance of words: for any semiotics, the gesture and the pause convey as much as words themselves in accounting for communication. So the problem is not that they can't account for the ways in which, say, a speaker's facial expression casts doubt upon the literal sense of the words they utter. Rather, it is that they can't account for the *quality* of consent given in different contexts and under different conditions.[7] The findings of Kitzinger and Frith suggest not that consent is not an issue, or is untheorisable, or legally irrelevant, or must always inevitably involve hidden power relations, but that consent is a far subtler, less literal, less linguistically based affair than a reductive concentration on the simple use of words could ever reveal.

At this level, I can't really see what the contribution of the 'rape as a script' school might be. Again, if everything is language, then the nuances of the actual, concrete lived experience of a situation of alleged sexual violence are not addressable in isolation from the playing-out of what for Marcus is a pre-scripted drama. They are, quite affirmatively, relegated to the level of 'empirical' evidence of which we should be deeply mistrustful. If – as the problems inherent in the term's definition suggest – a subtler, more nuanced, more contextual account of consent is in order, then post-structuralist approaches cannot provide it precisely because they have already rejected its possibility. Their methodology casts doubt on the slogan 'no means no', since the intentions of the speaking subject are not responsible for the workings of the language which, it's claimed, 'speaks through her' rather than being manipulated by her. But it seems unable to account for the possibility that *anything* could actually mean 'no' – or to address those extra-linguistic factors which, concretely, count as refusal. While right to insist that people's words or actions or gestures or expressions are never *simply* enough in themselves to signal consent, it seems to deny that they could *ever* count as evidence of willingness or otherwise.

It might be argued that this would be no bad thing – that for the reasons mentioned at the start, the very notion of consent is legally untenable. That is, to a degree, another question.

It does, though, seem worth it to raise a number of questions arising from my discussion here. Does registering that the word 'no' is not a necessary semantic component of refusals actually make more urgent an adequately critical assessment of the nature and scope of 'consent'? Does the viability of any notion of consent depend upon the possibility – denied under post-structuralist approaches – of an ontological gap between word and world? Does the possible intervention of a third, external force such as a 'date rape drug', and its effects, have implications for either the need for a viable notion of consent, or for its form? Is the attribution of *some* degree of authorship of speech-acts necessary for the demand that women be granted an equal right to be treated as authors of their own refusals – for them to be accepted, as Lovibond (1996, p. 106) puts it, 'as *meaning what they say* rather than summarily reinterpreted by men as (really) meaning something different'? My own answers to these questions are in each case a qualified 'yes'. Post-structuralism's 'no' to each question (if, of course, it really means 'no') seems to me to render it inadequate as an approach to the realities of alleged rape situations, and to put an unfortunate roadblock in the way of finding an adequately nuanced and concrete definition of 'consent'.

Notes

[1] These descriptions all feature in the same passage of Marcus's essay. I don't know whether something can be at the same time both a 'fact' and 'terrifyingly unnamable'. Nor can I see how something can be simultaneously 'a reality that lies beyond our grasp' and 'a fact to be accepted or opposed, tried or avenged'. While seeking to highlight the inconsistencies of 'common sense', Marcus also splices together various quite different opposing arguments to her own. More seriously, Marcus seems to argue by implication that rape *is* nameable, that it *is* within our grasp, but that it is *not* a fact. Hence it is fully knowable, because it is not a separate reality. There seems to be a thoroughgoing, positivistic nominalism at work here,

according to which the only reality is that which we name, and reality just is how we name it. I doubt Marcus thinks it would be equally valid to describe an act of proven sexual attack as 'rape' and as 'a constitutional walk in the park', but I'm not sure how she could object to the equation.

[2] I haven't the space here to deal with the radical differences, perhaps the tension, between these different senses in which Marcus claims that rape is a language. Cultural representations are one thing; the use of language in rape is another; the claim that rape is a 'linguistic fact' is a huge conceptual leap from the first two. For both of the first two are contingencies, and the latter is an *a priori* claim: it is in rape's *nature* (so it would seem) that it is a language, whereas it is not in rape's nature that perpetrators of sexual attacks use language as part of the violence, or that rape is represented culturally at all. Unless the claim is that rape is *only ever*, always already, a cultural construction (which Marcus does indeed seem to be suggesting sometimes, if sophisticatedly). But in that case it is not clear that the roles of those involved can be discussed other than as effects of a prior script. If the script is alterable through individual agency, does this mean that these actions must be linguistic too – that all such actions are in some deep sense linguistic? And if so, isn't it purely incidental that some would-be rapists use language in certain ways during their actions? A bit like saying 'Rapists usually have names, therefore rape is fundamentally linguistic'? One might equally well say 'Rape is fundamentally *physical* because all rape involves physical interaction.' It may be that Marcus is making a sort of argumentative capital out of sliding between two senses of the term 'language': between on the one hand, instances of its usage, and on the other, the cultural and political backdrop against which such usage takes place. This latter is more familiarly termed *discourse*, rather than language *simpliciter*.

[3] J.L. Austin's benchmark discussion of performative utterances defines them thus:

> A. they do not 'describe' or 'report' or constate anything at all, are not 'true or false', and B. the uttering of the sentence is, or is a part of, the doing of an action, which again would not normally be described as , or as 'just', saying something.'

He gives as examples: 'I promise', 'I name this ship. ..', 'I bet you sixpence it will rain tomorrow'. See Austin (1962), especially p. 5 ff.

[4] See, for instance, Butler, 1993, pp. 9-10:

> What I would propose ... is a return to the notion of matter, not as site or surface, but as *a process of materialisation that stabilises over time to produce the effect of boundary, fixity, and surface we call matter*. That matter is always materialised has, I think, to be thought in relation to the productive and, indeed, materialising effects of power in the Foucauldian sense.

This is Butler's reformulation of the traditional precedence of sex to gender: for her, in a *real, material* sense, gender (as cultural construction) determines sex.

[5] See, on this point, Giminez, 1995, p. 257, and also Hennessy, 1995, pp. 270-271.

[6] Moi points out (1999, p. 51) that it's a lot easier to change an island into a peninsula than it is to change your understanding of, say, what counts as giving directions to a stranger: nature needn't signify that which is immutable, even in comparison to cultural factors.

[7] For further consideration of the imperative to address the quality of consent – and an approach which (to my mind) complements my own preliminary conclusions here – see Paul Reynolds' chapter in this volume.

Bibliography

Austin, J. L. (1962), *How To Do Things With Words*, Oxford: Oxford University Press.

Butler, J. (1992), 'Contingent Foundations', in Butler, J. and Scott, J. W. (eds) *Feminists Theorise the Political*, London: Routledge.

Butler, J. (1993), *Bodies That Matter: On the Discursive Limits of 'Sex'*, London: Routledge.

Butler, J. (1996), 'Gender as Performance', interview with Peter Osborne and Lynne Segal, in Osborne, P. (ed.), *A Critical Sense: Interviews with Intellectuals*, London: Routledge.

Butler, J. (1997), *Excitable Speech: A Politics of the Performative*, London: Routledge.

Fraser, N. (1989), *Unruly Practices: Power, Discourse and Gender in Contemporary Social Theory*, Cambridge: Polity Press.

Gimenez, M. E. (1995), 'The Production of Divisions: Gender Struggles under Capitalism', in Cullenberg, S. and Brewer, C. (eds), *Marxism in the Postmodern Age: Confronting the New World Order*, New York: The Guilford Press.

Haslanger, S. (1996), 'Objective Reality, Male Reality, and Social Construction', in Garry, A. and Pearsall, M. (eds), *Women, Knowledge, and Reality: Explorations in Feminist Philosophy*, London: Routledge.

Hennessy, R. (1995), 'Incorporating Queer Theory on the Left', in Cullenberg, S. and Brewer, C. (eds), *Marxism in the Postmodern Age: Confronting the New World Order*, New York: The Guilford Press.

Hull, C. L. (1997), 'The need in thinking: Materiality in Theodor W. Adorno and Judith Butler', *Radical Philosophy*, 84, July/August.

Hume, D. (1994), 'Of the Original Contract', in Warner, S. D. and Livingston, D. W. (eds), *Political Writings*, Indianapolis: Hackett.

Kitzinger, C. and Hannah F. (1999), 'Just say no? The use of conversation analysis in developing a feminist perspective on sexual refusal', *Discourse and Society*, Vol. 10, No. 3.

Lovibond, S. (1996), 'Meaning What We Say: Feminist Ethics and the Critique of Humanism', *New Left Review*, No. 220.

Marcus, S. (1992), 'Fighting Bodies, Fighting Words: A Theory and Politics of Rape Prevention', in Butler, J. and Scott, J. W. (eds), *Feminists Theorise the Political*, London: Routledge.

Moi, T. (1999), 'What Is a Woman? Sex, Gender, and the Body in Feminist Theory', in her *What is a Woman? and Other Essays*, Oxford: Oxford University Press.

Temkin, J. (1987), *Rape and the Legal Process*, London: Sweet and Maxwell.

Various (1990), *Chambers English Dictionary*, Edinburgh: Chambers.

Chapter 5

The Age of Consent and Sexual Consent

Matthew Waites

Introduction

Why do we have age of consent laws, and how should the legal age for sexual behaviour be determined? This chapter addresses these questions, developing a historical critique of past rationales for age of consent laws in the United Kingdom in order to reconceptualise how we should think about these laws in the future. It illuminates the origins of the present legal age of 16 which applies to most sexual behaviour, and hence puts it in question. The particular analytical focus is the historical influence of biomedical and psychological knowledge-claims upon debates over age of consent laws, particularly their changing conceptions of young people's decision-making competence. The chapter also discusses how sociological theory suggests better ways to conceptualise age of consent laws in the future. The analysis draws upon and develops previous work which has examined the changing rationale for age of consent laws in the UK.

'Age of Consent' is a term I use to refer to any law, past or present, which prohibits young people's involvement in any form of 'assenting' and/or 'consenting' sexual behaviour below a particular age. Whereas the term 'consent' carries a legacy of association with being the 'positive, intentional action' of a fully self-determining, self-actualising subject, as David Archard has noted in his study *Sexual Consent* (Archard, 1998, p. 4), 'assent' tends to suggest a less decisive action by a less coherent subject (a use distinct from that of Archard: cf. Archard, 1998, p. 5). Use of the term 'age of consent' to cover a variety of laws applying to diverse sexual acts and identities mirrors its recent public usage, but should not disguise its specific historical meanings. For example, the term was avoided by the Wolfenden Committee when they proposed a legal age for sex between men in 1957, described as a 'minimum age' (C.H.O.P., 1957).

The chapter discusses a series of historical moments at which age of consent laws have been formulated, from the late nineteenth century to the present day, and demonstrates the historically changing forms of knowledge which have been invoked in their contestation. It then critically examines the forms of knowledge-claim which structure existing attempts to rethink the basis for age of consent laws, and thus outlines an agenda for theorising and researching how age of consent laws should be determined in the future.

The chapter's focus upon the changing forms of knowledge which have been regarded as sources of authority in debates over age of consent legislation facilitates linking age of consent debates to wider debates in social theory, including debates over epistemological transformations associated with modernity and a shift to 'post' or 'late' modernity (Giddens, 1991, Seidman, 1998). This presentation of the issues can be seen as a useful side-step away from established 'libertarian' versus 'protectionist' political standpoints which dominate both popular and academic debates over the age of consent, as with many other debates over the regulation of sexuality.

Why Reconsider the UK's Age of Consent Laws?

The age at which almost all sexual behaviour becomes legal in the UK is 16. There are exceptions: sexual behaviour which does not involve physical contact (such as 'flashing') is regulated by the offence of 'indecency with a child' in the Indecency with Children Act 1960, which applies only to children aged under 14. There are also differences in how various forms of behaviour are regulated by the variety of offences which act as 'age of consent laws' (for overviews, see: Waites, 1999a, pp. 12-30; Home Office, 2000, pp. 143-150); and some forms of sexual behaviour, such as 'incest', are illegal at all ages. Nevertheless, where an age of consent exists, in almost all instances it is 16.

However, a number of contemporary developments suggest that a reconsideration of the age of 16 might be desirable. Struggles to equalise the so-called 'gay age of consent' with the age for male/female and female/female sexual behaviour, culminating in the passage of the Sexual Offences (Amendment) Act 2000, were dominated by claims for equality (Waites, 2003), yet also generated dissenting currents of argument questioning the rationale for a universal minimum age of 16. For example, some 'protectionists' proposed 'levelling up' the law to achieve 'equality at 18', while prominent queer activist Peter Tatchell has advocated 'equality at 14' (Tatchell, 1996; Tatchell, 2002).

Several social trends and shifting priorities in public policy suggest the desirability of reappraising the age of consent. For example, the prioritisation of strategies to reduce the UK's high rate of teenage pregnancies by the Social Exclusion Unit (Social Exclusion Unit, 1999); the increasing threat of HIV/AIDS to young people (Department of Health, 1999); and the fact that recent research reveals 'an increasing proportion of young people are sexually active below the age of consent' (Wertheimer and Macrae, 1999, p. 19; see also Johnson et al., 1994), all suggest that a reconsideration of whether the current legal age of 16 is appropriate might be beneficial. International perspectives also suggest the possibility of re-examining the current law, since the age of consent remains high in the UK by the standards of western Europe, where the age of 14 or 15 is typical (West and Green, 1997; Graupner, 1999, p. 29; ILGA, 1999).

Yet challenges to the age of 16 were ruled off the political agenda in the recent Home Office review of Sexual Offences (Home Office, 2000), and hence no change to the age of 16 is proposed in the Sexual Offences Bill 2003. Can this confidence in the age of 16 be justified? My aim in the discussion which follows is to demonstrate, through a historical analysis, that the present age of 16 is founded upon problematic forms of knowledge-claim concerning young people's decision-making competence, their sexual behaviour and the relationship of both to the role of the law.

Historically Changing Rationales for Age of Consent Laws

To achieve a complete perspective upon changing rationales for age of consent laws requires an analysis focussing upon a variety of themes, including understandings of citizenship; the structuring effects of patriarchal power, gender and heterosexuality; and changing attitudes towards the role of the law, the state and individual liberty. However, in the historical analysis which follows I wish to focus primarily upon the changing role of medical and psychological knowledges in producing rationales for age of consent laws. This encompasses a number of themes, including theories concerning what constitutes healthy sexual behaviour, and changing theories of the constitution of sexual identity. But in particular I wish to analyse how understandings of young people's decision-making 'competence' – 'the capacity or potential for adequate functioning-in-context as a socialised human' (Jenkins, 1998, p. 1) – have informed rationales for age of consent laws (for discussion of the meaning of 'competence' in cross-cultural perspective, see Jenkins, 1998). The medical and psychological sciences have been crucial in influencing understandings of sexual competence.

The ascendance of medicine and the psychological sciences as institutionalised forms of authority in modernity has been elaborated and critiqued by theorists including Michel Foucault and Bryan Turner (Foucault, 1967; 1980; 1981; Turner, 1995). Subsequent challenges to the authority of orthodox medicine and psychology have been linked to transformations associated with 'postmodern' or 'late modern' society. With this in mind, it is possible to analyse prevailing rationales for age of consent laws at a series of key historical moments when these laws were in question.

The Origins of the Age of Consent in the Nineteenth Century

The 'age of consent' for all sexual behaviour between a male and a female was legally codified at the age of 12 by the Offences Against the Person Act 1861 in England Wales and Ireland, then raised to 13 by the Offences Against the Person Act 1875. The age of consent to sexual intercourse (vaginal penetration with the penis) was then raised again to 16 throughout the UK by the Criminal Law Amendment Act 1885. Section 5 states:

Any person who:
1. Unlawfully and carnally know or attempts to have unlawful carnal knowledge of any girl being of or above the age of thirteen years and under the age of sixteen years; or
2. [...] shall be guilty of a misdemeanour...[...].

A separate, more serious offence, described as 'defilement' in the statute, covered intercourse with a girl under 13, and was punishable by life imprisonment. The age of consent to sexual intercourse has remained 16 until the present day.

These increases in the age of consent during the late nineteenth century took place in the context of popular campaigns by the Social Purity movement, which inspired a widespread tightening of sexual regulation in late Victorian society (Waites, 1999a, pp. 120-151; Waites, 1999b). Campaigns to raise the age of consent were particularly inspired by concerns over child prostitution (Walkowitz, 1992; Bland, 1995).

The age of consent to sexual intercourse was therefore legally codified in a highly gendered form reflecting a dominant form of heterosexuality (cf. Jackson, 1998). The law assumed male desire and aggressive sexual agency, in contrast to female purity, lack of desire, passivity and submission, a dichotomy suggested by the statute's language of 'carnal knowledge'. No minimum age was provided for boys to have sexual intercourse. The male, of any age, was assumed to be responsible and hence punishable for the offence of intercourse with any girl aged under 16. The female was assumed 'innocent', and therefore not guilty of any offence.

How was the age of consent's relation to women's decision-making competence understood? It is clear from an examination of late nineteenth century debates that dominant voices made little reference to models of women's decision-making competence in determining the age at which sexual intercourse with a woman became legal. The boundary was fixed at an age below which women were seen as requiring protection, rather than at an age at which they achieved the ability to make their own decisions. This is apparent from an understanding of the wider socio-political context, in which women gained few citizenship rights at 16, or at any other age (Walby, 1990, pp. 160-171). Women did not have the vote, and access to many forms of employment was prohibited. In marriage (from 16) girls were regarded as the property of men, with no legal right to 'consent' to sex, and no property rights of their own. Hence there was no question of equating psychological competence with the law itself. As Judith Walkowitz notes, a variety of proposed ages circulated in public debate, a fact suggestive of the lack of reference to clear boundaries delineating women's decision-making competence (Walkowitz, 1992, p. 284).

Biomedical authorities, including sexology, advanced understandings of female subjectivity which emphasised an extended period of childhood sexual innocence for women, blending into understandings of adult females as sexually passive and lacking desire (Bland, 1995). This model was associated with understandings of women as lacking strong rational capacities in adulthood. Medicine and psychology thus provided little guidance to an age when women were regarded as gaining decision-making competence which might be relevant to age of consent laws. Lack of reference to women's competence in determining the law was also a product of the prevailing conception of sexual intercourse as something 'done to' passive women. Hence the current legal age of 16 for sexual intercourse was originally formulated as an age of protection for girls, with little reference to capacities for decision-making competence.

Other forms of male/female sexual behaviour such as oral sex and masturbation (with the exception of buggery, which was wholly illegal) remained subject to a lower age of consent until the passage of the Criminal Law Amendment Act 1922, which in response to continuing campaigns by the Social Purity movement, removed 'consent' as a defence to 'indecent assault' (Offences Against the Person Act 1861, s.52) for people aged under 16. This raised the minimum age for all sexual behaviour involving physical contact to 16, including the minimum age of 16 for sexual acts between women (though the legislation was rarely applied to consensual sexual behaviour between women until more recent years) (Waites, 2002). It is clear from analysis of parliamentary debates in the 1920s that the age of 16 established as the age of sexual intercourse in 1885 provided the foundation for the subsequent reform of the law on indecent assault. Hence the creation of a universal minimum age of 16 applying to all sexual behaviour involving physical contact derived its rationale from the protectionist perspectives of the 1880s.

The Policy Advisory Committee on Sexual Offences

In 1975 a Home Office Policy Advisory Committee on Sexual Offences was created as part of a wider review of sexual offences, with the specific purpose of reviewing age of consent laws. This was the only post-war official investigation concerning age of consent laws, the first since the 1920s. The committee recommended no change in the age of 16 as minimum age for sexual intercourse with a female, or in the law on indecent assault regulating other sexual acts (though it gave little explicit attention to the latter: Policy Advisory Committee on Sexual Offences, 1981). However, it proposed reducing the minimum age for sex between men, previously set at 21 when male homosexuality was partially decriminalised in 1967, to 18 (for discussion, see: Moran, 1996; Moran, 1997; Waites, 1999a, pp. 223-258).

The Policy Advisory Committee advanced several arguments in favour of its proposal that the age of consent to sexual intercourse should remain at 16. First, it emphasised the 'physical harm which may arise from premature sexual experience and the undesirability of pregnancy at too early an age' (Policy Advisory Committee, 1981, p. 6). Increased risks of cervical cancer were cited, together with risks of complications in pregnancy and the adverse effects of abortion upon the future fertility of girls under 16 (pp. 6-8). The committee thus drew upon problematically medicalised understandings of adolescence and sexual health. These arguments, invoking biological factors in opposition to a lowering of the age of consent, asserted physiological constraints upon the possibilities for young women's choice and agency, rather than exploring the possibility of promoting the social conditions and availability of resources for young women to make informed choices. The body was represented as placing absolute material constraints upon possibilities for agency.

Secondly, the committee emphasised the 'emotional and social harm which a girl may suffer when she has sexual relations at an age when she is not mature enough to cope with the consequences of a sexual relationship' (Policy Advisory Committee, 1981, p. 6). The repeated utilisation of the concept 'maturity' by the committee suggests the subtle influence of developmental models of adolescence, which have been widely critiqued in sociological research on youth and childhood (James, Jenks and Prout, 1998, pp. 1-25). However, the committee distinguished psychological maturity from any straightforward link to physiological development, noting that: 'although there had been a gradual fall in the average age at which the menarche occurred in girls [...] there had been no significant increase in recent times in the level of psychological maturity of girls under 16' (Policy Advisory Committee, 1981, p. 7). Nevertheless, the committee did clearly articulate the age of 16 as an age of psychological maturity with reference to medical and psychological expertise. While the degree of maturity required was discussed in the context of a complex discussion of various aspects of the social and cultural context, apparent in the committee's reports, the rationale for the age of 16 was not directly theorised or justified in relation to this context, but rather was asserted alongside invocation of evidence from the British Medical Association and Royal College of Psychiatrists (Policy Advisory Committee, 1981, p. 7). Medicine thus provided the review with a form of expertise which could define a particular age of psychological maturity at the age of 16, but without any systematic exposition of how this would relate to determination of the law in a social context. The average age of psychological maturity acquired through developmental processes was assumed to be the correct age for the removal of legal prohibitions.

   The committee's arguments made considerable reference to evidence submitted by the British Medical Association, which argued that that 'emotional and psychological development do not significantly outstrip physical growth' (quoted in Policy Advisory Committee, 1981, p. 16). The BMA's evidence claimed that 'the age of 18 for men would reflect, in general, their slower rate of biological development' because boys achieved puberty two years later than girls (cited in BMA 1994, p. 2; cf. Policy Advisory Committee 1981, pp. 16-17). The committee's advocacy of an age of consent of 18 for sex between men on the grounds of their later maturity, alongside the age of 16 for men having sex with women, can be convincingly argued to be confused and inconsistent (Hindley, 1986); but illustrates that developmentalist conceptions of adolescence were at play.

   It would be wrong to overstate the influence of developmental psychology, particularly since the British Psychological Society, the professional organisation responsible for representing psychologists, did not submit evidence. It is also important to note the distinct role played by psychiatry: the Royal College of Psychiatrists supported a universal age of 16, but without assuming the reductive links between biological development, psychological competence and the law operating in the understandings of the BMA (Royal College of Psychiatrists, 1976; for discussion of the conflicting evidence, see: Hindley, 1986). Developmental understandings thus played a limited role in determining the age for sexual intercourse, and came to the fore primarily in the context of the committee's quest for a scientific rationale, however crude, to legitimise a distinct age of consent for sex between males. Nevertheless, the evidence of the British Medical Association and the Royal College of Psychiatrists was invoked to argue that 16 represented an age of psychological competence and 'maturity' which could be verified by medical science, and could in turn be used to determine the appropriate legal age.

The review thus marked a significant shift from the previous epistemological frameworks which had underpinned the age of consent. In contrast to the prevailing rationale of the late nineteenth century, when the age of 16 had been conceived as marking the end of a gendered conception of female childhood innocence, the policy advisory committee emphasised that the age of 16 represented an age of psychological maturity marking the attainment of decision-making competence. As a consequence the review did not draw upon sustained sociological and criminological research into young people's experiences in relation to the law. An emphasis upon the age of psychological maturity for decision-making tended to preclude, for example, any sustained analysis of whether and how the law worked as a deterrent.

However, the emphasis of the committee upon psychological competence defined by medical expertise can be interpreted in the context of wider transformations in social knowledges occurring in late modernity (Giddens, 1991; Seidman, 1998). Institutionalised constellations of medical and psychological knowledge were increasingly subject to critique by the late 1970s, deriving from both external resistance (e.g. from social movements) and from tendencies towards internal reflexivity. The claims advanced by the medical profession and psychological sciences concerning the age of consent were unsophisticated, heterogeneous and relatively cautious. The emphasis placed upon medical and psychological evidence by the Policy Advisory Committee can therefore be interpreted as a pragmatic strategy, an attribution of authority in order to rationalise and lend support to the committee's conclusions. Thus the review suggests not a straightforward assertion of medical and psychological authorities, but a more mediated appropriation of these authorities.

The attribution of authority to medical and psychological authorities was occurring simultaneously with an internalised critique of medical power/knowledge within medical paradigms. In the context of the 'detraditionalisation' of sexual norms, the Policy Advisory Committee's review embodied a search for new social knowledges to define age of consent laws in the context of epistemological uncertainty deriving, for example, from the decline of traditional views of gender and childhood sexual innocence. Moves towards tolerance of homosexuality following gay liberation demanded the articulation of more finely delineated boundaries between heterosexuality and homosexuality (Waites, 2003). Medical and psychological theories of competence and sexual identity provided forms of apparently 'scientific' expertise which fitted this necessity. Hence the legal age of 16 originally determined in the late nineteenth century was revalidated with a new rationale.

The Hegemony of Equality at 16

During the 1990s there was sustained campaigning and public debate surrounding the age of consent for sex between men. In 1994 parliament voted to lower the age for sex between men to 18 (Waites, 1995; Rayside 1998). Following its election in 1997, the Labour government facilitated a number of attempts to achieve equality, culminating in the passage of the government's own Sexual Offences (Amendment) Act (2000) (Waites, 1999a; Epstein et al, 2000; Waites, 2003). The UK witnessed the steady ascendance of arguments in favour of, and political support for 'equality at 16' (17 in Northern Ireland) which can usefully be interpreted and analysed in terms of the ascendance of a new 'hegemony' in age of consent debates (Waites, 1999a, pp. 291-294; Waites, 2003; cf. Gramsci 1971).

Describing 'equality at 16' as 'hegemonic' within contemporary debates over the age of consent helps to suggest that support for 'equality at 16' is being generated and sustained within a firm constellation of dominant knowledges and cultural meanings. Age of consent debates during the 1990s did not simply witness the success of arguments for lowering the gay age of consent from 18, reflecting a straightforward assimilation of homosexuality to an existing norm; rather, these debates also generated the production of new institutionally embedded epistemological support for sexual behaviour to be legal at the age of 16. Diverse social knowledges have been drawn together to argue the case for equality at 16, as is particularly evident in the arguments presented by the lesbian and gay lobbying group Stonewall (Stonewall, 1998; see Waites, 2003).

The emergence of a hegemony in favour of equality at 16 was the consequence of multiple developments. The ascendance of human rights discourses, and the appropriation of human rights in the service of equality with respect to sexual orientation have been evident in the successful invocation of the *European Convention on Human Rights* in the European Commission on Human Rights' ruling on the Euan Sutherland case (Sutherland vs. UK, 1997). Broader political transformations including the decline of traditional Conservatism and the establishment of a broad centre-left hegemony within the political mainstream, have moved claims for an equal age of consent onto the agenda of government, and into the political centre-ground. Multiculturalist tolerance of cultural diversity and the individualisation of sexual morality, as well as the commodification of sex in mass culture, have encouraged the retreat of legal prohibitions. And wider cultural transformations in attitudes towards homosexuality have been advanced by lesbian, gay and bisexual movements. More particularly, claims for an equal age of consent at 16 have corresponded to structural incentives for marginalised social groups to formulate their political demands as claims for equality in terms defined by established 'norms'. And transformations in attitudes among child welfare professionals have been particularly crucial in winning equality, though some of this support derives from a desire to pursue effective social policy interventions – with some regulatory effects which can be conceived in terms of 'governmentality' (cf. Monk, 1998) rather than a wholesale endorsement of the equal value of homosexuality and heterosexuality (cf. Waites, 2003).

However, the reductive rationales advanced for age of consent laws by the Policy Advisory Committee in the 1970s persist in influence, underpinning the heterosexual norm of 16 in relation to which claims for gay equality were organised. Debates over the 'gay age of consent' during the 1990s witnessed continuing invocations of the evidence of key medical interest groups including the British Medical Association and the Royal College of Psychiatrists, to provide support for a reduction to the age of 16. Arguments concerning psychological definitions of competence continued to be used, though emphasis on them declined (Waites, 1999a, pp. 273-276).

Arguments for equality at 16 also drew upon medical authorities to assert the fixity of sexual orientation for all by the age of 16. Biologically deterministic theories such as the 'gay brain' or 'gay gene' were not widely invoked in age of consent debates (for discussion and critique of these see: Rose, 1996). Yet it is significant that claims from opponents of equality that sexual identity is not fixed for all by the age of 16 were mocked with increasing scorn and vehemence by equality supporters, including leading figures among the new generation of young centre-left MPs (Waites, 2003). The notion of homosexuality as a distinct and fixed condition remained central to arguments for an equal age of consent.

Hence the current hegemony of 'equality at 16' has been achieved through an under-theorised assumption that the law should equate with the individual's sexual development and/or psychological capacity for consent. The age of 16, which acted as a baseline for equality-claims, has derived much of its legitimacy from the medical and psychological sciences. Yet even the British Medical Association now explicitly questions assumptions of a clear relationship between emotional and physiological development, and of a clear or uniform cause of homosexuality (BMA, 1994, p. 5). To a significant degree the medical profession is effectively disclaiming the authority attributed to it by others.

Lowering the age of consent from 16 has been ruled off the political agenda in the current Home Office Review of Sexual Offences (Home Office, 2000). However, the analysis provided here has demonstrated the problematic rationales which have historically been advanced to determine the legal age for sexual behaviour. The fact that such rationales are explicit in official discourses, however, does not necessarily mean that other perspectives have not been influential among policy-makers. Other perspectives may have informed the decisions of political elites; there is always the possibility of an 'after the fact' rationalisation, and it is clear that to a degree developmentalist understandings of male and female maturity certainly provided such a gloss for the Policy Advisory Committee's advocacy of a discriminatory age of consent for sex between males in the 1970s. The fact that the age of 16 was legitimated by the Policy Advisory Committee in reductive terms does not mean that the policy-makers involved were not interpreting the issues in a more sophisticated way. However, revealing the limitations of official discourse nevertheless opens new possibilities for official policy to explicitly and systematically engage with alternative perspectives.

Rethinking the Rationale for Age of Consent Laws

Reappraising age of consent laws entails a movement away from biologising and developmentalist understandings of sexual competence and sexual identity. Biologically determinist developmental models of how young people obtain competence in sexual decision-making can themselves be challenged. Within psychology this demands an engagement with debates over the socially determined, rather than biologically given, nature of subjectivity and competence. Critiques of developmentalist assumptions need to be pursued (White, 1998; James, Jenks and Prout, 1998). It is necessary to press home critiques of the ways in which adolescent development is medicalised (e.g. Griffin, 1997, Gillies, 1999). The basis for reductive understandings of how biological development is linked to competence in sexual decision-making is in any case increasingly implausible. Whereas the Policy Advisory Committee of the 1970s assumed puberty to occur on average at the age of 14, new research by Professor Jean Golding at Bristol University shows puberty to be occurring earlier, with the average age of menarche in girls now 12 years 10 months (*The Observer*, 18.6.2000; 'Generation Sex', Channel 4, Tuesday 27.6.2000).

In the remainder of this chapter I will provide some preliminary suggestions about how the rationale for the age of consent might productively be re-conceptualised. Reductive forms of biomedical authority in age of consent debates require critique in two crucial respects. First, it is necessary to rethink the nature of the subject with respect to both understandings of competence required for decisions about sexual behaviour, and understandings of sexual identity. But secondly it is necessary to rethink the social relationship between subjects and the law. This discussion will focus primarily upon the latter issue.

Existing Attempts to Rethink the Rationales for Age of Consent Laws

Though policy-making and debates over age of consent laws in the political mainstream remain clearly structured by reductionist thinking, social movements and associated intellectuals have been rethinking the rationales underpinning age of consent laws for several decades, particularly since the 1960s. Movements for sexual liberation, feminism, lesbian and gay liberation and children's rights have engaged with the social construction of subjectivity, identity, and competence, with sociological understandings of social structure, and with critiques of biomedicine and developmental psychology. They have contributed to transformations in academic fields including the emergence of a sociology of childhood (eg. James, Jenks and Prout, 1998), and the expansion of socio-legal studies relating to the fields of gender and sexuality (e.g. Moran, Monk and Beresford, 1998).

However, processes of rethinking remain generally underdeveloped in social movements which might be hoped to be taking these ideas into the policy mainstream. In various ways, different tendencies within these movements remain caught within reductive epistemological frameworks influenced by biomedicine and developmentalist assumptions. For example, the lesbian and gay movement continues to rely upon homogenising understandings of sexual identity as 'fixed' by the age of 16 in its demands for an equal age of consent, citing old evidence from medical authorities to the Wolfenden Committee, and new evidence from medical authorities such as the BMA (Stonewall. 1998; for full discussion see Waites 2003). Claims for adult rights and freedoms, including some of the ways in which 'human rights' are invoked in age of consent debates, are sometimes articulated as if the age of consent should equate with an age marking adulthood and decision-making competence.

Some more libertarian arguments for a lower (and equal) age of consent at 14, such as those proposed by the Sexual Law Reform Society and National Council for Civil Liberties in the 1970s (Sexual Law Reform Society, 1974) and more recently inherited by Outrage, emphasise the existence of pleasure in making the case for lowering age of consent laws (Tatchell, 1996). This can contribute to an elision of the gap between individual experience and the role of law, mediated by social reality. This is not to underestimate the ways in which these organisations have been at the forefront of introducing more sociologically sophisticated themes into public debates, particularly by emphasising young people's experiences of age of consent laws, and the laws' effects upon sexual health education. It is simply to suggest that the impulse towards a libertarian stance, whatever the merits of a lower legal age, derives too strongly from a recognition that children can be sexual and have pleasurable sexual relationships, rather than from a more socially contextualised analysis.

Theoretical work on childhood, law and competence has continued to develop and critically question the meanings of competence and the factors which mediate the relationship between the subject and the law. Without wishing to make any strong claims about the entire field of theoretical work on the regulation of childhood, I would suggest that the recent emphasis upon rethinking the subject has sometimes been at the expense of a sustained sociological understanding of the subject's location within social relations.

Whether of not this general characterisation of the field of socio-legal studies of childhood is accepted, it is certainly the case that sociological thinking has had a limited impact upon the small amount of literature which explicitly addresses the rationale underpinning age of consent laws. For example, David Archard's recent book *Sexual Consent* is conscious of issues raised by feminism, sexual liberation and movements for children's rights (Archard, 1998). Yet his discussion of age of consent laws mirrors similar tendencies in social movement literature, to equate the minimum legal age for sexual behaviour with an age at which competence to make decisions concerning sexual behaviour is acquired by a subject (Archard, 1998, pp. 116-129). He assumes that any legal age is an age at which 'capacity' is recognised, 'above which are adults presumed capable of consent and below which are children presumed incapable of consent' (p. 116). His discussion places considerable emphasis upon the attainment of 'maturity' – 'a certain level of cognitive development – that is an ability to understand the relevant facts, a certain degree of acquired knowledge, and a certain level of temperamental maturity' (p. 124). Archard's description of such legal age boundaries with the phrase 'age of majority' also tends to suggest that the law reflects recognition of certain forms of citizenship and competence – which also need to be distinguished from one another (p. 116).

Similarly, Archard also assumes that age of consent laws necessarily imply a denial of children's sexuality – in sex with an older party they 'refuse to acknowledge the expressed sexuality of one party to the activity' (Archard, 1998, p. 120). He also regards age of consent laws as denying the validity of a child's consent, and characterising all behaviour below a legal age as 'non-consensual' (p. 119). Yet while this may be the case in the formulation of some rationales, it is not necessarily the case for all rationales for legal age boundaries, as the distinction between UK laws on 'indecent assault' and 'unlawful sexual intercourse' illustrates (Sexual Offences Act 1956). Age of consent laws need not necessarily be premised on such assumptions, as can be seen when the issue of an individual's competence and subjectivity are distinguished from the role of the law in a broader social context.

Prohibitive laws may mark limits against social forces which act upon subjects independently of their agency or competence. Archard notes the importance of the social context (Archard, 1998, p. 129), but leaves the relationship between subjectivity and the role of the law under-theorised.

The task of theorising the basis of age of consent laws therefore demands analysis of the mediated relationships between individual subjectivity and competence and the role of the law through a more sustained engagement with themes in social and sociological theory. Through a critique of the epistemological paradigms within which the rationale for age of consent laws has previously been conceived, it becomes possible to identify the way forward for developing new thinking about age of consent laws in the future. New thinking on age of consent laws needs to theorise the complex relationships between individual psychological development and competence and the practical effects of the law upon young people. This needs to take place at a number of levels of analysis, through a variety of forms of research, across different academic disciplines. These shifts can be understood as requiring two kinds of change in the resources we draw upon to consider age of consent laws: first, a shift in the substantive focus of research, and second, a shift in the theoretical frameworks employed to conceptualise the rationale for age of consent laws.

Re-orienting the Substantive Focus of Research Informing Age of Consent Debates

Rethinking age of consent laws from a critical and sociological perspective demands a shift in the substantive focus of research, towards analysing young people's experiences of age of consent laws. We need new forms of empirical research, including much clearer data on what young people know about the law at different stages in their lives; whether or how it influences their behaviour, and how they experience its effects when applied.

Historically debates over the age of consent have largely drawn upon quantitative data relating to young people's sexual behaviour, such as the recent survey of *Sexual Attitudes and Lifestyles* which includes information on ages of first sexual intercourse (Johnson et al., 1994). There has been little sustained qualitative research into young people's attitudes towards age of consent laws or how the law influences their behaviour.

The Policy Advisory Committee on the age of consent did not commission its own research into young people's experiences. It drew upon other government funded research on girls who become pregnant at school, though this did not draw upon systematic analysis of interviews with girls themselves (Joint Working Party on Pregnant Schoolgirls and Schoolgirl Mothers, 1979). In any case the Policy Advisory Committee's emphasis upon psychological development, and the political consensus in favour of 16, precluded any sustained social analysis of the data available, and enabled it to reject the Joint Working Party's argument that the existing law failed to act as a deterrent to men, while inhibiting girls from seeking contraception, abortion and ante-natal care.

Recent qualitative research into young people's sexual behaviour such as work of the Women Risk and AIDS Project is suggestive of the potential for closer attention to young people's experiences, but does not seek to explore specific attitudes to the law or its effects, or to differentiate between respondents according to age in a manner which could closely inform age of consent debates (Holland et al., 1998). As Jackie West has recently commented, much contemporary research on young people's sexuality has tended to lack a systematic or theorised examination of age or generation as a social dynamic (West, 1999, p. 526).

This is beginning to change however. Recent age of consent debates have stimulated extensive public debate in which the experiences of young people have increasingly been voiced. Opinion polls have provided information on the specific attitudes of young people towards age of consent laws. Yet public reception of these new resources remains mediated by dominant cultural assumptions.

The ESRC-funded Youth Values: Identity, Diversity and Social Change research project ('Respect'), examining the values of 11-16 year-olds in a selection of schools, has produced new data on attitudes towards subjects including sex and the age of consent (Holland and Thomson, 1999). The first phase of the study involved a structured questionnaire, from which quantitative attitudinal data has been published on issues including 'sexual intercourse under the age of 16' as well others including 'sex outside marriage', 'unsafe sex' and 'homosexuality' (McGrellis et al., 2000). Only 30% of boys and 37% of girls in the study believed sexual intercourse under the age of 16 is always wrong (McGrellis, 2000, p. 14). The second phase of the study involved focus-group interviews, with questions which included specific reference to age of consent laws, thus providing the first data of this kind available for qualitative analysis. Rachel Thomson has recently begun to analyse this data on attitudes to age of consent laws (Thomson, 2000).

Criminology also has a vital role to play in analysing the mediating effects of the application of the law through the entire criminal justice system. Existing debates on the age of consent, including the Policy Advisory Committee review, have drawn to a limited extent upon quantitative research crime statistics and the sentencing of sex offenders (e.g. Walmsley and White, 1979; 1980). Yet there is a large gap for criminological research to explore how young people who are affected by age of consent laws experience the effects of their interactions when drawn into the criminal justice system, including experiences of older partners being prosecuted, appearances in court, experiences of imprisonment and partners' imprisonment. Far more understanding is needed of the ways in which prosecution authorities and courts exercise discretion and filter cases, as well as the ways in which criminal proceedings entail negative impacts on children (cf. Graupner, 1999, pp. 34-35). It is striking how little research on such issues informs past and present debates over age of consent laws, particularly the lack of systematic consideration of the efficacy of age of consent laws as a deterrent, given the rarity of prosecutions. The extent of under-age sex is not necessarily an argument for a lower age of consent, given that some young people are below the age of criminal responsibility, or positioned as 'innocent victims' by age of consent laws. Policing practices employing cautioning rather than prosecution are also significant. Such issues require more attention.

Re-orienting the Conceptual Basis of Age of Consent Debates

As suggested above, both public debates and some theoretical work on the legal regulation of childhood tend to assume that the legal regulations upon subjects should mirror the age at which a subject acquires relevant forms of competence, which are themselves often defined with reference to developmentalist assumptions. Several theoretical observations may suggest ways to move beyond this dominant epistemological framework.

Firstly, we need to question the tendency to believe that a sociologised conception of the subject's competence implies that competence is highly susceptible to short-term transformation through agency. When critiques of developmentalist understandings of subjectivity and competence are made, the consequence is often to then suggest that regulations be reduced to allow children to make decisions. This is the case, for example, with Priscilla Alderson's work on children's participation in health-care decision-making, in areas including sexual health (Alderson 1990, 1992a; Alderson and Montgomery, 1996). If the logic of such work were pursued with respect to sexual decision-making, it might well suggest reductions in the age of consent. Some sexual libertarians adopt similar arguments (although most paedophile groups emphasise the sexual innocence and natural immaturity of children alongside the harmlessness of sexual activity, rather than children's competence to understand the activity).

Arguments emphasising the potential of children to develop the competence to make judgements about sex if given appropriate resources, while employing socially constructed understandings of competence, can nevertheless underestimate the complexity of the risks and structural forces operating in a wider social context which require assessment by subjects.

Secondly, it is necessary to question the assumed equation between the subject's competence and the law. Analyses such as Archard's, discussed above, effectively assume that age of consent laws are optimally fixed at the moment when a subject acquires sufficient competence in assessing the pleasures and dangers in its environment, so as to be able to judge whether participation in sexual behaviour is wise or beneficial. An assumption operates that regulations should be determined with reference to the competence of the subject. At a given point the development of the subject's competence will enable it to make an informed judgement about its social circumstances, balancing risks and benefits, and this is the point at which age of consent laws and other similar regulations should be fixed. This form of thinking assumes that an optimal age of consent will occur when the competence of the subject is ideally matched to the realities of the social structure. Competence in judging risks is seen as the only issue, without distinction from the issue of protection from the effects of risks which may have disproportionately serious consequences for younger people.

But there is a disjuncture between the social forces generating the (average) subject's competence and the social forces generating risks. The disjuncture arises because however much we may improve the competence of young people to make decisions, by equipping them with skills and resources, the degree of dangers given the risks involved if something goes wrong (due to poor judgement or bad luck) are too great. Given the ever-present possibility that 'things go wrong', the age of consent must be determined at a level when the potentially negative consequences of sexual activity are reduced by the social consequences of reaching a higher age.

This is demonstrated by reference to a few examples. A young person's physical body places them in certain determinate relationships to adults who are stronger, independent of their sexual negotiating skills. Young people's lack of independent financial resources places them in a determinate relation to adults who have their own money. Young people's institutional locations, for example within families and schools, place them in a given relation to adults who have power over them. Regardless of a young person's skills and resources for negotiating safe sex, the objective consequences of becoming pregnant or HIV positive are more serious for younger age groups given their institutional circumstances. In each case there are limits to the extent that a young person can ameliorate these structural effects.

It may be conceivable that an age of consent law could be fixed at an age where a subject's competence in judging risks equates perfectly to the optimal age at which the law offers protection from 'when things going wrong'. But it may be more likely that age of consent laws will be optimised when they are conceived not only with reference to young people's competence in assessing risks, but also to the objective consequences of their actions. At a conceptual level, we may need to pay more attention to the differentially dangerous consequences of sexual behaviour and relationships 'when things go wrong' for young people, rather than their own competence in assessing the risks of such eventualities.

For example, irrespective whether or not a young person receives a good sex education and develops competence in sexual negotiations, there remain certain social forces which act equally upon them determined by their youth. With respect to sex, young people may become more competent in sexual negotiations through education and practice, yet they remain to a degree subject to certain patterns of risk determined by less malleable factors: their embodiment, their social and material context, financial and institutional circumstances.

There is a general tendency to conceptualise the rationale for age of consent laws in terms of an age at which an agent acquires competence, rather than an age at which risks acting upon a subject are diminished. Consequently, many conceptualisations of age of consent laws in mainstream debate, and also, though to a lesser degree in academic theory, place excessive emphasis upon the significance of *agency*, including the subject's interpretative understanding and their resources for action. Such approaches are inflected by rationalist individualism. By contrast, I am arguing that it is necessary to theorise age of consent laws with greater attention to the effects of *social structure*, the systematic social forces which act upon a subject. Age of consent laws apply in contexts where young people operate as social actors in the context of risks imposed upon them by social structures, to a significant degree independent of their individual competence and agency. Appreciation of this point opens the possibility for an explicit analysis of the degree to which such social structural contexts place young people at risk, and the ways in which age of consent laws intervene in these contexts.

As Margaret Archer argues, social structures and agency require conceptualisation as different levels of a stratified social reality, each possessing distinctive properties that are linked but irreducible to one another (Archer, 1995). Archer's argument that we need to examine the interplay between structure and agency without conflating them seems potentially a useful avenue of enquiry with respect to age of consent debates.

This emphasis upon the benefits of a conceptually clear application of sociological theory runs counter to a large amount of contemporary work in the social sciences on gender and sexuality. A large amount of work influenced by postmodernism and concerned with the significance of feminism, new social movements and the politics of identity has moved towards regarding sociological theory, including questions of action and structure, as largely irrelevant to its analyses. By contrast, I hope to have illustrated how this could inform current debates such as those surrounding age of consent laws.

Prospects for Influencing Policy-Making

What is the potential in contemporary mainstream policy debates for rethinking age of consent laws in the future, on the lines proposed here? With respect to the epistemological basis of policy-making and political conflicts over the age of consent, there may be increasing opportunities for theorising the age of consent more sociologically, especially if or when a new review of age of consent laws occurs. A number of strains of contemporary scientific and social scientific theory are now becoming increasingly established in policy-making circles and political movements, which will increasingly throw knowledges deriving from biomedicine and developmental psychology into question. Mainstream policy-debates have their own dynamics, and it cannot be assumed that academic theory will straightforwardly or explicitly inform policy-making. However, the epistemologies which structure contemporary policy-making and mainstream political debates are influenced by wider developments in the social sciences.

Furthermore, the epistemologies which structure age of consent debates are themselves subject to wider social transformations. The ways in which we seek to develop a new epistemological paradigm for rethinking age of consent laws in the future depends upon how we diagnose and respond to contemporary transformations.

Theorists including Anthony Giddens and Ulrich Beck argue that we are entering an era in which 'reflexivity' is increasingly embodied in institutionalised learning processes and reflection (Beck, 2000, p. 81; Giddens, 1991). If we accept Beck's emphasis upon the social sciences, particularly sociology, playing a key role in the generation of new reflexive knowledges in societies of the future, then we can expect sociological perspectives to inform age of consent debates more systematically in the future, and we can also find reason to push forward and contribute to this process. Rather than succumb to relativism, it should be possible to generate more explicitly sociologised thinking about the age of consent, even in the political mainstream. The emphasis here upon the ways in which a more explicitly sociological analysis could inform public debates contrasts with that of others, including postmodernists, who take a more sceptical view of the potential for social science to inform policy-making and public debate.

Conclusion

This chapter has demonstrated that debates over the age of consent are interwoven with a series of wider debates over the basis of social knowledge, including the transformations associated with modernity and 'post' or 'late' modernity. It has demonstrated how changing disciplinary knowledges have structured the rationale for age of consent laws, drawing particular attention to the role of medical authorities and developmental psychology as sources of expertise. The analysis shows that the present age of consent of 16 has historically derived its rationale from forms of medical and psychological knowledge which are now discredited.

By focussing upon *how* we think about age of consent laws, the chapter has sought to re-orient perspectives, pointing towards the forms of theoretical and empirical research appropriate for conceptualising age of consent laws. The themes raised have wider application to other debates over the legal regulation of sexuality and sexual consent.

Bibliography

Alderson, P. (1990), 'Consent to Children's Surgery and Intensive Medical Treatment', *Journal of Law and Society*, Vol. 17, No. 1, pp. 52-65.

Alderson, P. (1992), 'In the genes or in the stars? Children's competence to consent', *Journal of Medical Ethics*, Vol. 18, No. 3, pp. 119-124.

Alderson, P. and Montgomery, J. (1996), *Health Care Choices: Making Decisions with Children*, London: Institute for Public Policy Research.

Archard, D. (1998), *Sexual Consent*, Oxford: Westview Press.

Archer, M. S. (1995), *Realist Social Theory: The Morphogenetic Approach*, Cambridge: Cambridge University Press.

Beck, U. (2000), 'The cosmopolitan perspective: sociology of the second age of modernity', *British Journal of Sociology*, Vol. 51, No. 1, January/March, pp. 79-105.

Bland, L. (1995), *Banishing the Beast: English Feminism and Sexual Morality 1885-1914*, London: Penguin.

B. M. A./British Medical Association (1994), *Age of Consent for Homosexual Men: A Scientific and Medical Perspective*, Report to the Council of the British Medical Association from the Board of Science and Education, London: British Medical Association.

C. H. O. P. / Committee on Homosexual Offences and Prostitution, Home Office and Scottish Home Department (1957), *Report of the Committee on Homosexual Offences and Prostitution*, Cmnd.247, London: HMSO.

Department of Health (1999), *Prevalence of HIV in the U.K.: 1998*, London: HMSO.

Epstein, D., Johnson, R. and Steinberg, D. L. (2000), 'Twice Told Tales: Transformation, Recuperation and Emergence in the Age of Consent Debates' 1998, *Sexualities*, Vol. 3, No. 1, pp. 5-30.

Foucault, M. (1967), *Madness and Civilisation*, London: Tavistock.

Foucault, M. (1980), 'The Politics of Health in the Eighteenth Century', chapter 9 in *Power/Knowledge: Selected Interviews and Other Writings 1972-1977*, ed. C. Gordon, London: Harvester Wheatsheaf), pp. 166-182.

Foucault, M. (1981), *The History of Sexuality, Volume One: An Introduction*, London: Penguin.

Giddens, A. (1991), *Modernity and Self-Identity: Self and Society in the Late Modern Age*, Cambridge: Polity Press.

Gillies, V., with Ribbens McCarthy, J. and Holland, J. (1999), *Young People and Family Life: Analysing and Comparing Disciplinary Discourses*, Oxford: Centre For Family and Household Research, Oxford Brookes University.

Graupner, H. (1999), 'Love versus Abuse: Crossgenerational Sexual Relations of Minors: A Gay Rights Issue?', *Journal of Homosexuality*, Vol. 37, No. 4, pp. 23-56.

Gramsci, A. (1971), *Selections from the Prison Notebooks of Antonio Gramsci*, edited and translated by Quentin Hoare and Geoffrey Nowell Smith, London: Lawrence and Wishart.

Griffin, C. (1997), 'Troubled Teens: Managing Disorders of Transition and Consumption', *Feminist Review*, No. 55, pp. 4-21.

Helfer, L. R. (1990), 'Finding a Consensus on Equality: The Homosexual Age of Consent and the European Convention on Human Rights', *New York University Law Review*, Vol. 65, No. 4, pp. 1044-1100.

Hindley, J.C. (1986), 'The Age of Consent for Male Homosexuals', *Criminal Law Review*, September, pp. 595-603.

Holland, J.; Ramazanoglu, C. Sharpe, S. and Thomson, R. (1998), *The Male in the Head: Young People, Heterosexuality and Power*, London: The Tufnell Press.

Holland, J. and Thomson, R. (1999), *Respect – Youth Values: Identity, Diversity and Social Change*, Economic and Social Research Council Children 5-16 Research Briefing No. 3, October 1999, Swindon: Economic and Social Research Council.

Home Office (2000), *Setting the Boundaries: Reforming the Law on Sex Offences*, London: Home Office.

ILGA: International Lesbian and Gay Association (1999), *World Legal Survey*. Available at http://www.ilga.org/ (25/8/99).

Jackson, S. (1998), 'Sexual Politics: feminist politics, gay politics and the problem of heterosexuality'; in T. Carver and V. Mottier (eds.) (1998), *Politics of Sexuality: Identity, Gender, Citizenship*, London: Routledge, pp. 68-78.

James, A., Jenks, C. and Prout, A. (eds.) (1998), *Theorising Childhood*, Cambridge: Polity Press.

Jenkins, R. (ed.) (1998), *Questions of Competence: Culture, Classification and Intellectual Disability*, Cambridge: Cambridge University Press.

Johnson, A. M. et al. (1994), *Sexual Attitudes and Lifestyles*, Oxford: Blackwell Scientific Publications.

Joint Working Party on Pregnant Schoolgirls and Schoolgirl Mothers (1979), *Pregnant at School*, London: National Council for One-Parent Families.

McGrellis, S., Henderson, S., Holland, J., Sharpe, S. and Thomson, R. (2000), *Through the Moral Maze: A Quantitative Study of Young People's Values*, London: The Tufnell Press.

Monk, D. (1998), 'Beyond Section 28: Law, Governance and Sex Education'; in L.J. Moran, D. Monk and S. Beresford (eds.) (1998), *Legal Queeries: lesbian, gay and transgender legal studies*, London: Cassell, pp. 96-112.

Moran, L. J. (1996), *The Homosexual(ity) of Law*, London: Routledge.

Moran, L. J. (1997), 'Enacting Intimacy', *Studies in Law, Politics and Society*, Vol. 16, pp. 255-274.

Moran, L. J., Monk, D. and Beresford, S. (eds.) (1998), *Legal Queeries: lesbian, gay and transgender legal studies*, London: Cassell, pp. 96-112.

Policy Advisory Committee on Sexual Offences (1981), *Report on the Age of Consent in Relation to Sexual Offences*, Cmnd. 8216, London: HMSO. April, 1981.

Rayside, D. (1998), *On the Fringe: Gays and Lesbians in Politics*, London: Cornell University Press.

Richardson, D. (1998), 'Sexuality and Citizenship', *Sociology*, Vol. 32, No. 1, pp. 83-100.

Royal College of Psychiatrists (1976), Submission to Criminal Law Revision Committee, London: Royal College of Psychiatrists, unpublished.

Seidman, S. (1998) *Contested Knowledge: Social Theory in the Postmodern Era* (Oxford: Blackwell).

Sexual Law Reform Society (1974), 'Report of the Working Party on the Law in Relation to Sexual Behaviour'; copy held in Anthony Grey papers, file 2/1, at Hall Carpenter Archive, British Library of Political and Economic Sciences, London.

Social Exclusion Unit (1999), *Teenage Pregnancy*, Cm.4342, June 1999, London: HMSO.

Stonewall (1998), *The Case for Equality: Arguments for an Equal Age of Consent*, London: Stonewall Lobby Group.

Tatchell, P. (1996), 'Is Fourteen Too Young For Sex?', *Gay Times*, June, pp. 36-38.

Tatchell, P. (2002) 'The Case for Consent at 14', Legal Note 38, Libertarian Alliance.

Thomson, R. (2000), 'Legal, protected and timely: young people's reflections on the age of consent'; in Monk, D. and Bridgeman, J. (eds) (2000), *Feminist perspectives on child law*, London: Cavendish Press.

Turner, B. S. (1995), *Medical Power and Social Knowledge*, London: Sage.

Waites, M. (1995), *The Age of Consent Debate: A Critical Analysis*, dissertation on the 1994 age of consent debate for MA Culture and Society, awarded by the Department of Sociology, University of Essex.

Waites, M. (1999a) *The Age of Consent, Homosexuality and Citizenship in the United Kingdom, 1885-1999*, PhD thesis (London: South Bank University).

Waites, M. (1999b), 'The Age of Consent and Sexual Citizenship in the United Kingdom: A History'; in J. Seymour and P. Bagguley (eds.) (1999), *Relating Intimacies: Power and Resistance*, London: Macmillan.

Waites, M. (2000), 'Homosexuality and the New Right: The Legacy of the 1980s for New Delineations of Homophobia', *Sociological Research Online*, Vol. 5, No. 1, June 2000, <http://www.socresonline.org.uk/>.

Waites, M. (2002) 'Inventing a "Lesbian Age of Consent"? The History of the Minimum Age for Sex Between Women in the UK', *Social and Legal Studies*, Vol. 11, no. 3.

Waites, M. (2003) 'Equality at Last? Homosexuality, Heterosexuality and the Age of Consent in the United Kingdom', *Sociology*, Vol.37, No. 3, August.

Walby, S. (1990) *Theorising Patriarchy* (Oxford: Basil Blackwell).

Walkowitz, J. R. (1992) *City of Dreadful Delight: Narratives of Sexual Danger in Late-Victorian London*, London: Virago.

Walmsley, Roy and White, Karen (1979) *Sexual Offences, Consent and Sentencing*, Home Office Research Unit Study No. 54, London: HMSO.

Walmsley, Roy and White, Karen (1980), *Supplementary Information on Sexual Offences and Sentencing*, Home Office Research Unit Study No. 54, Paper 2, London: HMSO.

Wertheimer, A. and S. Macrae (1999), *Family and Household Change in Britain: A summary of findings from projects in the Economic and Social Research Council Population and Household Change Programme*, Oxford: Centre for Family and Household Research, Oxford Brookes University.

West, D. J. and R. Green (eds.) (1997), *Sociolegal Control of Homosexuality: A Multi-Nation Comparison*, New York: Plenum Press, pp. 145-167.

West, J. (1999), '(Not) talking about sex: youth, identity and sexuality', *Sociological Review*, Vol. 47, No. 3, August 1999, pp. 525-547.

Chapter 6

The Quality of Consent: Sexual Consent, Culture, Communication, Knowledge and Ethics

Paul Reynolds

Thinking Sexual Consent

As has been observed in the introduction of this collection, much that has been written about sexual consent has actually been written about non-consent – rape, forced sex, and sexual abuse – and does not discuss consent at all. This is understandable, since it seems logical to focus on what is seen as the 'problem' of sexual consent – the prevalence of cases where sex is forced or otherwise pursued without consent – in the social and cultural context of increasing reporting of rape and sexual violence, and sometimes less dramatic but potentially equally damaging hetero-patriarchal notions of sexual ownership and obligation. Non-consenting sex remains a significant social problem, with reported rapes rising and the legal system struggling to apply sanctions that have an impact on that trend (see Cook, 2002). Even with the more recent focus on sexual consent, much of the literature – and indeed most of the essays in this collection – centre on distinguishing problems and issues with the moment when a person consents to sex and the distinctions between that moment of consenting and the moment prior to it – when consent was not given (See, selectively Cowling, 1998; Francis, (ed.) 1996). This form of definitional work is important because it begins to focus attention on what it means to consent to sex and how we should understand the act or process of consenting sexually. Both the literature on non-consent and the literature on distinguishing non-consent from consent seek to contribute to developments in law, politics and culture in the last 40 years that have progressively recognised sexual freedom as a subject of human rights, equality and social justice rather than a 'private affair' governed by traditional conventions, customs and wisdoms (Adam et al., 1999; Bell and Binnie, 2000; D'Emilio et al., 2000; Dunphy, 2000; Richardson, 2000).

Important as these discussions are, they are not definitive of concerns about sexual consent, and in this chapter I wish to shift focus and develop a critical discussion on and exploration of the quality of sexual consent. The focus of this discussion is therefore upon sexual acts or relationships where there is no legal basis for claiming an absence of consent, where subjectively the participants would both agree they consented and where consent would be recognised as having taken place within contemporary social and cultural norms. Of course, this would not satisfy radical feminists like Jeffreys, who would argue that social and cultural norms are intrinsically hetero-patriarchal, and women's consent in hetero-patriarchal society is always the less violent end of a continuum of sexual ownership, control and use of women by men (Jeffreys, 1990; also Dworkin, 1981 and 1988; MacKinnon, 1989). Such structural and cultural analyses provide a strong caution against assuming that sexual consent is ever 'free', and will be reflected, to a degree, in this critical discussion. Nevertheless, this analysis will make the assumption that women's sexual consent is not simply predetermined and has a value in itself (for an elaboration of this argument, see Moore and Reynolds in this collection). Further, it will assume that part of the development of critical analyses involves a critical recognition of degrees of autonomy and freedom of expression in consent in contemporary society – that is balancing degrees of subject agency and autonomy with structural and cultural shaping or determination.

The focus on the quality of sexual consent moves away from an evaluation of whether consent has been given or not. It focuses instead on what the quality of that consent decision is, and what meaning it has as an act or process that characterises interpersonal intimate and/or sexual relations. So, for example, people in long term sexual relationships, people who engage in promiscuous sex with many partners or people who are in relationships where sexual pleasure characterises the relationship – such as extra-marital affairs, may all be involved in consenting sexual behaviour, but the quality and meaning of their consent decisions – consenting out of passion or desire, or in exchange within the relationship, or because they feel they should, or through obligation – will vary considerably. 'Bad sex', or specifically low quality consent decisions, are perhaps an invariable part to having sex with someone else, and most people will probably have some such decisions and experiences they can recall. When such decisions seem to characterise the majority rather than a small minority of decisions, however, and are extrapolated across sexual relationships within a society, they tend to raise issues of sexual health and ethics rather than simply happenstance or opportunity cost.

This essay does little more than sketch the parameters and draw together some current thinking on how we might address the question of the quality of sexual consent. The argument I will begin to sketch out and pursue here is that whilst we should take free sexual consent seriously, and recognise that 'bad sex' does not necessarily constitute non-consenting sex, there are significant problems and difficulties of culture, communication and knowledge in understanding sex and sexuality that persist in contemporary societies. These problems are manifest in a low quality of sexual consent decisions, which might constitute the giving of sexual consent but remain unsatisfactory as decisions that might be regarded as free, healthy or positive self-expression. Or put simply, the quality of sexual consent decisions, and the quality of sexual experience attached to those decisions, is too often debilitating, denigrating and unpleasant – we might argue it is 'bad sex'. What is at stake in such a discussion is not just what we criminalise as unacceptable – non-consent – but what we recognise as harmful, negative and unethical, which may be consented to, but is anathema to any conception of a free, healthy and positive sex life. Changing such a quality of consent involves more substantial cultural and political change to accompany the limitation of legal change, in the development of a public sexual ethics that enables and emancipates subjects from a fear or fetishised and distorted fascination with sex. This goes beyond legal change to more substantial changes in sex education, the way sexual knowledge is communicated and the sexual cultures that emerge in contemporary society (see Reynolds, 2002 for a critique of the limitations to legal change). An analysis of the quality of sexual consent deepens our understanding of sexual consent within a broader context of sexual ethics as a central aspect of social, cultural and political change.

Distinguishing Sexual Consent

The principal 'problem' of sexual consent has been seen as constructing a clarity of understanding of the distinction between sexual consent and non-consent. This requires an act, utterance or communicative process that signifies that a relationship has developed a sexual dimension. Of course, sexual consent involves not one but an ensemble of acts or affirmations that reflect the different forms of pleasure expressed and acts desired – one consent act is not enough to clarify the scope and limits to complex relationships of desire. So, for example, many cases of heterosexual women consenting to penetrative sex does not intrinsically involve consent to oral or anal sex, which are refused or further negotiated within the course of the relationship. Nevertheless, in each case, the problem of sexual consent is clarifying the point of affirmation, when consent is given. Even if a hierarchy is established between consent decisions that change the nature of the relationship from non-sexual and consent decisions as to the nature of the sexual act participated in, clarifying affirmation remains the same. The search is for an understanding of the identification and characterisation of that point of change or transformation, and how it is communicated effectively, mainly to establish a legal distinction by which sanctions can be made against those who do not respect an individual's right to consent or withhold consent, but also more broadly to understand the cultural regulatory regimes that govern sexual discourse and communication.

As well as a focus upon an act or utterance or process, it is also an issue of identity, as our characterisation of acts or processes of consent do not map upon universal and rational individuals. For example, Corteen, Beckmann and McCarthy and Thompson (in this volume) are all writing about identities that do not conform to the hetero-patriarchal norm of contemporary societies. Any discussion of the act or process of consent has to consider the subjects engaging in sex. This raises issues, for example, about sex education (see Cowling in this volume) and the low quality of public discourses of sex and people's sexual literacy and maturity in communicating about sexual desire, appetite and feelings around consent decisions.

The focus on both act or process and identity begs important questions, focused largely on how we recognise consent and what it means when it is given, and it is on these questions that different positions emerge within consent debates. Lois Pineau has developed a concept of 'communicative sexuality' that seeks to displace what she describes as the 'aggressive-acquisitive' model of seduction that underpins judicial discourse, and focuses not on the different characteristics of the participants in a contested case of non-consenting sex (Pineau concentrates here on heterosexual 'date rape') (Pineau, 1996). She observes that with communicative sexuality 'All that matters is the quality of communication with regard to the sex itself' (1996, p. 26). It is therefore incumbent, for Pineau, that this focus on communication within a hetero-patriarchal society recognises the need for men to show they have elicited a verbal utterance of consent, and that women's silence (through fear or intimidation) should not be construed as consent. This intrinsically requires an act of communication, the most specific and accurate being a verbal utterance.

Such an argument provides the foundations for current trends in law towards the standard of 'free agreement' in determining rape or consent, where both sexual narratives and communications are equally scrutinised judicially (see Cook, 2002). It also provides a basis for codifications that demand speech acts as proofs of consent, such as the Antioch College Sexual Offence Policy (for an outline and discussion see Cowling 1998, pp. 99-101). As a rational basis for understanding and distinguishing sexual consent from non-consent, is it very persuasive.

There are a number of cautions to this argument. Cowling has argued that Pineau's legal and philosophical clarity does not easily translate into emotionally charged moments of heightened excitement within the context of social cultures in which open verbal discourse about sex is absent or marginal (Cowling, 1998). This is, in many respects, an appeal to account for social identity and culture in rational and legal discourse about sex. It does, in part, build on earlier arguments that the nature of sexual cultures and conventions has to be considered as critical in understanding sexual conduct (or misconduct) and legal standards have to reflect these cultures rather than set otherwise rational standards that will criminalise 'normal' behaviour (Husak and Thomas, 1992). This requires a cultural mediation of the idea of reasonableness, which radical feminists would argue preserves and supports structural and cultural inequalities and the violence and abuse in 'normal' hetero-patriarchal society (MacKinnon, 1989).

Cowling also raises the issue of the diversity of sexual desires and appetites (again tied to the diversity of identities of sexual subjects), some of which will not conform to rational constructs of sexual communication. Cowling uses the conventional 'romantic' example conforming to masculine and feminine stereotypes, of men and women actively enjoying active and passive roles, but it could be extended to sado-masochistic sexuality. Here, consent is openly negotiated, but often there is much 'play' around the limits of consent given, and in its 'no-limits' form may involve a 'global' permission to dispense with consent decisions. He also argues that most consenting sex – that would be identified as consenting by those who participate in it – does not conform to Pineau's rational standard and involve speech acts. Whilst Pineau's analysis is feminist in character, radical feminists would also question whether even the presence of a speech act can be meaningfully understood as indicative of free will or a responsive conditioning in the context of hetero-patriarchal society (Jeffreys, 1990; MacKinnon, 1989). Bryson reflects a feminist scepticism that was applied to Cowling and could also be applied to Pineau when she observes:

> Writing from within a dominant paradigm, he is attempting to apply 'male-stream' or 'common sense' concepts to a rapidly developing debate without reference to its theoretical underpinnings in feminist thought...
>
> Many would argue that 'private' sexual relationships do not take place in a vacuum but within the context of a society in which we are surrounded by images of commodified sexuality and violence, in which many women are economically dependent upon men and in which complaints of rape will be responded to by male-dominated police forces, law courts and media (Bryson, 1995, p. 72).

Bryson's observation raises the question of whether any rational, philosophical or legal conceptions of changing the terms of sexual consent can ever be regarded as positive because they fail to recognise the complex, but in Bryson's view definitely hetero-patriarchal, nature of interpersonal relations in society. Abstractions that appeal to reasonableness fail to tackle this implicit problem of social context and identity. Bryson's critique of Cowling seems to suggest a difference in the analysis of how far identities and culture are structurally determined by particular foundations in contemporary society – in this case, hetero-patriarchy. Cowling's critique of Pineau seems to abandon the possibility that radical change can produce a better context for consent decisions, if it does seek to explore how incremental reform can change the terms of inequality to punish more rapists.

Both Cowling and Pineau might argue that such objections discount the possibility of or under-theorise women's sexual agency or personal and social autonomy. Here Cowling finds Walby's theorising of patriarchy as a 'sloping playing field' that frames and contextualises unequal gendered relations (Walby, 1990). Walby's theorising stresses both differences in gendered identities under patriarchy and patterns of power and subordination within the social context that contextualise communications and culture and provide a balance of structure and agency in feminist thinking. This allows Cowling to explore the possibility of legal and social changes that will better distinguish consent and non-consent in the current social context, without an attendant radical change in structural social and cultural gendered relations. Like all reformist solutions, it might be seen as further complexifying the problem or allowing apologias for unacceptable sexual conduct, whether labelled rape or sexual assault.

Archard, in contrast to Cowling, is more sympathetic to Pineau's position in that he leans towards the need for a specific consent act (Archard, 1998). His argument for this is underpinned by conceiving the act of consent not just as changing the terms of a relationship but morally transforming it (though he notes that consent does not have to morally transform a relationship – it is a sufficient but not a necessary condition in consent decisions (Archard, 1998, pp. 3-4) The foundations for thinking about consent for Archard are its normative value (what it brings to and how it changes a relationship), performativity (it is an act not simply a state of mind) and a positive, valid process of decision based on full knowledge and awareness of the meaning of consenting. Whilst it is possible to raise the issue of cultural conventions and the irrational subject in criticism of such a consent standard, Archard's critical engagement with the idea of sexual consent represents a thorough dissection of the idea and meaning of what it is to consent. In this respect, Archard's work extends debate in two important ways.

First, by stressing the normative aspect of change he changes the notion of looking at the debate around consent/non-consent sex as simply that of the conduct of negotiating boundaries around sexual activity – a tactical question of legal or moral legitimacy – and underlines the idea that a consent decision might or should constitute a transformative moment in the interpersonal relationship. Whilst undoubtedly some interpersonal behaviour around consent decisions is precisely about satisfying law and conventional morality whilst satisfying desires, Archard speaks to the notion that there should be an ethical import to the idea of sexual consent. This ethical import diverts attention to whether a consent decision is given or not to what it is constituted by – and therefore the quality of that consent decision. It also raises the issue that consent decisions should conform to other features of sexual ethics and therefore points to wider concerns about the state of sexual ethics, knowledge and understandings. This connection of social structure and culture and interpersonal conduct is reinforced as an important one.

Second, and aligned to that, Archard recognises that sexual consent is limited in itself as a guide to sexual conduct. He surveys incest, prostitution, sado-masochism, the age of consent and rape and forced sex in drawing attention to the limitations of evaluating sexual conduct simply on the basis of consent decisions, which again raises the issue of the place of consent within broader understandings of sexual ethics (Archard, 1998, pp. 98-147).

The Parameters for Understanding Sexual Consent

The foregoing discussion reviewing different attempts to understand how we should distinguish sexual consent is important because it allows us to draw out a number of parameters that shape and determine consent decisions. First, there are the contextual parameters of different juxtapositions of structural and cultural determinations and personal agency and autonomy. These are important not just in respect of understanding a particular consent decision at a particular time, but in understanding the subjective development of the participants in that decision. These parameters apply, therefore, not just to evaluating the quality of consent decisions within a hetero-patriarchal society with a strong cultural impetus towards women's passivity and men's pro-active behaviour in negotiating consent. It also applies to consent decisions by people whose biographical experience has involved different degrees of encouragement of their autonomy and agency or suppression in the family, previous relationships and so forth. Whether consent is affirmatory (said positively to yourself), expressive (said in a publicly recognisable act) or tacit (implied by attitudes, responses and actions), these contextual issues are important in interpreting particular consent decisions and understanding how consent is given cumulatively in society (where expressions of personal biography map onto social and cultural characteristics of sexual knowledge, understanding and conduct in society).

Second, there are the parameters that juxtapose rationalism and irrationality in sexual conduct and the pursuit and enjoyment of pleasure and desire. The inherent rationalism in studies of sexual consent require tempering with an appreciation – if not an approval – of sexual cultures, knowledge and understanding amongst those engaged in sexual conduct. Some, as with evolutionary psychologists, would also argue that the juxtaposition is between human rationality and the inherent irrationality of the human subject as a biological organism (Thornhill and Palmer, 2000).

Thirdly, there is the juxtaposition of the idea of sexual consent as an act or contractual issue, and consent as part of a process of negotiation that moves beyond a focus on a given act to evaluating a series of acts of negotiation with the context of a relational process. The example of a particular sexual encounter that is so often used in discussing the nature of consent decisions does not conform to people's experience, with the exception of exceptional conduct such as 'one night stands'. Consent decisions are often part of a relationship in which there is a history of and context to incidences of negotiation, both of which feed into and directly impact upon negotiations. This reinforces the importance but not predetermination of context, because many of these processes of negotiation will be embedded in relationships that are not just defined by sexual conduct, such as partnerships and marriages.

Finally, there are the parameters of the development of sexual knowledge, understanding and communication in society. This in itself is part of the broad structural and cultural context that conditions sexual conduct at a particular time, but it requires abstracting in and of itself for two good reasons.

First, it raises issues of how sex is conceived and understood in society. Attitudes to and 'mindsets' at play when participants are based in negotiating sexual consent and sexual play are critical to understanding and decoding how they see their desires, their pursuit of their desires, and the relationships within which desires are pursued. What participants know and understand by their actions, the knowledge and understanding – common or otherwise – of those they play with, and what they regard as desirable or undesirable, or ethical or unethical, is at the centre of understanding their attitudes to sexual consent. Social and cultural knowledge and understanding condition action, and action, in how it is responded to, conditions the biographical knowledge and understanding carried with participants in consent decisions.

Second, it focuses much of the discussion around sexual consent away from the sex that may form the substance of consent decisions and the subject of thinking and feeling through the process of consent negotiation and sexual-play and towards the medium of consent being used. This refocuses attention upon consent as communication. When sexual consent is being discussed, and consent decisions analysed, sexual consent is the substance of discourse and forms the material consent for discourse, but the discourse itself is communication. When Cowling and Pineau debate what constitutes the giving of sexual consent, they are debating the validity and reliability of different forms of communication. Hence consent is constituted in and constructed through communication – specifically, the communication of participants knowledge and understanding of what they are engaged in as well as their desires, wants and preferences.

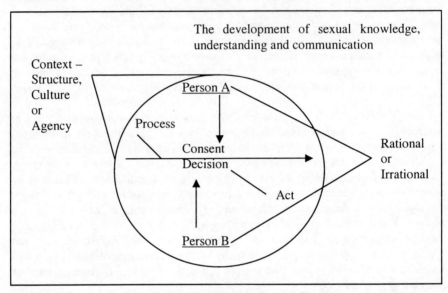

Figure 1 The Parameters for Understanding Sexual Consent

These parameters suggest that the participants in consent decisions could be seen as the subjects of an almost bewildering number of variables in making sense of their own consent decisions and the negotiations they make with others. A caveat should be immediately offered. Both radical feminists and those who defend traditional hetero-patriarchal culture and customs in sexual role and conduct might point to such parameters as reinforcing their arguments. The radical feminist argument would stress the limits on women's free consent, not just in terms of male power but in terms of contextual factors – structure, culture, knowledge, hetero-patriarchal 'institutions' or relationships (such as marriage) – that condition women's choice. They certainly provide a caution against post-feminists such as Katie Roiphe, and her assertion of women's agency and autonomy in the face of contextualising parameters (Roiphe, 1993) In a different sense, traditional patriarchs might themselves argue that such parameters are so complex as to form the basis for a defence of traditional conduct as something people know and as culturally ingrained, Hence if the picture is made more complex or changed, is it the man's fault if he is confused? (see Bly, 1990; Whitehead, 2002; Whitehead and Barrett (eds.), 2001 *passim*).

Stressing the contextual parameters to understanding sexual consent, and acknowledging that they make the issue of understanding sexual consent decisions one that is complex and 'messy' should not be regarded as an 'apologia' for poor sexual conduct or a defence for rape. Legal lines never rest upon uncomplicated ground, and such an analysis, on the contrary, might argue that higher standards of conduct enshrined in legal codes (such as stricter and more punitive laws on rape), may be a basis for giving an ethical impetus to the social, cultural and communicative changes necessary for less rape to take place (Reynolds, 2002). Whilst context is important, at any given moment the agency of social actors remains something that has to be judged partly against culture and convention, but also partly against the aspirational ethical standards that are desired in social change. Agents engage in interpersonal relationships and in negotiating sexual relationships and consent decisions. However much 'society is to blame', it does not mean pragmatic steps in sanctioning prohibited or unethical behaviours should not be addressed.

These four sets of parameters are important in disciplining thinking about sexual consent, and the evaluation of the quality of sexual consent. Whilst sexual consent may be a messy subject, they allow the mess and complexity to be organised. They also identify key variables that influence consent decisions and tensions within those consent decisions – factors that might, on balance, lead to a consent decision being affirmative or negative. In their representations as juxtapositions or tensions, these parameters allow for the representation of consent decisions as subject to tensions – a judgement accounting for different factors that effectively create a balance sheet of 'pro's and con's' upon which a decision is made.

The parameters also point to the importance of seeing consent as constituted in and constructed through communication. This is not, as Calder (in this collection) cautions, an invitation to dissolve consent into a post-structuralist preoccupation with language and discourse. It is, however, to recognise that any consent decision – sexual or otherwise – is formal and procedural, a communicative signifier that implies change (superficially, the change to new activity – from no sex to sex – or more deeply a moral transformation) mediated by a communicative act. This formal and procedural concept of consent is coupled with the substantive content of sexual pleasure, desire and practice. The substantive subject will influence the formal and procedural – if people are not used to talking about and negotiating their pleasures verbally, for example, it makes the communication more complex, less rational and arguably of a poorer quality in clarity. Consent decisions may also be part of the substantive content of sex, such as the 'play' around consent in role play or sado-masochistic play (though this should be regarded as distinct and of a second order to consent decisions that govern the negotiation of that play). Nevertheless, the abstraction of the formal from the substantive can be useful in clarifying conditions around sexual consent decisions, in four respects.

First, if consent is communication, and can be regarded as a formal and procedural aspect of communication integrally contextualised by the substance of sexual desire, identity and sexual behaviour, then it begs the question of why sexual consent should be any different from other forms of consent, and evaluating consent. Why should deciding to consent sexually be different to deciding whether to choose one financial option or another for purposes of investment, for example? If desire is a factor, why should deciding to consent sexually be any different to choosing what and how much to drink or eat? This reminds us that if sex is so different that consent decisions cannot be judged in the same way, it is necessary to evaluate what factors (or parameters) make it so, and judge whether the context to making consent decisions encourages decisions that are ethical or moral or otherwise. It also reminds us that the substantive – sex – has a symbiotic relationship with the formal and procedural communicative. This is partly represented in negotiating consent, but equally negotiated in other aspects of sex, such as encouraging the satisfaction of particular desires in respects of sex acts such as positions, postures and movements that fall within consent decisions. Certainly, both these factors are avenues through which, for example, the argument that people who are sexually stimulated might 'not be able to help themselves' in pressing their desire forward can be challenged. For if communication is an integral part of sex – both in sexual consent and in the communication of wants, desires and pleasures – the argument of a 'non-communicative moment' seems particularly problematic.

Second, it clarifies that if consent is formal and procedural communication, it is also *a priori* – before the act. Hence consent decisions precede acts, by the presence or absence. If consent is absent, such as in cases of force, discussion moves in the direction of the need to minimise rape or sexual violence through prohibition and sanction. If it is present, then guilt, regret or unhappiness after the event is indicative of the quality of the consent decision. Of course, the distinction between presence and absence can be complex, since it does not easily seem to account for acquiescence or submission to the unwanted, and perhaps it requires the caveat that the status of consent as a priori the act is a caution to sexual partners to seek consent prior to the act, leaving themselves open to sanction if they do not. Nevertheless the distinction is important in distinguishing between non-consenting sex and poor consent decisions, and in locating where consent should be located in the process of negotiating and enjoying sexual pleasure.

Aligned to that and third, it clarifies that consenting to an act carries with it no qualification as to whether the act is ethically good or bad. Here again, separating the formal procedural communicative construct of consent from the substance of sex is important in that it separates the ethical question of consent from other ethical questions related to sexual behaviour. It is possible to consent freely to what might be morally debated as unethical, but this is not a problem of consent as such. It may become a problem that is addressed by prohibiting the activity on ethical grounds regardless of consent (at present in the UK, sado-masochism might be subject to prosecution on the basis of harm, regardless of consent), but the problem in respect of consent is then one of the relationship between consent decisions and the ethical or legal import of the law on consent decisions (as with heterosexual anal sex, which was until recently formally illegal in the UK but arguably not unethical). The problem with constraining consent to legal prohibition is that, as the case of sado-masochism shows, there might be severe objections to its characterisation as unethical (see Beckmann in this collection; Thompson, 1994). Consent is one of the principal criteria for ethical behaviour, and thereby has a significant influence as a standard by which activities are considered to be ethical or not.

Finally, it reinforces the notion that in evaluating consent decisions, the formal and procedural communication that constitutes consent decisions is socially and culturally contextualised. Individuals' consent decisions and negotiations are expressed through cultural mediums of communication that may be unclear, complex, and in the case of sex, perhaps absent in an explicit expressive form. In, for example, a culture where people do not talk about sexual desire even when engaged in sex play, indirect expressions of consent are a poor communicative procedure and the quality of such a procedure will invariably contribute towards a sense of how far the consent decisions themselves are of a good or poor quality.

The Quality of Consent

The foregoing discussion, abstract and complex as it might be, has direct bearing on sexual consent decisions, and so on how the quality of sexual consent decisions is evaluated. The assumption – and it is an assumption – is that the better the communication both of consent decisions and around sexual desires, the better the personal health and well-being of sexual subjects in society will be, and so the healthier sex in society will be. This is an ethical assumption. It is based upon the idea that sexually ethical behaviour will not simply bring about the consequence of a majority of sexual subjects health and happiness (as in utilitarian ethics – for example Bentham, 1970), but an intrinsically ethical basis for sexual behaviour between social subjects in society (a deontological ethic – for example Kant, 1989). An important part of sexual ethics is therefore sexual communication, and a critical part of sexual communication is how we communicate our decisions, the most important of which are whether we consent to sex or particular sexual desires or propositions. Hence the quality of consent decisions is important, because it is part of and indicative of ethical and healthy basis of sexual conduct in society.

Is the quality of consent high in contemporary society? Insofar as there is evidence for this, it is mainly in somewhat unreliable sources such as magazine surveys (for example, see Stephenson and Bromley (eds.), 1998). Most sex surveys, (for example Wellings, 1994) concentrate more on sexual health and the incidence of sexual activity than on eliciting ethical discourse about sexual decision-making. This is not to say that there is not evidence of public attitudes and ethical views, but it is often aimed towards sexual problems and not towards understanding what people might regard as the less problematic aspects of their own sex lives.

There are grounds for pessimism as to the ethical health and well-being of sexual conduct and understandings in contemporary society. Historically, sex has been a subject that has been shrouded in silence and regarded as dangerous, and therefore not been the subject of public discourse (Mort, 2000; Weeks, 1989, 1991). Sexual knowledge has been the subject of strict regulation by religious, medical and political authorities, and pathological in its representation of sexual openness (Foucault, 1979; Mort, 2000; Porter and Hall, 1994). There is still considerable evidence that hetero-patriarchy conditions hostility, prejudice and pathology against other sexualities, reflecting an absence of ethical thinking (Richardson,

2000; Stychin and Herman (eds.), 2000, Weeks, 1995). The structural and cultural, and knowledge and communication contexts to sexual discourse remains one more likely to shroud unethical behaviour than support ethical behaviour, although the development of diverse sexual communities – lesbian, gay, bdsm – has offered the space for the opening up of sexual discourse and ethical debate.

Another way of exploring the quality of consent decisions is to establish from the parameters what might constitute low quality consent decisions or bases for decisions that are cause for concern. A number of examples will suffice. There are questions of quality where sex is consented to because it is perceived that it is expected because media and peers represent sexual activity as appropriate, against personal feelings of reservation. There are questions of quality where consent to sex is given because some sexual activity has already taken place and the 'process' is now 'too far gone' to stop. There are questions of quality where sex is consented to keep the peace or avoid unpleasantness that is short of coercive threats for sex – not necessarily because it is demanded, but because it will reassure or distract or otherwise have an effect that is more the motivation of the sex than pleasure and desire. There are questions of quality where sex is consented to because it is expected, in response the assumption of mutuality either assumed thoughtlessly or not considered at all, or of a sense of obligation or duty, or as a part of a given relationship such as marriage. There are questions of quality where sex is consented to because a person feels they have to give it to receive any form of attention or affection, not because of desire, whether through past experience or personal esteem. There are questions of quality where sex is consented to on the basis of exchange within a relationship – for financial benefit, for fulfilment of other wants on a straightforward exchange basis.

None of these would necessarily be seen as 'out of the ordinary' experiences and many might speculate that they have experienced these consent decisions often, or these experiences are the 'reality' of sexual relationships. Neither, however, can they be described as ethically sound or sexually healthy bases of sexual behaviour (though not all sexual behaviour may require the same ethical standards – such as in the enjoyment of promiscuity), or indeed relationships. Here it is necessary to stress that it is highly probable that most sexual relationships sometimes involve elements of these sorts of consent decisions, and a discussion of the quality of sexual consent is not concerned to be overly critical of individual cases of negotiation that do not conform to an ideal of mutual, compatible and simultaneous desire. If, however, the common experience of many is of their sex lives conform to the terms of those examples most of the time, then it becomes an issue of sexual ethics and it becomes a problem that requires attention if society is to be composed of ethical subjects of good health and well-being.

Having opened up this question, the – albeit limited – evidence would on balance point to a problem of sexual consent that is part of a broader problem of sexual ethics and relates to general problems of sexual communication, culture and knowledge. Such a problem takes in both the reported experiences of sexual subjects and the social and cultural contours of the development of sexual knowledge, understanding and education in society. Part of the agenda for sexual politics should not just be to address the 'problem' of sexual non-consent, but the less visible problem of sexual consent that has a low quality, and reflects an ethical weakness in the social and cultural construction of sex in society. To that extent, there are a small but growing and sophisticated number of studies that seek to give ethical guidance on the construction of a more open and free sexual communication, culture, knowledge and understanding in society (Cartlidge and Ryan (eds.), 1983; Foucault, 1979, 1986a, 1986b; Plummer, 1995; Primoratz, 1999; Segal (ed.), 1997; Soble, 1998a, 1998b; Soble (ed.), 2002; Weeks, 1993). This literature has not concentrated on the quality of sexual consent, but covered ethical decisions and sexual values in a way that offers some possibilities for change.

Plummer, for example, has argued for the importance of sexual story-telling in the context of an intimate citizenship that breaks down the public silences on sexual experience, in a way that empowers rather than provides media entertainment (Plummer, 1995, pp. 144-166). Carmody – in this collection – explores the use of Foucault's *rapport à soi* and the constitution of the sexual self away from traditional moralities towards an ethics built on mutuality and self-regard (Foucault, 1986a). Both projects would be certain to have explicit benefits for the improvement of the quality of sexual consent.

More generally, there are broader political projects that might offer some import for ethical change around sexual culture, communications and knowledge. Feminist critiques clearly offer a means of theorising change through challenging gendered and hetero-patriarchal constructions of sex and sexuality (see Moore and Reynolds in this collection). Foucault's discussion of the will to knowledge and his 'microphysics of power' offer the basis for thinking about how 'internalised' contextualising parameters can be subverted and reconceived to be personally empowering (Foucault, 1979; Rabinow (ed.), 1984; Simons, 1995). The Gramscian notion of hegemony and counter-hegemony could be utilised to conceive effecting a cultural and political shift towards a more enlightened and ethical social context (Gramsci, 1971). Alternatively, Habermas's critique of 'systematically distorted speech acts in contemporary society' and his attempts to develop a universal pragmatics upon which to base a more enlightened and ethically informed idea of social justice offers possibilities for the improvement of sexual communication (Cooke, 1997; Habermas, 1989, 1996, 1998).

These are little more than the beginnings of bringing together extant social, philosophical and political analyses – some only tangentially considering issues of sexual ethics and social values – that offer frameworks for conceiving social and cultural change and more specifically changing the parameters to sexual consent decisions. In this chapter, the main purpose has been to clear the ground and begin to set the agenda for more substantial considerations.

Sexual Consent and Sexual Ethics

It may well be that some readers feel that much of the discussion of the quality of sexual consent bleeds back into debate into the distinction between sexual consent and non-consent – if the quality of consent is bad, should we call it consent at all?

There are others who might ask whether an attempt to dissect the quality of consent is worthwhile if we accept that humans are fallible, flawed creatures and the negotiation of sexual consent is messy – we all make mistakes and have bad sex, so why make a meal of it?

Both these views miss the point. What I have tried to do here is to talk about sexual consent apart from non-consent not because I see the divide as definite, but because it is important to understand the problems with sexual consent where no legal code would necessarily improve the quality of consent decisions. In order to address the question of sexual ethics as one that involves transforming sexual relations and understandings, it is necessary to focus on those sexual relations that are unproblematised, as well as those that are problematised. Further, however flawed people are and whatever philosophical discourse of human nature is applied, this discussion has been about establishing better ethical guidance for sexual conduct, with a focus on the social and cultural context within which sexual relations take place. However fallible the human condition may be, the notion of encouraging a greater knowledge, understanding and communicative ability of sex and sexual conduct – including ethics around consent decisions – is still important in the establishing of a sexually ethically healthy society.

The next stage of the emancipation of the sexual self – following on from the unfinished and partial sexual revolution of the 1960s and the subsequent legal, political and cultural changes towards greater openness and public discourse on sex, however sensational and fetishised – is to move from thinking about sexual 'problems' to thinking about sexual custom and practice. As important as discussions of the distinction between sexual consent and non-consent are, the quality of sexual consent is also critical importance if we are to think about and effect changes towards more ethical sexual communication, cultures, knowledge and understanding. A greater sense of ethical conduct in sexual pleasure will both encourage the setting of higher standards for consent decisions and encourage more open intolerance of those who engage in non-consenting sex. More simply and immediately, reflection on the quality of sexual consent decisions begins the movement towards owning our sexual pleasure and demanding sexual ethics in everyday life.

Bibliography

Adam, B., Duyvendak, J. W. and Krouwel, A. (eds.), (1999) *The Global Emergence of Gay and Lesbian Politics*, Philadelphia: Temple University Press.

Archard, D. (1998), *Sexual Consent*, Oxford: Westview Press.

Bell, D. and Binnie, J. (2000), *The Sexual Citizen*, Cambridge: Polity.

Bentham, J. (1970), *Introduction to the Theory of Morals and Legislation* (ed. J. H. Burns and H. L. A. Hart), London: Athlone Press.

Bly, J. (1990), *Iron John: A Book About Men*, London: Addison-Wesley Publishing.

Bryson, V. (1995), 'Comment' (from the editorial board) *Contemporary Politics*, Vol. 1, No. 2, p. 72.

Cartlidge, S. and Ryan, J. (eds.), (1983) *Sex and Love: New Thoughts on Old Contradictions*, London: Women's Press.

Cook, K. (2002), 'Rape Law.Consent@FreeAgreement.co.uk: An Assessment of the Legal Definition of Consent, in the light of the Current Review of Sexual Offences Law', *Contemporary Issues in Law*, Vol. 6, No. 1, pp. 7-22.

Cooke, M. (1997), *Language and Reason: A Study of Habermas's Pragmatics*, Mass.: MIT Press.

Cowling, M. (1998), *Date Rape and Consent*, Aldershot, Ashgate Publishing Ltd.

D'Emilio, J., Turner, W. and Vaid, U. (eds.) (2000), *Creating Change: Sexuality, Public Policy and Civil Rights*, New York: St Martin's Press.

Dunphy, R. (2000), *Sexual Politics: An Introduction*, Edinburgh: Edinburgh University Press.

Dworkin, A. (1981), *Pornography: Men Possessing Women*, London: The Women's Only Press.

Dworkin, A. (1988), *Intercourse*, London: Arrow.

Foucault, M. (1979), *The History of Sexuality Volume 1: The Will to Knowledge*, Harmondsworth: Penguin.

Foucault, M. (1984a), *The History of Sexuality Volume 2: The Use of Pleasure*, Harmondsworth: Penguin.

Foucault, M. (1984b), *The History of Sexuality Volume 3: The Care of the Self*, Harmondsworth: Penguin

Francis, L. (ed.) (1996), *Date Rape: Feminism, Philosophy and the Law*, The Pennsylvania State University Press.

Gramsci, A. (1971), *Selections from Prison Notebooks*, London: Lawrence and Wishart.

Habermas, J. (1989), *The Structural Transformation of the Public Sphere*, Cambridge: Polity Press.

Habermas, J. (1997), *Between Facts and Norms: Contributions to a Discourse Theory of Law and Democracy*, Cambridge: Polity Press.

Habermas, J. (1998), *On the Pragmatics of Communication* (edited by Maeve Cooke), Cambridge: Polity Press.

Husak, D. and Thomas, G.C. (1992), 'Date Rape, Social Convention and Reasonable Mistakes', *Law and Philosophy*, Vol. 11, pp. 95-126.

Jeffreys, S. (1990), *Anti-Climax: A Feminist Perspective on the Sexual Revolution*, London: The Woman's Press.

Kant, I. (1989), *Foundations of the Metaphysics of Morals*, New York: Macmillan.

MacKinnon, C. (1989), *Towards a Feminist Theory of the State*, Harvard: Harvard University Press.

Mort, F. (2000 – 2nd edition), *Dangerous Sexualities: Medico-Moral Politics in England Since 1830*, London: Routledge.

Pineau, L. (1995), 'Date Rape: A Feminist Analysis', in Francis, L (ed.), *Date Rape: Feminism, Philosophy and the Law*, Pennsylvania: Pennsylvania State University Press.

Plummer, K. (1995), *Telling Sexual Stories: Power, Change and Social Worlds*, London, Routledge.

Porter, R. and Hall, L (1994), *The Facts of Life: The Creation of Sexual Knowledge in Britain, 1650-1950*, New York: Yale University Press.

Primoratz, I. (1999), *Ethics and Sex*, London: Routledge.

Rabinow, P. (ed.) (1984), *The Foucault Reader: An Introduction to Foucault's Thought*, Harmondsworth: Penguin.

Reynolds, P. (2002b), 'Rape, Law and Consent: The Scope and Limits to Sexual Regulation by Law', *Contemporary Issues in Law*, Vol. 6, No. 1, pp. 92-102.

Richardson, D. (2000), *Rethinking Sexuality* London: Sage.

Roiphe, K. (1993), *The Morning After: Sex, Fear and Feminism*, London: Hamish Hamilton.

Simons, J. (1995), *Foucault and the Political*, London: Routledge.

Soble, A. (1998a), *The Philosophy of Sex and Love*, Minnesota: Paragon House.

Soble, A. (1998b), *Sexual Investigations*, New York: New York University Press.

Soble, A. (ed.) (2002), *Philosophy of Sex: Contemporary Readings*, London: Rowman and Littlefield.

Stephenson, H. and Bromley, M. (eds.) (1998), *Sex, Lies and Democracy: The British Press and the Public*, London: Longman.

Stychin, C. and Herman, D (2000), *Sexuality in the Legal Arena*, London: Athlone Press.

Thompson, B. (1994), *Sado-Masochism: Painful Perversion or Pleasurable Play?*, London: Cassell.

Thornhill, R. and Palmer C. T. (2000), *A Natural History Of Rape: Biological Bases Of Sexual Coercion*, Cambridge Ma: MIT Press.

Walby, S. (1990), *Theorizing Patriarchy* Oxford, Blackwell.

Whitehead, S. (2002), *Men and Masculinities*, Cambridge: Polity.

Whitehead, S. and Barrett, F. (eds.)(2001), *The Masculinities Reader*, Cambridge: Polity.

Weeks, J. (1989 – 2nd edition), *Sex, Politics and Society: The Regulation of Sexuality since 1800*, London: Longman.

Weeks, J. (1991), *Against Nature: Essays on History, Sexuality and Identity*, London: River Oram Press.

Weeks, J. (1993), 'An Unfinished Revolution: Sexuality in the 20th Century' in Victoria Harwood *et al.* (eds.), *Pleasure Principles: Politics, Sexuality and Ethics*, London: Lawrence and Wishart.

Weeks, J. (1995), *Inverted Moralities: Sexual Values in the Age of Aids*, Cambridge: Polity Press.

Wellings, K. et al. (1994), *Sexual Behaviour in Britain: The National Survey of Sexual Attitudes and Lifestyles*, Harmondsworth: Penguin.

PART 2
(MORE) SPECIFIC AND PRACTICAL THEMES

Chapter 7

'Risky' Women, Sexual Consent and Criminal 'Justice'

Margaret S. Malloch[1]

Introduction

This chapter examines the complexities which impact on the social construction and meaning of consent, as a direct result of the structural imbalance of gender relationships. The issue of 'consent' and its centrality to the social construction and meaning of 'rape' has been highlighted and analysed by feminist theorists[2] (Millett, 1970; Dworkin, 1987; MacKinnon, 1987; Kelly, 1988; Smart, 1989; Stanko, 1990; Edwards, 1996; Lees, 1997; Kelly and Regan, 2001). This chapter will highlight the ways in which issues of consent are constructed and contested within the criminal justice system, specifically in cases of rape.

By examining the presentation of women in court, it is argued that women who fail to conform to what are vague standards of 'respectability' are depicted as 'risky' and their authenticity in relation to issues of consent will be brought into question (Smart, 1989; Lees, 1997). Through an examination of the concept of 'risky women' it is possible to examine the structural imbalances which underpin judgements of what consent is, how it is presented and how it operates in the criminal justice system. More specifically, the structural context of patriarchy will be considered, as it is through patriarchal imperatives that the meaning of consent becomes defined and determined. This chapter will examine the ways in which women's behaviour, notably in relation to drug and/or alcohol use, is used in a social and legal context to challenge notions of 'consent'. It will re-emphasise the significance given to locating 'risk' in rape cases with women, thereby shifting the focus away from the perpetrator. Women have been portrayed in the court setting (as both victims of crime and as lawbreakers) as irrational and untrustworthy (Kennedy, 1992; Edwards, 1996; Lees, 1997). Their narratives are delegitimised and their rights to justice are frequently undermined through these negative representations. This chapter illustrates the operation of this process through an analysis of 'risky' women, and in doing so critically explores the status of consent.

A woman's right to withhold consent is frequently challenged should she fail to meet the standards of 'appropriate femininity' as depicted in social mores and institutional/cultural discourses of morality (Carlen et al., 1985; Malloch, 1999). Through the enactment of control within patriarchal society, women are expected to conform to often-vague standards of conduct and presentation in order to attain protection from the state and its agencies, and to afford them 'justice' should they be 'harmed' by sexual violence. However, factors such as class, 'race', sexuality and perceptions of 'respectability' are rooted in the structural determining contexts of society and form the basis for such mediators of social control.

While liberal democratic constructs portray the equality of all individuals before the law, in reality social, economic and political structural inequalities determine individuals' access to justice and the standards of justice they are likely to receive. This is evident when the experiences of women are examined within the context of the criminal justice system (Carlen, 1985, 1998; Kennedy, 1992; Edwards, 1996; Lees, 1997; Malloch, 2000a and 2000b; Jordan, 2001; Kelly and Regan, 2001) particularly when cases revolve around depictions of consent, most noticeable in rape cases. A woman's right and indeed, her portrayed ability, to withhold consent is dependent on reputation and status, on her perceived 'respectability' (Stanko, 1985 and 1990; Smart, 1989; Lees, 1997). Women are expected to avoid situations, which may hold some element of 'risk' for their personal safety, indeed 'victim status' is often a status that needs to be earned. In cases of contested rape, the evidence is frequently pared down to the issue of one person's word against that of the other, particularly when the issue presented relates to consent. For women who engage in 'risky behaviour' such as illegal drug use or 'drunkenness'[3] the harm of sexual victimisation is denied by legal agencies and society in general. As Elizabeth Ettorre (1992, p. 38) argues: 'a woman who drinks does not need to be a prostitute to have a promiscuous image. She is promiscuous by the very fact that she is a drinker'. This presentation of women is underpinned by the suggestion of the 'spoiled identity' and used to discredit women either by the suggestion of lowered inhibitions or an 'unleashed sexuality' (Lees, 1997, p. 82). This concept can be seen at a number of levels, from proscribed activity such as sex work to more 'normative' forms of behaviour. Wearing attire that meets with current fashion trends can be portrayed in different contexts such as the courtroom, as overly sexualised and therefore 'inappropriate' thus resulting in the wearer being depicted as 'risky'. As drug and/or alcohol use can lead to concerns about 'uncontrolled' women so too will attributes which are perceived as overtly sexualised.

'Risky' women are women whose conformity to social constructions of 'acceptable femininities' may be questioned and accordingly, the status of their consent is open to manipulation and disrespect. Social constructs are internalised to such an extent that all women recognise that failure to conform will result in the destruction of their reputation and the removal of their access and/or right to justice. Indeed Carol Smart (1989) questions how it can ever be possible for women to achieve justice in a system that represents the 'feminine' in such a distorted and problematic way. Hence many cases of violence against women are never brought to court. Both the assailant and the legal system often deny women who have voluntarily consumed drugs or 'too much' alcohol the right to withhold their consent. It is often suggested that being intoxicated or drugged as a result of her own actions removes a woman's ability to consent or withhold consent (she is 'at risk' as a result of her own actions), thus the legal system removes her right to consent or withhold consent.[4] She is seen as the embodiment of 'risk', in a way that is not applied to men.

Gender identities are represented throughout the criminal justice system. As Pat Carlen (1985), Elizabeth Stanko (1990), Helena Kennedy (1992), Susan Edwards (1996) and many other theorists have argued, the justice system operates in a particularly gendered way. Diane Richardson and Hazel May (1999) discuss the gendered and sexualised meanings which are used in the social construction of violence. They note (1999, p. 309):

> Social definitions of violence revolve around culpability, victimisation and what is deemed socially appropriate behaviour in particular contexts. (...)...such different meanings suggest that some individuals are seen as more 'deserving' of violence and less deserving of victim status than are others on the basis of their 'behavioural responsibility' for risk avoidance.

Certain victims are viewed as possessing some level of 'behavioural responsibility' and are expected to employ a range of avoidance strategies to minimise the risk of violence they may be subject to. Behaviour which is deemed 'problematic' (sex work, gay sex, intravenous drug use) subsequently denies those who participate, the status of 'innocent victim'. As Richardson and May (1999) point out, this was particularly evident in social reactions to HIV and AIDS (see also Davenport-Hines, 1990; Patton, 1990; Singer, 1993) where certain behaviour (unprotected sex, anal sex, injecting drug use) were associated with the spread of HIV. This in turn led to the attribution of levels of culpability to identifiable groups who became the focus for blame rather than victim status.

Richardson and May (1999) argue that this allocation of blame and responsibility distinguished between the murders of 'prostitutes' and 'innocent' victims (Smith, 1989). It is possible to see how this operates at a more pervasive level on the consciousness of individual women in terms of access to public space and self-presentation. It is clear that 'inappropriate behaviour' such as drug use, or being 'drunk' can have a significant impact on how a woman is judged and responded to by state institutions. Such judgements can also affect the resources she can access (Malloch, 2000a and 2000b).

In terms of rape cases, behaviour deemed 'inappropriate' for a woman can result in accusations that she was 'contributorily negligent' (Kennedy, 1992, p. 11). Such a claim serves to wholly or partially blame her for the injuries she has received, and enables the assailant to cast doubts that she withheld her consent. The suggestion of 'risk-taking' is enough to cast doubts on a woman's respectability.

Richardson and May (1999, p. 309) argue that the '...gender of the victim is significant in terms of expectations of 'behavioural responsibility' for avoiding social contexts commonly associated with the potential for violence'. They continue (1999, p. 313): 'Women are more likely than are men to be blamed for making themselves vulnerable to violence by being in the 'wrong' place at the 'wrong' time'. This is very evident in the portrayal of crime prevention literature, frequently directed at providing women with information on how to minimise risk and make themselves 'safe'. Thus, women are expected to modify **their** behaviour to avoid or minimise potential risks. Failure to do so, will deny them the right to be viewed and responded to as 'innocent victims'. As feminist writers such as Carol Smart (1989), Helena Kennedy (1992), Susan Edwards (1996) and Sue Lees (1997) have consistently argued, this is particularly evident in rape trials. In the court setting, women's behaviour and presentation are scrutinised, their narratives are challenged and discredited. Frequently, the perpetrator's version of events is given precedence over the victim's. This goes some way to explaining why only approximately 9% of cases originally recorded by the police as rape result in a conviction for rape. Although many factors impact on this, the issue of 'consent' is among the most problematic, with the *Morgan Ruling* representing the high point of subjectivity as far as rape cases in England and Wales were concerned (Heilbron Committee, 1975).[5] In Scotland, the use of force is still considered to be a central element in rape cases (Scottish Executive, 2001; Scottish Parliament, 2001), however this does not significantly negate the importance given to depictions of consent.

The Problem of 'Consent' in Rape Trials

While representations of sexuality and 'attractiveness' change over time, for feminists, a constant theme is the way in which sexual practice is socially constructed around notions of male, not female, desire (de Beauvoir, 1953; Millett, 1970; Dworkin, 1987). Sexuality is therefore a major site for male domination over women, and for the male imposition of notions of femininity on women, as well as masculinities on men (Newburn and Stanko, 1994; Collier, 1995). Discourses of gender change over time, however the impact of traditional presentations of gender has had a lasting legacy, particularly within the criminal justice system.

Victorian discourses of femininity were based on definitions of women as contained within the family, whether they were married or not. The presented image (for women of the upper classes, rather than black women and/or working class women) was one of selflessness, fragility and dependence on a husband or father. This presentation contrasted with the invasive and brutal methods of intervention, both social and medical (such as clitoridectomies) used to control female sexuality. At the same time, prostitution was a widespread phenomenon and women were the targets for measures of control, held responsible for the spread of venereal disease and other forms of vice (Mort, 1987; Smart, 1992; Mason, 1994). Masculinity on the other hand was seen to embody rationality and involved an orientation to the outside world, beyond the family and household (Seidler, 1989 and 1994). Similarly, male and female sexuality was seen to differ significantly (Hester, 1992). Prior to the Enlightenment, women were seen to be sexual creatures, indeed their sexuality was often feared as seen with the 'witch-hunts'. However, by the nineteenth century, women were seen to be non-aggressive and submissive in matters of sex. Male sexuality was considered to be active, based on drive and aggression. Today, representations of very different images of femininity are presented in the cultural realm.[6] Sylvia Walby (1990, 1997) argues that rather than containment within the domestic circle as the key image of femininity today, the predominant defining feature of femininity is attractiveness to men. Susan Bordo (1997) and Sandra Bartky (1998) discuss the often-drastic measures, both physical and surgical, which are used to attain the 'perfect' feminine form.

These standards impact on women in a range of ways (see Malloch, 1999). The bodily appearance of an individual woman influences judgements about her competence (Bordo, 1990 and 1997; Wolf, 1991; Bartky, 1998).[7] This has significant consequences for women in the criminal justice system in general (Taylor, 1993; Malloch, 1999) and in rape cases in particular. Furthermore, 'the structural divisions of class, 'race'/ethnicity and sexuality interact with relations of gender to mediate ideological constructions and representations of identity' (Malloch, 1999, p. 357). As a result, institutionalised myths and stereotypes of 'appropriate femininities' and correspondingly 'appropriate sexualities' are evident which significantly impact on the presentation of the defendant and complainant in rape trials (Smart, 1989; Edwards, 1996; Lees, 1997).

Such concepts have clearly been reflected in laws of rape where the active role is presumed to lie with men, while the 'victims' are required to show that they *did not* consent to sexual intercourse. In law, this reflects the traditional notions of active male sexuality and the more passive, female response. Undoubtedly, this dichotomy is under threat when there is any evidence of the woman complainant as an active sexual individual, the search for such evidence informing the basis for much of the defence cross-examination in court. Historical notions of femininity and contemporary representations of the 'respectable woman' are interspersed to determine women's experiences in court. This results in the woman being vilified and judged in place of the male rapist, it is *she* who is assumed to have behaved badly on the basis of this gendered notion of sexuality (Smart, 1989).

Delia Dumaresq (1981, p. 47) has noted that:

Feminists have for a long time claimed that there are two groups of women, one of which is granted social acceptability but denied sexuality, the other, freely expressing her sexuality but denied society.

In rape cases, Dumaresq (1981) argues that women are interrogated as to which category they fall into. She notes that the legal procedures in a rape trial are aimed at establishing *intent*. The intent of the rapist, and more specifically the victim, who is also cross-examined. Dumaresq (1981) notes that this is the only legal situation where the victim would be interrogated in this way. So in the specific context of rape, the victims sexuality, behaviour and 'respectability' is in question and correspondingly, her entitlement to the status of 'innocent victim'.[8] Sue Lees (1997, p. 71) notes that this interrogation of the woman's respectability transforms her into a 'spectacle of degradation' and suggests that 'the rape trial can be seen as a public spectacle which functions as a warning to all women against speaking out about male violence'.

The cross-examination, which many women have to endure, is evident in the debates surrounding the use of the complainant's sexual history evidence. Until the mid-1970s a woman's personal history could be used by the defence to undermine her credibility. Public outcry over this led to the Heilbron Committee in 1975, followed by the Sexual Offences (Amendment) Act 1976. This required that the defence prove, to the judge's satisfaction, that the victim's sexual history was relevant to the case. However, with the *Morgan Ruling*, the defendant is able to claim that he 'honestly believed' the woman was consenting. This shifts the onus of the case on to the woman. Her validity and 'respectability' become the focus of the proceedings. Use of the defendant's sexual history evidence is only allowed at the judge's discretion and is, in practice, rarely used even if he has been accused of similar behaviour.

In June 1998, the Home Office Report *Speaking Up for Justice* noted that judges allowed 75% of defence applications to question the complainant about her sexual history, generally to challenge the prosecution presentation of 'good' sexual behaviour and thereby to question or re-present the woman's 'good character'. Section 41 of the Youth Justice and Criminal Evidence Act, 1999 (which came into operation in December 2000) sought to place further restrictions on the use of sexual history evidence but judges still retained their discretionary powers. This section of the Act banned previous sexual history evidence where the issue of whether the woman had consented or not was in dispute, but left it admissible where the defendant *believed* that she was consenting.[9] This issue is steeped in controversy. As Beverley Brown, Michelle Burman and Lynn Jamieson (1993) note in their study of the use of sexual evidence in Scotland, there needs to be some distinction made between 'sexual history' and 'sexual character'. While 'sexual history' refers to specific information about events and actions which have taken place, 'sexual character' is a more subjective concept which 'involves the typing of a person, usually in moral terms of 'good' and 'bad' and evinces generalised tendencies or propensities' (Brown et al., 1993, pp. 1-2; Birch, 2002). In court, direct questions relating to sexual character may be prohibited, but this does not prevent the use of broader questions of character which may 'set the scene' such as questions around drug and/or alcohol use.[10]

The essential factor in determining rape is the absence of consent.[11] Rape is currently defined in England and Wales as an act of sexual intercourse with a person who does not consent to it. The reliance on the use of force in Scotland is intended to evidence a lack of consent (Scottish Parliament, 2001). To be found guilty, the assailant must know that the person does not consent or be reckless as to whether the person consents. The key issue is clearly 'consent'. However, for feminists, any oversimplification of this is inherently problematic. Different contextual factors and issues of power and inequality can impact significantly on a woman's perceived right and/or ability to give or withhold consent to sex. The existence of moral and philosophical debates around the 'age of consent' illustrates the interconnection between the right and ability of an individual to participate in sex and the problematics of individual judgement and communication. Frequently overlooked however, is the context of power and power relations, which characterise patriarchal society and which underpin the ability to give or withhold consent at any given moment (Dworkin 1987; MacKinnon, 1987). As Anderson (2000, p. 2) points out:

The legal notion of the ability to consent seems to be founded on the autonomous individual of liberal theory presupposed in criminal law. The power balance between the sexes, highly relevant in this context, does not seem to have been taken into consideration, be it in the statutory definition of rape or in case law.

In the broad context of rape trials, these inherently problematic assumptions are evident throughout the process, emphasising the importance of notions of 'respectability' and 'appropriate' femininity, as various research studies have illustrated. Jennifer Temkin (1996) has noted that research conducted throughout the 1970s, 1980s and 1990s has highlighted that police surgeons, in some cases, make their own assessment of the validity of the rape allegation, often affecting the thoroughness with which they conduct their medical examinations. While Temkin discusses the various factors in this process which impact on the women's experiences as either negative or positive, she notes that the issue of being 'judged' by medical professionals at the stage of being medically examined clearly impacted on many of the women. One of the respondents quoted by Temkin stated (1996, p. 12): 'I felt that I was being judged...I felt cheap and guilty as if it were my fault'. Sue Lees (1997) also notes that in her study of rape trials it was not unheard of for medical 'experts' to suggest that alcohol acted as 'an aphrodisiac' on the woman, further illustrating the presentation of 'medical knowledge' as underpinned by distorted views of women's sexuality.

Similarly, Keith and Debbie Soothill (1993) examined media reporting of rape trials by five major newspapers during 1951, 1961, 1971, 1978 and 1985. Their analysis indicated that barristers for both the prosecution and defence, as well as trial judges, were responsible for making comments in court which were damaging to, and impacted negatively on, the presentation of the woman in court. Comments based on damaging stereotypes of appropriate female behaviour, and others which questioned the woman's plausibility, illustrated that the entire court system is saturated with such assumptions. The use of these stereotypes as a basis with which to interrogate victims leads Sue Lees (1997, p. 78) to go so far as to suggest that this constitutes 'judicial rape'. This was disturbingly evident in the High Court in Glasgow where a 17-year-old rape victim, Lindsay Armstrong was made to hold up the underwear she had been wearing when assaulted and to read out the logo embossed on her pants. Her parents later stated that Lindsay said she had been made to 'feel like a tart who deserved to be raped' (The Scotsman, 1 August, 2002). These events only came to public attention after Lindsay took her own life following the conviction of her attacker. This led one 'senior legal figure, who declined to be named' to state:

What advocates and barristers are trained to do is use people's prejudices to influence the case. It's not about evidence. When the defence got Lindsay Armstrong to hold up her knickers in court, there was a message there that people who wear knickers, or thongs with the words 'Little Devil' on them, are somehow less worthy. It's a classic middle-class male cliché, that somehow a woman wearing a particular kind of underwear is 'asking for it' (*Scotland on Sunday* 4 August, 2002).

Damaging attitudes are reflected beyond the defence barrister who uses them in the defence of their client and are further reinforced through media coverage. These judgements are evident when women appear in court as both 'victims' and law-breakers, illustrating the prevalence of institutionalised bias and structural inequalities within the criminal justice system. The justice system itself can be seen to embody patriarchal power structures.

Women and 'Risk': Drug and Alcohol Use as 'Risky' Behaviour

Illegal drug use and 'excess' alcohol use is seen as inherently 'unfeminine', therefore women who engage in such behaviour are seen to conflict with, or distort norms and expectations of 'appropriate' feminine behaviour (Ettorre, 1992; Skeggs, 1997; Malloch, 1999). Portrayals of 'risk' are different for men and women, so too is the responsibility for engaging in risky behaviour. And of course, it is impossible to clearly distinguish between 'acceptable' and 'risky' behaviour given the subjective nature of appropriate social forms. There would appear to be a continuum of behaviour which may be viewed differently in different social contexts. The representation of behaviour in court (i.e. the wearing of particular underwear, or 'drunken' behaviour) clearly decontextualises it from broader social circumstances existing at the time, re-presenting particular factors as 'risky'.

'Risk' is everywhere and is often the term used to describe situations which are best avoided (Beck, 1992; Franklin, 1998). Risk and harm are implicitly linked. However, it would appear that risk might not simply be an external danger that individuals may encounter, but can actually be created by them. Individuals are expected to assess any risk that may be in their vicinity. Notions of being 'at risk' tend to be applied to children (the 'at-risk' register) or at risk of offending (risk-assessment procedures) (Castel, 1991). For women, the likelihood that their own behaviour will 'put them at risk' is regularly implied and frequently used in mitigation for defendants in rape cases (see Castel, 1991). 'Risk' in sexual behaviour is discussed by Frank Mort (1987), Cindy Patton (1990) and Jeffrey Weeks (1995). Robert Castel (1991, p. 287) argues:

> A risk does not arise from the presence of particular precise danger embodied in a concrete individual or group. It is the effect of a combination of abstract *factors* that render more or less probable the occurrence of undesirable modes of behaviour.

In turn, this promotes a 'new mode of surveillance' (Castel, 1991 p. 288) which is clearly reflected in the regulation and surveillance of women in the 'age of sexual epidemic' (Singer, 1993 p. 83). When examining concepts of consent and rape, this dichotomy is clearly evident. Women are expected to meet the expectations of the 'respectable' woman to ensure protection from the state and criminal justice agencies. If she has failed to meet these (highly subjective) standards then she may not merit protection. This also varies somewhat for working class and middle class women, with the latter being more likely to be treated with greater respect (Lees, 1997). This distinction is particularly evident in situations where women are judged to have put themselves 'at risk', where they may be assumed to have been 'asking for it' should they be raped or assaulted. However, contemporary culture is saturated with contradictory images of how women should and should not behave and continuums of behaviour that are deemed acceptable or unacceptable are not concisely distinguished.

The cultural messages directed at women, and indeed young men, are inherently mixed. Germaine Greer, in an article she wrote in *The Observer Review* (19 October, 1997) laments the expectations placed on women, particularly young women, to be active participants in a 'penetration culture' (Carol Smart, 1989, p. 27 had previously referred to a 'phallocentric culture'; both depict cultural norms organised around male desire and the primacy of male sexuality):

> The advertisements in such teen mags are for clothes, make-up, hair-dye, condoms – and pregnancy-test kits. This is the culture that the liberated young women of the Nineties are being inducted into. The statistics seem to show that they seldom succeed in getting the boys to use condoms. They are not in a position to demand even basic consideration from the men they are told to 'go out and shag' especially as it is understood that getting drunk is a prerequisite. Article after article offers ways out when you wake up after a drunken encounter to discover that the male totty you raced off with is an absolute plonker and the chances that you succeeded in getting him to use a condom are pretty slim.[12]

The onus on the woman to take responsibility for her behaviour and often for men's behaviour is reflected in law. Prior to the 1976 Sexual Offences (Amendment) Act, previous rulings had set standards for the recognition that rape could occur when a woman was asleep, or overcome by drink and therefore insensible. Consent was seen to be absent. In 1981, a ruling was made (see Temkin 1999) which required the jury to decide the issue of consent in individual cases. As a result, rape may not be acknowledged in cases where the woman has voluntarily taken alcohol or drugs. Indeed, under Scottish law, being intoxicated or drugged as a result of one's own behaviour only merits the charge of sexual assault or 'clandestine injury' (Scottish Parliament, 2001). This is viewed as an alternative charge to rape which, under Scottish law, is based on sexual intercourse 'by force and against her will'. 'Against her will' meant that if a woman was unconscious through alcohol, drugs or sleep, there was a need to show that she was unwilling to have intercourse prior to becoming unconscious.[13]

A woman who has been forced or duped into consuming alcohol or drugs by her assailant is seen differently and can legally be deemed to have been raped, although there are often difficulties in proving this (see Sturman, 2000). However, this does reinforce the distinction between the 'deserving' and the 'undeserving' victim. Again, however, the responsibility is on the woman to protect herself.

Current fears about 'spiked' drinks are evident on college campuses, pubs and clubs where women are warned to keep a close eye on their drinks. This reflects the contradictory images and messages aimed at young women in particular, about the need to be 'in control' while the cultural images of sociability (ladettes) encourage young women to 'keep up with the lads' in their drinking habits. Similarly, the focus of danger is directed away from men (as potential assailants) and alcohol (as a potentially intoxicating medium) towards the 'polluted' drink which the individual should be alert to and vigilant in their avoidance strategies.

Temkin (1999) in her literature review for the Home Office Sex Offences Review identifies that alcohol is often an issue in rape cases in two main ways. The 'victim' may 'lose her inhibitions' and consent to something she would not otherwise have agreed to, or she may have become drunk and unable to give consent (or presumably to have withheld it). As Temkin (1999, p. 93) notes, ' In a rape trial, the defence will always seek to argue that the former was the case'. She continues 'The position of the common law is that it is rape for a man to have sexual intercourse with a woman who is insensible through drink but there is a point well before this when (the victim) may be incapable of giving a true consent' (Temkin, 1999 p. 93). It is this continuum which makes it easier to represent the act of rape as 'bad sex' (for either or both individuals) in court, where the woman's claim of rape is disbelieved. This continuum can be likened to Liz Kelly's continuum of sexual violence (Kelly, 1988) and can be drawn upon to examine the extent to which women are expected to avoid any 'risky' or dangerous encounters by maintaining control over their own behaviour. Male responsibility and accountability are, of course, disengaged from this process.

'Danger' is clearly a subjective concept. Women have long been considered as 'dangerous' when displaying their active sexuality. Women who are 'out of control' are feared as irrational and viewed as in need of regulation (Hester, 1992; Faith, 1993; Karras, 1996). These images permeate the criminal justice system where women appear as both victims and lawbreakers (Carlen, 1985; Worrall, 1990; Kennedy, 1992; Lloyd, 1995). Indeed women are frequently punished by the courts for offences relating to drink and drugs (Carlen, 1998; Devlin, 1998; Social Work Services and Prisons Inspectorate for Scotland, 1998; Malloch, 2000; Prison Reform Trust, 2000). This has also been the situation historically.[14]

While 'laddish' behaviour by men is seen as 'fun' (i.e. exposing their backsides in public) this is seen very differently when women engage in lewd behaviour. Germaine Greer, writing in *The Guardian* (5 March, 2001) provides a graphic account of the 'Essex Girl' who is 'tough, loud, vulgar and unashamed. (...) when she and her mates descend on Southend for a rave, even the bouncers go pale'. Furthermore, 'the Essex girl neither knows – or cares – that she is the target of the nastiest kind of misogyny'.

Under patriarchal conditions, women need to be seen as controlled and regulated individuals and these images are evident when women enter the criminal justice system as both victims and offenders. Women who are out of control are a danger, they present a 'risk' – and this risk is to men, illustrated in the ongoing debates about 'date-rape'. The UK Men's Movement went as far as to submit a petition to the Scottish Parliament in 2000, calling for the creation of a new crime of False

Rape Allegation, which the Movement demanded should attract sentences of equal length to those facing men convicted of rape, which carries a maximum sentence of life imprisonment (*Scotland on Sunday*, 3 September, 2000).

The severity with which unsubstantiated or false accusations of rape are responded to is already reflected in law. In February 2000, Martin Garfoot was awarded £400,000 after a colleague falsely accused him of rape. This sum is considerably greater that the average £7500 women can expect to receive as damages following a rape (*The Guardian*, 10 February, 2000). In such contexts, portrayals of risk become ways of discounting rape, rather than mere measurements of responsibility.

'Risk' and the Removal of Consent

It subsequently follows that if any 'risk' that is experienced by a woman can be attributed to her own behaviour, then she is seen to be at fault. This is particularly applicable for women who use illegal drugs, have consumed 'excess' amounts of alcohol or are considered overtly sexual. In cases of rape, this endorses the ambiguity of the concept of consent. If consent is seen to be a process rather than an act, then in cases such as this, the woman loses her right, if not her ability, to withhold consent at the point of intoxication, and significantly, loses her entitlement to be believed. However, definitions of intoxication are often very broad and can extend from one drink to a state of collapse. This is re-presented as 'consent confusion' when cases where women are assumed to have taken some amount of 'risk' are dealt with by the criminal justice system. Such depictions operate as forms of social control, both formally and informally.

If force is used to determine rape (police and court emphasis on significant injuries) then physical injuries may not be immediately obvious. The focus is displaced from the man's behaviour to the woman's. She is required to prove that she did not consent to sex, and somehow to prove that she is 'truthful'. He, on the other hand, is only required to show that he believed that she had consented (and even if she didn't, it is sufficient that he genuinely believes that she did), with any use of drugs or alcohol by him often accepted as mitigating circumstances for his behaviour. It is this very issue that is so problematic when women are judged in court through the socially constructed meanings and broader value-laden assumptions attached to representations of 'risky' women.

Women are presented as responsible for their own behaviour and for the behaviour of the men around them. Those who take risks (drug users, sex workers, and women in general) are seen as responsible for the harm that their 'risky' behaviour may potentially or actually result in. The harm they experience is viewed as partially or wholly the result of their own risk-taking behaviour and it thus follows that the entire issue of consent is made increasingly ambiguous.

Women are expected to behave in a way which minimises risk (not going out alone, dressing modestly), they are assumed to have the ability to calculate potential risks and to mitigate those risks accordingly. At the same time, contemporary cultural images present a very different reality to what is fashionable and acceptable, social images which are not reflected positively in court. It is evident that any failure to curtail behaviour in response to perceived risk results in the woman herself being held as partially or wholly culpable for any harm that subsequently befalls her. This is further endorsed should the risk-taking behaviour be her own.

This can apply to drug use in the same way. Sturman (2000) argues that rape complainants should not be prosecuted for their use of 'recreational drugs' should it come to light that they have used drugs. However notions of being 'drugged' voluntarily are unlikely to receive a sympathetic hearing. Most women will be aware of this (through media reporting, women's own perceptions of criminal justice responses) and it may well reduce the likelihood that a rape will be reported.

The relationship between gender stereotypes and preoccupations with morality influence the treatment women receive by the criminal justice system. In cases of rape, the significance of consent is crucial. It often seems however, that the right to give/withhold consent is dependent on a woman's perceived respectability and conduct, mediated through relations of class, 'race' and sexuality (Skeggs, 1997). There is a clear integration of these notions of conduct and 'appropriate behaviour' into decisions and judgements made within the criminal justice system. This is reflected in the exclusion of certain groups from a clearly defined entitlement to state protection, on the basis of their supposed conduct.

For women, sexual history and behaviour is presented as a basis for judgement as is drug use and/or use of alcohol, despite legislative attempts to curtail this. Such judgements are indicative of the status of legal equality/citizenship as conditional, as a result of moral discourses and pathologies. The woman who behaves in such a way as to 'put herself at risk' becomes the focus of attention, deflecting the focus from male abuses of power and often trust, and whether or not consent was obtained. These flawed images and expectations are used to reinforce the male notion of a 'reasonable belief' and to deny women the right to refuse – and to be entitled to refuse – sex and more importantly to be believed. Social constructions underpinned by patriarchal structures lead to the devaluing of women's narratives. Women who are viewed as 'risky' are reconstructed in the lens of criminal justice, it is they who are interrogated and presented as the 'spectacle of degradation'. This process must be analysed and understood in order to highlight the inherently problematic way is which women's non-consent is portrayed and judged.

Notes

1 Thanks to Karen Corteen, Elizabeth Stanley, Helen Jones and Paul Reynolds for their constructive comments.
2 It is now recognised both socially and legally that men can be the victims/survivors of rape. However, for the purposes of this discussion the focus is on women.

[3] While the consumption of alcohol is legal, the acceptability of women drinking, and particularly of appearing to be drunk in public, is conditional. While use of alcohol does not merit the sanctions of illegal drug use, the moral approbation which can ensue has a similar basis and can lead to similar judgements being made about the woman. The similarity would appear to relate to the inappropriateness of women utilising chemical substances that can result in a perceived loss of control.

[4] Criminal justice agencies often facilitate such judgements by routine questioning processes and evidence collating procedures. In Finland, for example, police routinely measure the blood alcohol level of rape complainants.

[5] The Morgan Ruling provided a legal ruling that if a man honestly believes that a woman is consenting to sex, even if that belief may be unreasonable, then he is not guilty of rape.

[6] Images of women are frequently presented in the media, and more specifically in advertising, as the mothering 'homemaker' or as active, independent, glamorous individuals.

[7] Writers have debated whether it is a sign of resistance for women to display and exert their sexuality, whether it is evidence of incorporation into a patriarchal system, or if it indicates the occurrence of both simultaneously.

[8] It could be argued that Dumaresq underestimates the extent to which this impacts on other women, outside the court sphere, as a generalised form of social control.

[9] This has since been contested and on 26 March 2001, the House of Lords housed a challenge to this protection offered to the woman on the basis that it could breach the defendant's right to a fair trial under the Human Rights Act 1998 which came into operation in 2000. The Court of Appeal allowed this case to proceed on the basis that where the complainant and defendant had 'recently engaged in consensual sexual activity' any failure to bring this to the attention of the court and the effect it may have had on the defendant's state of mind, could 'unfairly distort the trial process' (*The Guardian*, 6 February, 2001).

[10] Recent changes are being introduced in Scottish courts (Scottish Executive, 2001).

[11] This varies in different international contexts. For example, in Scotland and Sweden definitions of rape are based on the use of *force* to make someone have sexual intercourse or engage in a comparable sexual act (see Anderson, 1999 for a detailed discussion of legislative differences between Sweden and England/Wales; see also Temkin, 1999 for other international comparisons).

[12] Calls to make the 'morning-after pill' available to women free of charge have led to considerable debates. High street fashion outlets sell 'morning-after' packs with an emergency make-up kit and Alka Seltzer for those nights when you just don't make it home!

[13] If no evident force was used to overcome unwillingness, then legally a woman could not be raped. In Sweden, a woman who is too drunk/drugged to give or withhold her consent to intercourse can not be raped, while in Tasmania a 'rational and sober person' is required to give their consent freely (Temkin, 1999).

[14] Joe Sim (1990) cites the Prison System Enquiry Committee of 1922, which noted that drunkenness with aggravation was the most common crime for which women were imprisoned, followed by prostitution.

Bibliography

Anderson, U. (2000), 'The Unbounded Body of the Law of Rape'. Paper presented at *Making Sense of Sexual Consent Conference*, Edge Hill, June 29-30.

Bartky, S. (1998), 'Foucault, Femininity and the Modernisation of Patriarchal Power', in Diamond, I. and Quinby, L. (eds), *Feminism and Foucault*, Boston: Northeastern University Press.

Beck, U. (1992), *Risk Society: Towards a New Modernity*, London: Sage Publications.

Birch, D. (2002), 'Rethinking Sexual History Evidence', *Criminal Law Review*, May, pp. 531-553.

Bordo, S. (1990), *Femininity and Domination*, New York and London: Routledge.

Bordo, S. (1997), '"Material Girl": The Effacements of Postmodern Culture', in Lancaster, R. and di Leonardo, M. (eds), *The Gender Sexuality Reader*, Routledge: New York and London.

Brown, B., Burman, M. and Jamieson, L. (1993), *Sex Crimes on Trial: The Use of Sexual Evidence in Scottish Courts*, Edinburgh: Edinburgh University Press.

Carlen, P. (1998), *Sledgehammer*, London: Macmillan Press.

Carlen, P., Hicks, J., O'Dwyer, J., Christina, D. and Tchaikovsky, C. (1985), *Criminal Women*, Cambridge: Polity Press.

Castel, R. (1991), 'From Dangerousness to Risk', in Burchell, G., Gordon, C. and Miller, P. *The Foucault Effect*, London, Toronto, Sydney, Tokyo, Singapore: Harvester Wheatsheaf.

Collier, R. (1995), *Masculinity, Law and the Family*, London and New York; Routledge.

Davenport-Hines, R. (1990), *Sex, Death and Punishment*, London: Collins.

Devlin, A. (1998), *Invisible Women*, Winchester, Waterside Press.

De Beauvoir, S. (1953), *The Second Sex*, London: Cape.

Dumaresq, D. (1981), 'Rape – Sexuality in the Law', *M/F*, Vols. 5 and 6, pp. 41-50.

Dworkin, A. (1987), *Intercourse*, London: Arrow Books.

Edwards, S. (1996), *Sex and Gender in the Legal Process*, Hampshire: Blackstone Press Ltd.

Ettorre, E. (1992), *Women and Substance Use*, Houndmills: Macmillan Press.

Faith, K. (1993), *Unruly Women*, Vancouver: Press Gang Publishers.

Franklin, J. (ed.), (1998), *The Politics of Risk Society*, Oxford: Polity Press.

Greer, G. (2001), 'Long Live the Essex Girl', *The Guardian*, 5 March.

Harris, J. and Grace, S. (1999), *A Question of Evidence?* London: Home Office Research Study 196, Home Office.

Heilbron Committee (1975), *Report of the Advisory Group on the Law on Rape*, Cmnd 6352 London: HMSO.

Hester, M. (1992), *Lewd Women and Wicked Witches*, London and New York: Routledge.

Home Office (1998), *Speaking Up For Justice*, London: Home Office.

Home Office (2000), *Setting the Boundaries: Reforming the Law on Sex Offences*, Volumes One and Two, London: Home Office.

Jordan, J. (2001), 'World's Apart? Women, Rape and the Police Reporting Process', *British Journal of Criminology*, Vol. 41, pp. 679-706.

Karras, R. (1996), *Common Women*, Oxford: Oxford University Press.

Kelly, L. (1988), *Surviving Sexual Violence*, Cambridge: Polity Press.

Kelly, L. and Regan, L. (2001), *Rape: The Forgotten Issue?* London: Child and Woman Abuse Studies Unit.

Kennedy, H. (1992), *Eve Was Framed*, London: Vintage.

Lees, S. (1997), *Ruling Passions: Sexual Violence, Reputation and the Law*, Buckingham: Open University Press.

Lloyd, A. (1995), *Doubly Deviant: Doubly Damned*, Harmondsworth: Penguin.

MacKinnon, C. (1987), *Feminism Unmodified*, Cambridge (MA): Harvard University Press.

Malloch, M. (1999), 'Drug Use, Prison and the Social Construction of Femininity', *Women's Studies International Forum*, Vol. 22, No. 3, pp. 349-358.

Malloch, M. (2000a), 'Caring for Drug Users? The Experiences of Women Prisoners', *The Howard Journal*, Vol. 39, No. 4, pp. 354-368.

Malloch, M. (2000b), *Women, Drugs and Custody*, Winchester: Waterside Press.

Mason, M. (1994), *The Making of Victorian Sexuality*, Oxford: Oxford University Press.

Millett, K. (1970), *Sexual Politics*, New York: Doubleday and Company Inc.

Mort, F. (1987), *Dangerous Sexualities*, London: Routledge and Kegan Paul.

Newburn, T. and Stanko, E. (eds) (1994), *Just Boys Doing Business?* London: Routledge.

Patton, C. (1990), *Inventing AIDS*, London: Routledge.

Prison Reform Trust (2000), *Justice for Women: The Need for Reform*, PRT.

Richardson, D. and May, H. (1999), 'Deserving Victims?: Sexual Status and the Social Construction of Violence', *The Sociological Review*, Vol. 47, No. 2, pp. 308-333.

Scottish Executive (2001), *Redressing the Balance: Cross-Examination in Rape and Sexual Offence Trials*, Edinburgh: Scottish Executive.

Scottish Parliament (2001), *The Legal Definition of Rape* Research Note: RN 01/46. Edinburgh: Scottish Parliament.

Seidler, V. (1989), *Rediscovering Masculinity*, London: Routledge.

Seidler, V. (1994), *Unreasonable Men*, London: Routledge.

Sim, J. (1990), *Medical Power in Prisons*, Milton Keynes: Open University Press.

Singer, L. (1993), *Erotic Welfare*, London: Routledge.

Skeggs, B. (1997), *Formations of Class and Gender*, London: Sage Publications.

Smart, C. (1989), *Feminism and the Power of Law*, London: Routledge.

Smart, C. (ed), (1992), *Regulating Womanhood*, London: Routledge.

Smith, J. (1989), *Misogynies*, London: Faber and Faber.

Social Work Services and Prisons Inspectorate for Scotland (1998), *Women Offenders: A Safer Way*, Edinburgh: The Scottish Office.

Soothill, K. and Soothill, D. (1993), 'Prosecuting the Victim? A Study of the Reporting of Barristers' Comments on Rape Cases', *The Howard Journal*, Vol. 32, No 1, pp. 12-24.

Stanko, E. (1985), *Intimate Intrusions*, London: Unwin Hyman.

Stanko, E. (1990), *Everyday Violence*, London: Pandora.

Sturman, P. (2000), *Drug Assisted Sexual Assault*, London: Home Office and Metropolitan Police.

Taylor, A. (1993), *Women Drug Users*, Oxford: Clarendon Press.

Temkin, J. (1996), 'Doctors, Rape and Criminal Justice', *The Howard Journal*, Vol. 35, No. 1, pp. 1-20.

Temkin, J. (1999), 'Literature Review of Research into Rape and Other Sexual Assaults', in Home Office (2000), *Setting the Boundaries: Reforming the Law on Sex Offences* Volume Two, London: Home Office.

Walby, S. (1990), *Theorising Patriarchy*, Oxford: Blackwell.

Walby, S. (1997), *Gender Transformations*, London: Routledge.

Weeks, J. (1995), *Invented Moralities*, Cambridge: Polity Press.

Wolf, N. (1991), *The Beauty Myth*, Toronto: Vintage.

Worrall, A. (1990), *Offending Women*, London: Routledge.

Chapter 8

Prostitution and Consent: Beyond the Liberal Dichotomy of 'Free or Forced'

Barbara Sullivan

Introduction

Most of the current literature on prostitution and consent tends to – wholly or largely – reject the possibility of consent to prostitution sex (for sex workers). This is not an entirely unreasonable position. Economic and other coercions clearly play an important part in sex work – as they do in most other forms of work. From a traditional liberal perspective, coercion or the lack of autonomy makes valid consent impossible. However, more attention needs to be paid to the power relations which both coerce sex workers *and* construct their consensual capacities. An examination of recent case law addressed to the rape of prostitutes demonstrates that consensual capacity can and has been constructed in this arena over the last twenty years. Where once a prostitute could not pursue a complaint of rape her non-consent can (under some circumstances) now be registered in law. This suggests that a positive consensual capacity might also be constructed. This chapter argues that certain conditions will maximise the freedom and thus, consensual capacity of sex workers. These include safe and legal working conditions, access to other employment options (or other forms of income support), access to the criminal justice system and a politico-legal system that encourages the development of new rights as workers for prostitutes.

In the literature on prostitution, most authors suggest that consent to prostitution is deeply problematic if not impossible. For radical feminists like Kathleen Barry (1995) or Sheila Jeffreys (1997), this is because prostitution is always a coercive activity. Under world-wide conditions of male domination and endemic male violence, women are forced into prostitution sex. From this perspective, no consent is possible and prostitution should be regarded as a form of rape. However, even those authors who do not toe the radical feminist line suggest that there is a particular problem with consent and prostitution (see Freeman, 1990; O'Connell Davidson, 1998; Cowling, 1998; Archard, 1998). They contend that a whole range of 'normal' conditions – for example, gendered/patriarchal power relations, poverty, drug addiction etc – can and do compromise the consent of prostitutes.

For some years I have practised a deliberate non-engagement with this debate. I have argued that it is more appropriate to talk about prostitution in the realm of work and economics (rather than sexuality). In the realm of work there is a general lack of freedom and choice for most workers. So, why would we want to insist on the particular relevance of the liberal language of choice and consent in the area of sex work? If prostitution is to be judged according to liberal ideals of unimpeded choice and consent, why should factory work or commercial fruit picking not be judged in the same way? Of course, if these forms of work were judged according to similar criteria, it is likely that they might *all* be seen as coercive and as an impingement on human freedom (this is certainly the position that Karl Marx takes). In relation to prostitution, my own position has been that it is more useful to focus on improving the working conditions – and choices – of those who earn their living in prostitution, particularly poor and marginalised women. A focus on sexual consent would appear to be far too abstract to be of use in this very concrete task.

However, I can now think of at least two reasons why this position should be reviewed and why it is necessary to re-consider the theorising of consent in relation to prostitution. First, if sex workers get raped (by their clients, employers, pimps or others) it is important that these assaults can be made visible in the criminal justice system. If the consent – and therefore, non-consent – of sex workers is deemed impossible, then they are going to be even less able than other women to pursue complaints of rape. My overall point, then, is that thinking about prostitution as a form of work should also admit a consideration of the limits of consent and of the lived experience of consent and non-consent in the practice of sex work. Second, I think a consideration of prostitution and consent is necessary because this sort of liberal language already structures a range of literatures and debates about prostitution (theoretical, legal, policy, human rights etc). This means that it is not possible to engage in international or local debates about prostitution – or to advocate for sex worker rights – without also engaging a liberal language of freedom and consent. Clearly, then, feminists need ways of talking about prostitution that, while engaged with the current field (and thus using a liberal language), maintain a critical engagement with liberal notions of freedom and consent. My overall aim in this chapter is to open up the whole field of prostitution and consent for such a post-liberal and feminist reconsideration.

This chapter is in three main sections. The first section analyses some of the current literature on prostitution and consent. It explores the range of positions – both feminist and non-feminist – which are presently circulating about consent and prostitution. The second section of the chapter examines one concrete arena where authoritative determinations of consent have been made in relation to prostitution; it considers a range of British, Australian, New Zealand and Canadian case law and the fate of prostitutes or ex-prostitutes who have made complaints of rape. In this section I locate and discuss a significant change that appears to have occurred over the last twenty years. In the past, prostitutes were virtually unable to make complaints of rape; as 'promiscuous' women, their claims of non-consent were deemed unreliable. Thus, sex workers were legally constructed as women who could not be raped because they were 'always consenting'. In the present day, however, sex workers are increasingly able to launch successful rape prosecutions. This change is clearly a result of feminist activism, rape law reform and improvements in social attitudes towards women working in prostitution. At a theoretical level, however, it calls attention to the importance of context and power relations in the construction of consensual capacity. Feminist contestations of gender power and a changing legal context have constructed the possibility of sex workers' non-consent. In what sort of context, then, might a positive consensual capacity be constructed? This question is explored in the third and final section of the paper. I argue that certain contexts will maximise the freedom and consensual capacity of sex workers. These include safe and legal working conditions, equitable access to the criminal justice system, the availability of other forms of employment or income support and a politico-legal system which encourages the development of rights as workers for prostitutes.

The Current Debate About Prostitution and Consent

There are a small number of authors and activists who argue that consent to prostitution is relatively straightforward and unproblematic. In the theoretical literature this extreme liberal position is most clearly represented by Ericsson (1980) who argues:

> If two adults voluntarily consent to an economic arrangement concerning sexual activity and this activity takes place in private, it seems plainly absurd to maintain that there is something intrinsically wrong with it (1980, pp. 338-339).

For Ericsson, 'satisfaction of sexual desires is...*intrinsically good*, love or no love' (1980, p. 341). In his view, (hetero)sexual intercourse is a need as natural as 'our cravings for food and drink'; 'coition resembles nourishment...if it can not be obtained in any other way it can always be bought. And bought meals are not always the worst' (1980, p. 355). From this essentialist foundation, Ericsson argues that prostitution is a 'contractual relation in which services are traded'. What the prostitute sells is not her body but sexual services; thus 'the kind of relationship that exists between prostitute and customer is one that we find in most service professions' (1980, pp. 341-353). For Ericsson, then, prostitution is a straightforward liberal negotiation in which consent is not problematised. There is a (liberal) assumption about the inherent freedom, autonomy and equality of the contracting parties. While Ericsson admits that prostitutes are subject to some 'economic exploitation' (which – in his view – need to be addressed via law reform and better attitudes to sex and prostitution), this does not appear to compromise his view of prostitution as basically a consensual transaction. Under conditions of 'sound prostitution', prostitutes will 'freely choose' their occupation 'in the same sense of "freely" as anyone's trade or occupation may be said to be freely chosen'. That is 'prostitutes will be no more economically exploited than wage workers in general' (1980, p. 366).

A broadly similar position has been advanced by some prostitutes' rights groups. Freeman (1990) argues that groups like COYOTE (Call Off Your Tired Old Ethics), CORP (Canadian Organisation for the Rights of Prostitutes) and the NTFP (National Task Force on Prostitution) are 'essentially liberal and only reluctantly feminist'. This is because they see prostitution as a voluntary exchange of sexual services for money and begin with a presumption of consent (Freeman 1990, pp. 87-88). It is clear, however, that not all prostitutes' rights groups adopt this liberal position (and Freeman acknowledges this). Over the last decade, sex worker advocates have developed much more nuanced accounts of consent particularly in the wake of new international debates about the distinction between free and forced prostitution, sex work and 'trafficking' for the purposes of prostitution (see Bindman 1997, p. 5, Doezema 1998, pp. 34-50). This trend has been particularly apparent among sex worker advocates outside the liberal strongholds of North America.

The liberal position on prostitution and consent has been thoroughly critiqued by the feminist theorist Carole Pateman (1983). Arguing against Ericsson, she contends that prostitution should not be regarded as a 'free contract'; it is a form of slavery because 'the prostitute cannot sell sexual services alone; what she sells is her body' (1983, p. 562). Pateman says that the representation of prostitution as a 'free contract' is simply another example of how women's sexual submission is confused with consent and free association. Prostitution, in her view, is 'unilateral subjection to sexual acts with the consolation of payment' (1983, p. 563). That is, payment occurs in place of real consent. In her 1988 text, *The Sexual Contract*, Pateman argues that the liberal language of contract and consent has been used – both historically and in the present day – to mask the operation of sexual power. It has led to an extension of men's freedom but to women's subordination (including in prostitution).

Pateman's analysis has been utilised by radical feminists such as Sheila Jeffreys (1997). However, the main intellectual sources for radical feminist accounts of consent and prostitution would appear to be Kathleen Barry (1979, 1995) and Catharine MacKinnon (1987, 1989). Radical feminists argue that 'consent is not a good divining-rod as to the existence of oppression, and consent to violation is a fact of oppression' (Barry cited by Jeffreys 1997, p. 135). Thus, even if women express their 'consent' to prostitution sex this will not be 'real consent'. Under world-wide conditions of male supremacy and endemic male violence, women are essentially unfree. They will therefore be forced into many abusive situations – including prostitution – in order to survive. It is men who are responsible for this abuse and women who are their 'victims'. Women and sex workers are likely to minimise or deny the abuse they have suffered as a way of coping. Thus, if sex workers offer any explicit 'consent' this should be regarded simply as a sign of their subjection because 'the ideology of consent has been used to obscure the real effects of women's multi-layered oppression on their ability to exercise individual free will' (Barry cited by Jeffreys 1997, p. 137). From the radical feminist perspective, then, prostitution should be addressed as rape and to do otherwise is to 'falsely' separate prostitution from rape. Note also that while the radical feminist approach delivers a trenchant critique of liberal approaches to freedom and consent, it also measures the presence or absence of these *by* a liberal standard. Thus, in order to register 'real' consent, women and sex workers need to be in a state of liberal freedom – that is, completely autonomous of power relations of any sort (economic, familial etc). So not only is this approach impractical (offering no concrete way of achieving 'real consent'), it also renders most women – and all sex workers – as *incapable* of 'real consent'. This means that no differences can be made visible between commercial and non-commercial sex, forced and consensual sex, prostitution and rape. As I argue below, the political ramifications of this sort of approach are extremely problematic.

The radical feminist approach to consent – and to prostitution – has been roundly criticised by a number of theorists (Archard 1998). Cowling (1998), for example, argues that the 'slope' on which prostitution sex is negotiated can vary enormously and that economic coercion is 'insufficiently powerful' in contemporary Britain to justify the (radical feminist) equation of rape and prostitution. However, in his view, the same cannot be said of poorer societies – 'In this context the slope on which sex is negotiated is so extreme as to render agreements suspect' (1998, pp. 118-119). Thus, while there may be room for consent to prostitution (where economic and other coercions are minimal), most prostitution in the world should probably be regarded as 'suspect' or non-consensual.

O'Connell Davidson (1998) is also critical of radical feminist accounts of prostitution. She argues that it is politically and morally 'dangerous' to regard prostitution and rape as the same thing. She says:

> If prostitution is rape, then it is logical to define prostitutes as women who are publicly available to be raped, and this is precisely the position taken by many police officers, judges and jurists around the world who refuse to accept that a woman who works as a prostitute can ever be raped' (1998, p. 122).

O'Connell Davidson's work presents an empirically rich account of the diversity of prostitution practices. She describes the very different situations of prostitutes working independently or in massage parlours in Britain, women confined to brothels in Turkey and the bar system in the Philippines. However, across all these different arenas, O'Connell Davidson remains 'firmly of the opinion that prostitute use (by clients) is an oppressive act' (1998, p. 121). What distinguishes prostitution from other oppressive acts (including, we might assume, rape) is a 'veneer of consent':

> prostitution is most usually organised as if it involved a mutual and voluntary exchange, and the various formalities which surround the prostitute-client transaction (such as payment and contractual specification...) make it possible for the client to read his sexual contact with the prostitute as consensual. Even where a client has negotiated with and made payment to a third party, rather than to the prostitute, he can tell himself that the woman concerned has agreed to work in this way. The veneer of consent makes prostitute use appear to be something quite other than rape or battery (1998, p. 121).

Thus it is the veneer of consent that constructs the particular power relation between prostitute and client and which distinguishes prostitution from rape. I think O'Connell Davidson is making an important point here about the discursive construction of prostitution and of the power relations under which many prostitutes earn their living. However, to talk about the 'façade' of consent implies that consent to prostitution can never be solid or 'real'. In effect, this means there is little real difference between prostitution and rape; both are non-consensual practices. Like the radical feminists, then, O'Connell Davidson measures real consent by a liberal standard. Real consent can occur only in the absence of power relations, that is when individual freedom and autonomy is untrammelled by power relations.

At the same time O'Connell Davidson says:

> For the actual participants in prostitution...the notion of contractual consent, and the formal and tacit rules which surround and produce it, does separate prostitution and rape at the level of subjective experience. When formally 'free' prostitute women say that they have been raped by a client, they rarely mean that he has simply failed to pay (1998, p. 121).

Thus the 'subjective experience' of sex workers is that they negotiate consent within a particular set of power relations and are able to distinguish between their 'consensual' work as prostitutes and non-consensual rape. This suggests to me, not that sex workers are the deluded victims of false consciousness (or the 'veneer of consent'), but that the nature of their consent – and their specific non-consent – needs to be taken more seriously by feminist and other theorists of prostitution.

Rape Law and Prostitution

The argument that real consent is impossible in prostitution clearly has some significant problems. In particular, from this perspective, it is impossible to distinguish between rape and prostitution. However, sex workers – like all people – need to be able to pursue complaints of rape within the criminal justice system. Several recent studies have indicated that sex workers may have a greater need; they suffer a high incidence of rape in their work but rarely report sexual assaults to the police (O'Connell Davidson, 1998). Sex workers fear that their complaints of rape will not be taken seriously by the police and/or that they will be charged for practising prostitution. There is clear evidence to support the reasonableness of these fears.

Until recently, there were also significant legal barriers that prevented sex workers from prosecuting their rapists. In nineteenth century British law it was recognised that a prostitute could be the victim of rape (Edwards, 1981, p. 62). However, as Edwards (1981) has argued, it was in fact very unlikely that a man would be convicted of rape on a woman known to be a prostitute. Despite various judicial utterances to the contrary, in the trial process the fact that a woman was a prostitute was seen as relevant to whether she had consented to the sexual intercourse or not. Before feminist-inspired reform of rape laws (in the 1980s in Britain, Australia and Canada), all rape complainants could be extensively cross-examined about their sexual reputation and experience. They could be asked about their sexual reputation and past sexual activities. They could be asked if they were 'promiscuous' and evidence of prostitution – of being 'a common prostitute' or 'of notoriously bad character' – was deemed relevant to the charge of rape (See *R v Bashir* [1969] 1 WLR 1303; *R v Krausz* (1973) 57 Cr App R 466; *R v Barker* (1829) 3 Cand P 589 [172 ER558]). The courts accepted that a lack of 'normal' female sexual morality made it more probable than not that a woman had *not* been raped but had consented to the sexual conduct under consideration. Evidence of prostitution was, therefore, deemed relevant in determining whether the complainant's denial of consent was worthy of belief – see *Thomas v David* (1836) 7 Car and P 350 [173 ER 156]; *Cargill* (1913) 8 Cr App R 224; *R v Richardson* [1969] 1 QB 299.

A case heard by the British Court of Appeal in 1973, *R v Krausz*, is broadly representative of this situation. The complainant in this case was a woman of 22 years of age who said she met the defendant in a public house called the Ducks and Drakes. After drinking 'three gin and tonics and one beer' and dancing with Krausz, the woman said she left alone to go home. Krausz followed, helped her locate a taxi and then joined her in the taxi. She told the driver her address but Krausz instructed the driver to go to Shepherds Bush where he persuaded the woman to go to his flat for a coffee. She claimed that soon after they arrived, Krausz forced himself upon her; when she pushed him off, he struck her 'some hard blows on the face'. When she regained her senses, she was naked, the lights had been turned off and the defendant was pushing her onto the bed. She said she allowed him to have sexual intercourse with her because she said she was terrified. Afterwards, when she tried to get away by going to the lavatory, the defendant hit her in the face again. The defendant claimed the woman had consented to sex, demanded money after the intercourse and refused to leave the flat until she had been paid, saying she would make trouble for him. He had then slapped her face. She had gone to the lavatory and fallen downstairs causing her nose to bleed. In cross-examination, however, Krausz admitted that he had been angry and had hit her in the face.

Krausz's conviction for rape was subsequently quashed by the British Court of Appeal although his conviction for 'assault occasioning bodily harm' was upheld. The Court found that certain evidence – which 'tended to show that the prosecutrix was a prostitute' – had wrongly been deemed inadmissible by the original judge. This evidence included the claim that the Ducks and Drakes was a public-house where prostitutes met customers and that the prosecutrix had previously engaged in sex for money. While, in general, a woman could not be cross-examined about sexual acts unrelated to the one under judgement (for example, with other men at other times), evidence that she had engaged in prostitution in the past constituted an exception to this rule. The Court of Appeal found that the prosecutrix in this case was 'not a prostitute in the strict sense' but was still 'a woman who is in the habit of submitting her body to different men, whether for payment or not'. The conviction was quashed, therefore, because:

> the prosecutrix was a woman of loose morals, in that she was not merely promiscuous, but was further in the habit of having sexual intercourse with first acquaintances for

money and that her practice included a first demand for payment after intercourse had taken place; that (this) evidence was, accordingly, relevant as tending to prove not merely consent, but consent in special circumstances and as being probative of the defendant's account of what had taken place (*R v Krausz* (1973) 57 Cr App R 466).

This situation has changed significantly in the last twenty years. In a number of western countries, working prostitutes and those with a history in the sex industry are now, under some circumstances, able to prosecute their rapists. While clear problems remain (see below), there are a growing number of cases where men have been convicted of raping prostitutes and ex-prostitutes. Evidence of prior history as a sex worker is no longer automatically relevant or admissible (in Australia see *Marotta v R*, *R v Maxwell*, *R v Lear*). Moreover, prostitutes raped in the course of practising their occupation have successfully pursued complaints of rape – in Australia (see *R v Lear*, *R v Myers and Ward*, *R v Hakopian*), in the United Kingdom (see *R v Charles Grenville Shaw*, *R v Arjumand Hussein*, *R v Kevin Davis*), in New Zealand (see *R v Clark*) and in Canada (*R v Gateman and Vansickle*, *R v Resendes*, *R v Dhak*, *R v Buteau*).

The Australian case of *R v Hakopian* is broadly representative of this recent trend. The defendant was charged with rape with aggravating circumstances, indecent assault with aggravating circumstances and kidnapping. The complainant was a 28 year-old woman, a drug addict who worked as a street prostitute in Melbourne. On the evening of the assault, she had serviced two previous clients before meeting the defendant. He said he had gone to St Kilda in order to solicit a prostitute. After they met, a discussion ensued about the type of sexual services being sought. The complainant quoted the defendant a price of $50 for oral sex and a further $40 for vaginal sex. He handed her $90 and they went in his van to a secluded laneway. Consenting intercourse took place at first. After 15-20 minutes of providing oral sex the complainant suggested the activity had gone on long enough and that it was apparent he was not going to ejaculate. At this point, the defendant forced her head back onto his penis and she resumed her actions for a short time. When she again discontinued and claimed that she had fulfilled her end of the bargain, he insisted that he was still 'owed' vaginal sex. He became aggressive and the complainant offered to return $50. She attempted to leave the van but he produced a knife and prevented this. The defendant then forced her to resume the oral sex. He later accused her of stealing his credit card and indecently assaulted her as she lifted her clothes to indicate that she was not hiding his credit card under her clothes. The complainant again attempted to leave the van and this led the defendant to drive off with her still in the vehicle. He drove dangerously fast around suburban streets, collided with another car and eventually ordered the complainant to get out of the car.

Hakopian was found guilty on all three counts. However, what is particularly remarkable about this case is that the complainant was a sex worker and a drug addict raped in the course of practising her occupation. It is only in the last two decades that such a complainant would have been able to get her case to court let alone achieve a successful prosecution. In *R v Krausz*, the victim was not even a 'prostitute in the strict sense' but her 'loose morals' were clearly seen to completely compromise her credibility as a witness. What made possible the legal visibility of the rape of a prostitute in *R v Hakopian*, were social changes (in particular, a feminist activism) which problematised the view that it was impossible to rape prostitutes and other 'bad' women. Changes to statutory law – and the erection of a so-called 'rape shield' – had also limited the use of evidence pertaining to sexual reputation and sexual experience (see Henning and Bronitt 1998). Thus, Hakopian's barristers were less able to use evidence of her occupation as a sex worker to undermine the credibility of the complainant's testimony.

This is not to suggest that most of the problems faced by prostitutes pursuing complaints of rape have been solved. As Henning and Bronnit (1998) have argued in the Australian context, rape shield laws may be structurally flawed in some jurisdictions and non-compliance with the law, commonplace. Hence, evidence of sexual reputation and experience will still sometimes be presented to undermine the credibility of rape complainants (a situation particularly affecting, we might assume, complainants who work as prostitutes). As Schulhofer (1998) has argued in the North American context, it is also clear that rape laws continue to require evidence of abnormal violence (in addition to that imposed by an act of non-consensual sex). In *Hakopian* it was clearly significant that the complainant received visible injuries and that the accused was witnessed driving in a dangerous manner. Moreover, Hakopian was given a lighter sentence than normal *because* his crime was directed at a prostitute. The judge argued that a very moderate sentence (three years and four months with a minimum term of sixteen months imprisonment) was justified because the victim was a prostitute. The likely impact on the victim was therefore 'much less a factor in this case and lessens the gravity of the offences'.

The Director of Public Prosecutions in Victoria later filed an appeal against the inadequacy of the sentence imposed suggesting 'that the judge had erred in placing too much weight on the fact that the complainant was a prostitute'. Consequently, the Victorian Supreme Court increased Hakopian's sentence to four and a half years with a two and a half year minimum term. However, the lower court judge was not found to be 'in breach of any sentencing principle when he dealt with the matter as he did on the basis that the complainant was a prostitute' (because his decision was seen to be in line with a previous judgement – *R v Harris*).

A significant debate then ensued about the correctness of this sentencing decision and, in a recent case in the neighbouring state of New South Wales, the Hakopian/Harris principle was explicitly rejected. The case of *R v Leary* involved the sexual assault of a street prostitute by three men in Kings Cross, Sydney. The victim was soliciting in the street when approached, abducted and raped by the men. Both the original judge in this case and the New South Wales Supreme Court specifically rejected the Hakopian/Harris principle in the sentencing of the men. Judge Kirby said: 'prostitutes, male or female, were entitled to the same protection of the law as any other citizen. They have their human dignity and their privacy and ought not unconsensually to have that invaded by fellow citizens, and that is what occurred in this case'. The Victorian Law Reform Commission has also recently rejected the sentencing principle in *Hakopian* and *Harris*. They argued that:

> If sentences are to be differentiated on the basis of the psychological effect of the crime on the victim, these assessments must be based on information about the actual impact of the offence on that particular victim, not simply on the fact that the victim comes from a particular social or occupational group... a court must not make any assumption about that impact that is based on the fact that the complainant was, or had been, a prostitute (LRCV 1992, pp. 5-8).

Rethinking Consent

So what does this legal story indicate? It certainly suggests a significant change has occurred over the last two decades in the legal position of sex workers. Prior to this sex workers were not able to pursue complaints of rape. Evidence of their occupation (or of a promiscuity 'resembling' prostitution) automatically cast any claimed non-consent into doubt, apparently for the remainder of one's life. Thus a sex worker's explicit non-consent was constructed as irrelevant. However, in the last decade in particular, some sex workers have been able to successfully pursue rape complaints (albeit in exceptional circumstances, where the assault has been accompanied by violence, and often with lesser sentences for their assailants). This means that sex workers have been (re)constructed as citizens with new rights and as subjects with new capacities – to make their non-consent visible and legally relevant. These capacities are not unreal or ideological. They are an effect of changing power relations and, in particular, of those feminist challenges to gendered power relations which led to both statutory reform and new social attitudes to prostitutes.

The capacity to register non-consent is, therefore, socially, politically and legally constructed as an effect of power relations. If this is the case then we might also look to a similar process in relation to consent. Liberals, and some feminists, see consent not as a process or construction but as a state which may be achieved only in the absence of power relations, that is when individuals are completely free and autonomous. Consent, then, becomes a marker of the distinction between legitimate and illegitimate exercises of power. The liberal approach to consent has recently been critiqued by feminists engaged with critical legal theory. Freeman (1990, p. 98), for example, argues:

> The fixed nature of liberal consent fails to appreciate the importance of social context and human mediation...we must look at the factors that minimise, undermine or extinguish it in order to work toward authentic consent.

For Freeman (1990, p. 96) consent is always 'relative and socially contingent'. Similar arguments have recently been made by both Cowling (1998) and Archard (1998). But Freeman also emphasises that we participate in processes which construct the meaning of consent in any given context. This suggests that processes of consent are always implicated in power relations.

The issues here might also be drawn out via an examination of Foucault on freedom, power and liberalism. Foucault (1982) argues that power is immanent in all relations and that it operates to construct the possibilities of human action, including 'free' action. Thus, 'at the very heart of the power relationship' will lie a 'recalcitrance of the will and the intransigence of freedom'. For Foucault, then, there is not an 'essential freedom' – untrammelled by power – which may be achieved (for example, in a Marxist, liberal, anarchist or feminist utopia). Instead, freedom is to be understood as a practice conducted in resistance to power, a process which involves an 'agonism' or 'reciprocal incitation and struggle' (Foucault 1982, pp. 221-222). Except in conditions of domination (see Hindess 1996, pp. 98-104), human subjects will be able to practice freedom. There is no reason why negotiations around sexual consent, including in prostitution, should not be seen as part of this.

To say that sexual consent will always be constructed within power relations is not to suggest the impossibility of 'real consent' but it is to call into question liberal consent (that is a consent negotiated in the absence of power). Women and men working in prostitution will not be without power or (in most cases) the freedom to resist power. Indeed, their capacities as subjects – including their capacity to practice freedom – will be constructed as an effect of power relations (Foucault 1982). Thus, in any specific culture, the meanings associated with prostitution will constitute the identity (and experiences) of being a prostitute. This process will not be seamless or completely predictable and there will usually be some room for sex workers and their advocates to resist. For example, emphasising the ordinariness of sex workers and the 'work' of prostitution can be used to resist the dominant representation of prostitutes as abnormal/bad women who deserve punishment. For feminists, this sort of approach – rather than an outright and principled opposition to prostitution – calls attention to the possibilities of resisting power and dominant representations of prostitution (Sullivan 1995). It looks to enhancing the freedom of sex workers – that is, their capacity to resist power. One way this might be pursued is by feminists working to establish conditions which support and enable the consensual capacity of sex workers.

What would these conditions look like? It is clear that sex workers who operate in an environment where there is a range of adequate employment options (or other adequate forms of income support) will have more consensual capacity. In an environment where prostitution is legal, prostitutes will not be subject to arrest, imprisonment and/or deportation simply for working in prostitution. They will also be more able to register their consent or non-consent if they are able to use the same official channels as other workers when sick, robbed, assaulted or mistreated. Moreover, if prostitution is addressed as a form of work then sex workers may also gain consensual capacity from the construction of new worker rights. Over the last two decades, for example, several Australian jurisdictions have moved to reform their prostitution laws and to extend the space of legal prostitution by permitting (and/or licensing) the establishment of legal brothels, escort agencies and street prostitution. The nature of these changes has differed significantly between jurisdictions (see

Sullivan 1997). In the Northern Territory brothels are outlawed but licensed escort agencies can operate openly and can legally employ sex workers to conduct 'out calls' at hotels and private homes. In order to fulfil the licensing requirements, escort agencies owners have to submit to the scrutiny of the Prostitution Control Board. This Board requires applicants for a license to submit copies of the 'Terms and Conditions' under which they employ sex workers. These written agreements set out the terms of the employment 'contract'; they specify, for example, the percentage of client fees that will go to the sex worker, the owners' responsibility to provide condoms and lubricants, and an employee sex worker's right to take sick leave, to refuse certain clients and to go to the police for assistance if clients assault them. The main advantage of this sort of employment 'contract' is that it institutes new employment conditions for sex workers and creates new (worker) identities for women working in prostitution. Traditionally, sex workers have not been regarded as workers but as criminals or 'fallen' women. Their wages and working conditions have not been subject to state or federal labour law or been the object of union scrutiny. Employers have been able to exploit their workers' illegal status and to manipulate the informal, verbal arrangement which have usually set the terms of the employment relation. While sex workers often earn much higher pay than other women workers they are 'normally' subject to stigmatisation, a lack of recourse to the law in cases of violence and fraud, and a lack of safe and healthy working conditions. The institution and supervision of employment 'contracts' in the legal prostitution industry represents a clear step forward for women employed in this area because it allows for the development of new rights for this group of workers. Thus, the legalisation of prostitution and the institution of labour rights for sex workers also allows for the development of consensual capacity.

Conclusion

Most of the current literature on prostitution and consent tends to – wholly or largely – negate the possibilities of consent to prostitution sex (for sex workers). This is not an entirely unreasonable position. Economic and other coercions clearly play an important part in sex work – as they do in most other forms of work in capitalist societies. From a traditional liberal perspective, coercion or the lack of autonomy makes valid consent impossible. However, more attention needs to be paid to the power relations which both coerce sex workers *and* construct their consensual capacities. An examination of recent case law addressed to the rape of prostitutes demonstrates that consensual capacity can and has been constructed in this arena over the last twenty years. Where once, by definition, a prostitute could not pursue a complaint of rape her non-consent can (under some circumstances) now be registered in law. This suggests that a positive consensual capacity might also be constructed. This paper argues that certain conditions will maximise the freedom and thus, consensual capacity of sex workers. These include safe and legal working conditions, access to other employment options (or other forms of income support), access to the criminal justice system and a politico-legal system that encourages the development of new rights as workers for prostitutes.

Acknowledgements

I would like to thank Julie Mackenzie for her excellent work as a research assistant in the preparation of this chapter. Also Mark Cowling and Paul Reynolds for comments on an earlier version of this chapter.

Bibliography

Archard, D. (1998), *Sexual Consent*, Boulder, Colorado: Westview Press.

Barry, K. (1995), *The Prostitution of Sexuality*, New York: NYU Press.

Bindman, J. (1997), *Redefining Prostitution As Sex Work on the International Agenda*, London: Anti-Slavery International.

Cowling, M. (1998), *Date Rape and Consent*, Aldershot: Ashgate.

Doezema, J. (1998), 'Forced to Choose. Beyond the Voluntary v Forced Prostitution Dichotomy', in Kempadoo, K. and Doezema, J. (eds.), *Global Sex Workers. Rights, Resistance, and Redefinition*, New York: Routledge, pp. 34-50.

Edwards, S. M. (1981), *Female Sexuality and the Law*, Oxford: Martin Robertson.

Ericsson, L. O. (1980), 'Charges Against Prostitution; An Attempt at a Philosophical Assessment', *Ethics*, Vol. 90, pp. 335-66.

Freeman, J. (1990), 'The Feminist Debate Over Prostitution Reform: Prostitutes' Rights Groups, Radical feminists and the (Im)possibility of Consent', *Berkeley Women's Law Journal* Vol. 5, pp. 75-109.

Henning, T. and Simon, B. (1998), 'Rape Victims on Trial. Regulating the Use and Abuse of Sexual History evidence', in Esteal, P. (ed.), *Balancing the Scales. Rape, Law Reform and Australian Culture*, Annandale (NSW): Federation Press.

Hindess, B. (1996), *Discourses of Power: from Hobbes to Foucault*, Oxford: Blackwell.

Jeffreys, S. (1997), *The Idea of Prostitution*, Melbourne: Spinifex Press.

Law Reform Commission of Victoria (1992), *Rape: Reform of Law and Procedure: Supplementary Issues Report No. 46*, Melbourne: Law Reform Commission of Victoria.

MacKinnon, C. (1987), *Feminism Unmodified*, Cambridge: Harvard University Press.

O'Connell Davidson, J. (1998), *Prostitution, Power and Freedom*. Ann Arbor: University of Michigan Press.

Pateman, C. (1983), 'Defending Prostitution; Charges Against Ericsson', *Ethics* Vol. 93, pp. 561-65.

Schulhofer, S. (1998), *Unwanted Sex. The Culture of Intimidation and the Failure of Law*, Harvard: Harvard University Press.

Sullivan, B. (1995), 'Rethinking Prostitution', in Caine, B. and Pringle, R. (eds) *Transitions. New Australian Feminisms*, Sydney: Allen and Unwin, pp. 184-197.

Sullivan, B. (1997), *The Politics of Sex. Prostitution and Pornography in Australia Since 1945*, Melbourne: Cambridge University Press.

Chapter 9

The Construction of Sexual Consent in Male Rape and Sexual Assault

Philip N. S. Rumney and Martin Morgan-Taylor

Introduction

The issue of sexual consent as it applies to male victims of rape and sexual assault has been given only limited attention within the legal literature. By contrast the social science literature on the nature and meaning of male victimisation has significantly expanded in more recent times (Isely, 1998). Within the legal literature attention has been given to issues such as the policing of male rape (Gregory and Lees, 1999); sentencing (Rumney and Morgan-Taylor, 1998); the use of 'Male Rape Trauma Syndrome' (Rumney and Morgan-Taylor, 1997b); and the legal definition of rape and its enforcement (Morgan-Taylor and Rumney, 1994; Rumney and Morgan-Taylor, 1997a). Several criminal justice-related agencies have also given specific attention to the issue of male sexual victimisation. Recently, the Sentencing Advisory Panel published its advice to the Court of Appeal concerning the revision of the *Billam* (1986) 8 Cr App R (S) 48 rape sentencing guidelines. The Panel recommended that any revised sentencing guidelines should generally apply equally to cases of male and female rape (Sentencing Advisory Panel, 2002, para. 12). The Metropolitan Police Authority report on rape investigation and victim care has also made specific reference to the needs of male victims (Metropolitan Police Authority, 2002), as has the recent joint inspection report on the investigation and prosecution of rape (HMCPSI/HMIC, 2002, pp. 35-36). Despite these developments, male sexual consent and the problem of male rape and sexual assault continues to be neglected (Rumney, 2001a). The need for legal analysis of sexual consent in this context is emphasised by the increased number of males reporting rape to the police and by the fact that so little of the discussion on the nature and dynamics of sexual consent has actually considered the problems faced by adult male victims (Estrich, 1987; Schulhofer, 1998).

This chapter will examine the relationship between rape supportive attitudes and the prevalence of male rape, male sexual victimisation within the prison system and the construction of male sexual consent in the courtroom. It will also explore the similarities and differences between male and female rape and make suggestions for future research.

Defining Male Rape and Sexual Assault

In order to assess the construction of sexual consent in cases of adult male rape and sexual assault it is essential that these terms are defined. Section 1 of the Sexual Offences Act 1956, as amended by s. 142(1) of the Criminal Justice and Public Order Act 1994 provides: 'It is an offence for a man to rape a woman or another man.' Section 142(2) provides:

> A man commits rape if:
>
> (a) he had sexual intercourse with a person (whether vaginal or anal) who at the time of the intercourse does not consent to it: and
> (b) at the time he knows that the person does not consent to the intercourse or is reckless as to whether the person consents to it.

This reform was a significant departure for the domestic law on sexual offences as previously 'much of the legislation concerning sexual crimes involving males [was] designed to regulate consensual homosexual behaviours rather than to protect males from sexual victimisation' (Adler, 1992, p. 120). Prior to the 1994 Act the crime of non-consensual penile-anal penetration was designated as non-consensual buggery for which there was no consent defence (s. 12 Sexual Offences Act 1956; *Gaston* (1981) 75 Cr App R 164). This offence was attenuated with the decriminalisation of homosexuality in 1967. Section 1 of the Sexual Offences Act 1967 provided that two consenting males of or over the age of 21 could commit buggery in private.[1] At the same time however, Parliament reduced the maximum sentence that could be imposed for non-consensual buggery that had previously been life imprisonment. The 1967 Act introduced a series of penalties depending upon the age of the participants, rather than the issue of consent. The maximum penalty was life imprisonment where the assailant was over 21 and the victim under the age of 16, or ten years where the assailant was over 21 and the victim over the age of 16. The maximum sentence of life imprisonment was retained for all cases involving the buggery of a woman of any age. In 1994 this structure was changed with the recognition of male rape. The offence of buggery was retained with a maximum sentence of life imprisonment where buggery is committed against a victim under the age of 16 or with an animal. A five year sentence is imposed where the assailant is over 21 and the victim under 18, with a two year sentence in all other cases.

Under existing law not all non-consensual sexual assaults perpetrated against males are legally classified as rape. Non-consensual oral sex, anal penetration with objects or parts of the body other than the penis are all classified as indecent assault, as are instances where a woman forces a man to penetrate her (Rumney and Morgan-Taylor, 1997a). The Home Office review *Setting the Boundaries* has recommended that non-consensual oral sex should be defined as rape, and that other non-penile penetrative sex acts should continue to be excluded from the legal definition of rape (*Setting the Boundaries*, 2000; Rumney, 2001b). These recommendations have recently been incorporated within the government White Paper *Protecting the Public* (Home Office, 2002a), and the Sexual Offences Act (2003).

Consent in the Law of Rape

The leading modern authority on consent in rape is the Court of Appeal decision in *Olugboja* [1981] 3 All ER 443. Here, it was held that there was a distinction between consent and submission and that in determining the issue of consent, the emphasis must be on the victim's state of mind, that is, did the victim consent to the act of sexual intercourse or did they merely submit? The Court also abandoned any suggestion that consent in rape could only be vitiated by force, fear or fraud. Dunn LJ stated: 'It is not necessary for the prosecution to prove what might otherwise appear to have been consent was in reality submission induced by force, fear or fraud, although one or more of these factors will no doubt be present in the majority of cases of rape' (p. 448f). In so doing, Dunn LJ appeared to recognise that consent might be vitiated by blackmail, moral and economic pressures (pp. 446d-e, 448j-449a).

In the later case of *McAllister* [1997] Crim LR 233, there was an attempt to provide additional guidance to jurors on the distinction between consent and submission. Brooke LJ stated:

> The circumstances of a possibly reluctant consent may be infinitely varied, and on each occasion the jury has to decide whether an alleged agreement to a sexual act may properly be seen as a real consent or whether it should be regarded as a submission founded on improper pressure which this particular complainant could not reasonably withstand from this particular defendant.

Recent authorities have also made clear that there is no requirement that the victim of rape communicate his or her non-consent. In *Malone* [1998] 2 Cr App R 447, Roch LJ made clear: 'the *actus reus* is complete if there is sexual intercourse without consent and the demonstration or communication of the lack of consent is not part of the *actus reus*' (p 457f). Earlier authorities had suggested that there was a need for resistance on the part of the victim (*R v Howard* [1966] 1 WLR 13). However, such a view cannot be taken to represent the current law. The approach set forth in *Malone* can be justified on the ground that it recognises the reality of rape. As will be apparent in some of the cases discussed later in this article, some victims of rape are so terrified by their experience they are unable to resist their attacker. A resistance requirement would therefore deny these victims protection from the criminal law.

This 'fleshing out' of the notion of consent by the courts was developed in three cases involving female victims. In principle, however, there appears to be no particular reason why the existing law of consent cannot be equally applicable to instances of male rape – certainly no detailed counter-argument has been made within the scholarly literature thus far. However, it has been suggested that: 'to refer to "non-consensual buggery" as the same as female rape (i.e. that the crime is gender neutral), is to render invisible the gendered power relations between men and women through men's sexual violence to women' (Gillespie, 1996, p. 151). The issue of 'gendered power relations' may be relevant when considering men as the perpetrators of sexual violence and women as victims and may help to explain why and how rape occurs. However, in terms of male *victimisation* it is evident that males, like females, experience a wide range of pressures and coercion that operate to vitiate consent. Indeed, Gillespie does not explain why her notion of 'gendered power relations' in relation to male sexual violence against women, should not be relevant to the analysis of male sexual violence against other males. In terms of how consent is constructed in the trial process, there are, as will become apparent later in this article, significant similarities between male and female rape. Yet, it would also be naïve to assume that notions of consent, submission, acquiescence or agreement will be constructed in identical ways in all cases of male and female rape. There are likely to be differences, for example, because facts and defence tactics vary between cases, just as there are likely to be significant differences between cases where the victims are of the same gender. Such issues will be discussed later in the chapter.

The Prevalence of Male Rape and Sexual Assault

It has only been in the last decade that reliable data has been produced on the prevalence and nature of adult male rape and sexual assault in this country. In a recent study of 2,474 males in England, Coxell et al. found that 2.89% of research participants reported non-consensual sexual experiences as adults, that is, over the age of 16. Most of the assaults did not involve penetrative sex acts, although some males did report being raped or subjected to other non-consensual penetrative sex (Coxell et al., 1999 p. 848). In an earlier study of homosexual males, Hickson et al. found that a significant number were victims of rape or sexual assault. Of the 930 homosexual males from England and Wales who were surveyed, it was found that 257 (27.6%) reported that they had been 'subjected to non-consensual sex at some point in their lives'. Of these, it was found that 45.2% (99) had been anally penetrated, and in another 11 cases (5%) there had been an unsuccessful attempt at anal penetration (Hickson et al., 1994 p. 286). Amongst those men who were over the age of 21 years when the assault took place 65.4% (52 cases) were assaulted by 'regular or casual sexual partners' (Hickson et al., 1994 pp. 288). The Coxell et al. study also highlighted the prevalence of rape amongst homosexual men, finding that men who had experience of consensual sex with other men were six times more likely to have been raped or sexually assaulted as adults than males who had not (Coxell et al., 1999 pp. 849). Despite the previous lack of information on the prevalence of male rape and sexual assault in this country, such research has not necessarily been welcomed. In response to what would later become the Coxell et al. study, Gillespie argued that because not enough was known about female rape, this study was 'a matter of some concern' since no equivalent survey of female rape was being conducted (Gillespie, 1996 p. 161). This reaction is unfortunate given that the Coxell et al. study is the only general population survey of men's non-consensual sexual experiences carried out in Europe,[2] and only the second such general population survey anywhere in the world. The other study was of both males and females in the United States (Sorenson et al., 1987).

These victimisation surveys provide crucial evidence on the prevalence of male rape and sexual assault. By contrast, evidence from official criminal statistics has historically been limited. This is partly a result of the fact that most men do not report experiences of rape and sexual assault. From the limited samples available it has been suggested that between 2% and 20% of males report rape and sexual assault to the police (Hillman et al., 1990, p. 503; Mezey and King, 1989, p. 207; Huckle, 1995, p. 190). Reasons for this low reporting rate vary. It has been suggested, for example, that some men fear that the police will be unsympathetic (McMullen, 1990, pp. 114-115; Scarce, 1997, ch. 10, pp. 216-218). Other men do not disclose their experiences because they feel that they will not be believed, that they are in some way to blame for the assault or are too embarrassed to report (Huckle, 1995, p. 190). It has also recently been suggested that some men may fail to report to the police because they do not realise their experiences constitute a crime (HMCPSI/HMIC, 2002, p. 35). Improvements in the police response to male rape and sexual assault however, has led to a significant increase in reports (Gregory and Lees, 1999, ch. 5; see Table 9.1 below) and may also reflect a 'changing social climate' of which the legal recognition of male rape is a part (Forman, 1982, p. 236; Crome et al., 1999). While the overall number of reports is significantly lower, this year-on-year increase in reporting of male rape mirrors the substantial percentage increase in reports involving female victims since the 1980s (Harris and Grace, 1999). The latest criminal statistics, which were released in 2002, indicate that reports of male rape constitute 8% of all recorded rape offences (Home Office, 2002).

Making Sense of Sexual Consent

Table 9.1 Recorded Rapes of Males in England and Wales

Year[3]	Number of Reports[4]
1995	150
1996	231
1997	347
1997/1998	375
1998/1999	502
1998/1999	504
1999/2000	600
2000/2001	664
2001/2002	735

In addition to statistics on male rape, the figures for 2001/2002 indicate that there were 3,613 recorded offences of indecent assault upon a male, compared with 21,765 upon a female (Home Office, 2002). Though females still make up the vast bulk of rape and sexual assault victims, this combination of victimisation surveys and criminal statistics suggests that a significant number of males have experience of sexual assault, though a minority of these are victims of rape. It is also worth noting for the purposes of this study that criminal statistics include reports of rape irrespective of the victim's age, in other words, they are not an exclusive measure of adult victimisation.

Despite the increase in the number of cases of male rape being reported to the police, the level of under-reporting may have serious implications for issues of sexual consent. It can be argued that unless men are held to account for the acts of sexual violence they perpetrate the acceptability of sexual coercion will remain unchallenged and ingrained within our society. Low reporting levels mean that it is difficult to engage legal mechanisms of accountability, while the inability of the criminal justice system to convict a greater number of rape defendants who are prosecuted undoubtedly add to a societal culture that excuses or normalises male sexual violence. Unsurprisingly, such issues have been raised in the context of the rape of women. Repeated studies have shown that very high numbers of women report non-consensual sexual experiences (Hall, 1985; Painter, 1991; Russell and Bolen, 2000; Myhill and Allen, 2002), most do not report to the police (Myhill and Allen, 2002) and a significant number of males also admit they might carry out a rape if they thought they could get away with it (Russell and Bolen, 2000, pp. 4-5, 260-261). Linked to these findings is the fact that many men, as well as some women, seek to minimise, excuse or normalise sexual violence committed by males (Finkelhor and Yllo, 1985, ch. 4; Ward, 1995; Burton et al., 1998). Such attitudes may also help to explain the extent of rape within the gay community (Hickson et al., 1994; Scarce, 1997; Coxell et al. 1999). Indeed it has been noted that:

> Fantasies of the sexually forceful man, the pleasure of 'being taken', and the excitement of power-driven sex are very common in gay culture and pornography. All these collective sexual fantasies normalise sexual abuse and rape of gay men by gay men, providing motivation, justification, and normalisation for the assault. It is difficult to see how a climate of intolerance towards sexual aggression can be achieved when sexual aggression is one of the mainstays of collective sexual fantasies' (Hickson et al., 1994, p. 293).

Societal attitudes toward male sexual violence take various forms and in this respect there appears to be significant overlap between male and female rape. In the context of female rape Stanko has argued that '[many] of the traditional assumptions about women's and men's sexuality ... continue to hold a powerful grip in our understanding about rape' (Stanko, 1985, p. 36). She argues that society's understanding of rape is shaped by beliefs that blame women for their victimisation and excuse men for committing acts of sexual violence, for example, by claiming that males have difficulty controlling their sex urges. Victim-blaming attitudes towards cases of male rape also appear quite common (Eigenberg, 1989; Pelka, 1995; Scarce, 1997, ch. 10, pp. 216-218; Human Rights Watch, 2001; Robinson, 2002). In the context of female rape, victim-blaming can involve finding fault with a complainant's lifestyle, dress and behaviour (Burton et al., 1998). Similarly, Fred Pelka, a victim of male rape, has recalled the reaction of one of the police officers who was assigned to his case: 'The bad cop asked me why my hair was so long, what was I doing hitchhiking at seven o'clock in the morning? Why were my clothes so dirty? Did I do drugs? Was I a troublemaker?' (Pelka, 1995, p. 252). Another victim who was raped by a man with a gun has recalled being asked by police officers: 'Do you have any friends who are gay?' and then 'Why didn't you just run? He wouldn't have shot at you, it's hard to hit a moving target. I would have just started running. Why didn't you run?' (Scarce, 1997, ch. 10). In a discussion of the situation prior to 1990 McMullen has also argued that '[male] victims are rarely believed [by the police], are assumed to be gay and thought to be responsible for not being man enough to fight off an attacker' (McMullen, 1990, p. 114). In the context of female rape Stanko has argued that societal attitudes 'focus on women's behaviour as an explanation of men's behaviour' (Stanko, 1985, p. 36). This linkage is equally applicable to male rape where, on the basis of the limited evidence available, there appears to be a pre-occupation with the complainant, in particular his sexuality. Such victim-blaming attitudes appear to result in a failure on the part of the police to take action or to act in a supportive manner (McMullen, 1990; Temkin, 1999). Pelka, for example, was told by one police officer: 'that the best thing to do would be to pull up my pants "and forget it ever happened"'. The other complainant told a police officer that he was unsure as to whether he wanted to press charges and was told: 'well, we're not your taxi service'. Ultimately, these societal attitudes serve to excuse male sexual violence, or at least leave it unhindered by legal or social sanction. Given the prevalence of male sexual violence and rape supportive attitudes this should be a matter for serious concern.

The Dynamics of Non-Consent in Male Rape and Sexual Assault in Prison

One of the most problematic areas of male sexual consent relates to the rape and sexual assault of incarcerated males. Much of the evidence on prison rape comes from the United States, where a number of detailed studies have been conducted on the problem. The earliest comprehensive study was of male rape and sexual assault within the Philadelphia prison system that produced a 'conservative estimate' of 2000 sexual assaults during a twenty-six month period. This represented around 3% of the inmate population (Davis, 1973). Other studies suggest that the rape and sexual assault of males within prison is extremely rare (Lockwood, 1980; Tewksbury, 1989). More recent research from the United States has found a much greater rate of non-consensual sexual contact. For example, Struckman-Johnson and Struckman-Johnson found that 21% of those inmates questioned in seven prison facilities had been coerced into unwanted sexual contact (Struckman-Johnson and Struckman-Johnson, 2000). The US courts have also, on occasion, commented upon the prevalence of sexual assault in specific institutions. In the Supreme Court decision of *United States* v *Bailey* 444 US 394, 421(1980). Blackmun J. commented: 'a youthful inmate can expect to be subjected to homosexual gang rape his first night in jail, or it has been said, even in the van on the way to jail.' In an earlier case before the same court, Stevens J., in describing the conditions of one Arkansas prison noted: 'Homosexual rape was so common and uncontrolled that some potential victims dared not sleep, instead they would leave their beds and spend the night clinging to the bars nearest the guards' station': *Hutto* v *Finney* 437 US 678, 681 n 3 (1978). One of the reasons for the large discrepancies in the number of rapes and sexual assaults found within the research literature is that a variety of definitions and research methods have been adopted (Coxell and King, 2000). It is undoubtedly also the case that rape and sexual assault varies between institutions and is dependant upon such factors as the nature of inmate accommodation, the type of offender imprisoned and staff attitudes to sexual violence (H. In addition, some studies have adopted a particularly narrow definition of rape or sexual assault (Tewksbury, 1989; McGurk et al., 2000) and have failed to explore particularised notions of consent and coercion within prison settings (McGurk et al., 2000). However, there have also been criticisms of the methods adopted in studies that have found higher rates of victimisation (Coxell and King, 2000, p. 87-88). One prison researcher has noted that 'Prison and jail conditions vary widely over place and time. Concerning rates of victimisation, it is quite improper to extrapolate from one prison to another' (Lockwood, 1994; Human Rights Watch, 2001, pp. 138-139). Consequently, while the rate of victimisation may be difficult to discern, the studies that have been conducted thus far can provide useful information on the nature of sexual consent within a prison setting. These studies also provide a useful comparator when considering the British evidence on rape and sexual assault in prison.

The only large-scale study of prison sexual assault conducted in Britain found that of 979 incarcerated 15-17 years olds, it was found that 0.3% of participants 'had observed someone doing something against their will' and another 0.3% said that 'they had been made to do something sexual against their will in the previous month' (McGurk et al., 2000 pp. 15). Although 8% of participants 'had heard of inmates doing something sexual against their will', the study authors argued that: 'Many of the incidents that inmates merely heard about ... appeared to refer to the same incident. There is no way of determining that they occurred. The fact that descriptions are similar may simply reflect the fact that rumours of the "Chinese Whispers" variety occur' (McGurk et al., 2000, p. 15). On the surface, these findings are encouraging in that they suggest low levels of rape or sexual assault amongst the group under study. This rate may be partly explained by the age of the participants and the fact that most inmates were located in individual cells (McGurk et al., 2000, p. 10) which may reduce opportunities for sexual assaults to take place.

There are, however, a number of reasons why these findings should be questioned. These reasons tend to centre on the issue of consent. First, there are problems with the questions the inmates were asked. The study did not provide a standard definition of 'against their will', which might be interpreted by some participants to include only those incidents accompanied by the use of violence. Interpreted in this way, the behaviour being measured is potentially narrower than definitions of rape or sexual assault used in a number of other studies of prison rape and sexual assault (Struckman-Johnson and Struckman-Johnson, 2000). Another problem is that interviewees were asked how many incidents of sexual assault they had experienced 'in the previous month', thereby excluding any incidents that occurred prior to this period. This study also failed to recognise the various forms of coercive behaviour that can exist within institutional settings. It did not ascertain whether economic coercion was used to pressure inmates into sex, or whether the atmosphere of tension and bullying also reported by McGurk et al. undermined notions of consent. Second, the study did not attempt to ascertain the level of 'consensual' homosexuality that may mask coerced behaviour (Davis, 1973; Wooden and Parker, 1982). Rather, the authors of this research state: '[m]any comments were made to the effect that anyone trying anything sexual would themselves be the victim of threats and physical attacks' (McGurk, et al., 2000, p. 17). The problem with this assertion is that the evidence from US prison studies is that homophobic attitudes are rife. This antagonism towards homosexuality, however, does not prevent rape and other sexual assaults from occurring (Human Rights Watch, 2001). Consequently, McGurk et al.'s willingness to assume that the inmates' dislike of homosexuality makes acts of sexual violence unlikely may be misplaced, and indicates a lack of understanding of the dynamics of prison sexual assault. The researchers were also of the view that it was unlikely that interviewees would be reluctant to disclose incidents of rape or sexual assault: '[T]here was no indication that inmates were shy to respond [to questions involving non-sexual bullying] ... There is no obvious reason why this should change when sexual behaviour is examined rather than violence' (McGurk et al., 2000, p. 17). However, if one examines the research literature it is found that many men are reluctant to disclose experiences of rape or sexual assault. These assaults raise issues of humiliation, male inadequacy, homosexuality, embarrassment and self-doubt, which other acts of violence may not (McMullen, 1990; Scarce, 1997; Mezey and King, 1992; Huckle, 1995). In addition, if it is a fact that there was widespread antagonism toward those who engaged in sexual behaviour with other inmates, as this study claims, it is foreseeable that at least some interviewees might as a consequence be unwilling to disclose non-consensual experiences because many male victims mistakenly believe themselves to be gay (Mezey and King, 2000). Finally, the rate of disclosure might also be affected by the study methodology. An attempt by the researchers at gathering information by the use of questionnaires was dropped as a result of the lower than expected rate of inmate literacy (McGurk, 2000, p. 9). It has been argued, however, that the use of interviews in order to get information about 'potentially shameful or embarrassing material' may result in fewer reports of sexual assault (Coxell and King, 2000, p. 85). The Human Rights Watch study also suggests 'differing methodologies-inmate interviews vs. anonymous surveys ... may also account for much of the inconsistency in the findings [of US prison rape studies]' (Human Rights Watch, 2001, p. 138).

The complexities of male sexual consent within prison have not always been recognised within the academic literature. Stanko, for example, has claimed that 'the studies of [sexual assault] in prison show that rape is, in fact, a rarity there. Sexual exploitation and coercion is far more common' (Stanko, 1990, pp. 123-124). Even if one ignores the way in which Stanko discounts the possibility that the sexual exploitation or coercion of males in prison could constitute rape, a number of studies have recognised that the notion of sexual consent within prison is fraught with difficulties. In addition to the problems of getting inmates to admit to sexual victimisation (Davis, 1973), researchers have also repeatedly acknowledged the difficulties of distinguishing between consensual sexual behaviour and contact that results from coercion. Davis for example, noted:

in our study of sexual assaults we excluded any that were cases of truly 'consensual' homosexuality. Nonetheless, it was hard to separate consensual homosexuality from rape, since many continuing and homosexual liaisons originated from a gang rape, or from the ever-present threat of gang rape. Similarly, many individual homosexual acts were possible only because of the fear-charged atmosphere. Thus, a threat of rape, expressed or implied, would prompt an already fearful young man to submit (Davis, 1973, p. 228).

Similarly, in their study of prison sexual assault, Wooden and Parker found that inmates utilised various strategies to avoid being repeatedly victimised or raped. They noted that the best survival strategy for vulnerable inmates 'is to "hook up" with a jocker, an inmate dominant enough to protect them' (Wooden and Parker, 1982, p. 18). Research from the United States suggests that prison rape victims are frequently younger males with so-called 'feminine' characteristics such as being slightly built, having long hair or a non-aggressive personality. They are also normally serving their first prison sentence and lack knowledge of how the prison system works and are victimised primarily because of their susceptibility to violation and control. As with the Wooden and Parker study, a recent Human Rights Watch report on prison rape and sexual assault in the United States found that it is common for a male who has been raped or 'turned out' to meet the subsequent sexual demands of the rapist in return for protection from other inmates. Some males are also locked into a form of economic extortion by other inmates. This can occur where the perpetrator provides: 'food, drugs, or other desirable items to a potential victim, allowing the victim to build up a debt. At some point, the perpetrator insists that the debt be repaid via sexual favours. Again, if the victim hesitates, the perpetrator may make it terrifyingly clear to him that refusal is not an option, but this last step is often unnecessary' (Human Rights Watch, 2001, p. 89; Struckman-Johnson et al., 1996).

These strategies suggest that at least some apparently voluntary homosexual relationships within prison occur as a result of coercion and exploitation. Since several studies of prison rape and sexual assault have not attempted to measure the extent of such relationships (McGurk et al., 2000), it may be that the rate of victimisation has been under-estimated. In addition to this problem, the recent Human Rights Watch report noted that within the prison setting notions of consent and coercion 'are extremely slippery':

> Prisons and jails are inherently coercive environments. Inmates enjoy little autonomy and little possibility of free choice, making it difficult to ascertain whether an inmate's consent to anything is freely given. Distinguishing coerced sex from consensual sex can be especially difficult... For some prisoners, the atmosphere of fear and intimidation is so overwhelming that they acquiesce in their sexual exploitation without putting up any obvious resistance (Human Rights Watch, 2001, pp. 83, 84).

There are other significant difficulties in attempting to ascertain the sexuality of either the victims or perpetrators of prison sexual assault. For example, a person's sexuality cannot necessarily be subject only to the polar definitions heterosexuality and homosexuality. While polymorphic sexuality (bisexuality) had been addressed by Freud *inter alia* as a developmental phase through which children grow to a state of post-pubertal heterosexuality (Evans, 1993, ch. 6), the more recent Kinsey seven point sexuality scale showed that only 50% of the population claimed to be exclusively heterosexual throughout adult life, 4% was exclusively homosexual, leaving 46% with tendencies to both sexes (Kinsey et al., 1948). Later work has suggested that sexuality is not static, fixed at birth or in childhood, but instead can be fluid throughout life (Klein et al. 1985, cited in Evans, 1993, p. 156). In addition, it has been argued that those who perpetrate acts of male rape and sexual assault may prefer to identify themselves as bisexual, rather than as homosexual in a homophobic world (Russell, 1984, p. 72). Consequently, the dynamics of male rape and sexual assault within the prison environment mean that researchers must take great care in their use of research methods and in the conclusions that they draw from interviews with research participants. The problematic notion of consent within prison settings creates specific difficulties for the legal process. As will be discussed later in this chapter, outside of assaults that involve significant levels of additional violence and resulting physical injury, male victims of rape or sexual assault may have difficulty explaining the nature of coercion within the prison system.

The problem of prison rape and sexual assault in the United States is made more difficult because of the unsupportive attitudes of prison officials that results in few inmates having the confidence to report their victimisation (Davis, 1973, pp. 226-227; Human Rights Watch, 2001). In the United States it is clear that the authorities have generally failed to deal with either overt acts of rape, or more subtle forms of sexual threats and coercion (Robertson, 1999; Struckman-Johnson, 1996; Dumond, 1992). In reality there appears to be little regard for the sexual autonomy of inmates and their right to be free of violence and sexual coercion. The Human Rights Watch report found that prison staff will:

> frequently ... intimate that any sexual contact that may have occurred was consensual ... gay inmates, or those perceived as gay, often face great difficulties in securing relief from abuse. Unless they show obvious physical injury, their complaints tend to be ignored and their requests for protection denied' (Human Rights Watch, 2001, p. 152).

Other research indicates a willingness amongst prison staff to blame prisoners for their own victimisation. In a study of correctional officers' attitudes to prison rape, Eigenberg found that of 166 officers, 46.4% 'believe that inmates deserve rape if they have consented to participate in consensual acts with other inmates' (Eigenberg, 1989 pp. 50). The attitudes of prison officials are doubtless informed by societal attitudes that fail to recognise the seriousness of male rape and sexual assault. For example, research suggests that students are prepared to attribute more blame and pleasure and less trauma to a male rape victim who is gay, than one who is heterosexual (Mitchell, 1999). Such attitudes are particularly problematic because of the large numbers of gay inmates who claim to have been raped or sexually assaulted (Human Rights Watch, 2001). These attitudes are also in evidence amongst criminal justice officials and impact upon law enforcement and the protection of vulnerable males (Scare, 1997; Human Rights Watch, 2001). A recent example of an alleged failure by prison authorities in the United States to protect a vulnerable inmate has arisen from legal proceedings brought by Roderick Johnson, a gay black prisoner who is suing several Texas prison officials. Johnson claims that members of the prison classification committee, which decides whether prisoners should go into protective custody, told him: 'If you want to be a ho, you'll be treated like a ho' and 'You ain't nothing but a dirty tramp. Learn to fight or accept the fucking' (Robinson, 2002).

The Construction of Male Sexual Consent in the Courtroom

Under English law the parameters of rape are primarily defined by the complainant's consent or non-consent to sexual intercourse. This is problematic because the notion of consent tends to 'shift the inquiry from the behaviour of the accused to that of the victim.' (Hall, 1988, p. 74). As a consequence the behaviour, words and state of mind of rape complainants are central to the trial process (Lees, 1997; Temkin, 2000; Ehrlich, 2001). Until recently there has been little legal analysis of the treatment of male victims during court proceedings (Rumney, 2001a). The aim of this section is to discuss defence attempts to construct consent in four cases of male rape and sexual assault.

Carol Smart has argued that in rape trials women's experiences of non-consensual sex are 'disqualified' by the trial process and the notion of 'phallocentrism' is validated (Smart, 1989, p. 35). She describes phallocentrism as 'a culture which is structured to meet the needs of the masculine imperative' (Smart, 1989, p. 27; Carrington and Watson, 1996). Women's experiences are disqualified in a number of ways: through the use of language in the courtroom; the re-interpretation of women's words or behaviour, and through the legal definition of rape which, for example, states that a man cannot be guilty of rape so long as he has a genuine belief in consent, no matter how unreasonable that belief might be (*DPP* v *Morgan* [1975] 2 All ER 347). This analysis might also be applied to the problem of male rape and sexual assault. The question that arises is whether the mechanisms in the trial process that are used to disqualify women's experiences of rape are also utilised in cases involving male victims. This analysis potentially challenges a strain of feminist thought that is unwilling to recognise the significance of male victimisation. For example, it has been argued by some feminist commentators that rape should primarily be viewed as an issue of male violence against women, that the gender neutral rape laws 'cover-up for the gendered reality that ... [is] ... really going on' (Naffine, 1994), that favouring rape laws that recognise the rape of males is part of a backlash against feminism (Rush, 1990) and that once adopted gender-neutral law have 'fallen into disrepute' (Fennell, 1988, 117). Such approaches however, fail to recognise the complexities of sexual violence and the empirical fact that men victimise other men as well as women. The critics of gender neutrality also fail to identify any substantive harm that is done to women or the enforcement of rape law by recognising male victimisation and make factual claims that have little, if any, supporting evidence (Rumney and Morgan-Taylor, 1997a, pp. 205-218). Ultimately, male and female rape are substantially linked to male violence and domination (Graham, 2001) and 'can both be seen as forms of promoting dominant hegemonic heterosexuality' (Gregory and Lees, 1999, p. 131; Lees, 1997, ch. 5). Indeed, perhaps the most obvious linkage of male and female rape within an analytical framework of male violence and domination is in the context of the research literature on why men commit acts of rape (Rumney and Morgan-Taylor, 1997a). In both male and female rape, sexual aggression is a means of establishing or re-affirming the rapist's sense of self-image and manhood. In his small study of male rapists, for example, Groth found that for some: 'The victim may symbolise what they want to control, punish and or destroy – something that they want to conquer and defeat. The assault is an act of retaliation, an expression of power, and an assertion of their strength or manhood' (Groth, 1979, p. 126; Groth and Burgess, 1980; Scare, 1997, ch. 7). In the context of female rape the motives of punishment or control have been repeatedly identified (Groth, 1979, ch. 2; Levine and Koenig, 1980; Scully, 1990, chs 4 and 6). In cases of relationship or marital rape some men will rape in order to establish authority over their partner, or to punish her for some transgression (Groth, 1979; Finkelhor and Yllo, 1985, ch. 4; Russell, 1990, ch. 11). There is evidence of male rape being committed for similar reasons (Groth, 1979; Human Rights Watch, 2001). There is also evidence in cases of both male and female rape that some men strongly associate sex and the use of violence (Scare, 1997, p. 71; Levine and Koenig, 1980; Groth, 1979). As such, it can be argued that male rape and sexual assault further illuminates the combination of societal attitudes and practices that normalise, justify or excuse male sexual coercion. The question for this analysis is whether the legal process serves to validate such coercion by 'disqualifying' the experiences of men and thereby emphasising the 'masculine imperative'. It is to this issue that we now turn.

Early anecdotal evidence from cases involving buggery or indecent assault, suggested that: 'many male victims report that the treatment they receive by the police and in the courts is worse than the offence itself' (McMullen, 1990, p. 114). Despite this, it has been suggested that some male rape complainants have been treated more favourably by the courts then their female counterparts. This claim was made after the first case of male rape to come before the courts in this country resulted in a man being sentenced to life imprisonment for the attempted rape of an 18 year-old male (Rumney and Morgan-Taylor, 1996a). It was subsequently suggested that had the victim been female, then the defendant would not have received such a lengthy sentence (*The Guardian* June 12, 1995). It is clear however, that the sentence in *Richards* was entirely consistent with the sentencing principles developed in cases of female rape (Rumney and Taylor, 1998; *Richards* [1996] 2 Cr. App. R. (S.) 167). It was then argued by Helen Codd that there were 'anomalies between the experiences of the male complainant in *Richards* and the experience of many female complainants of rape'. It was also claimed that 'the complainant's sexuality does seem to have been in question, and there appears to have been little suggestion that the complainant consented' (Codd, 1996). It is apparent however, that these and other claims were inaccurate and not based upon the transcript of the case, which Codd seemingly had not read (Rumney and Morgan-Taylor, 1996b; Rumney, 2001a).

Similar attempts by scholars in the United States also fail for want of reliable evidence. In what is otherwise an excellent study of research on rape and sexual abuse in the United States, Russell and Bolen note that 'the law has consistently refused to effectively protect women who are subject to threats of death ... let alone threats of rape, particularly if the perpetrator is the woman's husband' (Russell and Bolen, 2000, p. 68). In the accompanying footnote they cite what they claim is an example of 'the sexist application of the law' in which they make reference to the arrest and conviction of a man who stalked and threatened to rape the film director Stephen Spielberg (Russell and Bolen, 2000, p. 86 n 2). They do not explain why the Spielberg case is an example of sexist application of the law, they provide no details of the case; of the stalking-related offence for which the defendant was convicted or how their claim stands against cases where men who have stalked and threatened women have been the subject of criminal sanction (Meloy, 1998). Neither do they consider the poor treatment male victims of sexual assault have experienced at the hands of the criminal justice system in the United States (Pelka, 1995; Scarce 1997). Without systematic and detailed analysis any suggestion that male victims of rape, or threats of rape, receive preferential treatment has to be considered with caution as the available evidence does not support such arguments.

This section will proceed by examining issues of consent that arise in three cases of male rape and one case of non-consensual buggery. This analysis draws upon two trial transcripts, along with interviews with two male rape complainants conducted by one of the authors of this article. The two male rape complainants were interviewed by phone and letter between July 1999 and April 2000. The first interviewee (SB), was raped by a former work colleague after a party in 1998. As they walked down a street together the assailant made suggestive comments to SB and tried to kiss him. When SB recoiled, he was punched and forced into an alleyway. At this point SB was terrified and simply froze as he was raped and indecently assaulted. The attack lasted for several minutes before the assailant ran away. SB reported the attack to the police within hours of its occurrence and his assailant was later convicted of rape. The second interviewee (DD), was attacked in 1997 whilst he walked home from a night out with friends. When walking near an embankment, DD was approached by a man whom he vaguely knew. He was threatened with violence, punched and then raped. Whilst DD did make some attempt to resist during the attack, he was physically weaker than his assailant. The attack left DD with bruising to his face and back. DD delayed reporting to the police for two days in an attempt to 'forget what had happened'. DD's assailant was later convicted of rape.

Constructing Consent From Complainant Behaviour

It is not uncommon for defence lawyers to utilise 'rape myths' as part of their strategy during cross-examination. In this context the term 'rape myth' is used to denote misconceptions concerning the behaviour of rape victims during and following an attack (Burt, 1991; Torrey, 1991). Several of the trials under review illustrate the use or influence of such myths. The use of rape myths also forms part of a wider strategy in which the defence 'set up expectations in the jury as to what happens in a "real" rape and then asks them to judge their cases with reference to that' (Adler, 1987, p. 118). This section will consider the use of myths and expectations in the context of the behaviour of male complainants.

The first case to be considered is that of *R* v *Armstrong* (Unreported, 10 April 1995, Weymouth and Dorset CC). In *Armstrong* the complainant, who was a remand prisoner, claimed to have been sexually assaulted in his prison cell by another inmate. During the alleged assault the complainant was fondled and had an erection, he was anally penetrated and was then allegedly forced to anally penetrate his assailant. When the assault began, the complainant allegedly told his assailant to stop, but claimed that he was too frightened to say or do anything else. At trial much of the cross-examination centred upon the complainant's physical response to the alleged assault. The defence suggested that by having an erection he gave the impression of 'being keen' and 'sexually aroused' and that he gave the 'signal' and 'message' that he was interested in sex. Following a defence submission, the trial judge directed the jury to acquit on the grounds that there was 'not sufficient evidence' of the complainant's non-consent and that the jury could not properly conclude that the defendant either knew or was reckless as to the complainant's consent.

The following exchange illustrates how the defence in *Armstrong* attempted to undermine the complainant's claim of being frightened by reference to his physical response and failure to physically resist:

Q: You did not struggle at all, or give him any physical indication that you did not want to do it?

A: No. I didn't struggle at all, no.

Q: You did not try and push him off ...

A: No, I just lied.

Q: Or put your hand over your penis ...

A: No, I just lied there like a plank of wood.

Q: Did you?

A: Yes, I froze – I was scared.

Q: Scared?

A: Scared, frightened ...

Q: You got an erection right at the beginning, did you not? ...

A: When he started playing with me ...

Q: All right. So you say: 'Stop,' according to you?

A: Yes.

Q: He plays with your penis and you get an erection – yes?

A: Yes.

Q: Although you are so scared you cannot say anything you get an erection?

A: Yes.

Q: Not a half-hearted one – a full-blown one, no doubt?

A: Yes, I suppose so.

There is a growing body of evidence that some male victims of rape or sexual assault experience involuntary physical responses during rape, involving erection and even ejaculation (Sarrel and Masters, 1982; Seabrook, 1990; McMullen, 1990). Involuntary physical responses during rape can worsen victim trauma and have also been noted in cases of female rape (Sarrel and Masters, 1982; Lees, 1997, pp. 117-119). In a small-scale study of male rape victims and offenders Groth and Burgess found that:

A major strategy used by some offenders in the assault of males is to get the victim to ejaculate. This effort may have several purposes. In misidentifying ejaculation with orgasm, the victim may be bewildered by his physiological response to the offence and thus discouraged from reporting the assault for fear his sexuality may become suspect. Such a reaction may serve to impeach his credibility in trial testimony and discredit his allegation of nonconsent. To the offender, such a reaction may symbolise his ultimate and complete sexual control over his victim's body and confirm his fantasy that the victim really wanted and enjoyed the rape. This fantasy is also prominent in the rape of females' (Groth and Burgess, 1980, p. 809).

Groth has also argued that male rapists tend to misinterpret such physical responses as 'indicating that the victim is homosexual and, therefore, a legitimate victim' (Groth, 1979, p. 127). The reaction of the complainant in *Armstrong* to the alleged assault and the defendant's eventual acquittal in this case can be linked to a point made by Smart that 'the denial of enjoyment [in rape trials] is vital because if there is any suggestion that she might have taken pleasure, then lack of consent becomes immaterial' (Smart, 1989, p. 36). Indeed, there is evidence of a failure by the judiciary to recognise that a sign of sexual consent and pleasure in a male, may also result from fear or stress. In *Armstrong* the trial judge stated: 'Is [having an erection] consistent with being scared? Can one really behave like that while really scared ... This is something that ... requires some very active expenditure of energy.' Similar comments were made in an earlier divorce case in which a man claimed that his wife used violence in order to force him to have sexual intercourse. In considering whether the husband had voluntarily engaged in sexual intercourse with his wife, Willmer LJ stated:

It might be otherwise in the case of a wife, but in the case of a husband who has sexual intercourse it can only be said of him that what he does he does on purpose, and that sexual intercourse with his wife must be a voluntary act on his part ... However much the husband disliked what he was doing, he did in fact voluntarily have intercourse with his wife ... (*Willan* v *Willan* [1960] 2 All ER 363).

It could be argued that the prosecution case in *Armstrong* was undermined by a conception of consent that fails to emphasise the notions of mutuality and communicative sexuality. That is, a sexuality in which there is agreement between sexual partners and a respect for sexual integrity (Schulhofer, 1990; Remick, 1993; Lacey, 1998; Rumney, 2001b). The prosecution case in *Armstrong* may therefore have been strengthened by the implementation of proposals in *Setting the Boundaries* (2000, para. 2.10). The Review recommended that consent be defined in terms of 'free agreement' and that jurors be given instructions that the absence of physical or verbal resistance on the part of the complainant does not necessarily provide evidence of freely given consent (2000, para. 2.11.5). On the basis of the complainant's testimony in this case the defendant did not seek the complainant's agreement to sex, and that even if there was an agreement, it would not appear to have been entered into freely. It should also be recalled that this alleged assault took place in prison. As noted earlier, prisons are intimidating environments where the notion of freely given consent must be considered with care. In contrast, the defence in *Armstrong* suggested that a verbal agreement was unnecessary and that the complainant had communicated consent by having an erection and failing to resist. At one point the complainant was asked whether having an erection gave the impression of being 'keen' or 'sexually aroused':

A: Yes, it most probably would have given that impression, but then he should have waited for my permission first.

Q: In what form – sort of written permission, or asked you, or what?

A: Like, he should have asked me, shouldn't he, really, to find out if I really wanted it, but I didn't, did I?

Q: Instead you rolled over and presented your backside to him, did you not?

A: Yes.

Q: Again, a signal that you agreed this to happen?

A: I didn't agree – I just done what he said because I was scared, mate, all right?   ...

Q: In what way did you show you were frightened and scared? ... You were not crying or saying: 'No, don't,' or whimpering, or anything like that, were you? ...

A similar strategy, involving the use of complainant behaviour, was adopted in the case of *R* v *Richards* (Unreported, 4 May 1995, Central Criminal Court), where an 18 year-old male was the victim of an attempted rape and indecent assault in a park. Having commented on the fact that the complainant went to a park that he did not know late at night, defence counsel then proceeded onto what happened after the attack. The implication being that if he had been assaulted, the complainant would have behaved differently:

Q: When you left, you left together, there was no violence, there was no threat?

A: That's all wrong ...

Q: He did not hold you?

A: No ...

Q: Were there people around in Marylebone Road at that time? I am not suggesting it was crowded.

A: No.

Q: But there were people?

A: A couple of people ...

Q: Did you try and run away at any stage?

A: No.

Q: He might have stopped you. I am not suggesting, if you ran, he would not try, but did you try, even try, to run away?

A: Well, I tried to walk off after the incident into a building, but he said, 'Where are you going?' That's the only time ...

Q: He said, 'Where do you think you are going?' or words to that effect, all right? He did not prevent you from going, did he?

A: He said it threateningly.

Q: He did not grab you and pull you along, did he?

A: No.

Q: The fact is, you never tried to get away? That is the truth?

A: I didn't know where I was in the park ...

Q: Is the answer to my question that, along the Marylebone Road, the main road, you did not even try to get away?

A: I was scared.

Q: Yes?

A: Of running away?

Q: You may have had reasons, according to you. I suggest there might have been other reasons ... (inaudible) ...

In the case involving DD he was questioned by the defence on why he had talked to his assailant after the rape. At one point defence counsel suggested that was an unusual thing to do. When interviewed DD stated: 'I couldn't really explain why I did that. I suppose I needed to [do] something to try and pacify him. I don't think you can ever tell how someone will react until it happens.' The behaviour of SB was also the focus of defence questioning. Defence counsel noted that SB was physically bigger than his assailant. SB recalled: 'The barrister asked me why I hadn't thrown him off, why I hadn't resisted or really struggled ... what he [the barrister] didn't understand is the fear. I couldn't move ... I tried to block it out.' It is clear that the responses of many male victims are influenced by the fear that sexual assaults generate. In *Armstrong* the fear to which the complainant repeatedly referred may have been worsened by the fact that the alleged assault took place in a prison cell where there was no immediate means of obtaining help.

During cross-examination the complainant pointed out in response to questions about why he had not resisted that: ' ... he was doing 15 years, and he could have done anything to me and just not cared because he's in there for most of his life anyway'.

In cases of female rape evidence suggests that defence lawyers will use a woman's lack of physical resistance during rape as evidence of consent (Lees, 1997). Indeed, it is sometimes argued that a lack of physical injury is inconsistent with being raped (Adler, 1987, pp. 113-116). Likewise, in *Armstrong* the lack of physical resistance on the part of the complainant was repeatedly stressed by the defence as the following questions indicate:

> Q: You did not struggle at all, or give him any physical indication that you did not want to do it?
>
> Q: You did not, for example, make his entry of your body more difficult, by gritting your buttocks, or anything like that, did you?
>
> Q: But you did not try and prevent him entering you by gripping your buttocks together, or folding your legs, or turning over, or anything like that, did you?

This questioning along with the complainant's earlier testimony that he was too scared to resist are good examples of the kinds of expectations that are placed on complainants by the defence (Ehrlich, 2001). Such expectations may also be shared by jurors. There is evidence that jurors are more reluctant to convict in rape cases where there is little evidence of violence or resistance (Adler, 1987, pp. 119-120) and attitude surveys suggest that some people are less unwilling to believe that a woman has been raped where she has failed to resist their attacker (Feild and Beinen, 1980, p. 50-51; Ward, 1995). Yet, such expectations can be contrasted with evidence that some male rape and sexual assault victims are so fearful during the assault that they are unable to resist and simply freeze in terror or disbelief (Mezey and King, 1992; Huckle, 1995).

Constructing Consent from Sexual History Evidence

The use of sexual history in cases of male rape and sexual assault has been a long-standing problem in the United States. The use of sexual history evidence by the defence has led state courts to extend restrictions (so-called 'rape shield laws') on the use of such evidence in cases involving female complainants to their male counterparts (see for example, *Commonwealth* v *Quartman* 312 Pa. Super. 349; 458 A.2d 994 (1983)). Such decisions have been justified on the basis that they will encourage reporting to the police and restrict irrelevant defence questioning. It has also been claimed that '[i]nformation about the victim's sexual orientation and history should be minimised in order to prevent anti-gay bias from being directed at either the victim or the defendant' (Kramer, 1998, p. 331). However, the use of 'rape shield laws' in cases of male rape has also been the subject of criticism. It has been argued for example, that some of these laws may unjustly prevent the disclosure of the complainant's homosexuality where the defence claims that there was a consensual sexual relationship between the defendant and complainant (Hill, 1998).

The use of sexual history evidence has also arisen in some cases of male rape and sexual assault in this country (Mezey and King, 1992, p. 207). In *Richards* the complainant was asked several questions about his sexual history without gaining the permission of the trial judge as statute law stipulates (Rumney, 2001a, p. 209). He was asked 'Were you gay?' and he was also asked: 'You tell us that never anything like this had happened to you? No such experience before, either willingly, or unwillingly with anybody, right?' Reference was also made to the complainant's room-mate at the hostel (who was gay). The following extract sets out how the defence developed two themes. The first concerned homosexuality and the second was the suggestion that the complainant had sex for money:

Q: Did you become aware that amongst the people [at the hostel] there were people who were ... gay?

A: I wasn't one of them, but yes ...

Q: Was [your roommate] gay?

A: Yes ...

Q: So you know what being gay means?

A: Yes.

Q: Undoubtedly, you know that, if I may use the phrase, 'The gay scene,' do you understand what I mean by that?

A: Yes.

Q: In London, it is quite a large one? Different places, but quite a large one?

A: Yes.

Q: Were you gay? I am not suggesting you are, I am asking?

A: No ...

Q: Do you know, or have you heard the phrase, 'Rent boy'?

A: Yes, I have heard the phrase, yes.

Q: What do you understand by the phrase, 'Rent boy'?

A: It's a person who takes money for sexual.

Q: For sexual favours?

A: Yes.

Q: You were aware of that?

A: Yes I am aware of that ...

It has been suggested that in cases of male rape 'presumptions about male sexuality will no doubt be implied only where the complainant is homosexual' (Edwards, 1996, p. 363). This would appear not to recognise the kinds of tactics used in *Richards* where the defence will suggest that the complainant is homosexual in order to make more credible the argument that he consented. Such tactics clearly do not rest upon a requirement that the complainant be homosexual. Indeed, in other cases it is possible that a victim may be bisexual, or uncertain of their sexuality. Such uncertainties might be used by the defence to suggest that the complainant, rather than being a victim of rape, had willingly engaged in sex, but then felt shame or regret which led to an allegation of rape. Similar tactics were used in *Richards* and the case involving SB which are discussed in the next section. The defence may also link involuntary physical responses to homosexuality on the basis that they could only occur when a man consents to sex. In such circumstances a complainant's homosexuality may be assumed and it is therefore essential that the prosecution offer expert evidence to explain that such reactions do not necessarily result voluntarily.

False Allegations and a Consent Defence

While there can be no doubt that men sometimes fabricate allegations of rape or sexual assault, there is very little evidence as to the scale of this problem (Hays, 1992; 'Man "lied" about rape': 1992). It is also evident from the prison research discussed earlier that some officials are prepared, without good reason, to label complaints as false (Human Rights Watch, 2001, p. 152). Indeed, in the Roderick Jones case that was discussed earlier, one member of the prison classification committee stated that there was a note in Johnson's file labelling him as a 'manipulator who makes false complaints'. Other officials also described his allegations as 'unfounded' (B. Robinson, 2002).

In arguing that a complainant did consent to sexual intercourse, the defence in each of the cases under review also provided reasons why the complainant would fabricate an allegation of rape or sexual assault. In *Armstrong* the defence suggested that the complainant had made a false complaint by claiming that he used his alleged victimisation to gain a more lenient sentence when the charges for which he was on remand came before the courts. In the case involving SB it was suggested that he had fabricated the rape allegation because he was terrified that his partner would discover he had consensual sex with another man. In *Richards* the defence suggested that the complainant made the false allegation because he was ashamed of having sex for money:

> Q: [you] became ashamed of it quickly, and could not really believe it of yourself, and you thought this was a way of getting it out of your system, and to ascertain to your own self, in your own mind, that in fact it was not your fault?

Another defence strategy is to link the post-rape behaviour of the complainant to the claim that the allegation is fabricated. In cases of female rape for example, it is claimed that a delay in reporting to the police is inconsistent with being raped, as a genuine victim would report immediately (Adler, 1987, pp. 116-118). In the case involving DD his delay in reporting to the police was linked to a claim by the defence that the allegation had been fabricated. During cross-examination the defence suggested that the delay in reporting could be explained on the basis that the allegation took time to 'think-up'. DD also recalled repeatedly being asked 'if this happened, why didn't I go straight to the police?' It has been noted that a significant number of male rape and sexual assault complainants delay reporting their rape to the police (Gregory and Lees, 1999, p. 119). DD delayed reporting his rape for two days and only came forward after encouragement from friends: 'I was terrified of the whole thing, the police were very good, but the whole thing was very difficult. Telling strangers about the rape made me feel sick.'

Conclusion

This chapter has addressed the issue of sexual consent in cases of male rape and sexual assault. Due to the nature and limitations of the available data this analysis can only act as a starting point for further, and one hopes more detailed research in the future. Despite this, we have begun to examine the 'differences in the construction of male and female consent to sexual acts arise and ... comparative legal constructs of "legitimate victims"' (Bridgeman and Millns, 1998) and as a consequence, we believe that the following points can be made.

First, the problems experienced by female rape complainants within the legal process are not, on the basis of this data, unique. That does not mean that the treatment of men and women is identical. Rather, defence tactics that were developed and refined in cases of female rape have also been applied to the cases of male rape and sexual assault discussed in this study. At the same time there are also discernible differences in the tactics adopted. For example, while in cases of male rape the defence may use the issue of homosexuality as a means of casting doubt upon a complainant's claim of non-consent, women have to endure questions concerning such issues as birth control and abortion (Adler, 1987; Lees, 1997). The use of actual or alleged homosexuality as a defence tactic may feed into societal beliefs that gay male complainants are more blameworthy and therefore less deserving of legal protection than heterosexual males (Eigenberg, 1989; Mitchell, 1999), in the same way that women may be viewed as less deserving of protection because of their sexual history or perceived moral character (Temkin, 2000; Lees, 1997). In future, we might also see the crossover of other tactics from female to male rape, such as the normalisation of coerced sex (Adler, 1987, pp. 91-92) and the use of force being sexualised (Edwards, 1996, pp. 351-354). Another feature of rape trials is defence questioning of the medical history of female complainants in an attempt to characterise them as unreliable or dysfunctional (Temkin, 2002), a tactic that has been used in cases of male rape in other countries (*Farrell*, 1996).

In the context of Smart's notion of phallocentrism it would appear that only the experiences of the complainant in *Armstrong* could be said to have been 'disqualified'. His reactions to the alleged assault were entirely consistent with a non-consensual sexual encounter, yet his behaviour was re-interpreted as indicating consent. Ultimately his experiences were viewed in light of the defendant's *mens rea* when the trial judge held that that the jury could not properly conclude that the defendant either knew or was reckless as to the complainant's consent. In the other cases the defence tactics were ultimately unsuccessful. However, one can still view various strategies that were used in an attempt to disqualify men's experiences of rape. For example, there was the suggestion that the complainant was gay or prepared to have sex for money. On the basis of the limited number of cases under consideration, it is difficult to come to firm conclusions as to whether cases of male rape will see the disregard for men's experiences that we have seen in cases of female rape. Future analysis of cases that result in acquittal would be particularly helpful in this respect.

The second issue to arise out of this analysis relates to our understanding of male sexual consent. Over several decades there has grown a vast literature on the complexities of sexual consent arising out of women's relationships with men. In contrast, little has been written on the subject of male sexual consent, particularly in the context of men as victims of sexual aggression. Such a difference in emphasis is understandable given that most victims of rape and sexual assault are female and it is only relatively recently that there has been significant legal recognition of males' non-consensual sexual experiences, particularly in cases involving adults. Thus the complexities of male sexual consent and associated problems within the legal process are likely to become increasingly apparent. In order to properly respond to such issues it is of central importance that the misunderstandings and simplifications that have been discussed in this chapter are challenged. This could take the form of training criminal justice professionals, as well as the use of expert evidence during rape trials to educate jurors about the responses of rape victims to rape and sexual assault (Tetreault, 1989; Rumney and Morgan-Taylor, 1997b; Rumney and Morgan-Taylor, forthcoming). In order to address the problems set out in this analysis, it is to be hoped that the needs of adult male victims of rape and sexual assault will be specifically considered in any future revision of rape law and its enforcement.

Notes

[1] Prior to the 1994 reforms, consent could still arise as an issue in male sexual assault trials because s. 1 of the Sexual Offences Act 1967 permitted certain acts of *consensual* buggery.

[2] The Hickson et al. study examined a particular group of males as defined by their sexuality and therefore does not count as a general population survey.

[3] The 1997/1998 period and the two references to 1998/1999 denote a change in the method for counting reported offences from the calendar year, to the financial year.

[4] Source: Home Office, 2002.

Bibliography

Adler, Z. (1987), *Rape on Trial*, London: Routledge and Kegan Paul.
Adler, Z. (1992), 'Male Victims of Sexual Assault – Legal Issues', in Mezey, G. C. and King, M. B. (eds.), *Male Victims of Sexual Assault*, Oxford: Oxford Medical Publications.
Bergen, R. K. (1996), *Wife Rape: Understanding the Response of Survivors and Service Providers*, London: Sage Publications.

Bridgeman, J. and Millns, S. (1998), *Feminist Perspectives on Law*, London: Sweet and Maxwell.

Burt, M. R. (1991), 'Rape Myths and Acquaintance Rape', in Parrot, A. and Bechhofer, L. (eds.), *Acquaintance Rape: The Hidden Crime*, New York: John Wiley.

Burton, S. et al. (1998), *Young People's Attitudes Towards Violence, Sex and Relationships: A Survey and Focus Group Study*, Edinburgh: Zero Tolerance Charitable Trust.

Carrington, K. and Watson, P. (1996), 'Policing Sexual Violence: Feminism, Criminal Justice and Governmentality', *International Journal of the Sociology of Law*, Vol. 24, No. 3, pp. 253-272.

Codd, H. (1996), 'The Treatment of Complainants' *New Law Journal*, March 29, p. 447.

Commonwealth v Quartman, 312 Pa. Super. 349; 458 A.2d 994 (1983).

Coxell, A. et al. (1999), 'Lifetime prevalence, characteristics and associated problems of non-consensual sex in men: cross sectional survey', *British Medical Journal*, Vol. 318, pp. 846-850.

Coxell, A. and King, M. K. (2000), 'Behind locked doors: Sexual assault of men in custodial environments', in Mezey, G. C. and King, M. B. (eds.), *Male Victims of Sexual Assault*, Oxford: Oxford Medical Publications.

Crome, S. et al. (1999), 'Male rape victims: fact and fiction', *Law Institute Journal*, Vol. 73, p. 60.

Davis, A. J. (1973) 'Sexual Assaults in the Philadelphia Prison System', in Gagnon J. H. and Simon, W. (eds.), *The Sexual Scene*, 2nd ed., New Brunswick, Transaction Books.

'Do courts view rape more seriously when it is a man who is the victim?' *The Guardian*, June 12, 1995.

Dumond, R. W. (1992), 'The Sexual Assault of Male Inmates in Incarcerated Settings', 20 *International Journal of the Sociology of Law*, Vol. 20, No. 2, pp. 135-157.

Edwards, S. S. M. (1996), *Sex and Gender in the Legal Process*, London: Blackstone Press.

Ehrlich, S. (2001), *Representing Rape: Language and Sexual Consent*, London: Routledge.

Eigenberg, H. (1989), 'Male Rape: An Empirical Examination of Correctional Officers' Attitudes Towards Male Rape in Prison', *Prison Journal*, Vol. 69, p. 39.

Estrich, S. (1987), *Real Rape*, Cambridge: Harvard University Press.

Evans, D. T. (1993), *Sexual Citizenship*, London: Routledge.

Farrell (1996) 16 TAS LEXIS 510.

Field, H. S. and Beinen, L. S. (1980), *Jurors and Rape: A Study in Psychology and Law*, Lexington: Lexington Books.

Finkelhor, D. and Yllo, K. (1985), *License to Rape: Sexual Abuse of Wives*, New York: The Free Press.

Forman, B. D. (1982), 'Reported Male Rape', *Victimology: An International Journal*, Vol. 7, p. 235.

Gillespie, T. (1996), 'Rape crisis centres and "male rape": a face of the backlash', in Hester, M. et al. (eds.), *Women, violence and male power*, Buckingham: Open University Press.

Graham, R. (2001), 'Deconstructing Reform: Exploring Oppositional Approaches to Research in Sexual Assault,' *Social and Legal Studies*, Vol. 10, No. 2, pp. 257-271.

Gregory, J. and Lees, S. (1999), *Policing Sexual Assault*, London: Routledge.

Groth, A. N. (1979), *Men Who Rape*, New York: Plenum Press.

Groth, A. N. and Burgess, A. W. (1980), 'Male Rape Offenders and Victims' 137 *American Journal of Psychiatry* 806.

Hall C. (1988), 'Rape: the Politics of Definition', *South African Law Journal*, Vol. 105, p. 67.

Hall, R. E. (1985), *Ask Any Woman: A London inquiry into rape and sexual assault*, Bristol: Falling Wall Press.

Harris, J. and Grace, S. (1999), *A question of evidence: Investigating and prosecuting rape in the 1990s*, London: Home Office.

Hays, P. (1992), 'False But Sincere Accusations of Sexual Assault Made by Narcotic Patients', *Medico-Legal Journal*, Vol. 60, p. 265.

Hickson, F. C. I. et al. (1994), 'Gay Men as Victims of Non-Consensual Sex', *Archives of Sexual Behavior*, Vol. 23, No. 3, pp. 281-294.

Hill, C. E. (1998), 'Chicken-Hawk!: Evidence of Complainants' Homosexuality Under Vermont's Rape Shield Law', *Vermont Law Review*, Vol. 23, p. 711.

Hillman, R. J. et al. (1990), 'Medical and social aspects of sexual assault of males: a survey of 100 victims', *British Journal of General Practice*, Vol. 40, No. 341, pp. 502-4.

HMCPSI/HMIC (2002), *A Report on the Joint Inspection into the Investigation and Prosecution of Cases involving Allegations of Rape.*

Holocomb, D. R. et al. (1991), 'Attitudes about date rape: Gender differences among college students', *College Student Journal*, Vol. 25, p. 434.

Home Office (2002), 'Crime in England and Wales 2001/2002'.

Home Office (2000a), *Protecting the Public*, London: Cmnd. 5668

Huckle, P. L. (1995), Male Rape Victims Referred to a Forensic Psychiatric Service', 35 *Med. Sci. Law*, Vol. 35, No. 3, pp. 187-192.

Human Rights Watch (2001), *No Escape: Male Rape in U.S. Prisons*, New York: Human Rights Watch.

Isely, P. J. (1998), 'Sexual Assault of Men: American research supports studies from the UK' 38 *Med Sci Law*, Vol. 38, No. 1, pp. 74-80.

Kaufman, A. et al. (1980), 'Male Rape Victims: Noninstitutionalized Assault', *Am J Psychiatry*, Vol. 137, p. 221.

Kinsey, A. C. et al. (1948), *Sexual Behaviour in the Human Male*, Philadelphia: W B Saunders.

Kramer, E. J. (1998), 'When Men Are Victims: Applying Rape Shield Laws To Male Same-Sex Rape' 73 *New York University Law Review* 293.

Lacey, N. (1998), 'Unspeakable Subjects, Impossible Rights: Sexuality, Integrity and Criminal Law', *Canadian Journal of Law and Jurisprudence*, Vol. XI, p. 47.

Lees, S. (1996), 'Unreasonable doubt: the outcome of rape trials', in Hester, M. et al. (eds), *Women, Violence and Male Power*, Buckingham: Open University Press.

Lees, S. (1997), *Carnal Knowledge: Rape on Trial*, London: Penguin Books.

Lees, S. (1997), *Ruling Passions: Sexual Violence, Reputation and the Law*, Buckingham: Open University Press.

Levine, S. and Koenig, J. (1980), *Why Men Rape: Interviews with Convicted Rapists*, London: W. H. Allen and Co. Ltd.

Lockwood, D. (1980), *Prison Sexual Violence*, Oxford: Elsevier.

Lockwood, D. (1994), 'Issues in Prison Sexual Violence', in Braswell, M. C. et al. (eds.), *Prison Violence in America*, Cincinnati, OH: Henderson.

'Man "Lied" about rape' *The Times*, 17 October 1992, 2.

McGurk, B. J. et al. (2000), *Sexual Victimisation Among 15-17 year-old Offenders in Prison*, RDS Occasional Paper No. 65, London: Home Office.

McMullen, R. J. (1990), *Male Rape: Breaking the Silence on the Last Taboo*, London: Gay Mens Press.

Meloy, J. R. (ed.) (1998), *The Psychology of Stalking: Clinical and Forensic Perspectives*, London: Academic Press Limited.

Mezey, G. C. and King, M. (1989), 'The effects of sexual assault on men: a survey of 22 victims', *Psychological Medicine*, Vol. 19, No. 1, pp. 205-209.

Mezey, G. C. and King, M. (2000), *Male Victims of Sexual Assault*, 2nd ed. Oxford: Oxford University Press.

Metropolitan Police Authority (2002), *Scrutiny Report: Rape Investigation and Victim Care*.

Mitchell, D. et al. (1999), 'Attributions of victim responsibility, pleasure and trauma in male rape', *Journal of Sex Research*, Vol. 36, No. 4, pp. 369-373.

Morgan-Taylor, M. and Rumney, P. (1994), 'A male perspective on rape', *New Law Journal*, October 28, p. 1490.

Myers, M. F. (1989), 'Men sexually assaulted as adults and sexually abused as boys', *Archives of Sexual Behavior*, Vol. 18, No. 3, pp. 203-18.

Myhill, A. and Allen, J. (2002), *Rape and sexual assault of women: the extent and nature of the problem*, Home Office Research Study 237, London: Home Office.

Naffine, N. (1994), 'Possession: Erotic Love and the Law of Rape' 57 MLR 10.

Painter, K. (1991), *Wife Rape, Marriage and the Law – Survey Report: Key Findings and Recommendations*, Manchester: Faculty of Economic and Social Studies, University of Manchester.

Pelka, F. (1995), 'Raped: A Male Survivor Breaks His Silence', in Searles, P. and Berger, R. J. (eds.), *Rape and Society: Readings on the Problem of Sexual Assault*, Boulder, CO: Westview Press.

Remick, L. A. (1993), 'Read Her Lips: An Argument for a Verbal Consent Standard in Rape', *University of Pennsylvania Law Review*, Vol. 141, No. 3, pp. 1103-1151.

Renzetti, C. M. and Miley, C. H. (1996), *Violence in Gay and Lesbian Domestic Partnerships*, London: Harrington Park Press.

Review of Sex Offences (2000), *Setting the Boundaries: Reforming the law on sex offences*, Volume 1 (London: Home Office).

Roberston, J. E. (1999) 'Cruel and Unusual Punishment in United States Prisons: Sexual Harassment Among Male Inmates', *American Criminal Law Review*, Vol. 36, p. 1.

Robinson, B. (2002), 'Sexually Enslaved', abcNEWS.com, April 18. Accessed 25th July, 2002.

Rumney, P. and Morgan-Taylor, M. (1996a), 'Sentencing for Male Rape', *New Law Journal* February 23, p. 262.

Rumney, P. and Morgan-Taylor, M. (1996b), *New Law Journal*, June 14, p. 872.

Rumney, P. and Morgan-Taylor, M. (1997a), 'Recognising the Male Victim: Gender Neutrality and the Law of Rape Part One', *Anglo-American Law Review*, Vol. 26, p. 198.

Rumney, P. and Morgan-Taylor, M. (1997b), 'Recognising the Male Victim: Gender Neutrality and the Law of Rape Part Two', *Anglo-American Law Review*, Vol. 26, p. 330.

Rumney, P. and Morgan-Taylor, M. (1997c) 'Male Rape Trauma Syndrome in the US Courts: *People* v *Yates*', *International Journal of Evidence and Proof*, Vol. 1, p. 232.

Rumney, P. and Morgan-Taylor, M. (1998), 'Sentencing in Cases of Male Rape', *Journal of Criminal Law*, Vol. 62, p. 262.

Rumney, P. (2001a), 'Male Rape in the Courtroom: Issues and Concerns' *Criminal Law Review*, pp. 205-213.

Rumney, P. (2001b), 'The Review of Sex Offences and Rape Law Reform: Another False Dawn?' *Modern Law Review*, Vol. 64, p. 890.

Rumney, P. and Morgan-Taylor, M. (forthcoming), 'The Use of Syndrome Evidence in Rape Trials', *Criminal Law Forum*.

Rush, F. (1990), 'The Many Faces of the Backlash', in Leidholdt, D. and Raymond, J. G. (eds.), *The Sexual Liberals and the Attack on Feminism*, Oxford: Pergamon Press.

Russell, D. E. H. (1984), *Sexual Exploitation: Rape, child sexual abuse, and work-place harassment*, London: Sage Publications.

Russell, D. E. H. (1990), *Rape in Marriage*, revised ed., Bloomington: Indiana University Press.

Russell, D. E. H. and Bolen, R. M. (2000), *The Epidemic of Rape and Child Sexual Abuse in the United States*, London: Sage Publications Ltd.

Sarrel, P. M., and Masters, W. H. (1982), 'Sexual molestation of men by women', *Archives of Sexual Behaviour*, 11, pp. 117-131.

Scarce, M. (1997), *Male on Male Rape: The Hidden Toll of Stigma and Shame*, New York: Insight Books.

Schulhofer, S. J. (1990), 'The Gender Question in Criminal Law', *Social Philosophy and Policy*, Vol. 7, No. 2, pp. 105-137.

Schulhofer, S. J. (1998), *Unwanted Sex: The Culture of Intimidation and the Failure of Law*, London: Harvard University Press.

Seabrook, J. (1990), 'Power Lust', *New Statesman and Society*, 27 April, p. 20.

Sentencing Advisory Panel (2002), *Advice to the Court of Appeal – 9: Rape*.

Smart, C. (1989), *Feminism and the Power of Law*, London: Routledge.

Sorenson, S. B. et. al. (1987), 'The Prevalence of Adult Sexual Assault: The Los Angeles Epidemiologic Catchment Area Project', *American Journal of Epidemiology*, Vol. 126, No. 6, pp. 1154-1164.

Stanko, E. A. (1985), *Intimate Intrusions*, London: Routledge and Kegan Paul.

Stanko, E. A. (1990), *Everyday Violence*, London: Pandora.

Struckman-Johnson, C. et al. (1996), 'Sexual Coercion Reported by Men and Women in Prison', *The Journal of Sex Research*, Vol. 33, No. 1, pp. 67-76.

Struckman-Johnson, C. and Struckman-Johnson, D. (2000), 'Sexual Coercion Rates in Seven Midwestern Prison Facilities for Men', *The Prison Journal*, Vol. 80, p. 379.

Temkin, J. (1998), 'Medical Evidence in Rape Cases: A Continuing Problem for Criminal Justice', 61 MLR 821.

Temkin, J. (1999), 'Reporting Rape in London: A Qualitative Study', *The Howard Journal of Criminal Justice*, Vol. 38, p. 17.

Temkin, J. (2000), 'Prosecuting and Defending Rape: Perspectives From the Bar', *Journal of Law and Society*, Vol. 27, No. 2, pp. 219-248.

Temkin, J. (2002), 'Digging the Dirt: Disclosure of Records in Sexual Assault Cases', *Cambridge Law Journal*, p. 126.

Tetreault, P. A. (1989), 'Rape Myth Acceptance: A Case for Providing Educational Expert Testimony in Rape Jury Trials', *Behavioral Sciences and the Law*, Vol. 7, p. 243.

Tewksbury, R. (1989), 'Measures of Sexual Behavior in an Ohio Prison', 74 *Sociology and Social Research*, Vol. 74, No. 1, pp. 34-39.

Torrey, M. (1991), 'When Will We Be Believed? Rape Myths and the Idea of a Fair Trial in Rape Prosecutions', *University of California, Davis Law Review*, Vol. 24, p. 1013.

Ward, C. A. (1995), *Attitudes toward Rape: Feminist and Social Psychological Perspectives*, London: Sage Publications.

Wooden, W. S. and Parker, J. (1982), *Men Behind Bars: Sexual Exploitation in Prison*, London: Plenum Press.

Chapter 10

Beyond (Hetero)Sexual Consent

Karen Corteen[1]

Introduction: Consent, Not So Straightforward

Contemporarily, the problems and complexities surrounding the issue of sexual consent have been highlighted in relation to HIV/AIDS. On Friday March 16th 2001 Stephen Kelly was found guilty of knowingly infecting his girlfriend with the HIV virus (Scott, 2001). He was jailed for five years for 'culpable and reckless conduct' (Scott, 2001, p. 9). This is the first time that anyone in the UK has been convicted of deliberately infecting another person with the virus. Anne Craig, Stephen Kelly's girlfriend contends that she was unaware of Kelly's HIV status, however, Kelly maintains that he had been honest about his heroin use and HIV infection. This event raises various concerns on numerous levels with regard to the negotiation of consent such as: the extent to which consent is informed consent; who and what individuals are consenting to; individual/shared responsibility for safer sex; concealment, deceit, disclosure, revelation and inquisition. Is the onus on the individual/s with HIV/AIDS (or other sexually transmitted infections (STDs)), to disclose or on the prospective partner/s engaged in a sexual encounter or relationship to ask about an individual/s HIV/AIDS status? As can be discerned from the above, these issues also have great significance with regard to the criminal justice system in terms of whose interpretation and account of events will be accorded legitimacy.

The negotiation of consent within the societal context of HIV/AIDS also poses various concerns regarding individuals knowingly consenting to unprotected sex, especially if one of the participants has a sexually transmitted infection or HIV/AIDS. It poses considerations as to the extent to which the onset and prevalence of HIV/AIDS has had a positive or negative effect on the negotiation of consent. On a positive note, it is possible that the awareness of HIV/AIDS, (other STDs and unwanted pregnancy) has prompted greater negotiation with regard to safer sexual practices. Has this therefore, resulted in more communication and thus improved the degree to which consent is informed, sought and given? Yet, there is the potential that differential pressures have been put on and felt by specific populations. Gay men for example, are particularly encouraged to engage in safer sex practices. The role that the advocacy of safer sex practices within the gay community has played in the recent eroticisation of and demand for 'bare backing' (anal sex without protection), as can be evidenced in gay men's magazines (see the Pink Paper for example), requires exploration.

For heterosexual women safer sex with regard to unwanted pregnancies has always been an issue. This may or may not be significant to the negotiation of consent. The context of heteropatriarchy and heteronormativity cannot be ignored with regard to what extent heterosexual women are able to negotiate consent, safer sex and sexual practices. Thus, the organising principles of heteronormativity and heteropatriarchy and their impact on heterosexuals and more specifically on sexual minorities with regard to sexual consent must be considered.

The objective of this chapter is not to provide or suggest answers or explanations to the concerns and questions raised, but to draw attention to some of the complexities in relation to sexual consent, especially once the focus shifts beyond that of (hetero)sexual consent. The heteronormativity of theories and discussions around sexual consent must be challenged. It is the intention of this chapter to engage in this challenge.

Sexual Consent and Heteronormativity

Historically and contemporarily heterosexuality is rarely acknowledged or problematised as a sexual desire, practice, identity or category (Kitzinger and Wilkinson, 1993, Wilton, 1995; Corteen and Scraton, 1997; Dunne, 1997).[2] This is due to the prevalence of heteronormativity, wherein heterosexuality is naturalised to the extent that everyone in society is assumed to be heterosexual unless there is explicit reason to think otherwise.[3] Such heteronormativity is reflected in the more recent exploration of the issue of sexual consent.

At the present time, theorisation, societal and legal contestation of the issue of sexual consent is discussed primarily in terms of heterosexual consent. Theoretical, societal and legal concerns and disputes regarding consent can be seen in debates around, HIV/AIDS, the age of consent and sado masochism. However, at all levels, other than the debates around the age of consent and sado-masochistic practices, the primary focus of discussion is heterosexual consent. In part the heteronormativity exhibited in discussions surrounding sexual consent derive from the privileging of heterosexuality and the primacy of the phallus (Coveney et. al., 1984; Jackson, 1994) at the levels of theory, the social and culture.[4]

It is commonly believed that through sex individuals express their subjectivity and identity. However, in capitalist patriarchy sex is more than a source of personal pleasure or anxiety, it is as Weeks (1985) states, a moral and political battleground. 'Sex' therefore is a zone of contestation, its terrain constantly being expanded (Ibid.). What constitutes 'sex', sexual desire, practice and identity are also areas of controversy. As Skeggs (1997) notes, sexuality is a categorisation of many different things. It is important therefore to briefly revisit the social construction of 'sex' and sexuality when discussing sexual consent. Consideration needs to be given to what is meant by 'sex', and specifically what is it that individuals are consenting to. Further, when consenting to 'sex', how is consent negotiated in this context?

However, sexual consent is more complicated than consenting to 'sex'. Consent is an issue that manifests itself prior to and beyond the negotiation of consent of 'sex'. Therefore, sexual consent must be conceptualised as a continual process of negotiation.

The definitions, categorisations and explanations of late nineteenth and early twentieth century sexologists, twentieth century sex educators, and first and second wave feminists have prioritised heterosexuality and emphasised the centrality of the phallus. In so doing they have not simply reduced sexuality to heterosexuality, and 'real' sex to penile penetration of the vagina, they have contributed to and compounded the invalidation, disqualification and stigmatisation of sexual minorities (Jackson, 1994; Corteen, forthcoming).[5] It is fundamental that these processes historically and contemporaneously be incorporated in an analysis of sexual consent. The significance of such processes regarding sexual consent will therefore be schematically discussed below.

The terrain of sex and sexuality continues to be contested and expanded. This has resulted in contemporary challenges, theoretically, legally and culturally, to the supremacy of hegemonic heterosexuality and the centrality of the coital imperative. Since the late 1960s and 1970s, challenges to the negative portrayals of gay and lesbian sexualities, predominantly underpinned by criminological and medical discourses, have developed (Plummer, 1992). These challenges have focused on the 'naturalisation' of heterosexuality and the inherently unequal masculine and feminine gender roles which heterosexuality is predicated upon (and implicated in). In addition the primacy of penile penetration of the vagina as 'real sex' have been challenged (Rich, 1981; Jeffreys, 1985; Butler, 1990; Kitzinger and Wilkinson, 1993; Butler, 1993; Sedgewick, 1993; Jackson, 1994; MacKinnon, 1997).

Such challenges are predominantly the result of social constructionism, primarily through feminist and queer theory.[6] Theoretically and materially the significance of the reiterative and repetitive compulsory performances of heterosexuality have been highlighted and challenged through queer practices such as 'gender fuck' (Butler, 1990; 1993). The influence of such developments must be included in discussions around sexual consent and will be explored below. The awareness and existence of sexual minorities, especially lesbian, gay, transgender and transsexual desires, practices and identities respectively, require further investigation and prompt further issues and questions in relation to sexual consent. Not only what, and how, but who are individuals consenting to? Again there are issues surrounding the question of informed consent, disclosure, deceit and acquisition. Further, 'non-heterosexual' signifiers and codes regarding 'non-heterosexual' or sexual minority identity and practice are also relevant here. The significance, if any, of codes and signifiers to the negotiation and degree of consent is pertinent. As is the matter of how and where sexual minorities learn important signifiers and thereby know to whom and to what they maybe/are consenting to.[7] The issues raised in this section will be developed in more depth.

Not a New Phenomenon: (S)experts Implicit Concern with Sexual Consent

Debates relating to consent are not a recent area of concern and intervention but can be traced historically. During the late nineteenth and early twentieth centuries the naturalness, normality, desirability and legitimacy of heterosexuality, and the unnaturalness, abnormality, undesirability and illegitimacy of homosexuality were put on a scientific footing. They were constructed as scientific 'truth' by (s)experts including sexologists such as, Havelock Ellis (in Coveney et al., 1984; Jackson, 1994; 1994a) and Edward Carpenter (in Rowbotham and Weeks, 1977), psychoanalysts, principally Freud (1977a, 1977b) and sex educators for example, Marie Stopes (1918; 1928).[8] Sexologists' 'expert' status and claims to specialised knowledge concerning the issues of sex and sexuality enabled them to naturalise (Weeks, 1985) (and denaturalise) sexual patterns and identities (Corteen forthcoming). In the naturalisation of heterosexuality, the inequality between the sexes was also naturalised and eroticised. The prestigious position of sexology in defining gendered and sexual categories and distinctions meant that it was (and continues to be) far-reaching. Law, medicine, social welfare and religious organisations where influenced by sexologists' theories and propositions.

These propositions became popularised through sex educators such as Marie Stopes (1981; 1928) whose advice and theories were rooted in sexological suppositions.[9] Havelock Ellis and Marie Stopes' efforts to humanise heterosexual sexual relations rather than revolutionise them, placed great emphasis on consent. Such emphasis, it is argued, was not explicit but implicit. Stopes and other 'new feminists' recognised the violence inherent in many heterosexual relations and marriages.[10] However, the more radical criticisms put forward by first wave feminists, of marriage as an oppressive institution due to existing inequalities in the power relations between men and women, were displaced by Stopes and other 'new feminists' and viewed instead as sexual disharmony. Bachi (1998, p. 46) comments, 'Sex became the cement to hold marriage together'. Thus, sexual disharmony was portrayed as the root cause of all marital discord and Stopes therefore sought to rectify this.[11]

Although Stopes (1918; 1928) was influenced by feminism in that she critiqued the ideology and practice of male (hetero)sexuality and emphasised female (hetero)sexual autonomy, she failed to detach herself from the patriarchal sexological model of sexuality. Within this model there is an implicit acceptance of 'the biological necessity and inevitability of male dominance and female submission' (Jackson, 1994 p. 132). Thereby contradicting her championing of female autonomy. Stopes (1918) contended that with regard to (hetero)sexual relations and practices, instinct was no longer enough and therefore (hetero)sexual relations and practices had to be learnt. The assumed 'naturalness' of heterosexual desire and practice is somewhat undermined by this belief and by the popularity of sex manuals, such as those written by Marie Stopes. It could be argued that the reason so much effort was channelled into assuring and improving the sex life of heterosexuals, especially heterosexual women, was to ensure women's compliance to their husband's demands.[12]

Stopes (1918; 1928) in keeping with her predecessors was an essentialist. She conflated gender differences with sex differences based on anatomical distinctions. Stopes (1918, p. 44) maintained that (hetero)sexual desires were based on biological differences:

> Much of the sex attraction ... depends on differences between the two that pair; and probably taking them unawares, those very differences which drew them together now begin their undoing.

Stopes also believed that the very differences that 'draw' men and women together are also the cause of marital breakdown. Thus, Stopes (1918, p. 29) sought to 'increase the joys of marriage, and to show how much sorrow can be avoided'. Stopes (1918; 1928) refuted the myth that an erection must result in ejaculation yet, she held up the ideology of the intransigent, predatory male sexual urge:

> Now physical passion, so swiftly stimulated in man, tends to override all else, and the untutored man seeks one thing – the accomplishment of desire. (Stopes 1918, p. 49)

> ... in the majority of men desire, even if held in check, is merely slumbering. It is always present, ever ready to wake at the lightest call, and often so spontaneously insistent as to require perpetual conscious repression. (Stopes, 1918 p. 73)

Stopes recognises that male behaviour can result in women's spiritual, intellectual and physical suffering. However, according to Stopes this is not consciously committed. Men themselves are conceived as victims of uncontrollable physiological forces (Corteen, forthcoming).[13]

In contrast to men's unremitting sexual desire, women's desire is conceptualised as 'intermittent' (Stopes, 1918, p. 73) and is ruled by 'rhythms', rhythms which 'man has no more control than he has over the tides of the sea' (Stopes, 1918, p. 55).[14] Consequently, women's suffering was perceived as emanating from men's lack of recognition and understanding of these rhythms. Stopes contended that the fundamental cause of marital disharmony was men's lack of knowledge in 'the Art of love'. This is reminiscent of the work of sexologist Havelock Ellis (in Jackson, 1994).[15]

For Stopes (1918; 1928) male desire is primarily a forceful urge, amenable to rational control and capable of adapting to the female pattern of desire. Echoing first wave feminists, Stopes recognised and criticised the violence involved in the insistence by men of their marital rights. Stopes, (1918, p. 57) declared that such insistence for those women who were unprepared, was experienced 'as a rape'. Stopes (1918; 1928) was therefore arguing that sexual intercourse should be consensual and enjoyable for both men and women.

Stopes (1918; 1928) bestowed the responsibility for achieving this goal on the 'husband'. Drawing once again on the work of Ellis, Stopes (1918, p. 45) contended, 'Only by learning how to hold a bow correctly can one *draw* music from a violin' (emphasis added). Men were advised to adjust their desire to women's 'natural' rhythms and to exercise constraint outside of these times. Stopes (1918 p. 78) maintained that while this was 'hard to do', the husband 'who so constrains himself' will find that he is:

> ... a thousand-fold repaid not only by the increasing health and happiness of his wife, and the much intenser pleasure he gains from their mutual intercourse, but by his own added vitality and sense of command.

Nonetheless, Stopes continued the tradition of eroticising unequal gender relations. Echoing Ellis' concept of 'courtship', Stopes (1918, p. 79) suggested that the man plays the part of 'tender wooer', and that 'even at times when her passion would not spontaneously arise, a woman can generally be stirred so fundamentally as to a passionate return'. Stopes (1918, p. 79) stated:

> The supreme law for the husband is: Remember that each act of union must be tenderly wooed for and won, and that no union should ever take place unless the woman so desires it and is made physically ready for it.

This assertion is somewhat paradoxical. The consent of the woman is displaced if the woman has to be 'made' ready for 'each act of union' and if 'each act of union' is about the man winning. On the one hand Stopes (1918) advocates some level of constraint, on the other she compromises this stance in the counsel she forwards for those men who seemingly cannot wait. The man 'who wants his mate all out of season as well as in it' according to Stopes (1918, p. 82) has a 'double duty to perform'. For he must 'rouse, charm and stimulate her to local readiness', and stimulus at this time 'must be made through her emotional and spiritual nature and less through the physical than usual' (1918, p. 82). In other words, husbands are advised to wield emotional and spiritual manipulation when a wife cannot be 'wooed' and 'won' by way of physical manipulation alone (Corteen, forthcoming). As Jackson (1984, p. 65) rightly suggests 'foreplay' becomes 'conquest by manipulation', 'submission as pleasure' and '"consent" to conquest' (Jackson, 1984, p. 65). The full extent of consent on the part of the wife is thus questionable. Within patriarchy, sexuality is gendered and phallocentric, arguably consent therefore is constructed differently for men and women and consequently consent may mean different things to men and women. Thus, the full extent of consent on the part of women in heterosexual encounters or relations is debatable. There are also concerns here with regard to the criminal justice system and legal process in rape cases. Whose interpretation, meaning and definition of consent are given primacy and legitimacy? This is particularly significant given the male dominance of the criminal justice system and the presence of 'judicial misogyny' (Carlen 1985, p. 10).

Within Stopes' contentions, women's sexual autonomy is compromised, if not lost. Jackson (1994, p. 142) asserts, 'Female sexuality cannot be simultaneously autonomous *and* dependent on men for its expression and fulfilment'. Furthermore, 'The final sex act' (Stopes, 1918 p. 63), penile penetration of the vagina, is upheld as 'real' sex and inevitably (hetero)sexual acts other than coitus are positioned as mere 'foreplay' and preparation for the 'real thing'. 'Non-heterosexual' or sexual minority desires, practices, and identities are from here onwards disqualified and marginalised. Moreover, Stopes went on to stigmatise and to point out the dangers of abstinence, masturbation and female homosexuality. Female homosexuality in particular was denigrated (Corteen, forthcoming). Stopes compounded Ellis' distinctions of the 'invert' and the 'pervert' with regard to female homosexuality, arguing that there were 'real' female homosexuals and 'spurious imitations' (Stopes, 1928, p. 41). According to Stopes, female homosexuality was innate in 'very few women' and that women 'indulging in the vice', 'drifted into it' out of 'laziness', 'curiosity', or through 'allow(ing) themselves to be corrupted' (1928, p. 41).

In the reinstatement and reinforcement of the coital imperative, Stopes (1928 p. 42) maintained that women could only 'play' with each other:

> The bedrock objection to it is surely women can only play with each other and cannot in the very nature of things have natural union or supply each other with the seminal and prostatic secretions which they ought to have and crave unconsciously.

The positioning of penile penetration of the vagina as 'real sex' has implications in relation to the issue of consent and raises a number of important questions. When engaging in sexual practices other than coital activity what are individuals consenting to if this is not 'real sex'? To what extent does 'sex' play an important part in an individual's identity? Does a person remain a 'virgin' if they do not engage in this activity, even after as Richardson (1996, p. 6) states, 'a life time of "foreplay"'? Is consent necessary therefore, and how is it ascertained? It is also significant regarding the law and legal process in terms of what constitutes (and what does not constitute) sex, rape and sexual assault.

Despite the weakening of traditional bases of sexual authority such as religion and the family (Weeks, 1993; Stein, 1999) and the 'liberalisation of sex' (Weeks, 1993) these ideas still have resonance at the level of formal politics, ideology and culture (Corteen, forthcoming).

Sexual Consent in the Context of Heteropatriarchy

Socially, politically and theoretically heterosexuality has and continues to be privileged and the coital imperative remains central (Weeks, 1985; Richardson, 1992; Corteen, forthcoming). Within hegemonic discursive practices heterosexuality is naturalised as monolithic and heralded as the cornerstone of social relations, without which society could no longer function or even exist. Heterosexuality remains constructed as:

... a central and determining feature of our understanding of social life. The heterosexual couple is the raw material through which society may interpret and imagine itself (Richardson, 1996, p. 11).

The primacy of the phallus and the ideological and institutionalisation of 'compulsory heterosexuality' (Rich, 1981, p. 41) as natural, normal, desirable and legitimate prevails. Continuity can be discerned as 'real' sex constitutes penile penetration of the vagina and the daily eroticisation of women's subordination (MacKinnon, 1997) continues and is prolific. It can be evidenced in pornography and mainstream cultural representations such as newspapers, magazines, music, films, videos, DVDs, television and the World Wide Web.

Jackson (1999, p. 251) highlights that more recently the issue of 'what counts as sex' has made its way onto the public agenda in the context of the Clinton-Lewinsky affair. The majority of sexual contact between Clinton and Lewinsky comprised Lewinsky performing oral sex on Clinton. However, in his defence (or false denial) Clinton drew on the traditional and conventional conceptualisation of 'sex'. He contended that he did 'not have sexual relations with that woman' (Jackson, 1999, p. 251). Similarly, Lewinsky also described the act of oral sex as 'just fooling around' (Jackson, 1999, p. 251). It could be argued that the dominance of the institutionalised gender hierarchy of heterosexual desire and practice which remains 'constrained by the erotics of domination and subordination' (Jackson, 1999, p. 251) is exemplified in the Clinton-Lewinsky saga. Jackson (Jackson, 1999, p. 252) maintains this exchange of pleasure was not mutual or equal as Lewinsky serviced Clinton while he was on the telephone:

> He wasn't even fully engaged with the act; it is almost disembodied sex, as if his penis was being manipulated without him being implicated at all. Perhaps he was stating the truth when he said he did not have 'sexual relations'.

Clinton may not have had a relation as such, but did he have sex? Jackson (Jackson, 1999, p. 252) contends that this affair tells us much about 'male (hetero)sexuality, about the ability of men to divorce body and mind, to localise their sexuality in their genitals'. That male (hetero)sexuality potentially (if not actually) entails the disembodiment in terms of women's disembodiment and their own disembodiment in the separation of the mind and body raises concerns regarding consent. What are individuals consenting to – an act devoid of a subject, a relation? The separation of body and mind makes the relations of sex, identity and possibly trauma less clear. Seemingly, consent to sex acts is less important than consent to a sexual *relation*. Again, this raises considerations regarding legal processes. Also, the extent or possibility of the separation of the body and the mind, is debatable, for example were Clinton's protestations simply a convenient process of false denial?

Arguably, the above interpretation of Lewinsky performing oral sex on Clinton is buying into and reinforcing the centrality of penetration, traditional notions of women's sexuality and demarcating what 'respectable' women should and should not get pleasure from. There is an innate assumption here that Lewinsky did not derive any pleasure from performing oral sex. Disembodied sex for women in certain contexts may be pleasurable and perhaps therefore, there is some degree of mutual consent. These are interesting but potentially dangerous considerations given the controversy around consent and male sexual violence. Attention must be given to how consent is negotiated, articulated, communicated and understood.

The patriarchal construction of (hetero)sexuality, (hetero)sexual sex and eroticised unequal gender roles raises issues in respect of consent. The negotiation of consent is or should be an issue for both heterosexual men and heterosexual women. Social constructions of hegemonic masculinity and emphasised femininity (Connell, 1987) create the position wherein women consent to 'sex' and men (in theory at least) ascertain consent. Given the patriarchal construction of heterosexuality and heterosexual sex, with its implicit unequal gendered power relations, the issue of heterosexual women's 'consent' must be further examined. MacKinnon (1997) has raised the question as to whether consent can ever be fully and freely given, bearing in mind the inherent persuasion and coercion within hegemonic heterosexual desire and practice. Within the context of heteropatriarchy (Wilton, 1995) autonomous and absolute consent for heterosexual women is debatable.

Sex and Sexual Consent Without the 'Lock and Key'

Heterosexuality is based on both difference and complimentarity. As Richardson (1996, p. 7) asserts 'heterosexuality depends on a view of differently gendered individuals who complement each other, right down to their body parts fitting together; like 'a lock and key' the penis and vagina are assumed to be a natural fit'. Heterosexuality entails a desire for 'other' based on sexed anatomical differences. The 'other' is constructed through gender, class and 'race' and is predicated on inequality. Gendered power differences are eroticised and are assumed to be natural and necessary to sexual arousal and pleasure. From this generalised patriarchal conceptualisation of 'sex' it follows that in order for sexual desire to exist in 'non-heterosexual' relationships, desire must imitate that of heterosexual desire, founded on active/passive; dominant/submissive. The patriarchal heterosexualisation of desire and practice can be evidenced in the conception of lesbian and gay sexual practices.

Predominantly (but not exclusively) the localisation of sexuality within male genitalia could be (and still can be) discerned within the theoretical, legal and ideological conceptualisation of male homosexuality. Similar processes can be discerned with regard to the theoretical and ideological treatment of (heterosexual) Black women and men and (heterosexual) white working class women. Middle class women and lesbians have not been positioned as the sign of sex. However, the latter is sexualised and eroticised in pornography – appropriated for the male gaze.

According to Bloch and other sexologists, it was believed that the locus of male sexuality as genital, prevented heterosexual men from being diverted from their heterosexual path (Jeffreys, 1985). In contrast, it was contended that women's natural desire for 'tenderness and caresses' made it easier for pseudo-homosexual tendencies to manifest and get taken advantage of by 'real' female homosexuals (Bloch, cited in Jeffreys, 1985, p. 109).[16]

The conceptualisation of homosexuality through certain gendered sex acts, thereby devoid of emotion, and the heterosexualisation of homosexual desire and practice can be seen in relation to the treatment of anal penetrative sex between men. Indeed it could be argued that ideologically homosexuality is defined by anal penetration and this is the only sex that gay men are thought to have.[17] Thus, while both men and women have an anus, the male anus as part of the sexualised body, is encoded as a gay male body (Richardson, 1996). If the anus is potentially a homologue of the vagina (Bersani, 1987, in Richardson, 1996), a heterosexual understanding of penetrative sex between men is applied as the male anus is conceived as being equivalent to or substituting the vagina.[18] This conceptualisation is not only offensive to gay men; it ignores female anality and anal intercourse, as part of heterosexual or lesbian practice.

Lesbianism however, has been conceived not so much in terms of genital contact but intimate bonds *per se* between women (Stopes, 1928; Rich, 1981). Yet, there has been a questioning of the centrality of genital sexuality in defining the erotic content of women's relationships (Faderman, 1981; Jeffreys, 1985). There has however, been no parallel debate among gay men (Corteen, forthcoming). The question of the centrality of genital sexuality in defining the erotic content of women's relationships has been a site of contention within feminism itself. This can be evidenced in the debates and conflicts during the 1970s and 1980s regarding feminism, political lesbianism, lesbian feminism and libertarian lesbianism (for example see: Abbott and Love, 1972; Faderman, 1981; Rich, 1981; Califia, 1982; Clarke, 1982; English et al., 1982; Rubin, 1982; Nestle, 1987; Alice, Gordon, Debbie and May, 1988; Gutter Dyke Collective, 1988; Radicalesbians, 1988; Penelope, 1988; Hoagland, 1988; Califia, 1989).

With the exception of Califia (1982; 1988; 1989) and Rubin (1982), lesbians are either conceptualised as asexual and affectionate (Faderman, 1981; Rich, 1981; Jeffreys, 1985) or as '(hetero)-sex-role playing' (Faderman, 1992; Healy, 1996; Richardson, 1996).[19] In the positioning of lesbians as '(hetero)sex-role playing', same-sex relations are based on asserted gender differences. Herein, the 'butch' partner adopts the role of a man, predatory and active, and her partner the 'femme' embodies the female role, passive and submissive:

> Many lesbian relationships between two women become the equivalent of a husband – wife relationship. The mannish or overt lesbian likes to take on the role of the 'husband' and generally attaches herself to a female partner who is feminine in physique and personality. She regards her mate as her wife (Frank Caprio, from the first major study of female homosexuality, cited in Richardson, 1996, p. 3).

The over simplification of the butch-femme relation as 'role playing' reproduction of the heterosexual model has engendered much debate and (Nestle, 1987; Faderman, 1992; Bell, et al., 1994; Healy, 1996; Richardson, 1996).

Given the heterosexualisation of sexual minorities, including lesbian and gay desires and practices, the sexual practices and the importance of the practices which lesbians and gay men consent to require further examination. The lack of the complimentarity of otherness and the absence of the eroticisation derived from unequal gendered power relations in same-sex relationships raises questions regarding how it is that sexual interest and sexual practices are initiated. What are sexual minorities consenting to and how is consent negotiated? The resistance, transcendence or challenge of traditional unequal roles may result in a greater degree of consent. It may also create new problems and dilemmas regarding consent. Given the lack of visibility of lesbians and gay men and their desires and practices there are questions as to how lesbians and gay men learn about alternative ways to conduct sexual relations, and to negotiate consent. There are also considerations with respect to the spaces that such negotiations can be observed, tried and tested (Skeggs, 1999; Corteen, 2002).

Sexual Consent and Marginalised 'Sex' and 'Sexualities'

Various research studies have illustrated that what is allowed to be expressed in 'public', legally, ideologically and materially, differs according to whether it is in a homosexual or a heterosexual context. 'Public' space or 'the street' as noted by Valentine (1996, p. 146) is heterosexualised:[20]

> Heterosexual couples kissing and holding hands as they make their way down the street, to advertisements and window displays which present images of contented 'nuclear' families; and from heterosexualised conversations that permeate queues at bus stops and banks, to the piped music articulating heterosexual desires that fill shops, bars and restaurants.

Those individuals whose lives are not comprised of 'monogamous, heterosexual, procreative sex' are excluded (Hubbard, 2001, p. 51).[21] Lesbians and gay men are subsequently 'placed outside (the underworld) or at the margins (twilight zone) of the normative boundaries of the social realm' (Richardson, 1996, p. 13). Expressions and practices of 'non-heterosexuality', sexual minorities and 'scary' heterosexuality (Hubbard, 2001, p. 57), or what Rubin (1984, p. 60) described in her conceptualisation of the 'sex hierarchy', as those heterosexual practices in the 'outer limits' (prostitution, sado-masochism, masturbation and pornography for example), can therefore, only comfortably and safely be enacted within specific separate (and often secluded) spaces, such as, 'a sex dungeon, a 'cottage', a brothel or private sex club'.

The (hetero)sexualisation of the 'public' arena authenticates (white, able-bodied) heterosexuality as a socially comprised group (Rubin, 1984, p. 60). Sexual dissidents such as lesbians and gay men are only allowed 'to be in gay specific spaces and places' (Bristow, 1989, p. 74). Tolerance (which is significantly different to equality) (Weeks, 1993) rests on the premise that gayness or lesbianism should be restricted to behind 'closed doors' (Richardson, 1996; Corteen, 2002; Hekma, 2001):

> ... the private has been institutionalised as the border of social tolerance, as the place where you are 'allowed' to live relatively safely as long as one does not attempt to occupy the public (Richardson, 1996, p. 15).

However, it must be noted that the public/private divide is highly problematic. As Hubbard (2001) rightly observes that spaces considered as principally private spaces are in fact not so private. Research has demonstrated that the home, the brothel, 'cottages' and sex clubs are subject to state intervention and regulation.

Further, turning the issues of visibility and publicity on its head, Hubbard also argues that it is not a lack of publicity but a lack of privacy that is the problem for sexual dissidents (see Hubbard, 2001 for more detail). Hubbard (2001, p. 64) suggests:

> ...many sexual minorities have too much publicity (in that they can access a number of different spaces) but not enough privacy (because they lack the ability to exercise control over those spaces by not being able to exclude others from them).

The accumulative effect of the heteronormality and heterosexual ordering of space is that when gay men and lesbians (and other sexual dissidents) show affection in the public domain they risk verbal, physical and sexual abuse (Comstock, 1991; Berrill, 1992; Bell and Valentine, 1995; Duncan, 1996; Valentine, 1996; Corteen, Tyrer, Skeggs, Moran, 2000; Corteen, 2002). Incidents of homophobic violence or homophobic hate crime are influenced by the perpetrators' perception of the visible signs of sexual orientation (GALOP, 1991; Moran, 1995). Such readings or (mis)readings are based on 'victim' characteristics (Richardson and May, 1999) such as signs of 'lesbian-ness' (Smith, 1992) or gay-ness. For example, adorning gay signifiers or more significantly deviation from expected gender presentation (GALOP, 1991; Moran, 1995; Corteen, 2002). Richardson and May (1999) note that interpretative frameworks are influenced by social and interactional contexts. Being with a partner or gay friends therefore increases lesbians' and gay men's visibility and therefore the potential for abuse (Stonewall, 1996; Corteen, 2002).

The private/public distinction is therefore a sexualised notion. Ideologically and institutionally the 'public' arena is heterosexual and gay men and lesbians are confined to the margins, they are bound to the realms of the 'private'. Confining sex to the private desexualises the social or public sphere. Yet, as has been demonstrated above, the 'public' or the street is heterosexualised. Public and social expressions of (hetero)sexual desire and practice permeate society. Thus, to some extent the negotiation of (hetero)sexual consent to (hetero)sexual practice can be observed, discerned, tried and practised. Yet, due to the heterosexualisation of 'public' space and place and the subsequent fear of and actual violence against those not perceived as heterosexual, learning about consensual 'sex' and sexual relations in this way is primarily confined to the heterosexual population. As noted above sexual dissidents are confined to sequestered spaces. This raises issues in relation to consent. Concerns are raised as to the potential of sexual minorities being forced to put themselves in potentially dangerous situations regarding being able to test, express and act on their sexual desire. Consequently, the safety of sexual minorities and their position and ability to negotiate consent may be seriously undermined.

Hubbard (2001, p. 67) concludes:

> ...I have begun to explore the spatial construction of new models of sexual citizenship which rely on the celebration and acceptance of difference as well as the exclusion of those who threaten the ability of people to control their own bodies, feelings and relationships with other consenting adults.

Thus, consent is not just an interpersonal process, the process involves the negotiation of place, time, others (usually heterosexual) and the state in terms of the law. Hubbard's notion of the creation of 'transitory sites for sexual freedom and pleasure' (2001, p. 68) broadens out the issue of consent. The negotiation of consent is extended beyond the two (or more) consenting adults having a sexual encounter or relationship. The negotiation of consent may entail processes of inclusion and exclusion, those who can be included and excluded from the space. This raises concerns regarding how and by who is this to be managed.

As a result of queer theory and politics attempts have been made by sexual minorities to subvert and disrupt the heterosexual street (Duncan, 1996; Butler, 1990, 1993; Hubbard, 2001).[22] For example, through lesbian and gay marches, street celebrations such as Mardi Gras, the establishment of lesbian and gay villages and mimicry – 'lipstick lesbians' and 'gay skinheads'. Though the extent of their success is debatable (Bell et al., 1994; Whittle, 1994; Duncan, 1996; Skeggs, 1999; Bell and Binnie, 2000; Hubbard, 2001).

Resistance to the invisibility, stigmatisation, and marginalisation of sexual minorities, and ways of managing the pervasive heteronormitivity and homophobia can be discerned historically and presently through the development of or the re-signification of (Butler, 1990) codes and signifiers. Within the lesbian and gay community for example, there are signifiers that convey sexual status. For example, 'pinkie rings', pride badges, rainbows, black triangles and pink triangles. In the more recent past there were also signifiers that informed others of an individual's desires and practices. For example wearing a handkerchief or chain in the left or right pocket can indicate whether one is a 'top' or a 'bottom'. Different colours of handkerchiefs also indicate a person's willingness (and unwillingness) to engage in certain sexual practices. This was particularly the case for gay men. Butch-femme in its traditional sense, as conceptualised by Nestle not only conveyed messages to the general public but conveyed 'complex sexual and emotional exchanges' between lesbians (1987, p. 92). So there were stylised dress codes and other signifiers that lesbians and gay men in particular adorned that told interested others what they liked and what they were prepared to do (and thereby, what they would not do and what they did not like).[23]

This is relevant and interesting as it could be argued that for some sexual minorities the process of negotiating consent begins even before the exchange of any verbal or physical communication. It could be contended that to some extent at least, what an individual is consenting to has already been communicated and has been established. However, arguably such signification is but partial divulgence. The interpretation of that which is present (or absent) is still reliant upon subjective recognition and interpretation or misrecognition and misinterpretation. This in itself may pose further problems and miscommunication in respect of the negotiation of consent. Consideration needs to be given as to how lesbians and gay men learn what the signifiers and codes are and their meanings. There are issues regarding the lack of recognition, misrecognition, misreading and misinterpretation of signifiers and codes, as well as the assumption or misassumption that signifiers and codes have been read, understood and therefore agreed to. Again the confinement of sexual minorities to marginalised and potentially dangerous spaces may undermine the degree to which an individual can negotiate consent.

Learning About Sexual Consent at the Level of Culture

Hegemonic discourses continue to naturalise and eroticise heterosexuality and its inseparable unequal gendered constructions of masculinity and femininity. At the level of culture, implicit and explicit representations of heterosexuality and 'hegemonic/dominant masculinity and emphasised/subordinate femininity' are 'all-pervasive':

> Television, newspapers, advertising, music and cinema guarantee a popular culture obsessed with heterosexual relations and intrigue in which the boundaries of fantasy and reality are purposefully blurred (Corteen and Scraton, 1997, p. 76).

Such images however, require an audience. The audience comprises individuals who although confined within and influenced by determining contexts such as gender, sexuality, class and race are agenic subjects. Consequently the pervasiveness and persuasiveness of this heteronormality may be challenged at an individual, collective, personal or professional level.

Further, the challenges, complexities and contradictions regarding sexuality as highlighted by feminists and queer theorists have been reflected to some extent in contemporary cultural representations of sexual desire, practice and identity. Books such as *Men are from Mars and Women are From Venus*, illustrate that heterosexual sexual relations are not so straightforward. They often comprise mixed messages, miscommunication, lack of clarity in relation to who should do what, when and with whom. The complexities and confusion surrounding heterosexual 'dating' rituals, various sexual practices, and consent pervade our screens. For example, real and fictional stories around heterosexual dating and falling in and out of relationships permeate terrestrial and satellite television, *Blind Date*, *Street Mate*, *Temptation*, *Ally McBeal* and *Sex in the City* to name but a few. On the one hand, these representations reinforce heteronormitivity, heterosexuality and the sexed and gendered roles with regard to sex and sexual relationships. But on the other hand, by presenting the complexities, contradictions and diversity within heterosexual experiences they can also challenge the seemingly apparent monolithic and universalised heterosexual ideal and the inherent demarcated gender roles.

Further, the reinforcement and the challenge to hegemonic heterosexuality in cultural representations that pervade our screens (cinematic as well as television) does mean that heterosexuals have access to witnessing the playing out of the negotiation of consent to heterosexual acts of intimacy and pleasure.

At the level of culture, lesbians, gay men and other sexual minorities are increasingly featured and given greater visibility (Gibbs, 1994; Cottingham, 1996; Hawkes, 1996; Allen, 1997). According to Stimpson (in Jenness, 1992 p. 73), the times when a 'lesbian identity' 'entailed invisibility because no one wanted to see her', have disappeared. There are magazines aimed specifically at the lesbian and gay community – *Gay Times*, *Diva*, and *Girlfriend* to name but a few. Greater cultural visibility can be seen in television programmes such as, *Queer As Folk* and *Meterosexualities*, *Eurotrash*, *Chained*, *Tipping the Velvet*, in soap operas such as *Coronation Street*, *Emmerdale* and *Brookside* and in films namely, *The Birdcage*, *Bound* and *The Opposite of Sex*.

That is not to say that these representations are not contentious. In keeping with capitalism's unremitting containment, commodification and appropriation of 'other', lesbians are appropriated and commodified (Hennessy, 1995; Cottingham, 1996) largely for the male gaze and mainstream palatability in representations of 'lesbian chic'. 'Other' sexual identities, desires and practices are often presented in a voyeuristic manner. They are therefore, projected in a somewhat alienated and detached manner as something 'other' as opposed to eroticised potential additions to or alternatives to compulsory heterosexuality and sexual heteronormativity. They therefore, do little if anything, to address or enlighten individuals with regard to consent (or lack of consent) in sexual minority relations.

More recently there have been greater cultural representations of not only lesbians and gay men but also transgendered and transsexual individuals. For example, in *Ally McBeal*, in films such as *Priscilla Queen of the Desert* and *Boys Don't Cry* and even in *Coronation Street*. Attention is thus, drawn to further complexities in relation to the issue of sexual desire, practice and identities and subsequently consent. The recognition that sexual identity *and* gender identity, both subjectively and bodily are fluid and flexible, raises complex questions and issues in relation to consent. If a heterosexual woman has 'sex' with a lesbian, but does not take on the subject position or identity of a lesbian, what and who is the lesbian consenting to, and vice versa?[24] In relation to transgenderism if an individual meets a male with a vagina or a female with a penis there are considerations with respect to at what stage the individual should be made aware of the person's transgenderism. Similarly, questions are raised as to what stage in an encounter, in the negotiation of sex, or in the development of a relationship should as person disclose their transsexuality. This has implications in terms of informed consent when beginning and/or during a relationship with a transgendered or transsexual relationship. There are issues regarding the onus being on the transgendered or transsexual person to disclose their transgenderism or transsexuality as opposed to the other person/s in the encounter or relationship to ask. This is significant when considering the fear of and actual violence that sexual minorities encounter. The process and acquisition of consent therefore becomes even more complex, consenting to a relationship and 'sex' in terms of to whom (subjectively/objectively and bodily) and to what (practices/relationship). Issues around disclosure can be applied when married men and married women remove their wedding ring when on a night out or when individuals fail to disclose that they have a child/ren.

What is actually being raised and explored here are issues of concealment and deceit. Arguably some acts or incidents of concealment or deceit are judged worse than others, and that which is judged to be worse, maybe dependent on whether it is in relation to a heterosexual context or a 'non-heterosexual' context. Regarding the criminal justice system and processes of criminal and social justice these concerns are not merely theoretical or discursive, as the tragic story of Brandon Teena illustrates. Brandon Teena was assaulted and raped one week before his death in Nebraska. Brandon Teena was treated by the police department as a criminal rather than a victim. His crime was representing himself as male when biologically he was female. Indeed it was the police department who disclosed his transsexuality in the first instance. Individual, ideological, social and legal expectations in terms of what subjectively (identity) and bodily (physically – externally and internally) should be made known, and when, in order for consent to be informed requires deliberation.

Conclusion: Beyond (Hetero)Sexual Consent

It has been established that heterosexuality is predicated on and implicated in the social construction of masculinity and femininity. The predominant essentialist explanations rooted in anatomical differences naturalise gender inequalities as normal, natural and necessary to (hetero)sexual desire, practice and identity. Within this the masculine is conceptualised and represented as – male, knowing, predatory and active, while the feminine – female, is naïve, pursued and passive. Heterosexual penetration is represented as the appropriate and ultimate mode of sexual activity and the most fulfilling sexual relation. The negotiation of (hetero)sexual consent, while disputed and complex, is nonetheless influenced by the social construction of masculinity and femininity. This raises issues as to the nature and degree of consent within heterosexual relationships or encounters, especially for heterosexual women.

The predominant saturation, mediation and actual manifestations of heterosexual identity, desire and practice rooted in a sexed and gendered prototype has potential implications for sexual minorities regarding consent. There are issues around how and where sexual minorities, such as lesbians and gay men, learn or encounter alternative representations of sexual practice and the negotiation of sexual consent that are not couched in these sexed and gendered dichotomies.[25] There is also the danger that given the marginalisation of sexual minorities, sexual minorities including 'scary heterosexuals' are being forced into potentially perilous situations, exposed to harm and thus, their ability to negotiate consent may be seriously weakened.

As noted above, sexuality is a contested and ever expanding terrain. Recently more sophisticated theories regarding heterosexual identity, desire and practice have been developed. Heterosexuals are not a homogenous group (Kitzinger and Wilkinson, 1993) and heterosexuals themselves challenge and resist hegemonic heterosexuality and the dichotomous sex and gender roles inherent to heterosexuality. Simultaneously, the dominance of heterosexuality theoretically, culturally and socially is persistently challenged and resisted. As a result, further questions and potential problems arise concerning sexual minorities and the issue of consent, in respect of, who and what individuals are consenting to and responsibilities with respect to disclosure of internal and external factors which may effect or undermine the extent to which informed consent to a sexual encounter or developing relationship is given.

The extent to which the desires, practices, encounters and relationships of sexual minorities challenge, disrupt and transcend the notion of consent rooted in the conceptualisation of male/active – female/submissive dichotomies warrants further exploration. What examples are there, of informed consent and 'good' sex and does the former necessarily result in the latter? The extent to which consent is negotiated, (if at all), or established prior to verbal and physical communication through signifiers and codes and the consequences of misreading and misinterpretation of codes and signifiers are also important considerations. So too are how codes and signifiers are developed and learnt.

In addition the implication of the above complexities regarding consent in heterosexual and sexual minority sexual practices and relations in the production and application of laws, the practices of the criminal justice system and the legal progress is fundamental. The tragic mistreatment of Brandon Teena, mentioned above, is indicative of the serious implications regarding human rights abuses and injustice within the criminal justice system.

Yet, there are implications in such levels of disclosure in the negotiation of consent to a sexual encounter or a potential long-term relationship. Arguably the process of disclosure could diminish the potential for spontaneous, anonymous sex. Are there situations therefore, were disclosures are not necessary or are even undesirable? Are disclosures always necessary in order to achieve consent? The wrong timing of certain disclosures may also lead to the termination of what might have been long-term relationship. Further, regarding sexual minorities, certain disclosures may and do lead to violence interpersonally and institutionally.

The heteronormativity of theories and discussions relating to sexual consent must be challenged. It has been the intention of this chapter to be a part of this challenge and to begin to look beyond (hetero)sexual consent. Further empirical research is needed in this area in order to investigate and address the questions, issues and concerns raised.

Notes

[1] The author would like to thank the following for their support and feedback whilst developing this chapter: Margaret Malloch; Gill Hall; Beverley Skeggs; Paul Tyrer; Paul Reynolds; Ann Jemphrey; Helen Finney; Eileen Berrington; David Orr and Julie Keen.

[2] The common usage and understanding of the term heterosexuality is the desire for sexual relationships with person of the 'other' or 'opposite' sex. This is how this term is to be utilised here. In addition, heterosexuality is conceived as a social construction predicated on and implicated in unequal gender relations, and is naturalised, normalised and privileged at the levels of the social, political, cultural and economic. The author also recognises that whilst at the level of ideology heterosexuality is depicted as a coherent fixed and universal category, in reality heterosexuality is always in the process of being produced (Butler, 1993) and comprises a diversity of meanings and social arrangements. Further, determining contexts such as class, race, age and ability interact with heterosexuality.

[3] Heteronormitivity is a concept that encapsulates the institutionalisation of heterosexuality as a particular 'form of practice and relationships, of family structure and identity' (Richardson, 1996 p. 2).

[4] Feminists highlight the primacy of the phallus in the construction of what constitutes 'real sex'. Within common-sense thinking 'real sex' is conceptualised as penile penetration of the vagina. The penis is not only given primacy with regard to heterosexual relations it is ideologically emphasised in relation to gay men (see below). Butler (1993) has argued that the penis is *one* phallus and not *the* phallus, thus, it is not the sole possession of men and women can have it in their own right, as can be seen in attempt to parody of the phallus by 'chicks with dicks'. Nonetheless, within feminism the term phallus is traditionally understood to symbolise masculine authority. This is how the term is to be utilised in this Chapter.

[5] The term 'sex' is an ambiguous term, and can 'denote either the distinction between male or female (as 'two sexes') or as sex an erotic activity (to 'have sex')' [Scott and Jackson 2000, p 169] It is used here to denote erotic activity. 'Sex' whilst socially constructed and involving a range of behaviours is ideologically associated with heterosexual intercourse and reproduction. 'Sexuality' is also a categorisation of many different things [Skeggs, 1997]. The term 'sexuality' encapsulates the socially constructed facets of sexual desires, practices and identities as expressed personally and interpersonally. It is also recognised that sexuality 'is not a discrete sphere of interaction...It is a pervasive dimension of social life, one that permeates the whole, a dimension along which gender occurs and through which gender is socially constituted; it is a dimension along which other social divisions, like race and class, partly play themselves out' (MacKinnon, 1997, p. 60).

[6] It is also important here to note the influence of 'anti-gay' advocates. See Simpson (1996) for more detail.

[7] These considerations may also be significant with regard to sado-masochism. Califia (1988) for example, talks about the difficulties she encountered when trying to find other lesbian sado-masochists.

[8] It must be noted that this process was not straightforward. Ellis, Carpenter and Freud were at least ambivalent with regard to homosexuality. The attempts at this historical conjecture to humanise as opposed to revolutionise sexual relations meant that pleas for tolerance were

rooted in notions of the naturalness of homosexuality. Nonetheless, the end product was the projection of heterosexuality as the norm and homosexuality and lesbianism as 'other' (Corteen, forthcoming).

[9] The popularisation of the sexological model of sexuality can be traced through the many marriage manuals published and purchased during the inter-war years. For example, Stope's book *Married Love* (1918) was the 16th book (out of 25) most influential books over the previous fifty years (Jackson, 1994, p. 129). It sold more than 2,000 copies over the first fortnight and by the end of 1923 it had sold 400,000 copies. Numerous reprints and 28 editions, amounted to 1,032,250 copies by the end of 1955, with copies were translated into 14 languages (Jackson, 1994).

[10] The term 'new feminism' and 'new feminist' is a description of late nineteenth to early twentieth century feminism and feminists. It depicts the departure from first wave feminists who recognised and highlighted male violence against women. It is not to be confused with the contemporary development of new feminism and new feminists such as Natasha Walter and Jan Breslauer.

[11] The title of the book *Married Love* in itself demonstrates that it is not solely heterosexual (penetrative) sex that Stopes is advocating, but a particular form of heterosexual (penetrative) sex – sex within marriage. Thus, it is this form of heterosexuality that is desirable, acceptable and respectable.

[12] The production and dissemination of sex manuals must also be contextualised in the development and consolidation of capitalism and the inherent development of clearly demarcated gender roles which capitalism was implicated in and reliant upon for its success.

[13] Such arguments can also be discerned in the contemporary ideological and discursive construction of gay men as predatory. See for example the debates around the age of consent and the repeal of section 28 and school sex and relationship education (Corteen forthcoming).

[14] Women themselves also appear to have no control of such rhythms. Indeed, Stope's conceptualisation of heterosexual women, and the conceptualisation of female psuedo-homosexuals (see below) position women as passive objects, as opposed to agenic subjects. Women apparently have no agency and can be duped or manipulated by those that desire them.

[15] This conceptualisation of (heterosexual) women's sexuality consequently resulted in discussions and explanations of lesbianism which denied lesbians femininity and masculinised lesbians and their desires.

[16] Within the sexological tradition and within sex educators' propositions the 'invert' or 'real' homosexual which according to Bloch (cited above), is usually male, is accorded sexual autonomy, albeit predatory and misdirected. Whereas the 'pervert' or the 'pseudo-homosexual' usually female, as contended by Bloch, was denied any sexual autonomy (Corteen, forthcoming). Female pseudo-homosexuals were characterised as women who did not fit the masculine stereotype. They were generally feminine, naïve, of lesser intelligence and therefore easily seduced by 'real' homosexuals. This was Bloch's justification for his proclamation that 'original' homosexuality was less prevalent amongst women compared to men, while pseudo-homosexuality was more common amongst women (Jeffreys, 1985). Healey (1996, pp. 42-3) notes, 'The femme...there was something missing in her make up, she was either too ugly or too innocent to find a proper man. Or she was just visiting and would return to the arms of happy heterosexuality when rescued by a proper man'. Stephen and Mary Llewellyn, characters from Radclyffe Hall's, *The Well of Loneliness*, personify, embody and reflect these sexological categorisations and propositions. Stephen's sexuality

is innate and masculine. Her name alone conveys her masculinity. Mary Llewellyn however, is gentle, feminine or lesser intelligence and her homosexuality turns out to be a temporary divergence.

[17] This can be evidenced, in the obsession with anal sex on the part of some opponents to the repeal of this Section 28 of the Local Government Act 1988 (Corteen forthcoming).

[18] In relation to the heterosexualisation of penetrative sex between men Richardson (1996, p. 7) notes, 'Indeed the very use of the terms heterosexual – meaning vaginal – intercourse and homosexual – meaning anal – intercourse are revealing in this respect'.

[19] Both processes heterosexualise lesbian relations as the conceptualisation of lesbians as asexual is predicated on notions around 'lack', wherein lesbians lack the desire and lack a penis. When there is no penis it is assumed that there can be no sex or no 'real sex'. Queer theorists have challenged the primacy of the phallus by appropriation and parody, through packing and or wearing dildos. However, the success of such a challenge is debatable given power and resonance of the historical construction of lesbians. These transgressive performances and acts may be read by heterosexuals in particular, as imitating the 'real thing' – heterosexuality. The heterosexualisation of lesbian relations can also be evidenced in the production of lesbian bodies with astounding clitorises (Jeffreys, 1985; Richardson, 1996).

[20] In utilising the term 'street' Valentine (1996) is referring to the pavement, sidewalk and public places such as shops and cafes. Valentine prefers to the term 'street' in place of the concept 'public' as she contends that the term 'public' is no longer appropriate. Valentine forwards three reasons for this. One, many 'public' places are actually privatised or semi-privatised. Two, many places exclude people on the grounds of age, race, sexuality and so forth. Three, the term 'public' obscures the fact that so many so-called 'private' relationships are part of public space.

[21] The western public street is also white and gendered.

[22] According to Bristow and Wilson, 1993, queer theory developed out of queer politics which emerged in April 1990 in New York. Queer politics signifies a shift away from a politics of identity to a politics of difference. Queer politics and theory endeavours to debunk, subvert or transgress gender and sexuality categories through the political project of 'gender fuck' and 'anti-gay'.

[23] Within the lesbian and gay community these signifiers do not appear to be the case contemporarily, however, the points made here may have some significance with regard to other sexual dissidents, for example, with respect to sado-masochism.

[24] As Skeggs (1997, p. 122) asserts 'Heterosexuality consolidates respectability'. It is therefore difficult for women to take on a lesbian identity. Thus, it can be argued that the feminist phrase of the 1970s that 'any woman can' is highly simplistic (Corteen, forthcoming). It is also important here and in light of queer theory to note that a distinction must be made between women who 'play' with lesbianism and those who take on a lesbian identity in a heteropatriarchal society.

[25] In relation to young people the question of how young people, especially lesbian and gay young people learn about matters sexual, including sexual consent is an important one. Particularly in light of the inadequacy of school 'sex and relationship' education for all young people but especially for lesbian and gay young people (Corteen, forthcoming).

Bibliogaphy

Abbott, S. and Love, B. (1972), *Sappho Was a Right-On Woman*, New York: Stein and Day.

Alice, Gordon, Debbie and Mary (1988), 'Separatism', in Hoagland, S. L. and Penelope, J. (eds), *For Lesbians Only: A Separatist Anthology*, London: Onlywomen Press.

Allen, L. (1997), *The Lesbian Idol: Martina, kd and the Consumption of Lesbians Masculinity*, London: Cassell.

Bacchi, C. (1988), 'Feminism and the "Eroticisation" of the Middle-Class Woman: The Intersection of Class and Gender Attitudes', *Women's Studies International Forum*, Vol. 11, No. 1: 43-53.

Bell, D. and Binnie, J. (2000), *The Sexual Citizen: Queer Politics and Beyond*, Cambridge: Polity Press.

Bell, D. and Valentine, G. (1995), 'Introduction', in Bell, D. and Valentine, G (eds), *Mapping Desire*, London: Routledge.

Bristow, J. (1989), 'Being Gay: Politics, Pleasure, Identity', *New Formations*, Vol. 9, pp. 61-81.

Bristow, J. and Wilson, A. R. (1994), 'Introduction' in Bristow, J. and Wilson, A. R. (eds), *Activating Theory: Lesbian, Gay, Bisexual Politics*, London: Lawrence and Wishart.

Butler, J. (1990), *Gender Trouble: Feminism and the Subversion of Identity*, London: Routledge.

Butler, J. (1993), *Bodies That Matter: On the Discursive Limits of Sex*, London: Routledge.

Califia, P. (1988), *Sapphistory: The Book of Lesbian Sexuality*, Tallahassee: Naiad Press.

Califia, P. (1982), 'A Personal View', in Samois (1982).

Califia, P. (1989), *Macho Sluts*, Boston: Alyson.

Carlen, P. (ed.), (1985), *Criminal Women*, Cambridge: Polity Press.

Clarke, W. (1982), 'The Dyke, the Feminist and the Devil', *Feminist Review*, No. 11, June.

Connell, R. W. (1987), *Gender and Power*, Cambridge: Polity Press.

Corteen, K. and Scraton, P. (1997), 'Prolonging "Childhood", Manufacturing "Innocence" and Regulating Sexuality', in Scraton, P. (ed.), *'Childhood' in 'Crisis'?*, London: UCL Press.

Corteen, K., Tyrer, P., Skeggs, B. and Moran, L. (2000), *Citizens' Inquiry Reports: Lancaster and Manchester 2000*, ESRC 'Violence, Sexuality and Space' Research Project.

Corteen, K. (2002), 'Lesbian Safety Talk: Problematising Definitions and Experiences of Violence, Sexuality and Space', *Sexualities*, Vol. 5 No. 3: 259-280.

Corteen, K. (forthcoming), 'The Sexual Ordering of Society: A Critical Examination of Secondary School Sex and Relationship Education within One Local Authority', PhD thesis, Ormskirk, CSCSJ: Edge Hill.

Cottingham, L. (1996), *Lesbians are so Chic ... That We are Not Really Lesbians at All*, London: Cassell.

Coveney, L., Jackson, M., Jeffreys, S., Kay, L. and Mahony, P. (eds), *The Sexuality Papers: Male Sexuality and the Social Control of Women*, London: Hutchinson.

Duncan, N. (1996), 'Introduction: (Re)placings', in Duncan (1996a).

Duncan, N. (ed.) (1996a), *Body Space*, London: Routledge.

Dunne, G. A. (1997), *Lesbian Lifestyles: Women's Work and the Politics of Sexuality*, Basingstoke: Macmillan.

English, D., Hollibaugh, A., Gayle, R. (1982), 'Talking Sex: A Conversation on Sexuality and Feminism', *Feminist Review*, No 11, June.

Faderman, L. (1981), *Surpassing the Love of Men*, London: The Women's Press.

Faderman, L. (1992), 'The Return of Butch and Femme: A Phenomenon in Lesbian Sexuality of the 1980s and 1990s', *Journal of the History of Sexuality*, Vol. 2, No. 4, pp. 578-595.

Freud, S. (1977a), *On Sexuality: Three essays on the Theory of Sexuality and Other Works*, Translated by James Strachey, Richards, A. (ed.), Middlesex: Penguin Books.

Freud, S. (1977b), *Case Histories I: 'Dora and Little Hans'*, Translated by Alix and James Strachey, Richards, A. (ed.), Middlesex, Penguin.

GALOP (1991), *Survey on Homophobic Violence and Harassment*, London: GALOP.

Gibbs, L. (1994), *Daring to Descent; Lesbian Culture from the Margins to the Mainstream*, London: Cassell.

Gutter Dyke Collective (1988), 'Over the Walls, Separatism', in Hoagland (1988a).

Hall, R. (1928), *The Well of Loneliness*, London: Virago.

Hawkes, G. (1996), *A Sociology of Sex and Sexuality*, Buckingham: Open University Press.

Healy, E. (1996), *Lesbian Sex Wars*, London: Virago.

Hennessy, R. (1995), 'Queer Visibility in Commodity Culture', in Nicholson, L. and Seidman, S. (eds), *In Social Postmodernism: Beyond Identity Politics*, Cambridge: Cambridge University Press.

Hekma, G. (2001), 'Sexual Citizenship and Sexual Liberation in the Netherlands: Issues and Contradictions', Open lecture, 19th March 20001, Ormskirk, CSSS, Edge Hill.

Hoagland, S. L. and Penelope, J. (1988a) (eds.), *For Lesbians Only: A Separatist Anthology*, London: Onlywomen Press.

Hoagland, S. L. (1988), 'An Invitation' in Hoagland (1988a)

Hubbard, P. (2001), 'Sex Zones: Intimacy, Citizenship and Public Space', *Sexualities*, Vol. 4, No. 1: 51-71.

Jackson, S. (1994), *The Real Facts of Life: Feminism and the Politics of Sexuality c1850-1940*, London: Taylor and Francis.

Jackson, S. (1999), 'A Conventional Affair', *Sexualities*, Vol. 2, No. 2: 247-252.

Jeffreys, S. (1984), *The Spinster and Her Enemies. Feminism and Sexuality 1880-1930*, London: The Women's Press.

Jenness, V. (1992), 'Lesbian Identities and the Categorisation Problem' in Plummer, (1992a).

Kitzinger, C. and Wilkinson, S. (1993), 'Theorising Heterosexuality', in Wilkinson, S. and Kitzinger, C. (eds.), *Heterosexuality: A Feminism and Psychology Reader*, London: Sage.

MacKinnon, K. (1997), 'Sexuality', in Nicholson, N. *The Second Wave: A Reader in Feminist Theory*, London: Routledge.

Moran, L (1995), *Homophobic Violence and Harassment in Lancaster and Morecambe* (Copies available from the author, Birkbeck University, London).

Nestle, J. (1987), *A Restricted Country: Documents of Desire and Resistance*, London: Pandora.

Penelope, J. (1988), 'The Mystery of Lesbians', in Hoagland (1988a).

Plummer, K (1992), 'Speaking Its Name: Inventing a Lesbians and Gay studies' in Plummer (1992a).

Plummer, K. (ed) (1992a), *Modern Homosexualities; Fragments of Lesbian and Gay Experience*, London: Routledge.

Radicalesbians (1988), 'The Woman identified Woman', in Hoagland S. L. and Penelope, J. (eds.), op. cit.

Rich, A. (1981), *Compulsory Heterosexuality and Lesbian Existence*, London: Onlywomen Press.

Richardson, D. (1996), 'Heterosexuality and Social Theory' in Richardson, D. (ed.), *Theorising Heterosexuality*, Buckingham: Open University Press.

Richardson, D. and May, H. (1999), 'Deserving Victims?: Sexual Status and the Social Construction of Violence', *The Sociological Review*, 47(2), pp. 308-333.

Rowbotham, S. and Weeks, J. (1977), *Socialism and the New Life: The Personal and the Sexual Politics of Edward Carpenter and Havelock Ellis*, Southampton: Pluto Press.

Rubin, G (1982), 'A Personal History of the Lesbian S/M Community and Movement in San Francisco', in Samois (1982).

Rubin, G. (1984), 'Thinking Sex: Notes for a Radical Theory of the Politics of Sexuality', in Vance, C. (ed), *Pleasure and Danger: Exploring Female Sexuality*, London: Pandora.

Samois (ed.) (1982), *Coming to Power. Writings and Graphics on Lesbian S/M*, Boston: Alyson.

Scott, K. (2001), 'HIV Man Jailed for Knowingly Infecting Lover', *The Guardian*, March 17th 2000.

Scott, S. and Jackson, S. (2000), 'Sexuality', in Payne, G. (ed), *Social Divisions*, London: Macmillan.

Sedgewick, E. (1990), *Epistemology of the Closet*, Berkeley: University of California Press.

Simpson, M. (ed.) (1996), *Anti-Gay*, London: Freedom Editions.

Smith, A. M. (1992), 'Resisting the Erasure of Lesbian Sexuality: A Challenge to Queer Activism', in Plummer (1992a).

Skeggs, B. (1997), *Formations of Class and Gender: Becoming Respectable*, London: Sage.

Skeggs, B. (1999), 'Matter Out of Place: Visibility and Sexualities in Leisure Spaces', *Leisure Studies*, 18, (2), pp. 213-232.

Stein, A. (1999), 'Clinton, the Right Wing, and "Civilised" Sexual Morality', *Sexualities* Vol. 2, No. 2, pp. 247-250.

Stonewall (1996), *Queer Bashing: A National Survey of Hate Crimes Against Lesbians and Gay Men*, London: Stonewall.

Stopes, M. (1918), *Married Love* (29th edition), London: Victor Gollancz.

Stopes, M. (1928), *Enduring Passion*, London: G. P. Putnam.

Valentine, G. (1996), '(Re)Negotiating the 'Heterosexual Street': Lesbian Production of Space', in Duncan (1996a).

Weeks, J. (1985), *Sexuality and its Discontents*, London: Routledge.

Weeks, J. (1993), 'An Unfinished Revolution: Sexuality in the 20th Century', in Harwood, V. et. al. (eds), *Pleasure Principles: Politics, Sexuality and Ethics*, London: Lawrence and Wishart.

Whittle, S. (1994), 'Consuming Differences: The Collaboration of the Gay Body with the Cultural State', in Whittle, S. (ed.), *The Margins of the City: Gay Men's Urban Lives*, Aldershot: Ashgate.

Wilton, T. (1995), *Lesbian Studies: Setting An Agenda*, London: Routledge.

Chapter 11

'Sexual Rights' and 'Sexual Responsibilities' within consensual 'S/M' practice

Andrea Beckmann

Like many postmodern texts, this chapter should be understood as a tentative attempt to tackle a very complex subject-area, which seeks to open up a dialogue and does not aim to provide yet another meta-narrative. The content of this Chapter is derived both from a critical theoretical exploration of the notions of 'rights' and 'responsibilities', and on data collected during a criminological, methodologically mainly qualitative, social research project I carried out in London's consensual 'S/M Scene'. I conducted unstructured, focused interviews as well as participant observation with the aim of exploring the 'lived realities' of consensual 'S/M' and its 'subjugated knowledges'. (As is standard practice, names have been changed. For further details of the interviews contact the author. 'S/M' is in inverted commas throughout to emphasise that it is a social construction.)

The data collected provided information about the diversity of erotic experimentation and 'bodily practices' (Mauss, 1979) of consensual 'S/M'. These bodily practices (a term I find more adequate, in describing and understanding the empirical world of consensual 'S/M' as I encountered it, than the simultaneously value-laden and, in contemporary consumer society, meaningless term 'sexuality') often stand in deep contrast to the cultural imperatives of genital 'sexuality' and to the day-to-day wholesaling of 'sex' as a consumer product. My data also revealed the central importance of responsibility and rights within consensual 'S/M', an importance that escapes traditional understandings and interpretations of these notions.

'Responsibility' and 'rights' in this context are defined not by reference to any explicit or implicit morality but through the development of a personal ethics that is necessarily contextual and relational. Accordingly the sense of 'responsibility' and of 'rights' is a contextual one and therefore also implies the possibility of change, which I will relate to Foucault's notions of the 'practice of the self' and 'care of the self'. I will put forward the suggestion that the framework of consensual 'S/M' 'body practices' allows and even requires far more reflection (self- and contextual) about personal responsibility and rights than any 'normal' 'sexual' encounter.

Following the notion of a 'politics of difference' (Sawicki, 1991) I would like to attempt to provide a reading of the practices of consensual 'S/M' that understands the 'subjugated knowledges' and experiences of this still marginalised, selectively and indirectly criminalised, group within society as a resource. The conceptual and practically realised framework of consensual 'S/M' relationships does provide a resource for acquiring a more reflective, responsible and contextual understanding of the complexity and interdependence of rights and responsibilities in human relationships: an understanding that does not rely on or appeal to any universalistic code of morals.

Very much in contrast to western socio-cultural concepts of relationships, for example romantic love, that promote on a socio-legal level the institution of marriage – which until the late eighteenth century, even from the point of legal theory, allowed the practice of wife beating (Muncie and McLaughlin, 1996, p. 136f) – the 'bodily practices' of consensual 'S/M' that I observed within the 'new' Scene are not (as they used to be in the 'old Scene') prescriptive and objectifying, but rather promote and even require profound contextual reflection and relational negotiation.

Holland, et al. (1992, p. 142) write that '...controlling sexual safety can be problematic for young women if they play subordinate roles in sexual encounters.' This statement reflects the difficulty of distancing oneself within many so-called 'normal' situations or societal contexts from socio-cultural constructions that position individuals and groups, according to historically specific interpretations and representations of 'gender', 'class', 'race', 'age' etc., in relatively powerful or powerless 'modes of being'. As we shall see, the context (second socialisation in the Scene, the conduct code of Scene and its informal control) as well as the actual 'bodily practices' of consensual 'S/M' detach 'lived bodies' from their socio-cultural positions and limitations and foster an open, explorative and at the same time caring attitude towards one's 'self' and the other.

During an interview, Lara discussed the difference between the risks of abuse within so-called 'normal' society and within the context of consensual 'S/M'. For her and for me people that engage in consensual 'S/M' are not inherently 'better', more responsible people, but there are distinct differences and risks that make the framework provided by consensual 'S/M' far more safe:

> ...But the difference is when you're negotiating a contract and you're saying: This is what I want to do with you....

It appears thus that the explicit negotiations about the needs, wishes and pleasures within the 'relative freedom' of conditions of domination in the conceptual and often experienced context of consensual 'S/M' 'bodily practices' provides a relative safety concerning the abuse of power.

Although 'domestic violence' is criminalised in contemporary society, neither its practice nor the impact of the underlying inequality of 'rights' and 'responsibilities' in terms of often internalised social constructions of gender, class, race, age, etc., as well as material conditions, has yet been properly addressed within public discourses (whether in the context of straight, gay, lesbian, bi- or otherwise defined relationships). From a critical criminological and feminist perspective, what is depressingly evident within various societal relationships is the lack of a concept and practice – to use Foucauldian terminology – of 'care of the self', including attentiveness to the 'selves' of a diversity of partners. As I do not want (and I am afraid I am incapable of this split anyway) to separate the personal sphere from my professional and political agendas, I have to add that even the diversity of experienced relationships within my personal sphere confirms this observation.

Deconstructing the Liberal Notions of 'Rights/Responsibilities'

As already stated, the 'bodily practices' of consensual 'S/M' as observed within the 'new' London Scene (in contrast to the 'old' Scene, which did not foster reflection but merely prescribed role-reversals instead of exploration) escape conventional and traditional understandings and interpretations of 'rights' and 'responsibilities'.

If we were to adopt the notions of 'responsibility' and 'rights' from a liberal rights theory perspective, we would not gain an authentic understanding that accommodates the 'lived diversity' of the empirical world. The liberal view is limiting because it advocates or presumes a legal individualism which fundamentally lacks any consideration of contextuality. The traditional, conventional discourse on 'rights' and 'responsibilities' is thus existentially flawed and alienating because it is inherently individualistic, anti-social, competitive, de-contextualised and, last but not least, inextricably tied to the notion of 'formal equality'.

Not only does this ascription of 'equal rights' operate to veil the 'suffered inequalities' produced and reproduced by the 'conditions of domination' (Foucault) inherent in capitalist consumer (I could add sexist, racist, ageist, ableist, etc.) society, but further, and this its most destructive effect, in practice the notion of 'equal rights' often leads to an unreflective acceptance of the status quo and a feeling of false security on the part of human beings.

Nicola Lacey's *Unspeakable Subjects* offers the possibility of critically reconstructing the notions of 'rights' and 'responsibility' which have not only preoccupied feminist legal thought but were also, as I have said, revealed to be crucial within the context of my empirical research. Lacey proposes to adopt and apply a modification of Cornell's concept of 'relational autonomy' and 'sexual integrity' (in my perspective 'bodily integrity'). In Lacey's opinion this application would require, in the case of rape for example, a far more complex sexual assault law that moves away from the conception of 'proprietary autonomy' towards a contextual and relational conception of autonomy. In the context of defining the offence of rape, Lacey argues that such a definition should move away from an emphasis on 'lack of consent' in the abstract and asymmetrical terms in which it is traditionally understood to be the core determinant of 'sexual abuse'. She therefore suggests the development of a 'positive consent' standard in contrast to the inherently dangerous conventional legal assumption of mutuality.

My attempts of theorising also move away from liberal rights notions (including the decontextualised understanding of 'consent'; see Cowling, 1998) and are close to Lacey's notion of 'positive consent' as well as Sue Lees' concept of 'communicative sexuality' (1996), which I consider to be covered by Foucault's notion of 'care of the self' and 'ethics of the self'. In order to illustrate and relate these theoretical elaborations to the empirical world of consensual 'S/M', I will first turn to the Scene in London as I observed and experienced it and then return to my theoretical concerns later.

The Conceptual Framework and the 'Bodily Practices' of Consensual 'S/M'

There are several levels on which the crucial importance of reflection upon limits (responsibility) and an awareness of individual possibilities of pleasure (rights) in the context of consensual 'S/M' became visible.

'Responsibilities' and 'Rights' in the Set-up of 'Scenes' for Consensual 'S/M':

Consensual 'S/M' requires a high level of internal reflection and external communication even before a 'scene' is set up, not only because of the sometimes complex techniques applied but, crucially, in order to make the experience of play pleasurable and safe for both parties. In contrast to 'normalised' and usually unregulated relationships, there is a requirement for more explicit communication and negotiations relating to the specific preferences of both parties, to the setting of safe-words or -gestures and also to the way in which the process of 'coming down' after a 'scene' is to be handled. Even the set-up of the 'dungeons' or 'black rooms' that are used for these consensual 'body practices' clearly point to the heightened sense of care ('responsibility/rights') concerning safety and health within this setting.

Anthony:

> (...) Basically, I think good 'S/M'-sex is very controlled, very controlled. At every stage, extremely controlled. (...) If I'm having a 'scene' with my Asian 'slave' for example, I might plan for two hours what exactly is going to happen. From the minute he rings that doorbell, exactly what will happen. If it's for watersports for instance I have to set up the bathroom in a particular way, move things out, bring things in, change the lights, clean things up. It's a lot of hard work. (...) Like I keep saying it's a whole different mindset and people don't understand that. (...) People have problems with that I think because it takes sex onto other levels that people can't even imagine. (...) everything is discussed before we do anything, anyway. There are certain things that he told me he doesn't like and don't do that kind of stuff. Even though he is my 'slave' by contract, I respect him as a person – it sounds like a contradiction. I can say: 'Yes, he is my 'slave',

yes he is my 'bottom', but I still respect him as a person. I know that 'S/M' draws up contradictions and that's what people have problems with.

'Communicative Body-usage' and Responsibilities and Rights in Consensual 'S/M'

On the level of the 'body', consensual 'S/M' and the 'Scene' that developed around this 'body practice', a 'communicative body usage' (Frank, 1991, in Turner, 1996) is fostered which not only stands in contrast to the 'mirroring body usage' *(ibid.)* that is generated and reinforced by consumer society, but which also fundamentally requires self-awareness in terms of 'responsibility' and 'rights' in relation to limits and pleasures. Preconditions for 'communicative body usage' are locatable in shared narratives of the 'Scene', communal rituals, a 'Scene'-specific second socialisation and, most crucial of all, in the implicit and explicit (safe-words and safe-gestures) requirement to continuously reflect upon one's own possibilities of deriving pleasure as well as one's individual limits, which may change.

For Bette consensual 'S/M' and 'ordinary sex' are similar in that both

...happen to utilise sort of extreme physical sensations in order to bring pleasure,...'

but with very distinctive features. The meaning and existential importance of communication between the partners engaged appears to Bette a point of difference:

I think that 'S/M'-sex in a way is more conscious, more verbal and non-verbal communication between people throughout. I mean if somebody is being beaten, you ought to be looking at the person and trying to get it absolutely right. I mean that should be true in ordinary sex as well but I think it's more true of 'S/M'-sex than any other sex...Men just go for their own pleasure. I think that part of the thing is the difference between intercourse and beating somebody, with intercourse, man having intercourse with a woman, there's a very direct sexual path, there's a very sexually fixed pleasure. And therefore he has a motive for just getting what he wants. But if what he does is not directly genital or sexual. I mean it may give immense satisfaction but the satisfaction it will give will be in the communication with the other person. The fact to get it right with the other person. The fact that it's turning the other person on. Unless this man is just violent. But assuming it's a proper 'S/M'-person. There isn't a direct path ...

Therefore Bette concludes that empathy is more crucial in consensual 'S/M' than in 'ordinary sex' as consensual 'S/M' depends directly on the communication between the partners as it otherwise would not work out.

After reading the 'Hite report on male sexuality' Bette was astonished:

It's just so tragic in a way how limited, what they appear to enjoy is. And how little use, you know, they are just so genitally orientated. It's just so terribly, terribly sad. You just think, what they are missing out on. You haven't explored your mind or other parts of the body. Have you not been taught about being fucked yourself or what about your nipples. I mean all you do is with your penises. It's so sad. I mean putting your penis in isn't much communication. And I mean sex doesn't have to be like that. And being a man doesn't have to be like that.

This comment has clear parallels to Michel Foucault's criticism of the genital fixation of the concept of 'sexuality' and its effects of domination: how, for example it has often led to 'dominating body usages' on the part of human beings who need to prove (or maintain) their socially constructed 'masculinity', and has thus prevented 'communicative body usages'.

The use of the term *pleasure*, as opposed to *desire*, is crucial in this context because, as Foucault understood, these terms have different connotations:

> I am advancing the term [pleasure], because it seems to me that it escapes the medical and naturalistic connotations inherent in the notion of desire. That notion has been used as a tool, as a grid of intelligibility, a calibration in terms of normality...The term 'pleasure 'on the other hand is virgin territory, unused, almost devoid of meaning. There is no 'pathology' of pleasure, no 'abnormal' pleasure. It is an event 'outside the subject', or at the limit of the subject, taking place in that something which is neither of the body nor of the soul,..a notion neither assigned nor assignable. (in Halperin, 1995, pp. 93-94)

The Scene thus provides a space for a (re-)signification of 'lived bodies' through 'bodily practices' that are accompanied by 'dislocated' signs and symbols. The diversity of representations (discourses and narratives) thus created can moreover be used as tools for ongoing explorations and experiences of 'lived bodies' and their changing limits. The various possibilities of transgression and/or transcendence within the context of these 'bodily practices' in terms of societal hierarchies (e.g. class, gender, race, age) also relate alternative patterns of discourse.

Second socialisation: The learning process of consensual 'S/M'

The awareness that each individual on the 'Scene' expressed of 'responsibility' with regard to the limits of other and self in interdependence with 'rights' to pleasure is acquired through a learning process on the 'Scene' and is also informally controlled and reinforced within the 'Scene'. If, for example a 'top' does not 'play' safe no-one will 'play' with this person again. If people who are traditionally labelled 'male' behave according to the socio-cultural behaviour patterns and rules that conventional society has established, they will soon find themselves outside the Scene. This form of control, although only on an informal basis, has profound effects in terms of behaviour changes.

Jane confirmed that 'responsibility' and 'safe sex' are important issues in the Scene, more so than in mainstream society:

...it's a lot better, I mean, I much rather go to a party that is an 'S/M'-party than a 'normal' party because, you know, that if somebody harasses you that's considered unacceptable and it's going to be dealt with. People are much more responsible usually about sex and there's a lot more emphasis on safe sex.

Apart from individual self-responsibility which appears to be increased within the Scene, Jane mentioned the impact of the pressure of 'significant others':

Peer-pressure to behave. So people who may be not necessarily sensible and respectful will be pressured into behaving like that.

One of my interviewees, Bette, mentioned one of her female friends who went for the first time to a 'S/M'-club and then stated:

I can't believe it, these are men but they don't behave like I would expect them to behave.

Me:

So, do you think these men are more reflective in that surrounding?

Bette:

Oh, definitely, yes. And also because of all these negotiations...

The 'Scene'-specific code of conduct encourages respect for and reflective exploration of 'self' and others and, as societal categories count for less in this 'Scene', everyone is more or less thrown back onto his or her 'self'. Golding once described a lesbian Scene-club as '...a peculiar place of exile;...' and as a '...distinct arena whose parameters can blur the edges...' (in Kroker, 1993, pp. 147-8). This special feature is created by the distinct code of conduct within the Scene of consensual 'S/M' and through the limitlessness of 'bodily practices' based on fantasy. The socially constructed differences between individuals do not count in this environment (with the partial exception of 'race') and individual pleasures and limits count for everything.

Diabolo:

... I'm 48 years old and the 'S/M'-scene is more accepting of age-diversity as well as sexual diversity because they are not normal. And they don't have a normal age, there isn't a normal age to be an 'S/M'er for example. Whereas there is almost a normal age to be on a disco-dancefloor or in a backroom of some pub somewhere, you got to be twenty or something or at least pretend that you are. And I'm beyond all that. Yes, so there isn't ageism, there isn't sexism, as there is amongst the so supposed 'normal'. And it's all part of people breaking free from stereotypical thinking about themselves and others.

Apart from the very obvious socio-cultural categories like 'gender', 'class', etc., the cultural pressure of 'the body beautiful', the icon of consumerism, is transgressed within most Scene clubs; people of all ages, sizes and shapes do not hesitate to dress in skin-tight leather and rubber-outfits or to turn up in nude or half-nude states in order to explore themselves and others. During my 'participant observations' in London's Scene another remarkable difference I noted from conventional 'club-culture' was the presence and acceptance of disabled people as active participants in 'play'. Comparing this feature of the Scene with the usual social reactions towards disabled 'bodies' is quite striking as for example Kirsten Hearn's 'A Woman's Right to Cruise' illustrates for the lesbian movement and club-culture. As a lesbian disabled woman she accuses most of the lesbian movement of 'ableism' and notes about herself and other disabled lesbians:

> ...our experience demonstrates that the reaction of severely able-bodied dykes when being cruised by one of us is likely to be embarrassment and terror. We are generally not taken seriously in these situations, since we are not supposed to have any sexual feelings whatsoever, let alone the ability to carry them out...Different women with different disabilities have different needs and abilities before, during and after sex. Some of us can only lie in certain positions or may have to use different parts of our bodies. (Hearn, in McEwen and O'Sullivan, 1988, pp. 50-51)

The 'Care of the Self': Contextualising 'Rights' and 'Responsibilities' in Consensual 'S/M' within the 'Frames of Reference' of Practitioners

I do not want to attempt to give an impression of a 'perfect world' in the Scene. Like Polhemus and Randall, who researched within it, I also noticed: 'As in any cross-section of society there are givers and takers, the used and their abusers, those who find themselves and the unfortunate few who get hopelessly lost' (Polhemus and Randall, 1994, p. 202). What the 'new' Scene of consensual 'S/M' does do, however, is to provide a space for 'counterpractices', because it disrupts the fundamental philosophical pattern of the Western world which has tied 'sexuality' to 'subjectivity' and 'truth'. 'Sexuality', so conceived, in effect permanently shapes human beings' relationships with themselves.

The 'bodily practices' of consensual 'S/M' serve Anthony as a space for exploration of 'bodily' possibilities and choice:

> But we have to also separate fantasy from reality, I think that's what 'S/M' does for me as an individual. And also it is, I want to explore lots and lots of things, whether its 'S/M', being tied up, watersports or whether its scatting – it provides this space. Where I can say this is for me or this is not for me, you know what I'm saying?

Further these 'bodily practices' allow 'lived bodies' to experiment within the spaces of subject- and object-position to which they are usually assigned by the apparatuses of domination. 'Play' with socio-culturally dominating symbols and representations of power hierarchies allows for their change.

Anthony:

> Just finding out how far I can go with my own boundaries. 'S/M' actually provides that place to play out what I want to play out without feeling guilty. As a black gay person there's a lot of issues around slavery and bondage – black experience – dealing with those issues.

For some practitioners the ambition to change structures of domination does not stop with their own explorative transformation in terms of an acquired 'empowerment' but goes further than that:

Anthony:

> I think to me as a black guy engaging in 'S/M' might change certain ideas.(...) -it provides this space. Where I can say this is for me or this is not for me...

A Foucauldian reading of consensual 'S/M' as a 'laboratory of life' that allows for socio-political changes suggests itself in this context and was evoked by much of the content of several of my interviews.

The 'Care of Self/Other' in Consensual 'S/M'

In order to appreciate the respect and empathy for both limits and pleasures that many of the 'tops' had in relation to their 'bottoms', it is crucial not only to be aware of the profound interdependence of 'play' but also to know about the 'golden rule' of consensual 'S/M' that states: 'A good top has to be a bottom first.' Obviously this rule will generate empathy on an experiential level for being in positions that are characterised by a lack of control.

> (...) You know, I'm too strong a personality to come off as a bottom. You know, I've started off as a bottom because I believed that's what you're supposed to do. That's the best way to do it and I think I'm right but then I decided that I've learned enough and I didn't really enjoy that position, mostly because I didn't ...It's very hard to find someone who's skilled, and they have to be skilled not just in the physical thing but in the emotional safety, you know, that's also what Pat Califia and SAMOIS stressed, was emotional safety and what happens afterwards.

As the pleasure and safety of the partners engaged in consensual 'S/M' 'play' are existentially interdependent, a 'good top' will not only rely on the safe-word or gesture negotiated beforehand but continuously care for and monitor the 'bottom'. According to Anthony:

(...) if you are a 'top' you have to be aware of how your 'bottom' is feeling at every single stage. A 'top' has to take responsibility, like a 'bottom' has also to take responsibility. A 'top' has to be aware of how exactly his 'bottom' is feeling. Is he OK ,can he breathe OK...is he mentally OK? Sometimes a 'bottom' might say: 'Yes, I'm okay.' But they might not be OK as well. So it must be like a unit, you must have a sixth sense. You have to pick up on body-language, breathing. And you might say: 'Well, actually, I don't think you're okay.'

Another interviewee, Jane, explained that she was emotionally and physically abused within her family, before leaving home at an early age. A very widespread stereotype suggests that people who have been abused as children will be more likely to engage in 'sadomasochistic' activities, yet the empirical research revealed that many people in the Scene did not have any abusive backgrounds but, for example, were bored and fed up with 'sexuality' as genital and as a commodity.

Concerning the relationship between childhood abuse and consensual 'S/M' practice, Jane remarked:

There may be a few more taboos that make it a bit more fun to explore because for most of us it's about exploring taboo. It's about pushing limits.

And later she added:

I'm not going to turn around and blame the abuse.

'Play' with formerly painful and threatening situations which can be 'relived' and 're-experienced' within the trusting and safe, because controlled, context of consensual 'S/M' appears to have therapeutic effects for some practitioners. The experiential transformation of traumatic experiences allows for a process of re-memorising and my observations suggest that it increases self-confidence and assertiveness for many practitioners. Former abuse experiences can thus at times be transformed through erotic practice in combination with trust and emotional safety:

Lara:

...a lot of things that we work out sexually do have to do with [their] childhood that those fantasies that are the most taboo and the most exciting often have to do with things that have happened to us that we haven't resolved or ways that we have learned to deal with things that are abuse by eroticising it.

Me:

Like overcoming the pain through erotic?

Lara:

> Yeah. The psychic pain, it might not even have been physical pain but, you know, there's a lot of things that you can work out.

Towards a Critical Ethics : Foucault's 'Care of the Self'

Many feminist writers have suggested that consensual 'S/M' practice ought to be read as a copy or mirroring of societal inequalities and/or that these 'bodily practices' can only be consensual between 'equal' partners, 'equality' being usually defined according to socially constructed categories of 'gender' and/or 'sexual orientation'.

Yet when we understand personhood not as socio-culturally and/or bio-psychologically determined but as a project – as a process of becoming, which has an imaginary dimension and no definite end – the idea of determined personhood with which dogmatic/radical feminists seem to operate disintegrates. The notion of contextual, relational integrity '...promises to escape the dangers both of essentialising a particular conception of the body and of propagating a vision of feminine empowerment which is premised, paradoxically, on a victim status which accords access to "truth"' (Lacey, 1998, p. 120).

There are still therefore undertones of a very modern deterministic positivism in much of feminist, even so-called 'postmodern', thought, in terms of a (re-) inscription onto 'bodies' of positions of power/lessness which are taken to be casually related to physiological, socio-psychological and/or psychological attributes. If we consider the project of deconstruction on both the philosophical level and the existential level of the 'lived body' and recall Michel Foucault's description of consensual 'S/M' as a 'laboratory of life', a 'political experiment' and a 'limit experience', the potential capacity of this 'bodily practice' to engender an existential, fundamentally experienced perception and understanding of the impossibility of a fixed 'identity' becomes apparent.

In Derrida's view the 'impossibility of identity' opens up endless possibilities for disrupting dominant identity discourses. In my opinion, in contrast to e.g. Diprose (1994), Foucault's notion of an 'aesthetics of self' does not depend, especially when read and contextualised within the framework and 'bodily practices' of consensual 'S/M', on some kind of '...pre-social body of disorganised pleasures' (Diprose, 1994, p. 75).

In contemporary 'late modern' or 'postmodern' consumer societies of the Western world there is a decline in belief in moral or ethical codes based on religion and many people are opposed to legal interventions and rules intruding in their lives. But liberation movements have not managed to find any principles on the basis of which a new ethics could evolve, one that does not derive from so-called scientific power/knowledges of the 'self'. Alternative approaches therefore need to be found. On an empirical level this chapter tried to provide insights into the 'subjugated knowledges' of consensual 'S/M' practitioners and their understanding and practice of contextual and relational ethics; now, the remainder of this chapter shall briefly move into a more theoretical discussion.

As a starting point Foucault stated that we have to acknowledge, not that everything is bad, but that everything can be potentially dangerous: 'I think that the ethico-political choice we have to make every day is to determine which is the main danger' (Foucault, in Rabinow, 1984, p. 343). Every ethics that is critical and wary of mechanisms of subjection ought to try and point towards other possibilities. Foucault's suggestion in connection with this complex problematic is the development of an 'aesthetics of self': the re-creation or re-invention of 'self' as a corporeal work of art, without reference to an external or internalised moral (disciplinary) code.

The call for an 'aesthetics of existence' in the approach to life which Foucault elaborated in *La Volonté de Savoir* understands such an 'aesthetics of existence' as contrasted with, and in resistance to, a 'science of life'. For Foucault, to understand and appreciate human existence as a work of art '...is to take it out of the domain of the scientifically knowable and free us from the obligation of deciphering ourselves as a system of timeless functions which are subjected to corresponding norms' (Bernauer, in Armstrong, 1992, p. 262). Foucault's history of sexuality suggests the ethical task '...of detaching ourselves from those forces which would subordinate human existence [*bios*] to biological life [*zoe*]' (Bernauer, in Armstrong, 1992, p. 262).

The central concern of Greek ethics from which Foucault derived and developed his concept of 'Ethics of the self', is ethical conduct which is understood as involving people's relationship to themselves and to others. This ethics is thus a contextual, relational one (very much as practised in consensual 'S/M'), which is not fundamentally related to any socio-legal institutional system (e.g. in ancient Greece there existed only a few, not strongly compelling, laws against 'sexual' misbehaviour). The goal of this continuous 'ethical practice of the self' is the constitution of a kind of ethics that aims at an 'aesthetics of existence'. It is important to note that Foucault did not understand ancient Greek ethics as an alternative but as a starting point to develop a concept of ethics that would be more open, flexible and contextual than moral codes of conduct or legalistic notions of 'responsibilities' and 'rights'.

The 'bodily practices' of consensual 'S/M' depend to a large degree on a continuous reflexivity; in Foucault's terms, on a 'critical hermeneutics' of the construction of 'self'. Many practitioners of consensual 'S/M' thus engage in an active process of becoming ethical subjects through change which, again, Foucault would term a '*pratique de soi*' or 'self-forming activity' The 'ethics of the self' are therefore necessarily contingent, local, specific, experimental and never complete. The shared 'pleasures in limits' ('rights and responsibilities') of consensual 'S/M' practitioners concerning 'bodily integrity' and/or harm are contextual and relational and are based on respect, acquired trust and explicit negotiations. They do not depend on 'regimes of truth' but depend crucially on the reflexive awareness of the partners engaged.

A conception of 'postmodern ethics' requires, according to Bauman (1992), an ethics that is realisable in social practice and that is based on reflection. In my opinion Foucault's 'care of the self' and/or 'ethics of self' provide a crucial starting-point, while the 'subjugated knowledges' of consensual 'S/M' practitioners illustrate the potential practicability of such an approach.

This chapter has not only provided the space for a small percentage of the 'subjugated knowledges' collected during empirical fieldwork, but further has sought strongly to oppose the socio-political marginalisation and silencing of 'difference' and to engage itself on the side of the human right to express, represent and live the 'pleasures in limits' that human beings chose to engage in. To end this chapter it is useful to quote Foucault's understanding of resistance in contemporary political struggles:

> If one side of this resistance is to 'refuse what we are', the other side is to invent, not discover, who we are by promoting 'new forms of subjectivity' (Foucault, in Armstrong, 1992, p. 263).

It is hoped that this chapter demonstrated that consensual 'S/M' practice and conduct offer one possibility to do just that in an ethical way that does not depend on distorting and alienating liberal conceptions of abstract 'responsibilities' and 'rights'.

Bibliography

Aggleton, P., Davies, P. and Hart, G. (eds) (1992), *AIDS: Rights, Risk and Reason*, Brighton: The Falmer Press.

Bauman, Z. (1992), *Intimations of Postmodernity*, London: Routledge.

Bernauer, J. W. (1992), 'Beyond life and death: On Foucault's post-Auschwitz ethic' in Armstrong, T. J., *Michel Foucault Philosopher*, London: Harvester Wheatsheaf, pp. 260-279.

Cowling, M. (1998), *Date Rape and Consent*, Aldershot: Ashgate.

Diprose, R. (1994), *The Bodies of Women*, London: Routledge.

Foucault, M. (1990), *The History of Sexuality*, Vol. 1, Harmondsworth: Penguin.

Foucault, M. (1992), *The History of Sexuality*, Vol. 2, Harmondsworth: Penguin.

Foucault, M. (1990), *The History of Sexuality*, Vol. 3, Harmondsworth: Penguin.

Golding, S. (1993), 'The Excess: An Added Remark On Sex, Rubber, Ethics and Other Impurities', in *New Formations*, Spring.

Grosz, E. and Probyn, E. (eds) (1995), *Sexy Bodies*, London: Routledge.

Halperin, D. M. (1995), *Saint Foucault: Towards a Gay Hagiography*, Oxford: Oxford University Press.

Lacey, N. (1998), *Unspeakable Subjects: Feminist Essays in Legal and Social Theory*, Oxford: Hart Publishing.

Lees, S. (1996), *Carnal Knowledge: Rape on Trial*, London: Hamish Hamilton.

Mauss, M. (1979), *Sociology and Psychology*, London: Routledge and Kegan Paul.

McEwen, C. and O'Sullivan, S. (eds) (1988), *Out the Other Side*, London: Virago Press.

Merleau-Ponty, M. (1968), *The Visible and the Invisible*, Evanston: Northwestern University Press.

Merleau-Ponty, M. (1969), *Humanism and Terror*, Boston: Beacon Press.

Merleau-Ponty, M. (1963), *The Structure of Behaviour*, Boston: Beacon Press.

Merleau-Ponty, M. (1964), *Sense and Non-Sense*, Evanston: Northwestern University Press.
Muncie, J. and McLaughlin, E. (eds) (1996), *The Problem of Crime*, London: Sage.
Polhemus, T. and Housk, R. (1994), *Rituals of Love*, London: Picador.
Rabinow, P. (ed.) (1992), *The Foucault Reader*, Harmondsworth: Penguin.
Rabinow, P. (1997), *Michel Foucault: Ethics Subjectivity and Truth*, London: Allen Lane, The Penguin Press.
Sawicki, J. (1991), *Disciplining Foucault*, New York: Routledge.
Turner, B. S. (1996), *The Body and Society*, London: Sage.

Chapter 12

Understanding Sexual Consent: An Empirical Investigation of the Normative Script for Young Heterosexual Adults

Terry P. Humphreys

> I'll look at him and smile, he'll understand,
> and in a little while, I'll take his hand,
> and though it seems absurd,
> I know we both won't say a word.
> – *The Man I Love, G. and I. Gershwin*

After a few minutes of deep kissing and a little light fondling over her clothes Trevor placed his hand very hesitantly under Kim's shirt. Kim was expecting this and simply kept kissing him. Trevor tentatively continued his advances, even though Kim said and did nothing. He left his hand on her stomach a while longer, hoping for some kind of sign, before moving it up to caress the underside of her breast. He seemed quite nervous to Kim, but she was too – after all they had only gone out a few times before tonight. Kim thought maybe she should say something to make them both more comfortable but felt kind of weird talking in the middle of making out. Besides, she thought it might break the heady mood. Kim reached down to undo Trevor's jeans and again wondered briefly whether she should ask but simply proceeded because she thought of herself as a pretty good judge of character and knew in her heart that he wouldn't refuse.

The negotiation of sexual consent is intimately connected to the negotiation of sexual activity overall. In fact, consent can be viewed as one aspect of sexual negotiations, whether purposeful or unconscious. Indications are that most of us do not verbally communicate our wants, needs, desires or our consent to engage in sexual activity to our partners. Why? There are many reasons. We live in a culture that has an ambivalent attitude toward sexuality. Sexuality has overtones of shame and guilt attached to it. This has generally been the legacy of a traditional religious orthodoxy that viewed sex as 'sinful' if performed outside of marriage or for reasons other than procreation (Davidson, Darling and Norton, 1995; Reiss, 1990; Tannahill, 1980). We certainly have more sex flashing across our television screens and in our magazines, but the sensationalistic nature of media images of sex tells us little about how to negotiate our daily sex lives with partners whose reactions actually matter to us. This is what Claude Guldner (2001), sex therapist and professor emeritus, talks about in his sexuality therapy training workshops when he discusses society's sophistication and ignorance with sex. In one sense, we are sexually sophisticated because of the abundance of sexuality related images, language, and ideas in the mass media. Unfortunately, our sexual ignorance with respect to sexuality is still quite evident because the 'apparent' openness about sex in our society is filled with half-truths and tends to perpetuate many myths, gender-role stereotypes, and sexual double-standards of a bygone era (Reinisch, 1990; Tiefer, 1994). The music videos of today's female pop artists, like Britney Spears for example, and the sexual content of television shows like *Temptation Island* contain the same tired portrayals of women and men of 60 years ago. Women are Barbie dolls whose primary purpose is the sexual pleasure of men. The perpetuation of a belief in the unequal sexual power of women and men hinders the ability of either to effectively communicate sexual intentions to a partner.

We also tend to believe that sex is perfectly natural so we will automatically know what to do in a sexual encounter (Guldner, 2001; Tiefer, 1994), that somehow we will magically know how to please our partner and ourselves when the time comes. Historically this myth has prohibited parents from teaching their children about sexuality and has retarded the growth of sexology as a discipline. This widely held attitude about sex leads to the assumption that the best sexual experiences require little communication. The encounters should be spontaneous, not planned, and partners should be swept away by unbridled passion (Haffner, 1995/1996). The media certainly perpetuate this myth with notions of both love and lust being depicted as uncontrollable urges.

The ambivalence and myths held by society about sexuality filter down to the individual. Direct methods of sexual communication tend not to be very popular because they tend to be confrontational and make us feel vulnerable as we expose our innermost desires. Voicing these desires can be a risky proposition if our partner does not respond in kind. It is difficult to save face if you ask your partner for oral sex and they tell you that behaviour is unpleasant to them. Indirect methods, on the other hand, are much more favourable because they allow partners to avoid awkward situations and the risk of rejection. It seems that men and women avoid discussion because they believe it decreases the likelihood that a sexual interaction will take place (Haffner, 1995/1996). Waldby, Kippax, and Crawford (1993) found that the men they interviewed disliked 'sex talk' because they equated talking during sex with failure. They felt that if their partner was talking to them during sexual activity, then their expectations about the "normal" sequence of sexual events was disrupted. In other words, talking and sex were antithetical to one another.

Given this widespread reticence to talk about sexuality in general, how then is sexual consent communicated between partners? Unfortunately, the research area that should have the most to say on the issue of consent tells us very little. Research dealing with sexual violence and coercion has as its central criterion for definitions of sexual violation, the non-consent of the partner, acquaintance, or stranger. Curiously, sexual consent itself has remained an unarticulated concept in this literature. Without defining the key concept of consent the content validity of much of the literature on rape-supportive attitudes is placed in doubt (Lonsway and Fitzgerald, 1994).

It is the lack of knowledge surrounding sexual consent which was the primary impetus for this empirical investigation. The objective of this study was to explore sexual consent attitudes and behaviours in a mid-size university sample in an attempt to understand the normative consent scripts for young women and men. Research on sexual consent is very important for several reasons. First, consent is the key criterion for legal definitions of what constitutes sexual assault, influencing the guilt or innocence of the accused and the repercussions for the defendant. Second, research definitions of consent affect the design of assessment instruments and ultimately the prevalence of estimates for sexual violence which researchers find in the population (Muehlenhard, et al., 1992). Finally, campus programs are designed to educate students about issues of sexual violence, but as in legal cases, they rely on an incomplete understanding of sexual consent. Without a solid understanding of how sexual consent is negotiated and communicated, awareness programs may not be as effective as they could be.

Current conceptualisations of sexual consent are derived from three diverse areas of study: (1) obtaining informed consent from participants involved in human studies (2) sexual relations between people with developmental challenges, and (3) relationships involving unequal power, such as therapists and clients. In summarising this research, Muehlenhard (1995/1996) suggested that two main themes are important in any definition of sexual consent. First, consent requires knowledge. In order to be able to give consent, a person must understand what he or she is consenting to. This requires not only information about the sexual act requested, but also, information about the social meaning of the act. Different cultures ascribe different meanings to sexual activities. In North America, for example, the acceptable level of coercion among dating partners is an issue that is in transition (Heise, Moore and Toubia, 1995/1996). Many societies have forms of sexual coercion or violence that are socially (and legally) condemned and others that are sanctioned by social customs and norms. 'The social definition of acceptable behaviour is culturally defined and therefore subject to change' (Heise, et al., 1995/1996). The 'boys will be boys' mentality of sexual encounters 20 years ago is being replaced by the label 'date rape' today.

Second, sexual consent is meaningless unless it is given freely. Being free to say yes or no means being free of coercion or undue influence. This second point is important since the cultural scripts for women as *passive* and *limit-setters* and for men as *always ready* and *in charge* may prevent both from freely giving or withholding sexual consent (Muehlenhard, 1995/1996). Men may feel undue pressure to push for sex and women may feel undue pressure to resist. An adherence to a rigid cultural script of masculinity and femininity may result in relationships that possess inherent undue influence.

Another issue raised by Muehlenhard (1995/1996) is whether sexual consent is a mental or a verbal act. As a mental act, consent is problematic because one person can never know for sure if another person has consented (Muehlenhard, et al., 1992). While sexual consent as a verbal act may not seem problematic, most sexual encounters do not involve explicit verbal statements of any kind, much less a discussion of consent (Greer and Buss, 1994; O'Sullivan and Byers, 1992; Sawyer, Desmond and Lucke, 1993). What tends to occur is acquiescence (i.e., passive consent), not explicit consent (Muehlenhard, 1995/1996).

Insights into what consent should or could look like have been sparked in other arenas as well. In 1990, in response to a number of rapes on their campus, students and administrators at Antioch College in Yellow Springs Ohio, drafted a sexual consent policy that required all members of the Antioch community to obtain consent from their sexual partners prior to engaging in any sexual activity and, once sexually engaged, at 'each new level of physical and/or sexual behaviour in any given interaction, regardless of who initiates it. Asking 'Do you want to have sex with me?' is not enough. The request must be specific to each act' (Antioch College, 1996, p.3). Consent was defined as 'the act of willingly and verbally agreeing to engage in specific sexual behaviour' (Antioch College, 1996, p.2). The international media debate over the policy was far more critical than praising, stating that the policy was unrealistic and unenforceable.

In a response to the public's reaction, Alan Guskin (1994), President of Antioch College at the time, discussed Antioch's rationale for developing a sexual consent policy. Touting Antioch's 'free spirit[ed]' student population and history of cutting-edge policies, Guskin (1994) suggested that the goal of the policy was to get students actually talking about sex and thereby reduce sexual misinterpretations and possibly sexual coercion. They emphasised that in sexual situations students should assume a 'no' until they have heard a clearly articulated, verbal, 'yes'. One of the major oversights of such an explicit policy was neglecting to delineate exactly what different 'levels' of sexual behaviour look like, which reduces the process to the subjective interpretation of the individuals involved – which was what it was before the policy.

Antioch College has portrayed itself as a role-model for other colleges and universities to follow (Guskin, 1994). However, the key question remains, 'Does the policy actually work?' Has it improved sexual communication between women and men? Have students integrated it into their sexual scripts? For a policy to be effective, it must be consistent with the conditions it is designed to influence. Guskin (1994) has suggested that the policy is 'widely accepted at Antioch College' (p. 4); however, no follow-up research has been conducted at Antioch that can substantiate this claim (K. Pauly, Antioch College, personal communication, November 18, 1996; Hall, 1995). Actual attempts, such as Antioch's, to alter the scripted behaviour around sexual consent are disconcerting given the vague understanding of consent to date. However, it raises an interesting issue. Would young adults be amenable to instruction regarding their sexual behaviour? The current study examined some reactions to policy implementation and regulation.

Theoretical Perspectives

To start building a foundation for the social-psychological understanding of sexual consent it is constructive to extrapolate from theoretical perspectives in the area of sexual coercion and date rape. Most of the date rape literature focuses on three main theories: (1) feminist theory, (2) socialisation theory, specifically script theory, and (3) psychopathology. Psychopathology will not be discussed here because the intent of the present study was to identify attitudes and behaviours occurring in the day-to-day negotiations of sexual consent between heterosexual, non-clinical partners.

Since feminist theory does not offer a unified viewpoint to this issue, two dominant discourses within feminism, namely, Radical Feminism and Liberal Feminism will be discussed. Naomi McCormick (1994) has demonstrated support for this ideological division and while it is not perfect, it does provide an adequate characterisation for the current discussion. Radical Feminists emphasise the dangers inherent in heterosexual relations and the extent to which girls and women are sexual victims in need of protection from coercive men. Liberal Feminists advocate greater sexual autonomy and pleasure for women by removing the barriers imposed by our patriarchal society (McCormick, 1994).

Radical and Liberal Feminists both agree that the problem of sexual coercion is fundamentally rooted in an unequal power distribution in society that favours men (McCormick, 1994). Historically, our culture has enforced rigid sex roles, accepted interpersonal violence, and viewed women as male property. Many of these beliefs are still firmly entrenched today, although somewhat less overtly than in the past. This patriarchal system of beliefs and institutions has created a rape-supportive culture (Check and Malamuth, 1983). Societies, such as our own, tolerate and even glorify masculine violence, encouraging men and boys to be aggressive and competitive. Women in these societies tend to have less power in economic and political arenas (Sanday, 1981). Some Radical Feminists have extended the patriarchal argument to an extreme position, stating that consensual heterosexual relations are incongruent with our society because women can never truly be free to refuse men sexually if they possess more power physically, economically, and politically (Dworkin, 1987; MacKinnon, 1987). For Dworkin, this argument culminates in the suggestion that there is essentially no difference between consensual sexual intercourse and non-consensual intercourse (i.e., sexual assault). However, Liberal Feminists, in response to these extremist statements, believe that equating rape with all heterosexual sex is misleading and an exaggeration of feminist views (McCormick, 1994).

In an attempt to relate a Liberal Feminist perspective to the issue of heterosexual consent negotiations, a power analysis would emphasise the socialising influence of our patriarchal system. This system affords men a dominant position with respect to initiating sexual encounters, negotiating desired sexual activities and deciding the start and end of such encounters. In other words, men have the culturally ascribed authority to orchestrate sexual encounters. Although women have been ascribed the prerogative of refusal, it is unclear whether male power overrides this already restricted role for women. For many feminists, 'sex is socially constructed as something men do to women, not something that belongs to women' (McCormick, 1994, p. 176). However, similar to socialisation theory, it is not clear what situations would lead men to use their position of power to initiate sexual encounters by asking for consent and in what situations men would simply exert pressure or sometimes force on reluctant women to engage in sexual activity.

Socialisation theory suggests that beginning at birth we undergo a continuous process that shapes us to the surrounding environment. This process is both individual and social. Through socialisation we acquire an individual identity (self-concept, attitudes, and dispositions) and the dominant values and beliefs of society are transmitted to individuals to maintain social continuity. Through interaction with others, children learn how to be social creatures and this involves learning how to think, what to think, and the language of the culture (Richardson, 1988). The differential socialisation of the genders has been connected to the patriarchal system and the unequal sexual division of labour (Gecas, 1981; Hite, 1994). Within the family context, parents teach children gender appropriate conduct, drawn from their own understanding of their culture and experiences (Richardson, 1988).

Many adolescent males are socialised to view sexual access, through force (if necessary) as justified if, for example, they paid for all dating expenses, the couple went to the man's apartment, and/or the women asked the man out (Muehlenhard, Friedman and Thomas, 1985). Under these circumstances, men may feel that obtaining sexual consent from a dating partner is inconsequential because, from their perspective, the situational variables have already provided consent. Behaviours from women that are 'suggestive' of a sexual interest may be interpreted by men as the non-verbal granting of sexual consent.

The difference in the socialisation of women and men suggests that the issue of sexual consent is more important to women than to men. If women are socialised to be the limit-setters of relationships, then part of that role would be the giving or not giving of consent to engage in sexual activity. It is expected that women, more than men, should *decide* whether sexual activity will proceed. Men, on the other hand, have been socialised to seek sexual involvement at every opportunity which suggests that men are more likely to take on the role of *asking* for consent. However, it is not clear that this is what men do, given the fact that they are also socialised to dominate (sometimes aggressively) women to attain what they desire. Given these mixed socialisation messages, men may ask for consent in one instance, under specific situational variables and not ask for consent with different situational variables.

Sex role stereotypes have contributed to biased cultural beliefs about dating (e.g., a woman is not to be believed when she says no to sexual advances). These stereotypes can contribute to misunderstandings regarding sexual intent in a dating situation (Check and Malamuth, 1983). This is supported by the finding that many men and women accept statements such as, 'A woman who goes to the home or apartment of a man on the first date implies she is willing to have sex' and 'any healthy woman can successfully resist a rapist if she really wants to' (Burt, 1980; Gilmartin-Zena, 1988). Sex role stereotypes also have direct implications for sexual consent since for some people, the situational variables themselves communicate implicit assumptions about the couple's consent to sexual involvement. The sex role double standard for women places them in a bind with respect to giving or not giving sexual consent.

Research

There have been very few studies which have focussed specifically on sexual consent. Hall (1995) was the first researcher to investigate sexual consent behaviour for non-coital and coital activities. His research on routine consent giving in day-to-day sexual interactions supported the assumption that consent is more often an issue when the behaviour being considered is intercourse. He found that most often sexual behaviours occurred without overt consent being given, although participants did report giving verbal and non-verbal consent to each of 12 sexual activities some of the time. For participants who had engaged in particular behaviours, consent giving was reported most frequently for penile-vaginal intercourse (79%) and anal intercourse (73%). The rate of consent giving for other sexual behaviours was markedly lower. Of the 10 other sexual activities (e.g., 'she/he touched his/her genitals', 'she/he gave him/her oral sex', 'kissed') the average percentage of participants who gave verbal or non-verbal permission was 50%. When given, most consent was granted non-verbally. Behaviours that indicated non-verbal consent included 'kissing', 'getting closer', 'intimately touching', 'smiling' and non-behaviours such as 'not moving away'. Rates of verbal consent rarely exceeded 20%. Similar rates were found for women and men (Hall, 1995). Unfortunately, Hall did not examine how participants indicated their verbal consent.

Hickman and Muehlenhard's (1999) exploratory study investigated how young women and men inferred and conveyed sexual consent. Participants were presented with scenarios in which sex was initiated either verbally or non-verbally along with a list of 34 possible responses to the initiation. Participants rated how representative each response was of how they would give sexual consent and how their date would give sexual consent as well as how frequently participants used each response in actual situations.

Their findings indicated that consent is more complex than simply saying 'yes'. There was a wide diversity of behaviours or signals individuals used to communicate sexual consent. Factor analysis revealed sexual consent to be comprised of four categories of signals: direct, indirect, verbal, and non-verbal. Direct consent signals were defined as straightforward and unambiguous signals (e.g., stating 'I want to have sex with you') while indirect consent signals were roundabout and ambiguous (e.g., 'she/he touches and kisses you' or 'she/he asks if you have a condom'). Hickman and Muehlenhard (1999) found that the majority of consent signals could be organised using the categories from the factor analysis to form a matrix with direct/indirect as one axis and verbal/non-verbal as the other axis.

While studies done to date have answered some questions, many remain. The current study was designed to investigate heterosexual students' perceptions of sexual consent and possible gender differences in those perceptions. In addition, the meaning and importance which students attach to consent behaviour was examined. This study also expanded research on consent by examining whether situational variables such as the length of an intimate relationship affects if or how consent is negotiated. In addition, this study obtained student reactions to Antioch

College's sexual consent policy to assess the potential of policy for improving sexual relations between women and men on college and university campuses.

Method

Given the relative newness of the area, it was important to begin by gathering information using a qualitative research approach. Focus groups are especially suited for clarifying the perceived meanings and interpretations of social and behavioural issues, where little is known about the beliefs, behaviours and meanings of a specific population (Miles and Huberman, 1994). Sexual consent is certainly one such phenomenon. These groups provided a voice for those participants that, as scientists, we often ignore. The focus group sessions added a tremendous richness and insightfulness to the data that would not have been possible with a quantitative component alone. I will highlight these insights through quotes as I relay the findings. The major objective of this research was to develop a sexual consent survey measure. The information gathered from the focus groups was used to build this quantitative survey. In this way, many of commonly understood words and phrases used by young people to describe their personal experiences found their way into the survey and provided assurance of its relevancy to the wider young adult population. Two female groups and one male group of heterosexual individuals participated in the focus group interviews. On average, each group was comprised of six members.

Focus group transcripts were examined separately for each question. A sentence-by-sentence, line-by-line analysis was performed in which margin notes kept track of key words and ideas. Summary sheets were developed based on the ideas from the margin notes. The patterns noted in the summary sheet data lead to the development of major and minor themes for each question. These descriptive themes were subsequently used in the development of the survey. Themes were translated into one or more Likert-type questions which represented the core aspects of that theme. For example, when asked about how often verbal consent is obtained during a typical sexual encounter, focus group participants frequently talked about the length or stage of a relationship as being a determining factor. This theme of relationship context led to the development of survey questions such as 'Obtaining sexual consent is more necessary in a new relationship than in a committed relationship' and 'The necessity of asking for sexual consent decreases as the length of an intimate relationship increases'. The final survey was comprised of 3 major sets of questions: (1) attitudes toward Antioch's sexual consent policy, (2) attitudes toward sexual consent and, (3) sexual consent behaviours. A principal components analysis was performed on each of these three scales to reduce the number of items to a smaller set of more meaningful dimensions.

Clearly, securing a good sample size for the quantitative survey portion of this study was important if anything about the generalisability of sexual consent issues for a larger audience could be discussed. The questionnaire was mailed to a stratified random sample of 1200 students from the undergraduate population at a mid-size university in Ontario, Canada. Equal numbers of women and men were selected for the mailing and efforts were made to increase the response rate through the use of reminder cards and a monetary incentive. Five hundred and fourteen usable surveys were returned (330 female and 184 male) for a response rate of 43%. The average age of the sample was 21 years, with a range of 18 to 27. The demographic similarity of the sample to the undergraduate population, from which the respondents were selected, indicates that the respondents were representative of the population of undergraduate students at this university. In addition, comparable with other university samples (Siegel, Klein, and Roghmann, 1999), almost three-quarters of this sample reported ever having had sex, defined as penile-vaginal intercourse. The average number of lifetime intercourse partners was 2.8, for those who had ever had sex, consistent with past research for this age group (Laumann, et al., 1994). The similarity between other university data and this survey provides confidence that students were honestly reporting their own sexual behaviour.

Results and Discussion

Given that the qualitative and quantitative findings in this study each provide complementary insights into sexual consent, I will integrate them in the discussion that follows.

When asked about their own definition of sexual consent, students gave a diversity of responses. Generally, they focused on themes of mutual understanding, a willingness between partners to engage in agreed upon sexual behaviours, and a clear state of mind, free from excessive drugs or alcohol. These themes are similar to the components of consent described by Muehlenhard (1995/1996) and Archard (1998). It is quite likely that student exposure to campus date rape education campaigns have influenced their understanding of sexual consent issues. There were differences of opinion regarding the extent to which sexual consent needed to be verbally communicated. In particular, the students emphasised that how consent is obtained depends on the length or quality of the relationship. Female students tended to focus on sexual consent as a process in which negotiation and re-negotiation are ongoing. As Sara[1] commented, it was

> both non-verbal and verbal in a combination that included negotiation and communication. ... I would want to see it in a tier system. I would need to have verbal consent initially, then talk about my non-verbal [signals]. Yet I would have to renegotiate all the time.

Some females also defined consent according to the traditional female role of passive recipient of sexual advances from men and gatekeeper in sexual relationships. As Nicole indicated: '[It is] how much you allow another person to do sexually' and as Andrea concurred: 'Not resisting. Not only in a physical sense but in an emotional sense as well.'

Males, similarly, supported a definition of consent which emphasised mutually agreed upon sexual activity but they were more divided on whether sexual consent was a singular event or a process of negotiation. When discussing how often consent needs to be communicated during a one night stand, Jeffrey indicated specific guidelines about when consent should happen, namely, beginning with a brief invitation to go to one's place and then just prior to intercourse:

> ...there is one [consent] before it starts, especially if you are somewhere and you say 'Do you want to go back to my place?', and then there is one more just before intercourse occurs, almost like a safety net, like 'are you sure?'. You don't want to dwell on it because it takes away from it [the experience].

Some men indicated that while verbal consent may be used only once or twice, there are many non-verbal signals that happen throughout an encounter that contribute to the sexual activity continuing, ending or escalating. When asked whether the act of sexual intercourse was the only situation needing consent, Mark responded:

> I think it's the only one that requires verbal [consent]. I think as far as the other stuff goes, that those are mostly non-verbal and waiting to see if there is a reaction. You can, pardon me, grope your way through the situation. I see sex as being a major step that requires a little more special [attention], but the other stuff, not as much.

The finding that women view consent more as a process and men more as a single event is supported by the quantitative survey questions. Men, more than women, agreed with the following: (1) asking for consent at the beginning of a sexual encounter is enough, χ^2 (1, $\underline{N}$=511) = 29.1, $\underline{p}$=.001 (52% vs. 30%), (2) consent to begin a sexual encounter implies consent throughout the encounter, χ^2 (1, $\underline{N}$=508) = 9.96, $\underline{p}$=.007 (35% vs. 22%), (3) established consent for intercourse, implies consent for petting and fondling, χ^2 (1, $\underline{N}$=513) =16.68, $\underline{p}$=.001 (78% vs. 62%), and (4) that their own behaviour typically involves asking for consent only once during a sexual encounter, χ^2 (1, $\underline{N}$=505) = 10.16, $\underline{p}$=.006 (50% vs. 35%).

When students were asked if consent was an issue that was discussed and talked about between friends or partners, many indicated it was not. The students felt that it didn't seem natural to discuss consent and it could not easily be included in everyday conversation with friends. The male group joked about how it might possibly come up in conversation between male friends: 'It's not a question that comes up. Like, you are talking with your friends "had a good night last night, eh? Was there consent?" [laughter]. I don't think it really comes up.'. Students were quite aware of sexual consent as a public education issue having seen campus awareness posters on date rape; however, these campus campaigns had not translated into conversations with acquaintances, friends or partners. Generally, it was only when media attention was given to a dramatic event that students talked briefly about the issue of sexual assault, but not consent per se. As Rachael stated: 'Usually only when something comes up [media attention]. But generally speaking, it's not a topic of conversation with my peers.' Christina pointed out that even with an intimate partner, communication about consent seemed foreign: 'I just started my first long relationship this summer and it's really going well but we never discuss consent.'. In discussing why consent may not be talked about between intimate partners, one of the female groups raised the issue of discomfort, acknowledging that as a society we don't talk during sexual encounters and that we may not want to because doing so may spoil the mood:

> I think we're really uncomfortable with talk ... we don't talk about sex and when you say 'it kind of just happens', I think it's cultural. I like the element of surprise, I don't like discussing everything I'm going to do ... how romantic is that?

In the survey data, 65% of both men and women either agreed or strongly agreed that verbally asking for sexual consent is awkward. The limited discussions on the topic of sexual consent were supported by the quantitative data with only about one-half of students indicating any discussion of this topic. Specifically, 56% had discussed sexual consent with a friend and 43% reported that they had not given the topic of sexual consent much thought.

Other research has indicated that some individuals perceive discussion prior to sexual activity as a breakdown of the encounter (Haffner, 1995/1996; Waldby, et al., 1993) and some students believe that non-verbal signals are more accurate than verbal signals (Sawyer, et al., 1993). Thus, it is not surprising that students in the current study do not agree on the extent to which sexual consent should involve verbal rather than non-verbal behaviours as well as the reliance on non-verbal behaviours to assess sexual consent.

When presented with the Antioch sexual consent policy statement, the majority of both males and females responded that they were against the rigidity of a formal policy which dictated personal sexual behaviour and would not want this implemented on their own campus. Several commented that while they agreed with the premise behind the policy, they did not believe that it was practical to try to regulate sexual consent behaviour through the use of a formal document. Many believed that this policy would not be effective because of the difficulty in enforcing it. Nicole expressed puzzlement about the practicalities of the policy: 'Do you punish men on each sexual act that [they] violate? It seems totally unclear how you would be able to enforce it.' Similarly, Patricia asked, 'Who is there to make sure that the questions are asked and [that] the appropriate responses are given?'

Stemming from their concerns about enforcement, some students raised issues of personal freedom and questioned the university's role in prescribing appropriate sexual behaviour. As Andrea stated, 'I think it sets a precedent for institutional regulation of individuals' private lives. The university does not belong in the bedroom of their students, faculty, and staff.' Or as Paul bluntly stated,

There is no way in hell a university can tell me what I can and cannot do, whether it is right or wrong, especially in a situation like this cause if it goes to a judiciary it would be my word against their word.

Some students also commented that the required verbal negotiation dictated by the policy would reduce the intrinsic pleasure of sexual interaction and result in behaviours that were regimented, mechanical, and/or irritating. As Diana commented,

That's [Antioch policy] the most ridiculous thing I have ever heard. That's annoying. If someone [said] 'can I touch your breast?', 'can I do this?', and 'can I do that?' I'd [say] 'get lost'. It would get on your nerves.

When discussing the 'natural' progression of sexual encounters many students stressed the excitement involved in not knowing what the next move from a partner may be or how the progression of sexual events will play out on any given night. The Antioch policy of discussing and consenting to every sexual activity is contrary to the students' perception of sexual encounters as needing to be impulsive and uninhibited. A thoughtfully organised and planned sexual encounter was not perceived as exciting or romantic. Sara commented on her understanding of the conflict between ideal relationship progression and the Antioch policy:

Personally I think that the spontaneity of a first kiss is one of the most wonderful things in a blossoming relationship. There's no way that I would like to be denied of that 'tingly' feeling by having to practically sign a contract before having my first kiss with someone. ...What a way to ruin the mood.

Shawn stated it much more bluntly, 'So much for romance! Do you have to bring a clipboard with you?'

In the main campus survey, students also reacted negatively to the Antioch policy. Fewer than one-half of the students said they would endorse a similar policy on their campus (45%). The reasons given for the negative evaluation echo the qualitative comments. Most students agreed that the policy was unrealistic (74%), unenforceable (80%), and would be very difficult to implement effectively (86%). In addition, only 47% said they could easily incorporate such a policy into their own sexual interactions. A particular concern was that verbally asking for consent was viewed as awkward (65%). Despite those concerns, students were not totally negative and did endorse some aspects of the policy which they saw as being positive. Positive reactions to the Antioch policy focussed on the idealistic nature of the policy. Students agreed that the policy is a good way to get students communicating with their partners about sexual activity (69%) and could be more useful as an educational awareness tool (67%). Universities and colleges would be wise to take note of the negative evaluation of the Antioch policy on sexual consent and the reasons provided. Although favourable to the idea of more awareness, the policy's practicality seems to be a major obstacle against its acceptance. To design and implement programs that will effectively reach student audiences, campus officials must understand how students themselves think about and negotiate sexual consent. It is clear that telling students to verbally state their consent or non-consent to a partner ignores the contextual influences on consent and is bound to be ineffective for a significant proportion of them.

Focus group participants were asked which of two methods for obtaining sexual consent from partners they preferred to use: (1) ask a partner for a verbal yes before starting any sexual activity, or (2) initiate sexual activity and continue until the partner indicates otherwise (i.e., assume consent). Both males and females indicated that while asking for consent first is an ideal approach to sexual negotiations, in practice it is difficult to implement. Some of the reasons given why individuals may not ask for consent first, included the fact that being 'in the heat of the moment' makes one less rational and that consent may change during the moment, so there is a need for continuous communication.

Some males noted that the approach in which an individual assumes consent and continues until the partner indicates otherwise also has problems. They mentioned that it is frustrating to have certain expectations for an encounter only to be thwarted in midstream. It would be better to know ahead of time. As Tom stated:

> I think asking ahead of time should be followed, but that's not always realistic because the other way, I mean you get so far and then when you are told 'no' you're pretty frustrated and that can turn out to be a bad thing. That wouldn't happen if you always knew ahead of time where you were, instead of 'surprise, that's it'.

The survey data revealed that more students preferred to ask for consent first (60%) than to assume it (39%) before engaging in sexual activity. Females (65%) were more likely than males (53%) to prefer the method of obtaining consent which involved asking first prior to engaging in any sexual activity, whereas males (47%) were more likely than females (35%) to prefer assuming consent and continuing with sexual activity until the partner indicates otherwise, χ^2 (1, N=507) = 6.62, p=.01.

Focus group participants were asked how they thought students actually communicated consent. Both males and females believed that most of the time consent negotiations are non-verbal, involving the use of body language. They also agreed that negotiation around consent involves more verbal communication in a new relationship and less verbal communication as the familiarity and intimacy increases. As Patricia stated: 'I think you just move into non-verbal. Could you imagine a married couple every time you have to have sex [saying], 'are you ready for this?', 'do you want to do this?' ... you'd be there forever.' Students view the relationship's length as having a significant impact on a couple's ability to accurately interpret each other's non-verbal signals, which negates the need for permission: '...even before kissing if that's your first or second date. ...I can't see too many people that have been in a relationship for a long time being that verbal, because they don't feel they have to. They can read each other.'

Some students suggested that asking for consent may only occur the first time the couple engages in sexual activity, and then it can be assumed afterwards. The influence of relationship contexts is clearly demonstrated in the quantitative attitude questions. When asked idealistically whether 'consent is more necessary in a new relationship than a committed one' or whether 'a couple's long history of consenting relations reduces the need to ask for consent', 44% and 47% respectively did not agree. However, when asked the more practical question about everyday realities, 'that partners are less likely to ask for sexual consent the longer they are in a relationship', an overwhelming majority agreed (92%).

Clear and explicit consent negotiated early in a relationship, even if achieved through acquiescence, may be understood as establishing a precedent for future sexual relations. Students may feel that clear and explicit consent is less necessary in more committed relationships because intimate communication patterns are already established and accepted. Shotland and Goodstein (1992) have supported a precedence theory in sexual activity. They found that once sexual relations have been established, there are expectations on the part of both women and men that those relations will continue. Research on the expectations regarding sexual activity indicate that women and men are more likely to perceive a resisting woman as obligated to have sex if the couple has had sexual intercourse as little as 10 times before the current event (Shotland and Goodstein, 1992). In addition, Shotland (1992) has suggested that different forms of courtship rape are the result of context variables such as whether or not sexual ground rules have been established, the length of the relationship and whether the couple has engaged in prior sexual activity.

Some students suggested that a one-night stand would involve more non-verbal body language because the individuals involved would be too uncomfortable using verbal communication of a sexual nature with someone they did not know very well. For example, Jennifer suggested that:

> In a situation like a one-night stand, something where there is not a lot of trust, there's not a strong bond there, it would be more uncomfortable to use verbal communication so you would use physical, body language and I think that would be more the 'going to the point until someone said 'no' [method of consent negotiation]. Where if it is a long term relationship, or there is a lot of trust there, then the first time you say 'do you want to start sleeping together?' and then after that you would probably be comfortable just reading the person.

According to some of these students, the consent method used in one-night stands would assume consent is given and would continue until one of the partners said 'no'. One-night stands may represent a special case. Regardless of this contradiction, it appears that the method or process of negotiating consent is relationship specific.

The students indicated there were different ways in which verbal consent could be asked for, ranging from, very direct verbal questioning to somewhat evasive language, such as 'do you want to make love?', 'would you like to?' or 'should we?'. An explicit example of non-verbal behaviours, involved producing a condom. The giving of consent was generally understood as a direct 'yes' or 'no' answer to the questions posed or in some cases, a non-verbal non-response, such as not pushing away or just going along with the activity. Mark provided an example of passive consent from a partner:

> Here's an easy one, you're going to kiss someone and they don't move their head back, that's pretty much consent for me. If you are moving your hand in some certain place and they aren't pulling away, then that's consent for me.

It was also suggested that both partners should have the responsibility to inform the other if they feel uncomfortable in any specific situation. Shawn expressed his personal philosophy about each partner's responsibility to speak up: 'This is how I feel, that basically consent is always there and if my partner didn't want to have sex or anything then it would be a 'no I don't want to tonight'.'

Conclusion

The present study represents the first attempt at assessing more general attitudes and behaviours regarding sexual consent. To this point, the majority of research and educational programs have emphasised consent issues as consisting only of simplistic expressions of 'yes' or 'no'. The results of this study highlight the complexities involved in understanding sexual consent. The similarities between sexual consent definitions raised by the participants of this study and those of the research community (Muehlenhard, 1995/1996; Archard, 1998), suggest that there is not a lack of cognitive awareness about sexual consent as an intellectual idea. Most students understand the ingredients that ideally make up a consensual sexual encounter. The practical application of these ideas to lived experiences, however, is more complicated. The use of verbal consent, like sexual communication in general, seems to be limited. A preference for using non-verbal signals and situational cues to assess the consent of a partner predominates the current sexual script for young adults, at least those attending university. In addition, relationship length seems to be a very important factor determining how much verbal and/or non-verbal communication occurs. Future research will need to disentangle relationship length from relationship quality in determining their unique influences on the behaviours used to negotiate sexual consent.

Antioch College seems to have been the inspiration for a small, but growing research interest in how individuals negotiate sexual consent. Sexual consent needs to be recognised by researchers, policy makers, and lay people as a multifaceted process that can occur on numerous levels of expression but always within a specific, and influential, context.

Note

[1] Names changed to protect confidentiality.

References

Antioch College (1996), *The Antioch College sexual offense prevention policy*, Yellow Springs, Ohio: Antioch College.

Archard, D. (1998), *Sexual Consent*, Colorado: Westview Press.

Burt, M. R. (1980), 'Cultural myths and support for rape', *Journal of Personality and Social Psychology*, Vol. 38, pp. 217-230.

Check, J. V. P., and Malamuth, N. M. (1983), 'Sex role stereotyping and reactions to depictions of stranger versus acquaintance rape', *Journal of Personality and Social Psychology*, Vol. 45, No. 2, pp. 344-356.

Davidson, J. K., Sr., Darling, C. A., and Norton, L. (1995), 'Religiosity and the sexuality of women: Sexual behaviour and sexual satisfaction revisited', *Journal of Sex Research*, Vol. 32, pp. 235-243.

Dworkin, A. (1987), *Intercourse*, New York: Free Press.

Gecas, V. (1981), 'Contexts of socialisation', in Rosenberg, M. and Turner, R. (eds), *Social Psychology: Sociological Perspectives*, New York: Basic Books.

Gilmartin-Zena, P. (1988), 'Gender differences in students' attitudes toward rape', *Sociological Focus*, Vol. 21, No. 4, pp. 279-292.

Greer, A. E. and Buss, D. M. (1994), 'Tactics for promoting sexual encounters', *The Journal of Sex Research*, Vol. 31, pp. 185-201.

Guldner, C. (2001), 'Societal factors which contribute to a lack of sexual interest', symposium conducted at the meeting of the Guelph Conference on Sexuality, Guelph, Canada, June.

Guskin, A. E. (1994), *The Antioch Response: Sex, You Don't Just Talk About It*, Yellow Springs, Ohio: Antioch College.

Haffner, D. W. (1995/1996), 'The essence of "consent" is communication', *SIECUS Report*, Vol. 24, pp. 2-4.

Hall, D. S. (1995), *Consent for sexual behaviour in a College Student Population*, San Francisco, California, PhD Thesis, The Institute for Advanced Study of Human Sexuality.

Heise, L., Moore, K. and Toubia, N. (1995/1996), 'Defining "coercion" and "consent" cross-culturally', *SIECUS Report*, Vol. 24, pp. 12-13.

Hickman, S. E. and Muehlenhard, C. L. (1999), '"By the semi-mystical appearance of a condom": How young women and men communicate sexual consent in heterosexual situations', *The Journal of Sex Research*, Vol. 36, pp. 258-272.

Hite, S. (1994), *The Hite Report on the Family: Growing up under Patriarchy*, London: Bloomsbury.

Lonsway, K. A. and Fitzgerald, L. F. (1994), 'Rape myths: In review', *Psychology of Women Quarterly*, Vol. 18, pp. 133-164.

MacKinnon, C. A. (1987), *Feminism Unmodified: Discourses on Life and Law*, Cambridge: Harvard University Press.

McCormick, N. B. (1994), *Sexual salvation: Affirming Women's Sexual Rights and Pleasures*, Westport Connecticut: Praeger.

Miles, M. B., and Huberman, A. M. (1994), *Qualitative Data Analysis* 2nd edn, Westport Connecticut: Sage Publications.

Muehlenhard, C. L. (1995/1996), 'The complexities of sexual consent', *SIECUS Report*, Vol. 24, pp. 4-7.

Muehlenhard, C. L., Friedman, D. E. and Thomas, C. M. (1985), 'Is date rape justifiable?', *Psychology of Women Quarterly*, Vol. 2, pp. 297-310.

Muehlenhard, C. L., Powch, I. G., Phelps, J. L. and Giusti, L.M. (1992), 'Definitions of rape: Scientific and political implications', *Journal of Social Issues*, Vol. 48, pp. 23-44.

O'Sullivan, L. F. and Byers, E. S. (1992), 'College students' incorporation of initiator and restrictor roles in sexual dating interactions', *Journal of Sex Research*, Vol. 29, pp. 435-446.

Reinisch, J. M. (1990), *The Kinsey Institute New Report on Sex: What You Must Know to be Sexually Literate*, New York: St. Martin's Press.

Reiss, I. L. (1990), *An End to Shame: Shaping our Next Sexual Revolution*, New York: Prometheus Books.

Richardson, L. (1988) *The Dynamics of Sex and Gender: A Sociological Perspective*, New York: Harper and Row.

Sanday, P. R. (1981), 'The socio-cultural context of rape: A cross-cultural study', *Journal of Social Issues*, Vol. 37, No. 4, pp. 5-27.

Sawyer, R., Desmond, S. and Lucke, G. (1993), 'Sexual communication and the college student: Implications for date rape', *Health Values*, Vol. 17, No. 4, pp. 11-20.

Shotland, R. L. (1992), 'A theory of the causes of courtship rape: Part 2', *Journal of Social Issues*, Vol. 48, No. 1, pp. 127-143.

Shotland R. L. and Goodstein, L. (1992), 'Sexual precedence reduces the perceived legitimacy of sexual refusal: An examination of attributions concerning date rape and consensual sex', *Personality and Social Psychology Bulletin*, Vol. 18, No. 6, pp. 756-764.

Tannahill, R. (1980), *Sex in History*, New York: Stein and Day.

Tiefer, L. (1994), 'Three crises facing sexology', *Archives of Sexual Behavior*, Vol. 23, pp. 361-374.

Waldby, C., Kippax, S. and Crawford, J. (1993), 'Research note: Heterosexual men and "safe sex" practice', *Sociology of Health and Illness*, Vol. 15, pp. 246-256.

Chapter 13

People with Learning Disabilities[1]: Sex, the Law and Consent

Michelle McCarthy and David Thompson

Introduction

Within the learning disability field, there has for some time been an ongoing debate about how to balance people's rights to sexual autonomy with appropriate protection from abuse and exploitation. Some commentators argue that the balance has gone too far in favour of autonomy, whilst others argue 'this balance has continually fallen on the protection from harm side' (Kaeser, 1992, p. 36).

This chapter looks at what boundaries previous legislation in England and Wales put on the sexual lives of people with learning disabilities. It will be argued that these laws failed to protect people with learning disabilities from abusive sexual contact whilst simultaneously contributing to a prohibitive sexual climate. Consideration will be given to how well the proposals for change contained in the White Paper *Protecting the Public* will improve this situation (Home Office, 2002).

We argue that autonomy and protection should not be necessarily considered to be opposing factors in the sexual lives of people with learning disabilities. Rather we suggest that they are inextricably linked and that receiving protection from abuse is an essential part of being autonomous. Understanding autonomy only as the 'freedom *to*' (engage in desired activities) is a misunderstanding; ' freedom *from*' (undesired activities) is equally important.

In order for justice to be done, the law must improve on its poor record of punishing the perpetrators of sexual crimes against people with learning disabilities and have at its disposal more appropriate sentencing options. The law has to be fair and effective and to do this it must recognise the actual patterns of sexual abuse as it occurs against adults with learning disabilities.

However, the law, by which we mean the legislation itself and the forms and practices of the criminal justice system, has not traditionally been responsive to the actual nature of sexual crimes as most people experience them. For example, for centuries the law has responded more thoroughly to sexual crimes committed in a 'public' context (i.e. by strangers), compared to those committed in a private context. Yet it has long been recognised, and the most recent figures released by the Home Office confirm, that rapes of women by strangers account for only 12% of all rapes reported to the police (Vasagar, 2002) and even less (8%) when women have been asked directly about their experiences (Myhill and Allen, 2002). Contrary to popular belief rapes by known men are no less 'serious' than rapes by strangers; Lees' research in the 1990s showed that known men used high levels of violence and that 24% of women raped by known men were raped anally as well as vaginally (Lees, 1996). Many women report that anal rape is especially distressing, due to physical pain and psychological humiliation, although both these are also present in vaginal rape. Yet the police, courts, juries and especially the media, have traditionally been less sympathetic to rapes by known men, as opposed to the far less common 'stranger' rapes.

Sexual Abuse of People with Learning Disabilities

Whilst rapes and sexual assaults by strangers against people with learning disabilities do exist and must not be overlooked, these are also in the minority. Over the last decade a number of studies have been undertaken which have identified who perpetrates sexual abuse against people with learning disabilities and the nature / dynamics of that abuse. Research evidence (e.g. Brown, Stein and Turk, 1995; McCarthy and Thompson, 1997) shows that, broadly speaking, there are four main groups of perpetrators:

- Men with learning disabilities who use same services
- Fathers, step-fathers, and other male relatives
- Male staff
- Other trusted male adults e.g. friends, partners, neighbours, etc.

All available evidence suggests that women feature very rarely as perpetrators of sexual abuse against people with learning disabilities (which is why in this chapter we will refer to perpetrators in the male gender). Nevertheless, the law needs to be able to respond to such abuse when it does occur and to provide deterrents to women so inclined – principles which are embedded in the proposed law reforms (Home Office, 2002).

Problems with the Law as it has been Framed

Previous legislation in England and Wales presented three main ways in which perpetrators of sexual crimes against people with learning disabilities could be prosecuted:

- Laws which prohibited sex with people deemed unable to consent to sex
- Generic laws applying to sex without consent
- Laws which prohibited specific sexual relationships

The merits and limitations of these approaches will be discussed below.

Laws which Prohibit Sex with People Deemed Unable to Consent to Sex

The basis of such laws is that some people are so disabled as to be unable to give consent to any sexual relationship. This was enshrined in Section 7 of the 1956 Sexual Offences Act which made criminal sexual intercourse and assault of 'defective' women. The Sexual Offences Act 1967 extended this provision to 'defective' men. There has been little clarity as to who may or may not be equated to being a 'defective'. The legal definition has been understood to be a person suffering from a state of arrested or incomplete development of mind which includes severe impairments of intelligence and social functioning within the meaning of the Mental Health Act 1959.

Individuals may be judged as being incapable to consenting to any sexual relationship either because they are identified as having general deficits in understanding or specific deficits concerning sexual knowledge. The former of these, is known as a *diagnostic* approach to consent: where a person's capacity to make a specific decision is deemed inadequate because they have a certain level of learning disability. Another example of the diagnostic approach is the Republic of Ireland which takes a very broad definition by making it illegal to have sex with people:

> suffering from a disorder of the mind, whether through mental handicap or mental illness, which is of such a nature or degree as to render a person incapable of living an independent life or guarding against serious exploitation. (Sexual Offences Act , 1993)

IQ tests and other assessments of general ability have been used in this country, and others, to determine whether an individual is covered by such legislation (Sundram and Stavis, 1994). However, within England and Wales is it ultimately the jury which has decided whether or not individual women or men with learning disabilities come under these categories, although they may take advice from expert witnesses. This is problematic because most people sitting on juries will not have much, if any, personal or professional knowledge of people with learning disabilities (Brown et al., 1996).

Increasingly people have been critical of broad tests of ability being used to judge an individual's competence in specific areas of their lives (e.g. Murphy and Clare, 1997). However, concerns that such an approach is in danger of violating the Human Rights Act 1998 (Article 12 provides for the right to marry and found a family) seem unfounded, as this right is to be interpreted within the national law and issues of consent and capacity would still be relevant (Evans and Rodgers, 2000).

The alternative to the diagnostic approach is the *functional* approach, where a person's capacity to consent is judged on the basis of their ability to understand information relating to the matter in hand. This is favoured by the British Medical Association and Law Society (1995). The crucial question is precisely *what* knowledge and skills are required for a person to be able to consent to sex? This will be addressed below.

Another concern about the provisions concerning sex with 'defectives', has been the limited sentencing options they have provided; the maximum in Britain has been two years in jail. This relative leniency compared to other sexual crimes is replicated in other countries, for example South Australia (Sundram and Stavis, 1994). This has previously led to the accused being charged under generic laws regarding sexual assault (which carry considerably longer sentences) even though their guilt may have been harder to prove, as consent becomes the defining issue, not the alleged victim's lack of capacity.

Protecting the Public endorses the *functional* approach in the proposed offence of 'sexual activity with a person who did not, by reason of a learning disability or mental disorder at that time, have the capacity to consent' (Home Office 2002, p27). In recognition of the extreme vulnerability of such persons the proposed maximum sentence is life imprisonment.

Generic Laws Applying to Sex Without Consent

There is a consensus that where there is active resistance to a sexual act then an assault has been committed. Beyond this both individuals and the law have very different understandings about what constitutes sexual assault. Situations where people choose not to actively resist because of their fear of further consequences or where people lack the ability to offer resistance, challenge the law to take a much broader view of what constitutes sexual assault. However, traditionally the criminal justice system has taken a narrow view: 'The defence will argue that only extensive injury or evidence of [victim's] active resistance provides adequate proof of her non-consent' (Lees, 1997, p. 77).

The failure of generic sexual assault laws to protect the interests of people with learning disabilities was demonstrated in the *R v. Jenkins* held at the Old Bailey in January 2000 (see Murphy, 2000 for details). In this case, a woman with severe learning disabilities became pregnant and had a termination. DNA tests on the foetus showed that the father was a member of her residential staff, who subsequently admitted to having had sex with the woman on a number of occasions. He was charged with rape (rather than the lesser charge of sex with a 'mental defective'), but the trial was abandoned at an early stage, because Judge Coltart ruled that BMA and Law Society guidance (1995) was wrong and that free and informed consent was not necessary. He instead referred to case law from the nineteenth century where women yielding to their 'animal instincts' could be interpreted as effectively consenting to sex. This replicated a decision in the Court of Appeal in South Australia (*The Queen v Howard*, 1981).

The *R v Jenkins* judgement caused outrage in the learning disability and social care fields (e.g. Winchester, 2000) and much concern amongst those in the legal professions. Much of the concern was not only for the individual woman with learning disabilities in this case, but that the judge's ruling went against common sense and principles of natural justice and therefore left other people with learning disabilities extremely vulnerable.

Laws which Prohibit Specific Sexual Relationships

Sex with staff members Section 128 of the 1959 Mental Health Act (amended by the Sexual Offences Act , 1967) prohibited male staff from 'unlawful sexual intercourse, or commit[ting] an act of buggery or gross indecency' with either female or male 'patients'. The intention being to protect people in their care as a result of a mental impairment/ disorder including being in receipt of outpatient treatment. Aside from the obvious limitation of disregarding women staff as potential perpetrators, this has left staff working for social services or the private and voluntary sector outside the remit of this specific law. These deficits are addressed in the proposed new offence of 'breach of relationship of care' (Home Office, 2002). Further the maximum penalty for such an offence is set to increase to seven years.

Other countries have also sought to legally limit sexual contact between staff and the people they are paid to support, including the Netherlands, Germany and some American States. For example, Germany prohibits 'sexual contact with a person who has been entrusted into his/her care because of a mental or psychiatric problem, or a handicap including addiction, or who is in a situation of counselling or treatment' (Section 174 of the Criminal Code).

Sexual abuse by members of staff against the people they are paid to care for is not an uncommon experience, although there is evidence to suggest that this is one of the most difficult forms of sexual abuse for people with learning disabilities to disclose (McCarthy and Thompson, 1997).

Why is sex with staff wrong? In addition to the legislation stated above many organisations and authorities have guidelines and policies which prohibit all staff from having sexual activity with clients (e.g. Greenwich Social Service, 1991). Only rarely is it suggested by carers that sexual relationships should be allowed between staff and clients (Brandon, 1989). Research and anecdotal evidence suggests numerous cases where male staff members have exploited their authority to ensure the compliance of people with learning disabilities to sexual acts (e.g. McCarthy and Thompson, 1997). Staff rarely need to employ force, as many people with learning disabilities will comply with the request or demands of those in authority out of habit, fear, confusion or lack of understanding of what is happening. Absence of force is more a reflection of the power staff hold over people with learning disabilities and therefore should not be interpreted as evidence of their good character nor of the willing participation of the person with learning disabilities.

So great are the power dynamics between staff and people with learning disabilities, that it is difficult to imagine a scenario of a person with learning disabilities ever being an equal sexual partner. At best people with learning disabilities may comply, even those who, with different partners, could be considered to be able to give informed consent.

The specific power held by people in positions of authority which undermines the potential of free consent was recently acknowledged in the Sexual Offences (Amendment) Act (2000). This prohibits adults in certain positions of trust and authority from having sex with young people below the age of 18 in their care. This includes young people over the age of 16 who in other circumstances would be considered able to give consent to sex with adults. Although this is rather weakly referred to as 'abuse of trust', the maximum penalty being 5 years imprisonment gives an indication of how seriously it can be considered in law.

The wide consensus amongst professionals in the learning disability field about the unacceptability of sexual relationships between staff and clients is not shared by all people with learning disabilities themselves. People with learning disabilities are sometimes positive about the possibility of them having relationships with staff. Even those who, in some people's eyes, have been sexually abused by staff are sometimes unhappy when their relationship has been forcibly ended by the intervention of others. Although the sexual side of the relationship is likely to be exploitative and may be experienced as physically painful, people with learning disabilities are often taking a wider view by valuing the presence of that person in their life and the attention they receive. A broad concern about the welfare of people with learning disabilities needs to consider not only the damage done to them in such relationships, but also the damage done by ending such relationships. We suggest that lessons can be learnt from the field of child sexual abuse where, regardless of the feelings of the child, what the adult has done is always considered wrong and action taken to prevent it from re-occurring. However, good practice demands that the actions taken to end abuse are, as far as possible, not experienced as abusive by the child or vulnerable adult.

Sex with Family Members The law in England and Wales relating to incest has been sections 10, 11 and 54 of the Sexual Offences Act 1956. This has covered sexual intercourse between men and their mothers, sisters, half-sisters, daughters, and grand daughters. Consenting women could be prosecuted under this act. This prohibition of sex between family members stems from historical concern regarding the genetic make up of any children resulting from such sexual contacts. However, there is a now a wider concern about the morality of such relationships and a specific worry about the inherent power imbalances which exist in many family relationships.

These concerns were recognised in *Setting the Boundaries* (Home Office, 2000), which contained recommendations to replace the old incest laws with ones which would recognise a wide variety of family relationships (inc. step-parents, adoptive parents and siblings, foster carers, etc, as well as blood relations). *Protecting the Public* proposes that this is addressed by two new offences. The first being 'familial sexual abuse of a child' covering individuals living within the same household as the child and assuming a position of trust or authority in relation to the child (under 18). The second: 'prohibited adult relationships' – to include just blood relatives of adults. Together these would bring England and Wales into line with other countries which have broader legislation on incest (e.g. South Africa

[South African Law Reform Commission, 1999], and Scotland [The Criminal Law (Consolidation) (Scotland) Act 1995]).

Debate has been raised as to whether the law has a role in incestuous relationships between consenting adults. For example, the Australian Model Criminal Code Officers' Committee (1999) suggested that specific incest legislation would be unnecessary if there was adequate legislation both to protect children and for non-consensual sex between adults.

Adults with learning disabilities are vulnerable to incest in a way that many other adults are not. They frequently live for prolonged periods in the parental home and may not be able to 'escape' by leaving home as most other young adults do. Even where they do move into alternative accommodation, they may not have control over whether and how often they return home for visits or when their abusing relative may visit them (McCarthy, 1998).

What Constitutes Consent to Sex?

Whether people with learning disabilities are to be protected by either generic or specific laws on sexual assault, the challenge is to provide a workable definition of consent. Such a definition may relate to the particular circumstances on any one occasion when sex has taken place, or may provide a broad baseline of people unable to ever give consent to specific sexual acts.

There are competing forces in developing common ground on what constitutes consent to sex for people with learning disabilities. A perspective which seeks to redress the historical sexual repression of people with learning disabilities would be cautious about setting too high a standard. Conversely, if seeking to address the widespread abuse and exploitation of people with learning disabilities, a high standard would be expedient. There is however a consensus that legislation in England and Wales has been unhelpful by simultaneously failing to punish perpetrators whilst reinforcing a restrictive sexual climate for people with learning disabilities. Despite, the controversial *R v Jenkins* case, there is general agreement in the learning disability field that people must have free choice and that consent, if it is to be at all meaningful, must mean *informed* consent.

What is Free Choice?

For valid consent to sex people have to know that having sex is an option. In other words, people need to know that sex, especially when initiated by a more powerful person, is not required and compulsory. Many adults with learning disabilities, who have lived their whole lives being told what to do by others, do not know this: the following is a quote from a woman with learning disabilities 'The taxi driver touched me [sexually]. I didn't know if I could say no or not. He was much older than me' (quoted in McSherry, 1998).

Knowing that 'no' is an option is of little value if the person is unable to express this. Two factors are important here: firstly, people must have sufficient communication skills to be able to make their choice (to engage in sexual activity or not) known to the other party. This means either verbally, or through an alternative communication system known to both parties, to give/deny/withdraw consent at any stage in the activity. Silence or non-communication must not be interpreted as consent, as evidence suggests that men will successfully use this as their defence against allegations of sexual crimes (Lees, 1996).

Secondly, there needs to be reasonable degree of equality between the parties, so that both parties have sufficient power to make the choice to engage or not engage in sex, without fear of adverse consequences. In the context of ongoing relationships, where violence or abuse exists (and these need not be just between couples, but could include a bullying relationship between peers) then a person's ability to give 'free' consent to any individual sexual act must be strenuously questioned. In the domestic violence context this is well understood: 'when the female partner in the relationship knows the other can and will hurt her, she needs to take this into account in every aspect of the relationship, not only when the threat is immediate and imminent' (Eisikovits and Buchbinder, 1997, p. 488). To a lesser extent, similar dynamics occur where a relationship is based on dependency and authority, but which is not abusive.

Notions of free consent to sex are meaningless outside of conditions of equality (Pateman, 1980). In conditions of inequality the less powerful person can only realistically seek to limit and control sexual access by the more powerful person. The reality is that there are inequalities in power in most sexual contacts involving people with learning disabilities: evidence shows that women frequently lack power in heterosexual contexts (McCarthy, 1999): and that men lack power when having sex with more able men, including men without learning disabilities (Thompson, 2001).

What is Informed Consent?

Understanding is essential for consent, but what precisely is it that people have to understand to be deemed able to consent? There is no consensus on this, nationally or internationally (see however Murphy and O'Callaghan, 2002). Nevertheless here we attempt to set out the different elements of what it is people might be expected to understand if they are to be deemed capable or incapable of consenting to sex.

There are four potential areas of knowledge required:

- what the physical act(s) involve
- their meaning
- society's laws and norms concerning sex
- the potential consequences

People should have some understanding about what physical acts they are likely to be involved in. For example knowing that a man is going to insert their penis in one or more parts of their body. A true understanding would involve knowing that the sexual acts are distinct from other kind of behaviour that might involve the same parts of the body. For example, knowing that the contact is different from:

- having help going to the toilet, with menstrual care, or with washing and dressing.
- being examined by a doctor or nurse

If, for example, a person with a learning disability does not know that being masturbated is not a part of the necessary bathing routine, they cannot be said to have consented to the sexual activity.

In Victoria, Australia, women are said to lack capacity to consent if they do not understand 'that what is proposed to be done is a physical fact of penetration of her body by the male organ'. The other test of capacity in Victoria is a failure to comprehend 'that the act of penetration proposed is one of sexual connection as distinct from an act of a totally different character' (1970, *R v Morgan*, V.R.337, cited in McSherry, 1998).

Another dimension of understanding sex is recognising that it usually involves being part of another person's sexual gratification, i.e. one person will be using the other person's body for their own pleasure. This may be a mutual exchange, but of course it may not, and in the case of many women with learning disabilities, evidence suggests that it rarely is (Andron and Ventura, 1987, McCarthy, 1999). In other words, to be able to fully understand the nature and meaning of sex, people with learning disabilities need to have an idea about what motivates people to have sex, what gratification they can get from it and what their role in that might be.

When exploring a person's ability to consent, it is especially important to distinguish between their sexual *experience*, and their *understanding* of that experience. Everyone, whatever their degree of disability can experience sex. How they understand that experience is a critical point. For example, people who are continuously sexually abused may come to regard this experience as a normal aspect of their life – as normal as being helped with bathing, for example.

Thus people should also know something about society's laws and norms about sex, including those related to privacy. This includes, understanding that sex is something which is usually only done in certain places and within certain relationships. For example, not knowing that relatives and staff are prohibited from having sex with people with learning disabilities invalidates the potential for consent in such 'relationships'. Not knowing what is legal and illegal leaves people very vulnerable to exploitation, as they can be easily deceived into thinking that certain acts are normally accepted, when in fact most of society deems them to be transgressive of important boundaries.

As well as being able to distinguish between the legal and illegal, people with learning disabilities also need to know what is considered usual and unusual sexual behaviour. For example, the authors are aware of instances where people with learning disabilities have been approached for sex by complete strangers. Often individuals have complied with this (sometimes with small inducements such as a cigarette), without recognising that this is not usual behaviour. Of course in other contexts, for some people, sex with strangers is normal, e.g. men seeking anonymous sex with other men in public toilets, or for those engaged in prostitution. If people with learning disabilities are to be considered to have made an informed choice about having sex with strangers they need to know it is a choice many other people would not make. They would also need to be aware that one reason why strangers may be making sexual advances to them is because they may be perceived as 'easy targets' (McCarthy, 1999).

Reaching a consensus on what is the nature and/or meaning of sex and then producing a reliable test of a person's understanding of this is very difficult. This is particularly true, since the test needs to be conducted on people who will, to various extents, have limited intellectual and communication skills. In the United States, a person's understanding the *nature* of sex is a common feature of sexual abuse legislation. This has lead to high conviction rates of men who have exploited people with disabilities because even people with mild learning disabilities have shown very limited knowledge in this area. However it has simultaneously contributed to a prohibitive sexual climate for all people with learning disabilities (Sundrum and Savis, 1994).

Partly because of the difficulties of testing people's understanding of the *nature* of sex there has been a considerable interest in testing people's knowledge of potential *consequences*. For example, in a key Australian case where lack of capacity hinged on understanding either the nature or consequence of the act, the judge was unsure whether the women understood the first of these but was confident that she did not understand the latter i.e. the possibility of pregnancy arising from the assault (cited in McSherry, 1998).

As in the example above, assessing whether a person understands the consequences of sex usually focuses on what could happen physically, in particular the risks of pregnancy or sexually transmitted diseases. Emotional and social consequences are obviously also possible, but these vary considerably from person to person and are very difficult to either predict beforehand or measure afterwards.

Although it is easier to design tests for knowledge of potential consequences of sex (as opposed to the nature of sex), this is itself problematic because different kinds of sexual activity have different potential consequences and some sex has very few, if any, physical consequences. For example, if a woman with learning disabilities is post-menopausal or infertile, how important is it that she knows that penetrative vaginal sex can lead to pregnancy? Similarly if a man with learning disabilities is having sex with another man which doesn't involve anal penetration, how important is it that he knows about the risk of HIV?

Therefore one has to consider whether a test based on consequences should be related only to the risks associated with the specific sex which takes place and/ or the specific people involved. Being specific in this can lead to situations where, because there is neither risk of sexually transmitted disease of pregnancy, there is no requirement for knowledge. Not being specific in this way (i.e. expecting people to understand the broad risks attached to all sexual activity) leads to a situation requiring people to have information which is irrelevant for their circumstances. Consider what knowledge of consequences is appropriate for two women having sex together, neither having a history of sexually transmitted diseases?

A model whereby people are expected to understand the broad risks attached to all kinds of sexual activity has the advantage of removing any necessity of identifying in explicit detail what specific sexual acts took place and the sexual histories of the people concerned. However, in the debate about how high the standards of knowledge should be set, this appears to set the standard higher than the circumstances demand.

The recent recommendation by the Home Office (2000) on consent is to use the generic definition suggested by the Law Commission (2000):

(1) a person should be regarded as lacking capacity to consent if at the material time:
>(a) the person is by reason of mental disability unable to make a decision for themselves on the matter in question: or
>(b) the person is unable to communicate their decision on that matter because they are unconscious or for any other reason;

(2) a person should be regarded as being unable to make a decision on whether to consent to an act if:
>(a) he or she is unable to understand
>>(i) the nature and reasonably foreseeable consequences of the act; and
>>(ii) *the implications of the act and its reasonably foreseeable consequences; or*
>(b) being able so to understand, he or she is nonetheless unable to make a decision; and

(3) mental disability should mean a disability or disorder of the mind or brain, whether permanent or temporary, which results in an impairment or disturbance of mental functioning.

Even if this recommendation is transferred to the Statute books in the proposed Sexual Offences Bill people with learning disabilities will remain vulnerable to competing interpretations of what understanding is required; both in services for people with learning disabilities and in evolving case law.

Avoiding Tests of Capacity

Because of the difficulty of providing a valid and reliable working definition of informed consent, legislation which avoids tests of consent is attractive and may lead to higher prosecution rates. Prohibiting specific groups from having any sexual contact with people with learning disabilities (precisely because such contact is both considered and typically is abusive) is one option. As such the wider definitions of staff and familial sexual abuse proposed in *Protecting the Public* are welcomed by the authors and should lead to an increase in convictions. For example, in court the prosecution, having established that sex has taken place should find it easier to demonstrate a 'relationship of care' rather than the person with learning disabilities failing what will always be a subjective test of consent.

One group which has largely escaped attention in criminal law are those people who both deliberately and repeatedly target people with learning disabilities precisely because of their vulnerability to sexual exploitation. Such behaviour is illustrated in the following real life examples:

- Men driving into the grounds of learning disability hospitals looking for people with learning disabilities to have sex with.

- A man who drove around different learning disability services, picking up a series of women in his van and having sex with them, after getting them to sign 'consent' forms.

- A woman who visited, befriended, then had sex with a series of men with mild learning disabilities who lived in a secure unit.

In an attempt to address this kind of exploitation *Protecting the Public* introduces a radically new offence of 'obtaining sexual activity by inducement, threat or deception with a person who has a learning disability or mental disorder'. The text of the white paper acknowledges that:

> case studies show that it is possible for a person with a learning disability to be induced into sexual activity by offers of gifts. They can be seriously distressed by threats of withholding treats and favours or telling tales to their friends and family, and they can also be deceived by claims that sexual activity is all part of routine health care or a game that everyone plays. Seemingly implausible threats may be effective against a person who has a mental disorder, especially if they are targeted at known fears. Victims who are mentally impaired can thus be manipulated into unwanted or inappropriate sexual activity (p. 27).

One stated intention of this offence is to protect individuals with learning disabilities who with other people would be considered able to give their consent to a sexual relationship. This is a remarkable development towards striking a balance between sexual rights for people with learning disabilities and protection from exploitation. Also of huge significance here is the proposed maximum sentence of life imprisonment for offenders.

Laws and Practices Regarding a Defendant's Rights

Rather than a narrow focus on the capacity of people with learning disabilities to consent to sex, we suggest a more functional definition of consent would include an assessment of the context in which the act(s) took place, the environment and of the alleged perpetrator. In particular, it would be helpful to require defendants to demonstrate that they did have the consent of the person with learning disabilities. i.e. where the defendant is basing his defence on consent, the onus is for them to show how they had established this rather on the prosecution to show it was not present. This shift from proving lack of consent to proving consent has been proposed for the general population by many feminists who are concerned at the way rape trials are conducted:

> Feminists have proposed that a clear distinction needs to be made between 'voluntary agreement' and 'acquiescence' or submission as a result of threat or fear...Discovering that the woman gave her active consent should be investigated, rather than assuming that consent was given unless there is strong evidence to the contrary...The criteria would be absence of consent not presence of dissent. (Lees, 1996, p. 116)

In *Setting the Boundaries*, the Home Office (2000) has gone some way in addressing these concerns. Whilst it has not recommended reversing the burden of proof nor the presumption of innocence for the defendant, it has recommended defining consent to sex as 'free agreement' and also that:

> A defence of honest belief in free agreement should not be available where there was self-induced intoxication, recklessness, as to consent, or if the accused did not take all reasonable steps in the circumstances to ascertain free agreement at the time. (Home Office, 2000, p. 26).

The importance of revisiting some of the laws and practices regarding a defendant's rights is emphasised by the fact that, although in rape trials for example, jurors assume (and sometimes are directly told by the judges) that their role is to judge one person's word over another. In fact it is not as straightforward as that: the defence counsel (on the side of the accused man) has a number of vital advantages over the prosecution counsel (on the side of the woman making the accusations). These include:

- The defendant (accused man) can put his case together with his barrister, whilst the prosecution witness (woman or man making the accusation i.e. victim) is not allowed to meet or speak to their barrister before the trial;
- The defendant's counsel has full access to legal papers from both sides (including the victim's statement) when preparing the case, whilst the victim is not allowed to see even her own statement to the police (which she may have made over a year previously) until just before the trial starts;
- The defendant does not have to take the stand or give any evidence, whilst the victim must give evidence;
- The jury is not allowed to be told if the defendant has any previous convictions, whilst they can be told if the victim has any convictions;
- The defendant's sexual history is not allowed to be mentioned in court, whilst the victim's sexual history can be, and often is, mentioned. (Adapted from Lees, 1996)

In judging one person's word against another then and coming to a conclusion beyond reasonable doubt, there is clearly not a level playing field, especially when one considers that juries are not aware of the inherent imbalances in the system.

Factors such as these, and others such as the long delays in trials coming to court, which disadvantage *all* victims of sexual crimes, are likely to particularly work against the interests of victims with learning disabilities (McCarthy, 1999).

Conclusion

When considering sex and consent for people with learning disabilities, we need to acknowledge that the law is, and always has been, a `blunt instrument'. It is likely to remain so, despite recent improvements, e.g. the special measures and rules of evidence introduced in the Youth Justice and Criminal Evidence Act, 1999, which are designed to help vulnerable witnesses like adults with learning disabilities give evidence. Nevertheless, the fact remains that professionals in the learning disability field are going to continue to need to provide the 'fine-tuning', which the law cannot achieve.

Staff in learning disability services, alongside those in the social work, psychology and other professions, will still need to use their own judgement and refer to the appropriate policies and guidelines of their organisations in deciding what to do, if they suspect a person may have been involved in sexual activity without their informed consent. Whilst in most instances it will be absolutely right to inform the police and expect to see justice done in a court of law, in other cases it will be unrealistic to expect that the law could be applied. For example, where the sex involves another person with learning disabilities and there are no clear signs of threats or force. Those working directly with the person(s) with learning disabilities would still need to try to assess capacity to consent and take whatever steps were appropriate to ensure their safety.

Although we fully recognise the dangers in suggesting that staff in learning disability services should operate 'outside the law' (not least because of the ever present risk of abuse from staff themselves), the fact remains that everyday, in most learning disability services throughout the country, staff are required to make judgements and take decisions to ensure a person's safety or help them take calculated risks. There is often no legal basis for these everyday 'autonomy vs. protection' decisions. Staff work to a general notion of a 'duty to care' and in doing so, they have to weigh up risks and benefits to individuals. Different people need different levels of protection depending on their level of ability and the circumstances they are in. The same person may need different levels of protection at different times in their life (Brown, 1999). Whether we have disabilities or not, none of us is completely autonomous and few of us need complete protection at all times. Finding the right balance is difficult, but in seeking to do so, there is a clear role for the law.

Note

[1] Learning disabilities (or learning difficulties) are the accepted terms in Britain for what used to be called mental handicap. In an international context they can be used interchangably with intellectual disabilities or developmental disabilities.

References

The Queen v Howard (1981) 26 S.A.S.R, 481

Australian Model Criminal Code Officers' Committee (1999) – Report on sexual offences against the person

Andron, L. and Ventura, J. (1987), 'Sexual dysfunction in couples with learning handicaps', *Sexuality and Disability*, Vol. 8, No. 1, pp. 25-35.

BMA/Law Society (1995), *Assessment of mental capacity: guidance for doctors and lawyers*, London: BMA

Brandon, D. (1989), 'Can we breach the protective barriers of sexuality?', *Community Living*, April, p. 2.

Brown, H., Stein, J. and Turk, V. (1995), 'The sexual abuse of adults with learning disabilities: report of a second two-year incidence survey', *Mental Handicap Research*, Vol. 8, No. 1, pp. 3-24.

Brown, H. et al. (1996), *Towards Better Interviewing: a handbook for police officers and social workers on the sexual abuse of adults with learning disabilities*, Brighton: Pavilion Publishing.

Craft, A. (1987), 'Mental handicap and sexuality: issues for individuals with a mental handicap, their parents and professionals', in Craft, A. (ed.) *Sexuality and Mental Handicap: Issues and Perspectives*, Tunbridge Wells: Costello.

Eisokovits, Z. and Buchbinder, E. (1997), 'A phenomenological study of metaphors battering men use', *Violence Against Women*, Vol. 3, No. 5, pp. 482-498.

Evans, A. and Rodgers, M. (2000), 'Protection for whom? The right to a sexual or intimate relationship', *Journal of Learning Disabilities*, Vol. 4, No. 3, pp. 237-245.

Greenwich Social Services (1991), *Sexuality and Adults with a Learning Disability: policy and guidelines for staff*.

Home Office (2000), *Setting the Boundaries: Reforming the law on sexual offences, Volume One*. London: Home Office Communication Directorate.

Home Office (2002). *Protecting the Public*, London: Home Office Communication Directorate.

Kaeser, F. (1992), 'Can people with severe mental retardation consent to mutual sex?', *Sexuality and Disability*, Vol. 10, pp. 133-42.

Law Commission (2000), *Consent in Sex Offences*, February, Volume 2 Appendix C.

Lees, S. (1996), *Carnal Knowledge: Rape on Trial*, London: Hamish Hamilton.

Lees, S. (1997), *Ruling Passions: sexual violence, reputation and the law*, Buckingham: Open University Press.

McCarthy, M. (1998), 'Sexual violence against women with learning disabilities', *Feminism and Psychology*, Vol. 8, No. 4, pp. 544-551.

McCarthy, M. (1999), *Sexuality and Women with Learning Disabilities*, London: Jessica Kingsley Publishers.

McCarthy, M. and Thompson, D. (1997), 'A prevalence study of sexual abuse of adults with learning disabilities referred for sex education', *Journal of Applied Research in Intellectual Disability*, Vol. 10, No. 2, pp. 105-124.

McCarthy, M. and Thompson, D. (1998), *Sex and the 3R's: rights, responsibilities and risks*, Brighton: Pavilion Publishers.

McSherry, B. (1998) 'Sexual assault against individuals with mental impairment: are criminal laws adequate?', *Psychiatry, Psychology and Law*, Vol. 5, No. 1, pp. 107-116.

Murphy, G. (2000), 'Justice Denied', *Mental Health and Learning Disabilities Care*, Vol. 3, No. 8, pp. 256-257.

Murphy, G. and Clare, I. (1997), 'Consent Issues', in O'Hara, J. and Sperlinger, A. (eds) *Adults with learning disabilities: a practical approach for health professionals*, Chichester: J. Wiley and Sons.

Myhill, A. and Allen, J. (2002). *Rape and sexual assault of women: the extent and nature of the problem*, Home Office Research Study No. 237. London: Home Office.

O'Callaghan, A. and Murphy, G. (2002), 'Capacity to consent to sexual relationships in people with learning disabilities', Inaugural Conference of IASSID Europe, Dublin, 13th June.

Pateman, C. (1980), 'Women and Consent', *Political Theory*, Vol. 8, No. 2, pp. 149-168.

Thompson, D. (2001), 'Is sex a good thing for men with learning disabilities?' *Tizard Learning Disability Review*, Vol. 6, No. 1, pp. 4-12.

Thompson, D. and Brown, H. (1997), 'Men with learning disabilities who sexually abuse: a review of the literature', *Journal of Applied Research in Intellectual Disabilities*, Vol. 10, No. 2, pp. 140-158.

Vasagar, J. (2002), 'Rape trails may get expert prosecutors', *The Guardian*, April 2nd.

Winchester, R. (2000) 'Pressure builds to revamp consent laws in wake of failed rape charge', *Community Care*, 3-9 February, pp. 10-11.

Chapter 14

Sex is Violence: A Critique of Susan Sontag's 'Fascinating Fascism'

David Renton

Introduction

This chapter argues that violence should not be used in as the sole indicator of non-consensual sex. One argument which makes this link is addressed, namely Susan Sontag's essay 'Fascinating Fascism', which links the art of Leni Riefenstahl to the practice of S/M. Susan Sontag's claim that sexual violence is fascistic is rejected for two reasons. First, her argument is not a convincing account of the sexual dynamics of fascism. Second, Sontag also seems to misunderstand violent sex. The claim is made that it is wrong to see all violence as possessing one unitary set of properties. Violence is a broad term, whose common meaning is hard to pin down. Non-oppressive forms of violence can be envisaged. The most important question to ask of all sexual activity is 'did consent take place?' If this is the key issue, then the presence of violence is only a secondary question.

The question of whether violent sex can ever be consensual has already generated much discussion. Several authors have written about one-form of violent sex, S/M sex, and its treatment in law (Thompson, 1994; Reynolds, 1997; Archard, 1998, Andrea Beckmann in this volume). This chapter adds to the debate through an extended critique of one previous essay in particular, namely Susan Sontag's article, 'Fascinating Fascism', which was first published in 1975 in the *New York Review of Books* (Sontag, 1980, pp. 73-108). Ostensibly a critique of the art of the Nazi film director Leni Riefenstahl, Sontag's essay rapidly became an attack on the sexualisation of violence in all its forms. At its simplest, Sontag's argument claimed that all sado-masochism was 'fascistic' and hence illegitimate. Susan Sontag could be criticised for her misunderstanding of fascism, but here my target is Sontag's understanding of violence. I simply do not agree with her identification of fascism and sexual violence. The relationship is more complex than Sontag suggests.

Although I will be critical of Sontag's work, it is worth emphasising that Susan Sontag was a leading activist within a generation of feminist writers that rightly condemned the sexual mores of post-war Europe and America. In discussing the issue of sexual violence, it is always necessary to remember their point that sexual behaviour takes place in a society marked by structural division and relationships of inequality. As Sontag's contemporary, the libertarian sexologist Alex Comfort wrote:

> Both women and men have always run the risk of violence from a sexual partner. For evident reasons, women are overwhelmingly the more vulnerable – in our society, intensely so, since injury by a husband or lover is one of the commonest medical problems they experience. Society offers them remarkably little support. The police are traditionally uninterested in "domestic" violence, and folklore treats it as a sign of passion' (Comfort, 1973, pp. 212-213).

Thirty years on, the relationships within the family remain unequal, and the behaviour of the police unhelpful. If this chapter appears to give a partial affirmation of some forms of sexual 'violence', it does not in any way defend the many oppressive practices that have been justified by violent men in the name of 'fun'.

'Fascinating Fascism'

The occasion of Susan Sontag's article was an exhibition of the art of Leni Riefenstahl. Sontag argued that there had been a tendency since 1945 for liberal writers to discuss Riefenstahl's work apart from its political context. Leni Riefenstahl's most famous film, *Triumph of the Will*, was an open work of Nazi propaganda, a celebration of the 1934 Nuremberg congress, and it is hard to reinterpret this film as pure art. Instead, the focus of revisionism was on Riefenstahl's recent book, *The Last of the Nuba*, a series of erotically-charged photographs of this perfect, muscular, noble tribe. Although the images here of wrestling Africans seem a distant from the Nazi preoccupation with uniforms, Sontag observed that Riefenstahl pictures contained many familiar themes of Nazi art, including glorification of the masculine, love of violence, and contempt for thought. 'Fascist art glorifies surrender, it exalts mindlessness, it glamorises death' (Sontag, 1980, p. 91; Renton, 2000) For Sontag, fascist art was fascism, and art which plays with fascist imagery was the same.

Having criticised the reception of Riefenstahl's art, Susan Sontag went on to criticise what she saw as a process in which properly-fascist aesthetics had intruded into every-day art and culture. This is how she described the general themes of fascist imagery, 'Fascist aesthetics', she wrote, 'flow from (and justify) a preoccupation with situations of control, submissive behaviour, and the endurance of pain; they endorse two seemingly opposite states, egomania and servitude.' Because fascism had thrived on this aesthetic, any use of this imagery threatened to recreate the social conditions of fascism. To demonstrate the point that fascism was a deviant sexuality, Sontag examined the many picture books of the Third Reich. Of one publication Sontag wrote, 'One knows that its appeal is not scholarly but sexual. The cover already makes that clear. Across the large black swastika of an SS armband is a diagonal yellow stripe which reads 'Over 100 Brilliant Four-Color

Photographs Only $2.95', exactly as a sticker with the price on it used to be affixed – part tease, part defence to censorship – on the cover of pornographic magazines, over the model's genitalia' (Sontag, 1980, p. 98). In such histories, the depiction of aggressive masculine crimes have become something else, the glamorisation of brutality. Sontag's argument was a telling critique of an entire way of writing history, and one which continues today.

Having described the role of dominance and submission in Nazi art and the commodification of fascist imagery as a form of violent pornography, Susan Sontag went on to identify fascism with all forms of violent sexuality, 'Between sadomasochism and fascism', she wrote, 'there is a natural link'. Much of the imagery of far-out sex has been placed under the sign of Nazism, 'Boots, leather, chains, Iron Crosses on gleaming torsos, swastikas along with meat hooks and heavy motorcycles, have become the secret and most lucrative paraphernalia of eroticism.' Between fascism and sexual violence, one common theme was the glamorisation of military clothing, 'There is a general fantasy about uniforms. They suggest community, order, identity, competence, legitimate authority, the legitimate exercise of violence.' Another constant was the glorification of slavery. Thus for Sontag fascism can best be understood as the political sexualisation of violence, and if fascism was wrong – then so was any other practice which turned the processes of consent and domination into a sexual game (Sontag, 1980, pp. 99, 102, 108).

Susan Sontag argued that there was a strong link between the sexualisation of violence (sado-masochistic sex) and the imagery of fascism. It followed that violent sex could never be legitimate or properly consensual. Although this chapter will criticise Sontag's argument for this point, it should not be assumed that the argument here is a total rejection of Susan Sontag's case. There are many aspects of 'Fascinating Fascism' which should be endorsed. For example, Sontag's criticism of Riefenstahl's art was timely and well-observed. Also, Susan Sontag was not the only writer to have observed some overlap between violent sexuality and reactionary politics. 'Fascinating Fascism' could be compared to Klaus Theweleit's work on the culture of the German Freikorps, the pre-Nazi student bands and officer corps who opposed the German revolution of 1918-23. One difference is that Theweleit located fascism in the denial of sexuality, 'the core of all fascist propaganda is a battle against anything that constitutes enjoyment and pleasure.' Partly because Theweleit's work is based on a sustained study of primary materials (250 Freikorps novels and memoirs from the 1920s) it seems to capture the dynamic interplay between political and sexual reaction far more vividly than Sontag's essay (Theweleit, 1989, pp. xii-xiii; Theweleit, 1987; Mosse, 1985, pp. 153-181). Indeed Theweleit's theories have gained in popularity over the past few years, and several writers have attempted to apply them, not always successfully, to other forms of male aggression (King, 1997; Smith, 1999). So there is space for a comparison of fascism and violent sexuality – but Sontag missed the key dynamics, and is simplistic in her claim that all forms of violent sex were the same.

One of the several interesting aspects of Sontag's article is that it seems to pre-empt a certain radical feminist argument which would be expressed on several occasions through the late 1970s and early 1980s, namely that all violent sexual activity was male, aggressive and therefore non-consensual. Sontag's work could be seen as an early counterpart to the notion of 'gendered consent' defended by Catharine MacKinnon and Andrea Dworkin. For these later authors, all heterosexual sex takes place under conditions of domination (MacKinnon, 1989a; MacKinnon, 1989b; Dworkin, 1988). According to Dworkin all men oppress all women through the terror of rape, 'Men develop a strong loyalty to violence. Men must come to terms with violence because it is the prime component of male identity.' Or, to quote Dworkin more succinctly, 'Force ... [is] the essential purpose of the penis' (Dworkin, 1988, p. 55; Segal, 1987, p. 177). It follows that all heterosexual sex is rape, and that consensual heterosexual sex is a contradiction in terms. One key argument in this literature is that women can never enjoy heterosexual sex – a claim fiercely contested by Alison Assiter, among others (Assiter and Carold, 1993, p. 14). As this chapter will argue, the debate over violence and male sexuality has not been restricted to radical feminists, and nor has the discussion been restricted to the norms of polite, academic discussion.

Sontag Applied

One of the problems with the rejection of violent sex as a 'male' phenomenon has been how to understand this sex, when no men were involved. Across both sides of the Atlantic, through the 1970s and 1980s, there was a repeated debate between feminist opponents of all forms of violence and female supporters of sado-masochist sex. One controversy involved the San Francisco S/M group, Samois. In the early 1980s, they were practically the only visible lesbian S/M group in the US. To their surprise, the members of Samois were banned from renting rooms in the San Francisco Women's Building. This took place at a time when the building's owners were desperate for income, and rented space to virtually anyone else. The ban was overturned, but only in 1989 (Rubin, 1996). In the same year, another conflict involved the Michigan Womyn's Music Festival, which was closed to sadomasochist women. Lesbian separatists accused sadomasochists of being 'heteropatriarchal', that is, behaving like men. One exasperated activist, who found herself thrown out of the concert by female guards, described how she saw the debates,

> In the context of dyke S/M debates, *heteropatriarchal* is being used the same way young boys use the word *faggot*: it's thrown back and forth as a synonym for *bad*. Thus, debates consist of some women insisting, 'You are oppressive, heteropatriarchal, and trying to control other women's bodies and restrict women's sexual freedom,' while others respond, 'No you are heteropatriarchal and brainwashed, imitating male patterns of violence'. And somehow, in the course of those debates, the real heteropatriarchal gets forgotten and is no longer a target for resistance – a resistance that's vitally necessary (Kaplan, 1996).

The key phrase here is '*male* patterns of violence'. Some of the radical feminist critics of sado-masochism criticised by Rebecca Dawn Kaplan seem to have possessed a remarkably deterministic way of looking at the world, in which the bad was male and anyone they disagreed with could be placed in this category. But if women could become 'heteropatriarchal' like men – then what limits or meaning could be given to the term?

In Britain, the conflict between lesbian sado-masochists and radical feminists was expressed most clearly in the equally heated debate over whether sado-masochistic groups should be allowed to meet at the London Lesbian and Gay Centre (LLGC) which dragged on for six months from 1985 to early 1986 (Ardill and O'Sullivan, 1986). Despite any number of protests, the centre's management committee not only refused to allow S/M groups to meet on their premises, they also refused to debate the issue, declaring any vote unconstitutional. The management committee received the backing of a group which went under the name of Lesbians Against Sadomasochism (LASM). A typical LASM leaflet from this period expressed the same formula that was there in Sontag's piece, namely that violent sex is non-consensual sex, and non-consensual sex is fascism:

Q. But isn't Lesbian and Gay Liberation about freedom, not more limitations?
A. Total freedom is the freedom of the powerful to oppress – do you condone racism, anti-semitism, heterosexism?
Q. But I like wearing long spiked belts and dog collars – and I'm not into S/M.
A. So what. If you don't care that others see them as racist, anti-Semitic etc then you are being racist anti-Semitic, fascist (Ardill and O'Sullivan: 50).

Lesbian sadomasochists responded to this criticism from their opponents by asking 'Who are the Real Fascists?'. In their words:

To label SM fascist is to trivialise the real fight against fascism. To throw the word fascism about with no reference to what it means is to make the real fight more difficult. To use people's sexual revulsion as a scare tactic against sexual freedom is a real insult to fascism's victims' (Ardill and O'Sullivan: 50).

This debate became one of the key influences behind Sheila Jeffreys' important book, *The Lesbian Heresy* (Jeffreys, 1994; Walker, 1982). In an appendix, Jeffreys gave her own response to the GLC debate. A former activist in LASM, Jeffreys maintained that S/M represents 'the erotic cult of fascism'. As evidence of the link, Jeffreys' cited the presence of gay men among fascist circles in 1930s Berlin; she gave a graphic description of fisting from a 1980s S/M primer; she mentioned the wearing of the swastika; and the sadism of German fascism; Jeffreys also described a scene witnessed on American television in which one white (Hispanic) and one black women acted out a ritual of racial domination. Jeffreys concluded in terms resonant of Sontag's earlier argument:

Are S/M proponents fascist? Probably they are not members of fascist organisations and do not care for any aspects of fascism apart from the erotic one ... Most are not fascists, even though experiencing pleasure from the terrorising of other lesbians by wearing fascist regalia comes pretty close, but promoters of fascist values. The eroticising of dominance and submission, the glamorising of violence and of the oppression of gays, Jews and women, is the stuff of fascism (Jeffreys, 1994, p. 218).

The claim that S/M supporters promote fascism seems to rely on two misleading elisions, between fascism and fascists, and between violence and oppression. As to the first, fascism was not merely an accumulation of individual choices, it was a programme for government. To reduce the phenomenon to the sexual choice of individuals is to reduce and misunderstand fascism. Indeed Jeffreys seems to recognise this point, admitting in her words the distinction between fascist parties and 'the stuff of fascism'. As to the second point, it seems odd that 'the eroticising of dominance' should be confused with dominance itself. Those who make a theatre of power, are not generally the powerful. Often it is the worst victims of power who repeat the forms of their oppression, but when they do so the content is changed. Whether this notion of theatre as a means to revisit and overcome pain is accepted, the relationship is more complex than Jeffreys would suggest (Renton, 1999).

To return to the original GLC debate which sparked Jeffreys' intervention, it appears that the language on both sides grew sharper – but the tone of the radical feminist LASM was far more pointed, and even became intimidatory towards fellow activists. Indeed the naive claim that only men can be aggressive could not explain the sheer hostility of the debate. The similarity with events in America is striking.

More recently Linda Wayne has challenged the identification of fascism and sexual violence from the perspective of an activist within the lesbian S/M scene. Wayne's argument is with what she sees as a general tendency among feminists to treat all forms of violent imagery as if they were the same. In reply, she suggests that 'subgroup symbolism' can take symbols from the 'dominant imagery' of capitalism and subvert them. By removing them from their original historical context, these symbols lose their old meaning, and take on a different message, 'through group agreement'. Although there is much to be said for this approach, it does seem that the process which Linda Wayne describes is actually more complex than she suggests. The meaning of words can be challenged, but only to a certain historically-determined limit. The desire to use old signs differently does not determine the effect of these symbols on an audience which receives them in the light of its own understanding of the past. Interestingly, Wayne strongly defends the use of particular symbols of sexual domination which can be stripped of their older meaning (the belts and dog collars criticised by LASM above), while challenging the use of others (the swastika) which continue to be associated today with the far-right. For Wayne, one crucial question to ask is how great a 'distance' can be placed between meanings of the past and the meanings of the same symbols used in a different context today? Susan Sontag's simple equation, which identifies all forms of violence as being fundamentally the same, cannot provide any useful answer (Wayne, 1996, pp. 242-251).

Fascist Violence and Legitimate Violence

Before coming on to the key theme of this chapter – the claim that violent sex can never be legitimate, it is worth saying something more about the relationship between fascism and violence. As this chapter has shown, one of the main rhetorical strategies of those who regard all violence as identical has been to label all violence as fascist. Yet there have been writers who have attempted to elaborate a non-fascist understanding of violence. One example of a non-fascist defence of violence is Gorges Sorel's *Reflections on Violence* (Sorel, 1950). The best way to make sense of Sorel's philosophy is to follow his own distinction between force, which he believed was illegitimate, and violence, which he described as potentially just. 'Force' meant any attempt by a governing minority to impose the organisation of the established social order. 'Violence', for Sorel, referred to any form of collective activity which tended to undermine the capitalist order. Georges Sorel argued that violence was capable of providing a better world which could be created by no other means. New laws and new ways of living would result, based on what Sorel called 'free producers working in a factory without masters' (Sorel' 1950, p. 241). Although Sorel has been criticised for placing too much trust in the advocates of elite theory (Sternhell, 1984; Payne, 1995), the 'free' is not accidental, Sorel's belief in free association and self-determination was genuine. Georges Sorel distinguished between violence for its own sake, and violence against violence. Expressed this way, the point is not to ask whether all violence is fascistic, but rather how realistic it is to see violence as a means by which power can be opposed?

One of Georges Sorel's claims was that violence does not emerge in the minds of warped individuals, but rather in the structures of capitalism, which give violence a spur. Recently Penny Green has drawn our attention to the role of the capitalist state in creating violence. Her claim is that violence is an 'ideologically imbued concept', whose meaning is determined by the society we live in. When we think of violence, most of us do not think of the 400 people killed each year in Britain through violent 'accidents' at work, but rather of the violence of individuals, which is used to justify police and state supervision of society. Penny Green argues that 'Individual acts of violence are widespread in our society but rape, assault, and other forms of interpersonal aggression cannot be explained in any useful sense at the level of the individual. Like the violence systematically conducted by states and corporations against citizens and consumers, violence between individuals has its roots in the organisation of power in society.' Class, gender and racial divisions 'create a climate in which social violence is readily generated', while unemployment and poverty also make violence such an endemic part of our lives (Green, 1994, pp. 20-29).

The importance of Green's argument is that it reminds us that sexual consent takes place in a social context. The law treats the sexual decision as the prerogative of two independent adults, alternating between judgements based on intention (hence the importance of consent) and judgements based on effect (hence the distrust of S/M). In law, the missing consideration is equality and power. Despite my criticisms of 'Fascinating Fascism', I recognise this as a strength of Sontag's argument. Her distrust of S/M springs from a desire to take questions of power seriously. Sontag's failure is to equate the playing out of games based on power – with the functioning of real power in society.

Vanilla Sex and Violence

Perhaps the debate between radical feminists and sado-masochists was misplaced. The overwhelming majority of violent sexual acts takes place in the form of 'vanilla sex', that is heterosexual sex between socially-defined couples, and when intercourse is a consequence, it takes place usually in the missionary position. You could also argue that Sontag's assault on the sexualisation of violence was misplaced. Rather than discriminating between different forms of violent behaviour, Sontag tended to lump all violence in together. This begs the question of what constitutes 'violence'? It is a wide term, referring to different and often contradictory patterns of behaviour. Most societies are not based on a glorification of violence, but in all societies violence is endemic, 'an ordinary part of life' (Fawcett, 1996; Hall, 1978; Newburn and Stanko, 1994; Stanko, 1985; Witte, 1996; Stanko, 1990, p. 5). There is no society in which people have yet lived without war and violent rebellion, without crime, without private acts of violence, without street attacks, without police aggression and domestic violence. Surely it is not useful to treat violence as one and the same thing, irrespective of who committed these acts and why.

Instead, the best way to make sense of violence is to contextualise it, separating out different forms of violence according to the consequences of these acts. Two distinctions have already been made, between offensive and defensive violence, and also between the violence of private individuals and of corporations or the state. The differentiation between acts of aggression and self-defence should be familiar, as this distinction is entrenched in most moral and legal codes. As for the contrast between the violence of the state and the violence of the individual, this distinction reminds us just how violent most states actually are. Indeed our every-day definition of the state depends on its monopoly of armed power, and our use of language reflects these concerns. The government provides healthcare and education. By contrast, it is the state which jails and declares war (Malmo, 1998).

In the context of sexual violence, the English language already makes several useful distinctions. In addition to the two examples already discussed, one further distinction is the decisive contrast between consensual and non-consensual sex. The primary indicator of non-consensual sex is the absence of a clear spoken affirmation of consent. Several writers have discussed the status of the sexual contract, and the 'principle of communication' – the claim that communication is the *sine qua non* of legitimate sex – is the major theme of David Archard's book *Sexual Consent*, which has already been mentioned in this chapter (Archard, 1998, pp. 136-147). An acceptance of the overriding importance of consent raises further dilemmas, can consent be withdrawn? Can consent be degraded? Can anyone consent to 'bad' or unpleasant sex? To raise these dilemmas does not detract from the overriding importance of communication. The ultimate form of non-consensual sex is rape; and any rape is in some senses an act of sexual violence. Yet if the test of rape is the absence of consent, then it by no means follows that all sexual violence equals rape.

A fourth division exists between physical and emotional violence. When people commit acts of brutality on each other, these injuries very often take the form of emotional hostility. Here is Alex Comfort again:

> Both sexes need to realise that there is a healthy streak of hostility in all lasting adult love (where it's a defence against being too taken-over by another person) and that some sexual approaches are wholly hostile: notch-cutting by either sex, for example seduce-and-abandon operations by males, husband-hunting by females. Adults can often – but not always – recognise the state of play, but in adolescence once can far more easily get hurt or trapped' (Comfort, 1973, p. 57).

The language in this quotation is ambiguous. At one level Comfort regrets the importation into sex of confrontational behaviour which has emerged outside the sexual sphere. In another sense, the author acknowledges the damaging impossibility of a sexual behaviour solely dominated by romantic notions of monogamous love. In Alex Comfort's opinion, occasional hostility is better than the disappearance of either self. Whatever the origins of such emotional violence – it is often the most destructive form of violent sexual behaviour.

A fifth useful differentiation can be made between passion and cruelty. The point which this contrast highlights is a distinction according to intention. It is perfectly possible that violent sexual activity could occur in a context in which both or either partners saw themselves as continuing their passionate activity. Many people would view such sexual 'violence' rather differently from similar acts which came about because one individual had the specific intention of doing harm to another. Here, the traditional doubt should be mentioned which applies to all notions of morality based on intent. How can any third person truly know what was the intention of the participants at that time?

A sixth distinction exists between vigour, force and might. This is not a matter of intention, but of the level of physical pressure implied in the sexual process itself. Sex is a vigorous physical activity. It relies on heat, friction and rapid motion. Orgasm itself is frequently accompanied by muscle contraction, especially for men. Almost all sex involves some low level of 'vigour', and many consensual sex acts imply a greater energy, or 'force'. In *Rex v Donovan* (a discussion heavily cited in the later case of *Regina v Brown*), the degree of bodily harm was defined as that which while it need not be permanent, should 'be more than merely transient and trifling' (Archard, 1998, p. 112). To cause such harm, overbearing physical 'might' would need to have occurred.

From these six distinctions, it should be clear that any blanket criticism of sexual 'violence' runs the risk of conflating questions of communication, process, motive and outcome. In any lived situation, discord in one sphere is likely to imply discord in another. For example, a moment of violent and unwanted sex could easily take a form which combined every one of the aspects of violence listed above. Yet if this overlap of categories is a possibility at any one moment in time, it is not an *a priori* certainty.

Sado-masochism is one context in which the violence of outcome is often directly proportional to the level of prior communication. The more violence, the greater the prior discussion. This link is especially close when these acts involve active participants on the S/M 'scene'. Indeed this observation would suggest a further paradox, that pleasurable sado-masochist sex depends on the most obvious forms of sexual communication. Such are the levels of agreement required that conscious efforts must continuously be made to create and renew trust. Yet several writers have made the point that the high levels of scene communication can conceal a smaller number of individuals who do not conform to the necessary rules (Califia, 1996, pp. 264-277). It would be ridiculous to claim that all sado-masochists are necessarily better than all heterosexuals at sexual communication. But some are better, and maybe the rest of us have something to learn.

While sado-masochistic sex would constitute one example of violence with communication, it is equally possible to imagine non-communication without violence, or certainly non-communication without the physical intensity of 'force' or 'might' (given the meanings of these terms suggested above). Degraded consent can take place without requiring overt physical violence. Indeed, this is probably the condition of most sexual acts which take place in the societies we live in. In most steady relationships, whether gay, lesbian or heterosexual, there is not a high level of verbal communication prior to sexual behaviour. Such communication as exists is often non-verbal, when it is not merely assumed in the sense of 'I thought you'd like it, we tried this position last week'.

The consistent argument of this chapter has been that violence should not be used as the only indicator of non-consensual sex. Susan Sontag's claim that sexual violence is fascistic and hence illegitimate, has been rejected for two reasons. First, her argument is not a convincing account of the sexual dynamics of fascism. Second, Sontag also seems to misunderstand violent sex. The claim has been made here that it is wrong to see all violence as possessing one unitary set of properties. Violence is a broad term, whose common meaning is hard to pin down. Non-oppressive forms of violence can be envisaged, including the libertarian syndicalist violence defended as a principle by Georges Sorel. In the context of sexual activity, violence can be said to have taken place when there acts which were non-consensual, ill-intentioned or rough. Yet each of these instances is analytically distinct. The key question to ask of all sexual activity is 'did consent take place?' If this is the key issue, then the presence of violence is only a secondary question. Much violent sex is non-consensual or illegitimate – but some violent sex is based on consent.

Bibliography

Archard, D. (1998), *Sexual Consent*, Boulder, Colorado: Westview Press.
Ardill, S., and O'Sullivan, S. (1986), 'Upsetting an Applecart: Difference, Desire and Lesbian Sadomasochism', *Feminist Review*, Vol. 23, pp. 31-58.
Assiter, A. and Carold, A. (eds.), (1993), *Bad Girls and Dirty Pictures: The Challenge to Reclaim Feminism*, London and Boulder, Colorado: Pluto.
Califia, P. (1996), 'A House Divided: Violence in the Lesbian S/M Community', in Califia, P. and Sweeney, R., *The Second Coming: A LeatherDyke Reader*, Los Angeles: Alyson Publications, pp. 264-277.
Comfort, A. (1973), *More Joy of Sex*, London: Chancellor Press.
Dworkin, A. (1981), *Pornography: Men Possessing Women*, New York: Perigree Books.
Dworkin, A. (1988), *Intercourse*, London: Arrow.
Fawcett, B., et al. (1986), *Violence and Gender Relations: Theories and Interventions*, London: Sage.
Green, P. (1994), 'State and Violence: Redirecting the Focus', in Stanko, E. A., (ed.), *Perspectives on Violence*, London: Quartet, pp. 30-39.
Hall, S., et al. (1978), *Policing the Crisis: Mugging the State and Law and Order*, Houndmills: Macmillan.
Jeffreys, S. (1994), *The Lesbian Heresy: A Feminist Perspective on the Lesbian Sexual Revolution*, London: The Women's Press.
Kaplan, R. D. (1996), 'Sex, Lies and Heteropatriarchy: The S/M Debates at the Michigan Womyn's Music Festival', in Califia, P., and Sweeney, R., *The Second Coming: A LeatherDyke Reader*, Los Angeles: Alyson Publications, pp. 123-135.
King, A. (1997), 'The Postmodernity of Football Hooliganism', *British Journal of Sociology*, Vol. 48, No. 4, pp. 576-593.
MacKinnon, C. (1989a), 'Sexuality, Pornography, and Method: "Pleasure under Patriarchy"', *Ethics*, Vol. 99.
MacKinnon, C. (1989b), *Towards a Feminist Theory of the State*, Cambridge, Massachusetts: Harvard University Press.
Malmo, J. (1998), 'Beheading the Dead: Rites of Habeas Corpus in Shakespeare's *Measure for Measure*', *New Formations*, Vol. 35, pp. 134-144.
Mosse, G. L. (1985), *Nationalism and Sexuality: Respectability and Abnormal Sexuality in Modern Europe*, New York: Howard Fertig.
Newburn, T., and Stanko, E. A. (1994), *Just Boys Doing Business? Men, Masculinities and Crime*, London and New York: Routledge.
Payne, S. G. (1995), *A History of Fascism 1914-1945*, London: University College London.
Renton, D. (1999), *Fascism: Theory and Practice*, London: Pluto.
Renton, D. (2000), 'Think Again, Jodie Foster', *Searchlight*, December 2000.
Reynolds, P. (1997), 'Gay and Lesbian Politics, Collective Action and the Law: the Hoylandswaine Case', in Barker, C. (ed.), *Conference Proceedings: Alternative Futures and Popular Protests 1997*, Manchester: Manchester Metropolitan University.
Rubin, G. (1996), 'The Outcasts: A Social History', in Califia, P. and Sweeney, R., *The Second Coming: A LeatherDyke Reader*, Los Angeles: Alyson Publications, pp. 339-346.
Segal, L. (1987), *Is the Future Female? Troubled Thoughts on Contemporary Feminism*, London, Virago.
Smith, T. (1999), 'MUFC Fans, Sex and Football Violence: A "Preferred" Postmodern Past' *North West Labour History*, Vol. 24, pp. 55-69.

Sontag, S. (1980), 'Fascinating Fascism', in Sontag, S., *Under the Sign of Saturn*, Farar, Straus and Giroux, pp. 73-108.

Sorel, G. (1950), *Reflections on Violence*, trans. T. E. Hulme and J. Roth, intro. E. A. Shils, Glencoe, Illinois: Free Press.

Stanko, E. A. (1985), *Intimate Intrusions: Women's Experience of Male Violence*, London: Routledge.

Stanko, E. A. (1990), *Everyday Violence: How Women and Men Experience Sexual and Physical Danger*, London: Pandora.

Sternhell, Z. (1984), *The Birth of Fascist Ideology*, New Jersey: Princeton University Press.

Theweleit, K. (1987), *Male Fantasies I: Women, floods, bodies, history*, Cambridge: Polity.

Theweleit, K. (1989), *Male Fantasies II: Male Bodies: Psychoanalysing the Whiter Terror*, Cambridge: Polity.

Thompson, B. (1994), *Sadomasochism: Painful Perversion or Pleasurable Play?*, London: Cassell.

Walker, A. (1982), 'A Letter of the Times, or Should This Sado-Masochism Be Saved?', in *You Can't Keep a Good Woman Down*, London: Women's Press.

Wayne, L. (1996), 'S/M Symbols, Fascist Icons and Systems of Empowerment', in Califia, P. and Sweeney, R., *The Second Coming: A LeatherDyke Reader*, Los Angeles: Alyson Publications, pp. 242-251.

Witte, R. (1996), *Racist Violence and the State*, Harlow: Longman.

Chapter 15

'In the Field and In There': Some Ethical Dilemmas in Researching Sexualities

John Gibbins

Introduction

Since Bob Burgess published his epic text, *In the Field*, on the myriad problems involved in 'getting your hands dirty' in social research, much has changed to make matters more complicated. His reflections in chapter nine, on the ethical problems he encountered in the field, is the model I am using here – reflection *post hoc*, on what has been done with a view to sharing some ideas on how to do it better when researching the 'in there' (Burgess 1984, pp. 185-208). Amongst other things social scientists are now addressing the 'in there', the personal and intimate worlds, on a scale never before exhibited in the academic community. Next, they have widened the notion of what constitutes evidence to include personal in-depth interviews in such areas, content and discourse analysis of popular culture texts such as men's magazines, sex shop catalogues, sex and fetish internet web sites. In addition they are using more radical and diverse methods, such as semiotics, deconstruction, and such explosively catalytic theories as diverse as postmodernism and radical feminism.

The ethical stances of academics, in tune with the wider and global shifts in values and morals, have diversified, pluralised and become more incommensurable. This has widened scope for controversy and conflict in research. Meanwhile governments, responding to genuine calls to regulate immoral activities around sex, namely, trafficking of women, enforced prostitution, domestic violence, date rape, hate crimes, and paedophilia, have sought to extend legal governance and regulation. The academic community has witnessed the fall out of such a dangerous situation in recent debates over male rape, the evolutionary imperative of men to rape; male scholars' right and capacity to research and teach on rape and domestic violence; the rights of academics to access primary sources, in the field of paedophilia in particular (Crotty, 1998, pp. 173-182; Ashenden, 2002, pp.197-222; Hacking, 1999, pp. 253-288).

Researching any sexuality raises numerous ethical issues: around what we should and should not research; how we should do it; what evidence we should access and display; whose permission and consent is needed and how gained; and, what sensitivities should be addressed in the research and publishing process? This is complicated by a British 'Carry On' attitude to any discussion of sex, that trivialises on the one side and attracts prudish calls for censorship on the other. Most of the key concepts in the vocabulary of sexuality are also *essentially contested*, meaning that they are internally complex, have open rules of usage, contain appraisive elements, and invoke disputes over control of language, so groups can achieve or maintain power (Gallie 1962; Connolly 1983, pp. 10-41). Power/knowledge relations rule perniciously in discourses of sexuality and gender in ways rarely experienced elsewhere. One danger I wish to highlight is that while academics should embrace the call for ethical regulation and administration of research, we should seek to protect academic rights, and avoid the process of creeping governance through surveillance, discipline and control (Loader, 1997, pp. 12-15; Burchell et al., 1991).

It is not possible for me to review the whole field here, nor to espouse in detail a code of ethics for researching sexualities, but rather to reflect critically on some current issues facing researchers of intimate relationships, and to explore further, through a case study of what happened and what I experienced during the research for an essay entitled 'Sexuality and the Law: The Body as Politics' (Gibbins, J. 1998e, pp. 36-45). Similar matters arise in a relation to Andrea Beckmann's chapter in this collection. For the purposes of this book I will also bring some topical focus to issues revolving around two recent Home Office initiatives that affect researchers, and some topics around the dangers of unwitting or unanticipated non consensual practices, in using the internet as a research source. The essay seeks to construct an argument that balances the rights of the Academy for freedom to research and publish, the need for ethical and responsible exercise of this right, and the vital need, expressed in the letter of the relevant Acts and current Sexual Offences Bill (2003), that give voice to the right of women and children, to protection from abuse, and for victims to achieve redress.

My interest in everyday and popular culture was stimulated with my engagement with the founding and running of the journal, *Theory, Culture and Society*, from 1981, with amongst others Mike Featherstone, Bryan Turner, and Mike Hepworth. Bringing the discourses of philosophy, political, social and sociological theory to bear upon the everyday, was then a novelty. Bryan Turner on 'The Discourses of Diet', Ruth Levitas on 'Dystopian Times', and John Pratt on 'The Sexual Landscape: Repression or Freedom' in the first issue established an agenda for, and a genre of, cultural theory journals since (*Theory, Culture and Society*, 1982, Vol. 1, No. 1.). Three later issues on 'Consumer Culture' (1983), 'The Fate of Modernity'(1985), and 'Postmodernism' (1988) brought greater focus and interest in the dynamics and landscape of cultural change. My personal voice to these conversations was to apply the new approaches to politics, political values and citizenship, producing books in 1989 and 1999 and several conference papers and chapters in books (Gibbins, 1989a; 1989b; 1991a; 1991b; 1992a; 1992b; 1993a; 1993b; 1994b; 1995; 1996a; 1996b; 1998a; 1998b; 1998c; 1998d; 1999a, 1999b, 1999c).

My interest in teaching and researching sexuality arose from debates in this period about the politics of the personal, the body, sex and gender, a route shared by other social theorists such as Anthony Giddens, Ulrich Beck and E. Gernshein Beck; Judith Squires, Michel Foucault, Ken Plummer, Frank Mort and Jeffrey

Weeks. What does feminism mean for sexes, genders, sexualities and for masculinity? What do postmodernisation, postmaterialism, individualisation, globalisation and cosmopolitanism mean for sexes, genders, sexualities and for masculinity? Sexuality was to us a laboratory; sexes and genders the subjects; values and intimate relations were the focus of research, for those like me, who wanted to know where we were going, the processes of change in late modernity. Within this understanding, the new landscape would emerge first in personal identity and relationships, before impacting upon the public, and those interested in the public should therefore take an intense interest in the intimate. As with many researchers, course design and delivery, was adopted as a good way to get to know the field. A module called *Sexuality* being delivered from 1995, and a companion module, *Sexuality and Morality*, on value change and sexual ethics, began in 1996. A paper on the construction of sex, gender and sexuality in cartoons was given to the British Sociological Association and the at various Open University day and summer schools in the 1990s (Gibbins, 1994).

I came to write the conference paper (Gibbins, 1996b), after having identified an opportunity to link interests in sexuality and politics by joining in a workshop on the 'Politics of Sexuality' at the European Consortium for Political Research Annual Joint Workshop in Oslo in 1996 (Carver and Mottier, 1998). The rationale for the workshop centred upon the growing need for political scientists to focus on the politics of the personal and to address issues of injustice and exclusion around sexual minorities (ibid. pp. 1-9). The workshop attracted nearly equal numbers of males and females, was directed by one of each, and covered an array of themes, issues and topics that are now familiar to researchers in the field. Many papers were re-written and are published in the text above (Carver and Mottier, 1998). My original paper, entitled 'The Body as Politics: Discourses of Politics, Sexuality and the Law', was very well attended and attracted a thoughtful and helpful set of responses. The author of this paper has not had any subsequent adverse communications and has had only one correspondence overall, which I will refer to later. This essay is not about defending or justifying anything, rather exploring in public, the sorts of issues that arose at the time, during and after publication, as a device for encouraging wider ethical debate and the development of good practice in this field in the future. Similar concerns apply to other areas of research, for instance, research using the Internet of pornography, prostitution, hate sites by political scientists or historians, and terrorist sites by experts on security (Gillespie, 2000; Sharp and Earle, 2003; Whine, 1997).

That there was no ethical controversy about the modules at the time, and no hostile debate on the Conference Paper, could be construed as surprising, as the modules covered sensitive materials. The case study used in the conference paper to illustrate the core argument, was the substance, effects and appropriateness of the Spanner prosecutions of 44 males homosexual 'sadomasochists'. Sadomasochism sat uncomfortably at the interface of numerous and contentious linguistic and political structural binaries: sex and violence; consent and force; pleasure and pain; male and male; male and female; female and female (Thompson, 1994, pp. 188-241). My object in researching for the paper, had been narrow, to apply a post-structural and Foucauldian method of deconstruction of binaries, as a means to explore the moral and legal rights of consenting adults to do with their bodies what they wanted. The results suggested a set of reflexive moral principles of tolerance that should govern relationships between persons within global and civil worlds. These principles were compatible with existing democratic legal traditions and were elaborated in subsequent publications (Gibbins, 1998; Gibbins, 1999c).

But by the mid 1990s we had developed a protocol for teaching *Sexuality* at the University, which was applied to the Conference, and this may explain how potentially problematic problems around controversial subjects can be diminished, if not removed completely (see final section below, 'Good Practice in Researching Sexualities'). As the binaries I wished to deconstruct were pain/pleasure, play/actuality, fun/violence, I decided the Internet was safer than the participatory observation route taken by Beckmann (this volume). To protect myself, and the University, I adopted a protocol that involved not paying for site entry, not registering for a site, not using University servers, and avoiding any link or site that indicated children or animals. During an informal conversation I was given the name of a gateway site that linked the user to thousands of free pages of images and texts. Avoiding anything with 'Teens' in the title also seemed like a good idea.

Ethical Dilemmas in Researching Sexualities on the Internet

How was I to research a subject about which I knew little or nothing, where was I to start, and what sources was I to use? The subject was chosen on Foucauldian grounds, namely, the study of some extreme event or activity, deemed abnormal or perverted, will under deconstruction, tell us more about the normal, the process of normalisation, and the governance of that activity (Foucault, 1975; 1980, Burchell et al., 1991). What was so extreme, tainted with abnormality but not clearly illegal? Sadomasochism fitted the requirement well, it was pathologised by psychologists, criminalised by the police and courts, taboo to the mass media, a common but repressed and unspoken aspect of the intimate relationships of many couples and groups. The usual library sources proved very limited and the bookshops proved little better, offering a surprisingly wide and varied diet of soft-core bondage and flagellation themed novels, but little else. Should I turn to the Internet?

The Internet is one of the most influential tools for scholars and researchers, and will remain so for some time, in the new millennium. However, its use is fraught with ethical problems which neither the Internet industry, government nor professional bodies have yet addressed. Academic commentary and advice is uneven, Hamelink has a useful text on The *Ethics of Cyberspace*, that only touches briefly on research, but the author of a key text, *Research Using IT*, chose to ignore ethics altogether (Hamelink, 2000; Coombes, 2001). Two authors, and the editor of *Dot.cons: Crimes, Deviance and Identity on the Internet*, make a useful contribution on ethical issues around researching chat rooms (DiMarco, 2003), but Gillespie skirts around ethical issues in her survey and analysis of Pornography on the Internet (Gillespie, 2000). Davis' recent text on *Ethics and the University*, has no sustained account of research ethics policy despite having a chapter on 'Sex and the University', while Forester and Morrison in *Computer Ethics*, find about 4 pages for discussion (Davis, 1999, pp. 195-220; Forester and Morrison 1994, pp. 10-14). What controls that exist, tend to be self imposed or applied locally at the workplace by firms, schools and Universities. The University of Teesside is fortunate in having its main library focused around electronic sources and having its main Internet access siphoned through it *Learning Resources Centre*. The Library is hence able to invoke a code of practice and rules for staff and student access, can block access, monitor use, regulate and discipline offenders. Systems like this either do exist already or will do so as awareness of the issues raises and responsible authorities respond.[1]

Internet Service Providers are currently under pressure to replace their voluntary codes with more legalistic alternatives, and in Britain, the Home Secretary has pioneered a Bill that has the effect of requiring each ISP to fit a black box on machines that will allow the police, Customs and MI5 to have instant access to, and an annual log of, the web activities and emails of all users. What has failed in Germany, is likely to fail in Britain, and already ISPs are setting up sites on offshore gun towers, that will re-route web and emails around and away from the black box systems. While the Home Secretary defends the intrusion on personal privacy and rights on the utilitarian grounds that criminals, perverts such as paedophiles, hate site operators and commercial exploiters of the vulnerable cause harm to others, the opponents argue for the freedom and right to surf, espouse the positive benefits the a free internet provides (which outweigh the harms caused), and describe the practical and moral by-products of inappropriate and heavy handed regulation. ISPs in Britain claim that the net effect of black boxes will be to destroy their business and to oblige users to migrate to ISPs based in countries that won't operate the scheme.

However, even before the introduction of such legislation and enforcement, the researchers who use the internet are open to a number of potential and real risks which professionalism requires we should understand, debate and try to cover with clear guidance, training and support. What are these moral risks? Ought we to research such topics as date rape, paedophilia, prostitution, pornography or sadomasochism? Are they too immoral to be addressed? Are they better left excluded and un-researched?

The opponents of freedom to research use several arguments. Fundamentalists argue that we can leave such issues unexplored because a moral consensus and prejudice already exists that acts to deter such activities. The liberal replies that these are unreliable and immoral justifications and sources of disapproval. John Stuart Mill's argument, while challengeable, does have the advantage of revealing that prejudice is never enough to justify censorship; that we can still disapprove while researching; that the expansion of knowledge generally tends to produce more welfare and progress than censorship and regulation (Gibbins, 1990a; 1990b).

Arguments against using the net are legion. Firstly, by accessing sites it can be construed that we are encouraging the producers by encouraging demand. Many sites have access counters that are used to monitor and facilitate policy decisions. To access a site in pornography, even with an academic motive, could be said to encourage pornographers to supply more such sites. This is unlikely in this case, as sex sites are already the most numerous and accessed on the web, without considering the excursions of academics. Next, Kantian ethics suggests that good and bad motive is a deciding factor in making moral judgements, but motivation has no part to play in the law. Morally, it would not be accessing that was wrong *per se*, but accessing for the wrong motive. Academics' motives, if research and teaching based, can be said to change the judgement we would normally make about consulting primary sources of any kind. Academics researchers are not, according to my knowledge, seeking to expand the availability of pornography when researching that area, but to increase knowledge about its nature and effects. Accessing a chat room could be construed as presenting such activities hosted, as acceptable. Such an argument has difficulties, as it is rarely the aim of scholars to legitimate what they view, rather they aim to understand, explain, analyse, criticise and advise (Gillespie, 2000). Could it be construed that accessing a site was to give explicit consent that you approved of the contents of that site; contents that may involve prejudice, exploitation, encouragement of hate, or corruption? This issue of consent is a major one for this book. Does access to a site constitute consent to read the contents?

My solution to the problem of which images and text to analyse, was made easier with the publication of a text with images by the respected cultural theorists, Ted Polhemus and Housk Randall, gatekeepers to the world of fetish and SM. *The Rituals of Love* achieved mass media publicity at its launch and its subject and imagery had entered the public forum without me needing to locate, download, generate or publish my own materials (Polhemus and Randall, 1994). Thompson's book on *Sadomasochism* gave me access to the historical and contemporary debates (Thompson, 1994).

Case Study: The Politics of the Body

My brush with this problem arose because of the shortage of available sources on the *Spanner* case. I had one: Thompson's excellent *Sadomasochism*. From this I found my way to the legislation, the Court Reports and to several other books and articles on a subject about which I was naively and happily untutored.

But what did the public think? What did the networks, groups and movements who advocated SM feel and argue? What was the position in Europe, in the European Court of Human Rights, to which legal appeal was made? My first choice was to not to search for any sites on *Spanner* from the University site. The reasons for this choice were legion. It could have endangered the reputation of the University, if it was accused of hosting such access. At that point the University did not have its present *Policy, Procedures and Guidance Notes for Research Ethics*, so an official route was not available. Next, it was going to take time and energy to negotiate a one off permission before the various University bodies were geared up for the task. That we now have a *Policy, Procedures and Guidance Notes for Research Ethics*, and a Learning Resources Centre policy and procedure, would mean that work access would be more appropriate. This suggests that every university should adopt such a procedures to facilitate the interests of both researcher and institution, as well as the subjects of any research.[2]

When researching on the net the usual starting point is a Search Engine. Unfortunately, there are few dedicated academic Search Engines, most being private, commercial and built to access the entire web. No researcher can know or anticipate what will come up when they do a search for a topic. Once when looking up moral virtues to help test the MacIntyre thesis, that the virtues are 'dead' in the contemporary West, I inputted the term 'honour' (MacIntyre 1981). I was routed to a fetish wear emporium in south London. If this is the case, it is hard to see how it could be argued, that doing a search or opening a site, amount to consent to view the contents. Is visiting a site evidence of something, and specifically, a supportive interest in the contents? This is an improbable assertion, and a dangerous one for academic freedom. Visiting a church is not evidence of being a Christian and visiting a sex shop or web site is not evidence of being interested in buying or using its contents.

Accessing *'Spanner'* as my keyword, produced an interesting array of sites, many dealing with tools, others with firms or individuals with that name. I eventually found a web site, that the script informed me, was produced by a group dedicated to defending those prosecuted under *Spanner*, and advocate the decriminalisation of sadomasochistic behaviour amongst consenting adults: (was www.Spanner.demon.co.uk and is now http://www.barnsdle.demon.co.uk/span/span1.html; Stychin 1995, pp. 117-126). Could I have known the nature of the site before entering? The best answer is perhaps, 'Not with any degree of certainty'. Informed consent on the contents of a web site you are entering is not yet possible, and the few cursory lines under search engine rubrics rarely provide much help.

Matters get more complicated the moment the web site is entered. First, your entry may be logged by your host institution, by the Internet Service Provider (ISP), by an illicit third party, or indeed by the owner of the website. Are you aware of, informed about or consenting to these observations? Generally, the answer is, no, and the activities amount to unofficial or official covert observation amounting to or similar to policing. Arguments on the rights of authorities to observe covertly are hotly argued, but in academic scholarship the British Sociological Association, is in line with most other professional bodies, in advising against this measure, unless as a last resort, where no other methods will work, and where the benefits outweigh the calculable harms that covert observation always brings through the invasion of privacy and attendant consequences (BSA 1994; Bulmer 1974).

If you are not consenting to being observed, are you consenting to the contents of the site software that allow you to open the site and ease return? Many researchers are unaware of these 'cookies' and the 'cache' that are stored on the hard discs of their computers. It was the cache stores that were fundamental to the court case against Gary Glitter, for possessing indecent photographs, and Glitter's defence of ignorance was dismissed. Such cookies and the cache are impossible to erase, so researchers should be aware of the risks that are coincident upon visiting sites and even engaging in electronic communications where authorship anonymity has been promised, especially when they may contain morally reprehensible, illegal or private materials. It is unclear whether ignorant or non-consensual downloading of such materials onto a cache, amounts to possession. In the complicated case of an academic, Dr Atkins, guilt hinged on illegal possession of images stored about which he claimed ignorance. At the first appeal guilt was held to depend upon 'knowledge' of the storage, not just strict liability, based upon *de facto* possession. Lord Justice Brown upheld the appeal against the Magistrates guilty ruling based upon the 1988 Criminal Justice Act, that *de facto* possession was enough to convict; ruling instead that, 'the offence of possession under section 160 is not committed unless the defendant knows he has photographs in his possession (or knows he once had them)' (*Atkins v the Director of Public Prosecutions* (2000) 2 Cr. App. R. 248).

Next, do we consent to what may appear if we open up the box entitled 'Links' that may be attached to the site? On *Spanner* these linked sites contained an array of items spanning the academically helpful ones on similar legal cases, on the legality of *Safe, Sane and Consensual Spanking*, to the other extreme contents of fetish clothing shops, *Switchers Pervy Pages*, *Norwegian Leather Club*, and *Without Restraint, Bound to Please*, BDSM sites (Bondage and Sadomasochism). What can one reasonably expect to find if you open the site? Are you responsible for the contents if you do? Is opening the site evidence of consent to the contents? Again I suspect the right answers are in the negative.

What then happens if any part of the site contains unsavoury or even illegal materials which you discover on opening the page? What then are you to do? No agreed protocols exist for this eventuality. My own view is that the law and employers should only take seriously repeated entry where the motive for so doing cannot be construed as research. There should be a presumption that academics have good and legitimate reasons to open sites for research purposes, unless it can be proved that the motives or possession was unreasonable. It is possible that a researcher may have unreasonable possession of indecent images of children, in which case prosecution is justified, but it does not follow that all possession by all researchers should trigger prosecution. Justice Brown ruled, that it was always a question of fact, 'whether honest research into child pornography constitutes a "legitimate reason" for possession (or making) it'. What then happens if a site visit results in the receipt of unsolicited mailings of materials that are offensive or illegal? Many web and IST providers now use such methods as 'flaming' and 'spamming' which amount to the indiscriminate posting of unsolicited materials on the computers of site visitors and those with email accounts. Unscrupulous site designers create walls against leaving a site, make unsolicited and unavoidable links and mailing lists which could prove damaging to students and researchers.

It is a dubious a practice to assume that all the mail, e. or postal, that researchers receive is consented to, and doubly dubious to hold them responsible for unsolicited mail. But when you start a web search for a sex related topic are you consenting to support that activity? Does visiting a fetish or BDSM site amount to support for pornography, fetishism or sadomasochism? Such a suggestion sounds dubious, but is not without its advocates. Could it not be argued that the evidence of being interested in a topic and site is in itself evidence of interest in wanting to do or engage in that activity? Freudian psychology provides grounds for accepting and rejecting the hypothesis. Evidence that we consciously and explicitly identify an interest is not evidence for a real willed intention to act because evidenced interest is a rationalisation. But on the other hand, for Freud, our real 'id' based motives for doing things are generally suppressed but may be displaced into other neurotic or psychotic activities which replace them. The problem for these theses is that they can never be proved, that the whole argument is closed, and that it confuses motives and reasons in an illogical fashion (Stevenson, 1974, pp. 72-76). In addition, the logical consequence of such an argument leads to unacceptable and untrue conclusions. If it is true that anyone who shows an interest in, or researches a topic, must be said to want to do the activity researched, then most academics working are schizophrenic. All apparently law-abiding criminologists must want to commit crimes, all researchers on child abuse are repressed abusers, and all doctors must want to be ill, or create illness. In fact, it is untrue that all people interested in a subject wish to do the activities associated with that subject. One can research domestic violence and not want to subject partners to violence. You may wish to understand, criticise or advocate measures to alleviate the problem of domestic violence, or defend victims of such violence from future ill treatment.

Arguments about what usage of sexually explicit materials implies and causes, are legion and attract great conflict and debate.[3] The question of whether we are justified in researching such issues and areas is also a problem shared with other professionals and professions. Academic researchers are in good company in running risks. Andrea Dworkin, a radical feminist against pornography, has been accused by a journalist for being indecently obsessed with porn, having quoted lengthy passages in several texts (*Guardian* 6/20). Mary Whitehouse, the famed anti-porn activist was regularly accused of an indecent interest following her Commission's regular visits to strip joints, sex shops and long sessions watching pornographic videos (Whitehouse, 1977). Numerous popular television depictions (e.g. *The Bill, Vice*) of police vice squads display officers succumbing to the allure of the objects they wish to control. Tabloid newspapers that rail against indecency in all forms, regularly depict indecency in both their salacious reporting of cases and in page three images and advertisements. One poor Customs and Excise Officer reported to me that he was obliged to sit for hours per day watching pornographic films and books in his role of defending the public and he felt it was damaging his love life.

What we should keep in mind is that what is at stake in these debates is real harms to individuals and groups, and not just threats to academic freedoms, rights and harms of researchers. In this argument and in the moral advice I am giving, I am fully aware of the dangers to a variety of publics of uncontrolled access to the internet and other sources of information. Few academics, however radical or postmodern, will be non judgmental on the dangers of paedophile links, on hate sites, on the effects of pornography on children, on the exploitative effects of the pornographic industry on women, on the capacity of images to engender prejudice, injustice and exclusion. Considering these harms I am not against regulation of internet access as such, but wish to avoid any form of regulation that may inhibit or prevent useful and justified academic research of intimate relationships, and which may, in addition, endanger academics and academic freedom. Researchers should be made aware of such dangers, and be warned of the possible consequences. In addition it is a good idea for Universities and other research employers, to have a transparent policy on Internet usage, and communicate this to all staff. Many employers now have such a policy but not all communicate to staff and offer training on netiquette. Outside of the higher education sector, there are unofficial reports of a steady enforced exodus of staff found guilty of breaches of employment related to computer usage. At the University of Teesside, the *Learning Resource Centre* which includes the Library and numerous electronic data bases and gateways, has developed a transparent policy on access which is not by intention and design restrictive, but allows scholar friendly and sympathetic negotiation with users on access and usage. Access in private spaces with agreed protocols on agreed topics is one of the many solutions negotiated that create a fair balance between protection of the vulnerable and academic freedom. Self-regulation is a better, and a tried and tested, route to removing the ethical dangers associated with academic research.

Good Practice in Researching Sexualities

In this chapter I have highlighted some dangers for sex researchers from consensual and non consensual features of doing research on intimate relationships, with special reference to internet access. What would amount to good practice in our area, including course and module development, learning and teaching strategy, conference organisation and delivery, research and publication? Some of my detailed consideration of the sort of universal ethical rules that would apply on a global basis can be found in other publications and cannot be represented here (Gibbins, 2001; Gibbins and Reimer, 1999, pp. 155-160; Oliver, 2003). We need to weigh the needs for protection of stakeholders in research with the right, freedom and need to explore knowledge and understanding. Within the diverse and plural world that makes up scholarship on sexuality, no universal rules or prescriptions can achieve this. A better approach is self-regulation, focused on encouraging ethical awareness by ethical training, to develop procedures that oblige partners to engage and negotiate unique solutions to particular problems, and to have a policy and structures to make sure the former are fairly and effectively implemented.

Of primary importance is the obligation on academic and research institutions to develop and implement some kind of Policy, Procedures and Code for Research Ethics. The University of Teesside, *Policy, Procedures and Guidance Notes for Research Ethics* have application to all staff, postgraduates and final year undergraduates taking modules, such as the dissertation, which are primarily research based. Every research project has to have *Ethical Release*, achieved when a short form detailing the nature of the project, with evidence of discussion and agreement that harms will not follow, is signed off by the key parties and the Chair of the School Ethics Committee. If problems are identified then, after airing and negotiation, a more detailed *Ethical Approval Form* is submitted to detailed examination and amendment, until it is approved by the School Committee, or transferred onto the University Research Ethics Committee, where solutions to the ethical issues are negotiated, or the project rejected. The objects are to encourage all parties to own their own ethics, to generate and maintain ethical awareness, and to reduce the possibility that a project may harm any stakeholder, or bring the University or profession into disrepute. At Teesside the provision of such a code has reduced the scope for dangers and harms to a minimum, and solutions have been found to allow every research project to continue in some form, including many covering the areas of sexuality and gender. However, to have a code without attendant education, training and access to forums for debate is to encourage both irrelevance and avoidance. At Teesside, a *Gender Research Forum* exists in the University to encourage high quality research across disciplines. In addition we have a training Unit on *Research Ethics* which is compulsory for all new Directors of Studies and Research Supervisors. All Schools, Units, and Research Centres and specialist groups are obliged to conform to the University procedures and the general guidance on governance, harassment and equal opportunities. Our *Policy, Procedures and Guidance Notes for Research Ethics* insists that researchers consult the Codes of their affiliated Professional Bodies as they usually invoke rights and obligations for subjects, students, postgraduate researchers and staff on the netiquette for researching sexualities.

But rules and networks are not enough, good practice needs to be embedded in the wider university culture. To this effect it has become necessary to develop partner codes, training and procedures covering financial sponsorship of research in the university, and currently, the whole teaching and learning scheme, is being considered for ethical coverage. Perhaps all modules should have ethical clearance as part of the normal course development and validation process? Alongside the new governance codes and procedures it is likely that most research, teaching and management at the University can be geared and cleared for ethics, including research ethics, without the construction of over burdensome and restrictive effects. Research Ethics text books are not very helpful in the area of sexual ethics and we have to extrapolate from other areas for sexualities to get guidance. The most useful sources are Barnes (1982), Burgess (1984), Bulmer (1982), Heller (1986), Punch (1986), Wegner (1987) and Oliver (2003). However, there is still scope for much personal and interpersonal debate upon moral aspects of sex research.

Another practice colleagues may explore, is the formulation of informed consent and contracts between the stakeholders in a research or teaching project. When we opened our Workshop, and again when I began my presentation at the ECPR Oslo Workshop, we had an open forum and negotiated our methods of proceeding. We shared our plans, motives and methods and then gave informed consent for what we were to discuss, display and debate. This was given after few questions. When beginning my modules on *Sexuality* and *Sexuality and Morality*, we began by discussing the learning and teaching strategies, then explaining the Code of Practice contained in the module document. This was followed by small group discussion leading to an agreed *Module Contract*. Students usually agree to great scope for freedom, but ask for prior information of the contents of presentations, require anti-sexist and anti-racist practices, and guard against any form of intimidation and harassment. To safeguard students as participants at assessed presentations, presenting students had to complete a summary of contents, images and any handouts for ethical clearance at least a week prior to delivery. The *Sexuality* module ran across several degrees, courses and Schools. So far, and despite a massive range of topics covered and sources used, no cases of ethical impropriety or reported discomfort have emerged from the running of the two modules over a decade, due largely to the adoption of the above procedures and precautions. In the case of my presentation at Oslo, informed consent was obtained from those present, and the images shown were taken from a previously published academic text rather then unauthenticated sources taken form the Internet.

The principle of informed consent, must become, and remain the mainstay of any research in the fields of sexuality if we are to preserve the safety of subjects, students, academics, professions and Universities. I have argued, however, that for researchers there is always the present danger of unintended and unforeseen dangers, for instance, accessing materials, to which they have not consented. On this I have recommended care, good procedures and good practice, but also a recognition by authorities, that even with the best will and intention, researchers may inadvertently receive unsolicited correspondence, access, download or reproduce illegal or harmful materials, or have their computer or ID wrongly utilised.

This leaves the final dilemma, of the ability of many of the subjects of research, to give or withhold consent to information or images, of or about them, being viewed. Good practice dictates that no images or representations of others should be made available on the Internet without their consent, but viewers can never be sure of this. Indeed anyone using digital technology can copy and place images on the net, and some sites, such as *Celebrity Nudes*, aim to mislead by placing the heads of stars on the bodies of others. We can never be sure of what is said, under our names, and in our names, on the internet, and hence should be careful with placing information on the net and in using sources from the web that may not be there with the authors consent.

We may turn to two political issues arising from the Internet and Home Office policy, the policy, that allows surveillance of all internet users, and, in Clauses 52-52 of the *Sexual Offences Bill 2003*, the planned banning of anyone from holding and storing images of persons below the age of 18 defined as indecent. Should we as academics and researchers, agree to the monitoring of the Internet that is now in operation, or should we join Amnesty International, Censorship and other human rights bodies, in opposing such invasions of human liberty, with potential for limiting academic freedom? The answer to this last question I shall leave for the reader to debate, but I feel the spirit of Foucault revolting at this proposal. Free discourse amongst academics and the public on matters of sexualities, which are so close to the agenda of who and what we are, are preconditions for the success of the movements towards equal citizenship. We can at least consent to that.

The issues around Clauses 52 and 53 of the *Sexual Offences Bill* 2003 are even more complex. For a start the thorny issue of what we define, how and who does define indecency, remains focal and essentially contested. The media have already evidenced several demarcation disputes which test the boundaries e.g. the photographing of bathing pictures of Julia Sommerville's children by her partner, the photographing of her naked children by the artist shown at the Sally Mann exhibition, both raising similar issues to those provoked by the accusation of obscenity underlying the raid on the Mapplethorpe photographic exhibition in London.

Much of the imagery of children in classical art and architecture, if stored, circulated or sold digitally, could be prosecuted under the new laws. Even evidence used by group activists raising awareness about child abuse, could be subject to the law. The key argument against the storing of images is that there is no conceivable good reason for their possession, accept by the prosecuting bodies. However, I can imagine feminist researchers, civil rights bodies and child protection officers providing arguments on many grounds. One, is to do with evidence and inference, how can we determine indecency or harm without looking at a primary source? How, within normal liberal democratic society, can we question the 'official' view on indecency without access to the disputed materials? How, in a civil society, can we mobilise opposition to behaviours that cannot even be disclosed in public? The whole ethics and philosophy of 'archiving' also works on a principle that we should keep primary source evidence, because we don't know when it may prove invaluable in ways never considered today e.g. saving forensic evidence that later reveals compelling data via DNA testing. The provision in Clause 53, that five persons may provide authorisation, undermines the self-regulation procedures that operate in most universities and creates a culture of policing that is alien to academic environments. Whether, after normalising the age of consent to 16 for homosexual consent, we use 18 for images, is also contentious. Distributing, rather than making or owning is disallowed between 16 and 18. No exception can be taken with the motive of the law, to protect children and other victims and prevent their exploitation, *period*, but as citizens we need to keep to a norm, and this seems to settle on the age of consent as 16.

Finally, we can return to the one piece of correspondence I received after the publication of my essay 'Sexuality and the Law' and use it as a prompt for your own reflexive analysis on the unexpected outcomes of research. How are we to deal with unsolicited requests for advice and support on issues related to sexuality? In response to an unsolicited telephone contact, using an address provided to the caller without my consent, I found myself in a surreal discussion with a very distressed Ms 'A', who was seeking my advice on a personal problem. She had reviewed the recent literature on sadomasochism and was now seeking advice from authorities on how to help her 'Master, we can call 'M'. 'M' was described as a wonderful person and a brilliant 'Top' (meaning the dominant one in an SM relationship), and a popular 'Black Knight' (meaning a man who provided 'Top' services to a bevy or 'stable' of women and men, often for payment). According to the caller, 'M' was diligent in all his duties, including the acquisition and updating of consent from his 'Bottoms' (meaning the submissive members of his stable). One condition of entering his stable was to agree in writing that your body was at his disposal, subject to the use of a non-compliance clause triggered by a 'safe' word. 'M' had made a regular move in his repertoire with one 'bottom' we can call her 'B', and put her up for auction, apparently a popular game in 'SM' relationships and parties, without the safe word being utilised. The successful bidder, 'P', took away his purchase and proceeded to take over the role of 'Top'. After a period of time 'B' decided she had been abandoned by 'M' and took exception to her transfer and subsequent treatment by 'P'. She eventually approached the police and hence began a process of investigation, arrest and various accusations against 'M' and 'P' of assault occasioning bodily harm, battery, rape and 'living off immoral earnings' (Stone, 1999, pp. 103-126, 139-187). 'A' was distressed that her partner 'M' had become the victim of a wrongful and malicious accusation and was researching all sources to assist in his legal defence. I terminated the contacts and do not know if the case came to court or any outcome.

There are many questions you may ask about the case, and the ethical and legal advice to be given, and some advice is contained in the Beckmann essay above. But for researchers on human sexuality here are some questions for you to consider as a way of developing your own and your institution's policy and procedures:

- Within which paradigms and discourses can you to begin and end in understanding this scenario and the role of each actor?
- Who should we see as the victim, and the harmed and injured party, here?
- What ethical theory should we use to guide you and each party here?
- What advice would you give to the legal parties acting for 'A' 'B', 'M' and 'P'?
- What advice would you give to anyone considering playing any of the roles of 'A' 'B', 'M' and 'P'?
- What ethical advice would you give to anyone, such as Andrea Beckmann, David Renton, Martin Taylor (this volume), Terry Gillespie (2000), DiMarco and DiMarco (2000), or Martin Whine (1997) who have conducted, or are planning to research, unusual sexualities, such as sadomasochism, or violence?
- Should you reply to such a request for advice? Its clear it is not your duty to do so but it may be a supererogatory virtue? Or is it immoral to advise in such perverse circumstances?
- If you do reply, what qualifications and conditions of copyright would you place on the advice? What procedures would you follow?
- What policy and procedures apply to such research in your workplace?
- Are you informed of the rights of subjects and your duties to various stakeholders when researching sexualities?
- Who could you go to in your University or profession for advice on the above?

Notes

[1] University of Teesside, *Library and Information Services, Learning and Resources Centre Regulations, Learning Resources Centre* Home Page, http://www.tees.ac.uk

[2] University of Teesside, *Policy, Procedures and Guidance Notes for Research Ethics*, 2003. Can be obtained from Kathy Ludlow, University of Teesside, Middlesbrough, TS1 3BA k.ludlow@tees.ac.uk
[3] Two useful summaries of the debate, the first liberal and the second conservative are, Strossen (1996) and Russell (1993). Another useful discussion is in Gillespie (2000).

Bibliography

Ashenden, S. (2002), 'Policing Perversion: The Contemporary Governance of Paedophilia', *Cultural Values*, Vol. 6, pp. 1-2, 197-222.

Barnes, J. (1982), *Who Should Know What?* London: Penguin.

Bulmer, M. (1982), *Social Research Ethics*, London: Macmillan.

Burchell, G., Gordon, C. and Miller, P. (eds) (1991), *The Foucault Effect: Studies in Governability*, Hemel Hempstead: Harvester Wheatsheaf.

Burgess, R. (1984), *In the Field*, London: Unwin.

British Sociological Association, *Statement of Ethical Principles* (BSA Web Site, Home Page).

Carver, T. and Mottier, V. (eds) (1998), *The Politics of Sexuality: Identity, Gender and Citizenship*, London: Routledge.

Connolly, W. (1983), *The Terms of Political Discourse*, Oxford: Martin Robertson.

Coombes, H. (2001), *Research Using IT*, London: Palgrave.

Crotty, M. (1998), *The Foundations of Social Research*, London: Sage.

DiMarco, A. D. and DiMarco, H. (2000), 'Investigating cybersociety: a consideration of the ethical and practical issues surrounding on-line research into chat rooms', in Forester, T. and Morrison, P. (1994), *Computer Ethics: Cautionary Tales and Ethical Dilemmas in Computing*, Cambridge, Mass.: M.I.T Press.

Foucault, M. (1975), *I, Pierre Riviere, Having Slaughtered My Mother, My Sister, and My Brother: A Case of Parricide in the 19th Century*, New York: Pantheon Books.

Foucault, M. (1980), *Herculin Barbin: Being the Recently Discovered Memoirs of a Nineteenth Century French Hermaphrodite*, London: Harvester.

Gallie, W. (1962), 'Essentially Contested Concepts' in Black, M. (ed.), *The Importance of Language*, Englewood Cliffs N.J.: Prentice Hall.

Gibbins, J. R. (ed.) (1989a), *Contemporary Political Culture: Politics in a Postmodern Age*, London: Sage.

Gibbins, J. R. (1989b), 'Political Cultural Change in Western Europe: From Postmaterialism to Postmodernism', *European Consortium for Political Research Workshops*, Paris.

Gibbins, J. R. (1990), 'Mill, Liberalism and Progress', in Bellamy, R. (ed.), *Victorian Liberalism*, London: Routledge.

Gibbins, J. R. (1991a), 'Postmodern Politics and Culture', *American Political Science Association Annual Conference*, Washington D.C.

Gibbins, J. R. (1991b), 'Postmodernism and Values', *European Science Foundation Conference on the impact of Values*, Vienna: Austria.

Gibbins, J. R. (1992a), 'Postmodernism, Politics and Citizenship', *British Sociological Association Conference*, University of Kent.

Gibbins, J. R. (1992b), 'Principles of Postmodernism', *Northern Universities Philosophy Symposium*, University of Teesside.

Gibbins, J. R. and Reimer, B. (1993a), *'Postmodernism and Values'*, European Science Foundation Conference, Strasbourg.

Gibbins, J. R. and Reimer, B. (1993b), 'Lifestyles and Values', *European Science*

Association Conference, Strasbourg.

Gibbins, J. R. (1994a), 'Victorian Representations and Representations of Victorians: Constructions of Sexuality in Victorian Cartoons', *British Sociological Association Conference on Sexualities in a Social Context*, Preston.

Gibbins, J. R. (1994b), 'Value Change, New Politics and Postmodernism', *Conference on Political Cultures and Cultural Politics*, Lancaster.

Gibbins, J. R. and Reimer, B. (1995), 'Postmodernism', in *The Impact of Values*, Van Deth, J. and Scarborough, E. (eds), Oxford: Oxford University Press.

Gibbins, J. R. (1996a) 'Postmodernism, Values and Welfare', *Conference on Postmodernity and the Fragmentation of Welfare*, University of Teesside.

Gibbins, J. R. (1996b), 'The Body as Politics: Discourses of Politics, Sexuality and the Law', *European Consortium for Political Research Workshops*, Oslo.

Gibbins, J. R. (1998a), 'Postmodernism, Poststructuralism and Social Policy', in Carter, J. (ed.), *Postmodernity and the Fragmentation of Welfare*, London: Routledge.

Gibbins, J. R. (1998b), 'Social Policy and Citizenship in Postmodernity', *Conference on Welfare State, Fifty Years of Progress*, Ruskin College, Oxford.

Gibbins, J. R. (1998c), 'Postmodernism', Second edition of above 1998.

Gibbins, J. R. (1998e), 'Sexuality and the Law: The Body as Politics', in Carver, T. and Motier, V. (eds), *The Politics of Sexuality*, Routledge: London.

Gibbins, J. R. (1999a), 'The Principles for a Postmodern Cosmopolitan Political Morality', *Conference Workshop on International Distributive Justice, ECPR Annual Joint Workshops*, MZES, Mannheim.

Gibbins, J. R. (1999b), 'The Future of the Profession of Political Science', Political Studies Association Annual Conference.

Gibbins, J. R. and Reimer, B. (1999c), *The Politics of Postmodernity*, London: Sage.

Gillespie, T. (2000). 'Virtual Violence? Pornography and violence against women on the Internet', in Radford, J. et al. (eds), *Women, Violence and Strategies for Action: Feminist Research, Policy and Practice*, Buckingham: Open University Press.

Hacking, I. (1999), 'The Making and Moulding of Child Abuse', *Critical Inquiry*, Vol. 17, Winter, pp. 253-288.

Hamelink, C. J. (2000), *The Ethics of Cyberspace*, London: Sage.

Heller, R. (ed.) (1986), *The Uses and Abuses of Social Sciences*, London: Sage.

Jewkes, Y. (ed.) (2002), *Dot.cons: Crime, Deviance and Identity on the Internet*, Cullompton: Willan Publishing.

Kaase, M. and Newton, K. (eds), (1995) *Beliefs in Government*, 5 Vols, Oxford: Oxford University Press.

Loader, B. (ed.) (1997), *The Governance of Cyberspace: Politics, Technology and Global Restructuring*, London: Routledge.

MacIntyre, A. (1981), *After Virtue: A Study of Moral Theory*, London: Duckworth.

Oliver, P. (2003), *The Student's Guide to Research Ethics*, Buckingham: Open University Press.

Polhemus, T. and Randall, H. (1994), *The Rituals of Love: Sexual Experiments, Erotic Possibilities*, London: Picador.

Punch, M. (1986), *The Politics and Ethics of Fieldwork*, London: Sage.

Russell, D.E.H. (ed.), (1993), *Making Violence Sexy: Feminist Views on Pornography*, Buckingham: Open University Press.

Sharp, K. and Earle, S. (2003), 'Cyberpunters and Cyberwhores: Prostitution on the Internet', in Jewkes, Y. (ed.) (2002), *Dot.cons: Crime, Deviance and Identity on the Internet*, Cullompton: Willan Publishing.

Spanner – http://www.barnsdle.demon.co.uk/span/span1.html

Stevenson, L. (1974), *Seven Theories of Human Nature*, Oxford: Oxford University Press.

Stone, R. (1999), *Offences Against the Person*, London: Cavendish Publishing.

Strossen, N. (1996), *Defending Pornography: Free Speech, Sex, and the Fight for Women's Rights*, London: Abacus.

Stychin, C. F. (1995), *Law's Desire: Sexuality and the Limits of Justice*, London: Routledge.

University of Teesside, *Library and Information Services, Learning Resources Centre Regulations, Learning Resources Centre* Home Page, http://www.tees.ac.uk

Theory, Culture and Society (1982), Vol. 1, No. 1.

Thompson, B. (1994), *Sadomasochism*, London: Cassell.

Wegner, G. (1987), *The Research Relationship*, London: Unwin.

Whine, M. (1997) 'The Far Right and the Internet', in Loader, B. (ed.), *The Governance of Cyberspace: Politics, Technology and Global Restructuring*, London: Routledge.

Whitehouse, M. (1977), *Whatever Happened to Sex*, London: Wayland Publishers.

Index